AF352563

# Prosodic Variation (with)in Languages

The aim of this series is to provide both accessible and relevant texts to students of linguistics, phonetics and speech sciences, and to publish more advanced texts and edited collections. The textbooks aim to cover a wide variety of topics relevant for such an audience, and to introduce these topics in a practical way to enable students to undertake a range of analysis procedures. The more advanced books will present state-of-the-art research in the topic concerned. While we intend to cover a wide range of topics in phonetics and phonology, there will be an emphasis on phonetic studies of under-reported languages, or the bringing of new data to explore phonetic characteristics on the one hand, and on phonological studies that employ more psycholinguistic, cognitive and functional approaches on the other (and, of course, on the interaction between phonetics and phonology). The recent increase in interest in laboratory phonology we see as particularly to be welcomed. Each volume will be authored by leading authorities in the field, who have a grasp of both the theoretical issues and the practical requirements of the area and, further, are at the forefront of current research and practice.

Published:
*Challenging Sonority: Cross-Linguistic Evidence*
Edited by Martin J. Ball and Nicole Müller

*Phonology in Protolanguage and Interlanguage*
Edited by Elena Babatsouli and David Ingram

*Romance-Germanic Bilingual Phonology*
Edited by Mehmet Yavaş, Margaret Kehoe and Walcir Cardoso

*The Phonetics of Dysarthria: Studies in Production and Perception*
Ioannis Papakyritsis, Marie Klopfenstein and Ben Rutter

Forthcoming:
*Prosody in Practice: Non-segmental Phonetics in Typical and Atypical Speech*
Joan Rahilly

# Prosodic Variation (with)in Languages

## Intonation, Phrasing and Segments

Edited by Marisa Cruz and Sónia Frota

SHEFFIELD UK   BRISTOL CT

Published by Equinox Publishing Ltd.

UK: Office 415, The Workstation, 15 Paternoster Row, Sheffield,
South Yorkshire S1 2BX

USA: ISD, 70 Enterprise Drive, Bristol, CT 06010

www.equinoxpub.com

First published 2022



British Library Cataloguing-in-Publication Data

A catalogue record for this book is available from the British Library.

ISBN-13     978 1 78179 468 5        (hardback)
            978 1 80050 147 8        (ePDF)
            978 1 80050 175 1        (ePub)

Library of Congress Cataloging-in-Publication Data

Names: Workshop on Prosodic Variation (2015 : Universidade de Lisboa) |
    Cruz, Marisa, editor. | Frota, Sonia, editor.
Title: Prosodic variation (with)in languages : intonation, phrasing and
    segments / edited by Marisa Cruz and Sónia Frota.
Description: Sheffield, South Yorkshire ; Bristol, CT : Equinox Publishing
    Ltd., [2022] | Series: Studies in phonetics and phonology | This book is
    a collection of chapters that emerged from papers presented at the
    ProVar -  Workshop on Prosodic Variation, hosted by  the University of
    Lisbon, in July 2015. | Includes bibliographical references and index. |
    Summary: "This volume focuses on research on prosodic variation,
    comprising intonation, prosodic phrasing, and segmental phenomena that
    are prosodically motivated or constrained, in several languages and
    language varieties"-- Provided by publisher.
Identifiers: LCCN 2021049661 (print) | LCCN 2021049662 (ebook) | ISBN
    9781781794685 (hardback) | ISBN 9781800501478 (pdf) | ISBN 9781800501751
    (epub)
Subjects: LCSH: Language and languages--Variation--Congresses. | Prosodic
    analysis (Linguistics)--Congresses. | LCGFT: Conference papers and
    proceedings.
Classification: LCC P120.V37 W67 2015  (print) | LCC P120.V37  (ebook) |
    DDC 414--dc23/eng/20211222
LC record available at https://lccn.loc.gov/2021049661
LC ebook record available at https://lccn.loc.gov/2021049662

Typeset by Sparks – www.sparkspublishing.com

# Contents

# List of tables

# Introduction

**Marisa Cruz & Sónia Frota**

This book is a collection of chapters that emerged from papers presented at the *ProVar - Workshop on Prosodic Variation* (http://labfon.letras.ulisboa.pt/InAPoP/ProVar/), hosted by the University of Lisbon, in July 2015. The workshop provided a forum for discussion on prosodic variation in language, promoted by the *InAPoP – Interactive Atlas of the Prosody of Portuguese* team (http://labfon.letras.ulisboa.pt/InAPoP/), and gathering researchers interested on Prosody in language. These researchers' contributions discussed the properties of different prosodic systems and the extent to which prosodic systems may vary within and across languages.

This book focuses on prosodic variation, comprising intonation, prosodic phrasing, and segmental phenomena that are prosodically motivated or constrained, in several languages and language varieties. The book covers Portuguese (European, Brazilian, and African varieties), Romanian, Arabic, and Assamese (spoken in India and Bangladesh). Language coverage is thus diverse, including understudied languages/varieties. Importantly, all chapters share a common target: to add to the knowledge of prosodic variation in each of the languages and varieties studied, and to contribute to the understanding of prosodic grammar, in general.

The book is organized in two parts. The first part (*Intonation*) includes four chapters devoted to intonational variation in Arabic (Chapter 1), European and Brazilian Portuguese (Chapter 2 and Chapter 3), and Romanian (Chapter 4); the second part (*Prosodic phrasing and segments*) gathers three chapters exploring prosodic phrasing and prosodically constrained segmental phenomena in Assamese (Chapter 5) and European, Brazilian and African varieties of Portuguese (Chapter 6 and Chapter 7). In the following paragraphs, we provide a summary of each individual chapter, discussing its contribution to prosodic variation (with)in languages.

Chapter 1, authored by Sam Hellmuth, focuses on text–tune alignment in Tunisian Arabic yes–no questions, aiming to explore to what extent it resembles (or not) text–tune alignment strategies observed in Romance languages. Particularly, the author analyses the incidence of utterance-final vowel epenthesis in Tunisian Arabic yes–no questions to observe whether its occurrence varies by discourse context, prosodic contour, speech style, metrical structure, segmental content, and even by gender or individual speaker. Unexpectedly, the author concludes that the phenomenon described is not a case of 'text–tune' adjustment at all, but rather a 'question vowel' particle, thus setting aside the hypothesis that utterance-final vowel epenthesis in Tunisian Arabic yes–no questions was due to linguistic contact across the Mediterranean (with Portuguese or Italian). Instead, the author considers the possibility of older contact scenarios via historical migrations and/or substrate influence from varieties of Tamazight. The chapter nicely highlights how comparative cross-linguistic work on prosody may unravel the origins of grammatical phenomena previously not understood.

Also focused on the intonational contour of yes–no questions, Marisa Cruz, Verònica Crespo-Sendra, Joelma Castelo and Sónia Frota present, in Chapter 2, the first detailed phonological and phonetic analysis comparing neutral and counterexpectational yes–no questions between (and within) European and Brazilian Portuguese varieties, produced under two different speech styles. Nine varieties of European and eight varieties of Brazilian Portuguese are analyzed. The authors show that, independently of the communicative context, their results point to an asymmetry between European and Brazilian Portuguese varieties in conveying the two pragmatic meanings: in European Portuguese the nuclear configuration is changed to convey counterexpectation; by contrast, in Brazilian Portuguese counterexpectational yes–no questions are produced with the same neutral pattern, but with realizational (or phonetic) differences between the two pragmatic meanings. Thus, each variety expresses counterexpectational yes–no questions using different means – categorically (i.e., phonologically) in European Portuguese and gradually (i.e., phonetically) in Brazilian Portuguese –, which provides evidence to the co-existence of both strategies across language varieties. The chapter also explores the phonology-phonetics interface of yes–no question contours, showing that the phonetic findings support the phonological account which crucially relies on tonal alignment distinctions.

In Chapter 3, Marco Barone and Joelma Castelo also address phonological variation in Brazilian Portuguese, by looking into the intonation of Northeastern Brazilian Portuguese. Namely, by observing the nuclear contours of Brazilian Portuguese broad focus statements, and comparing them with the nuclear contours of the same sentence type produced in the southern variety of Italian spoken in Pescara, the authors suggest an ongoing process of reanalysis, or oversimplification by analogy. More precisely, in light of the theory of reanalysis and grammatical change, they argue that the complex rule of context-conditioned phonetic implementation of the intonational contour in Pescara Italian broad focus statements is being replaced over time by a simpler rule, aided by the fact that both rules produce the same surface outcome, thus providing an example of ongoing change in the grammar of intonation.

Chapter 4 closes part I of this book. In this chapter, Doina Jitca presents an innovative framework proposal for intonation analysis. Combining the functional perspective of Information Structure analysis (Halliday, 1967) with the phonological view given by the Autosegmental Metrical model and the ToBI annotation system (Ladd, 1996/2008; Pierrehumbert, 1980; *inter alia*), the author analyzes several examples of Romanian intonational contours. These illustrate how the new proposal, based on a communication act perspective, can add more clarity to phonological analyses, thus shedding light on issues related to nuclear accent assignment within intonational contour analysis. Since the framework presented deals with the notion of communicative unit, in which utterances are partitioned, this chapter also tackles prosodic chunking within utterances, thus bridging the two parts of the book.

Part II, focused on prosodic phrasing and segmental phenomena that are prosodically constrained and/or motivated, opens with Chapter 5, authored by Asim. I. Twaha and Shakuntala Mahanta. The authors examine how the realization of contrastive focus in two varieties of Assamese – an understudied language spoken in India and Bangladesh – impacts on prosodic phrasing. The authors show that the two varieties of Assamese employ different strategies to mark contrastive focus: the Nalbariya variety of Assamese (NVA) uses only intonation to express contrastive focus, whereas Standard Colloquial Assamese (SCA) applies a demarcative strategy to highlight a given constituent. Namely, in SCA the focused constituent forms an independent phonological phrase, which is the smallest tonally marked phonological domain in Assamese. Differently, in NVA the focused constituent forms a phonological phrase together with the post-focus material. These differences are evidenced by segmental phenomena that are licensed across prosodic words in NVA, but blocked in SCA. Although the phrasing strategies are different in the post-focus domain, both varieties present post-focal compression. In the pre-focus domain, by contrast, both varieties behave similarly, with the pre-focus constituents being generally phrased into a single phonological phrase. The chapter makes an important contribution to knowledge on the prosody of Assamese.

In Chapter 6, Flaviane Fernandes-Svartman, Nádia Barros, Vinícius dos Santos and Joelma Castelo also inspect phrasing strategies of declarative sentences, but on different varieties of Portuguese. Focusing on the European, Brazilian and Guinea-Bissau varieties of Portuguese, the same SVO sentences (with respect to the lexicon and syntactic structure) were analyzed with the goal of establishing how constituent length and syntactic and/or prosodic branchingness impact prosodic phrasing. The authors observe that, with the exception of the variety spoken in Braga and of central-southern varieties, European Portuguese displays [SVO]$_{IP}$ as the main phrasing pattern. The same applies in Brazilian Portuguese and Guinea-Bissau Portuguese. However, in the latter, [SV]$_{IP}$[O]$_{IP}$ is also attested, being triggered by prosodic branchingness and constituent length. Among the diverse cues to mark non-final intonational phrase boundaries, pause insertion and boundary tones are the most relevant ones across Portuguese varieties. The finding that prosodic phrasing patterns are differently affected by contituent length and branchingness across language varieties highlights the need to study language specific varieties to map prosodic phrasing variation.

Finally, Chapter 7 approaches hiatus resolution strategies across European Portuguese varieties. These strategies are constrained and/or motivated by prosodic structure. Nuno Paulino, Pedro Oliveira and Marina Vigário found that phonological processes used for hiatus resolution across European Portuguese varieties span the intonational phrase domain, are blocked by its boundary, and do not target the second vowel involved in the hiatus context, nor a stressed vowel. Importantly, this is not true for other Romance languages or even for Brazilian Portuguese. The authors found variation in the preference for different strategies of hiatus resolution, with the Northern varieties preserving the segmental material (e.g., through glide insertion), and the Southern varieties deleting segmental material (e.g., through back vowel deletion). External factors playing a role in the frequency of occurrence of the phonological processes analysed, namely, speakers' age-group and provenance from rural/urban locations, as well as speech style, were also inspected. The chapter thus offers a thorough analysis of vowel hiatus resolution in European Portuguese, from a prosodic perspective.

Differently from the most recent contributions to the field of prosodic variation, the studies in this book jointly aim to show that not all languages within the same linguistic branch behave similarly – the case of Portuguese, or Romanian, within Romance languages. Second, language varieties of a given language may display different prosodic grammars – as in the case of European, Brazilian and African varieties of Portuguese, or the Standard Colloquial Assamese and Nalbariya variety of Assamese varieties of Assamese. Third, although apparently unrelated, languages belonging to different families/branches – Romance and Indo-Aryan (Indo-European languages) and Semitic (Afro-Asiatic languages) – may share common prosodic properties. The non-genetic-relatedness patterning of prosodic variation is, thus, one of the points of interest of this book. Additionally, by offering different frameworks and both experimental and theoretical approaches to prosodic variation, the book aims to enrich prosodic studies and foster the development of bridges across methods and frameworks. Finally, the chapters in this book are a valuable resource not only to all those interested in prosody in language, but also to any reader interested on language variation and change, or on the interface between prosody and other areas of grammar, such as syntax, semantics, or pragmatics.

The editors of this book would like to make several acknowledgements. First of all, we are grateful to the authors, for their dedication to this project and eagerness to work on their chapters. A grateful word is also due to all those who generously acted as reviewers, listed here in alphabetical order: Anja Arnhold (University of Alberta), Annie Rialland (Université Sorbonne Nouvelle, Paris 3), Barbara Gili Fivela (University of Salento), Benjamin Schmeiser (Illinois State University), Carlos Gussenhoven (Radboud University), Celeste Rodrigues (University of Lisbon), Cinzia Avesani (Italian National Research Council), †Gisela Collischonn (Federal University of Rio Grande do Sul), Gorka Elordieta (Universidad del País Vasco-Euskal Herriko Unibertsitatea), Hubert Truckenbrodt (Leibniz-Centre for General Linguistics, ZAS Berlin), Ingo Feldhausen (Goethe-Universität, Frankfurt), João Moraes (Federal University of Rio de Janeiro), José Ignacio Hualde (University of Illinois at Urbana-Champaign), Kathryn Franich (University of Delaware), Marina Vigário (University of Lisbon), Martine Grice (University of Cologne), Anna Bruggeman (University of Cologne), Michelina Savino (Università degli Studi di Bari Aldo Moro), Nancy Hall (California State University), Oliver Niebuhr (Centre for Industrial Electronics), Paolo Roseano (UNED – National Distance Education University), Pilar Prieto (ICREA – University of Pompeu Fabra), Sameer ud Dowla Khan (Reed College), Samuil Marusca (SOAS University of London), Sasha Calhoun (Victoria University of Wellington), Sonia Colina (University of Arizona), Stefan Baumann (University of Cologne), Sun-Ah Jun (University of California, Los Angeles), Susanne Genzel (University of Potsdam), Teresa Cabré (Universitat Autònoma de Barcelona), Tomas Riad (Stockholm University), Yosuke Igarashi (National Institute for Japanese Language and Linguistics). Thank you for your work, that has greatly improved the quality of the book. We also would like to thank Pedro Oliveira, for his support to the editors in an initial stage of the book. We acknowledge the financial support provided by Fundação para a Ciência e a Tecnologia (FCT, Portugal) to *ProVar - Workshop on Prosodic Variation* (through grant PTDC/CLE-LIN/119787/2010 awarded to S. Frota), which was the seed of this book, as well as to the editors during the preparation of the volume (grants SFRH/BPD/94695/2013, UID/LIN/00214/2019, and UIDB/00214/2020). Last but not least, our special thanks to the editors of the Series *Studies in Phonetics and Phonology*, Martin J. Ball (Bangor University) and Pascal Van Lieshout (University of Toronto), for their constant support in the course of this (long) journey.

**Marisa Cruz** is Assistant Professor at the University of Lisbon. She obtained a PhD on prosodic variation in European Portuguese (phrasing, intonation and rhythm) in 2013, in the same institution. She is currently member of the Direction Board of Center of Linguistics of the University of Lisbon, where she investigates visual prosody in European Portuguese, by comparing the prosodic role of gestures in spoken language with the prosody of Portuguese Sign Language. Her research interests also cover language acquisition and language disorders.

**Sónia Frota** is Full Professor of Experimental Linguistics at the University of Lisbon. Her research seeks to understand the properties of prosodic systems (phrasing, intonation, and rhythm), the extent to which they vary across and within languages, and how they are acquired by infants and help to bootstrap the learning of language. She is the editor in chief of the *Journal of Portuguese Linguistics* (since 2002), Associate Editor of *Phonetica* (since 2015) and the Director of the Center of Linguistics at the University of Lisbon (since 2020).

# PART I: INTONATION

# 1
# Text–tune alignment in Tunisian Arabic yes–no questions

Sam Hellmuth

## 1    Introduction

Adjustment of the intonational 'tune' to the segmental 'text' has been observed in a number of languages in contexts of tonal-crowding, most commonly in the form of either compression or truncation of the tonal contour (Grabe, 1998, 2004). Nevertheless, a number of cases of the reverse phenomenon have been reported, in which the segmental 'text' is adjusted, through vowel insertion or lengthening, to accommodate the intonational 'tune'.

This chapter reports on a previously undescribed apparent 'text–tune' adjustment phenomenon observed in a corpus of Tunisian Arabic (TA) speech data, collected for a wider investigation of the intonational phonology of TA. In our data, the final nuclear accent in yes–no questions is commonly a (delayed peak) rise followed by a complex boundary tone (analysed here as L*+H H-L%). In such tokens, an epenthetic vowel is frequently appended to the last lexical item by some speakers (Figure 1.1).

This pattern of utterance-final vowel epenthesis has not previously been reported in the (small) literature on TA intonation, nor in any other work on the intonation patterns of neighbouring dialects of Arabic, to the best of our knowledge. In the present study we investigate the incidence of utterance-final vowel epenthesis in TA to see if its occurrence varies by discourse context, prosodic contour, speech style, metrical structure or segmental content, as well as by individual speaker. These are all factors which have been reported to condition text–tune phenomenon in one or more varieties of Romance languages spoken across the Mediterranean from Tunisia. In addition we explore a new potential factor, the sociolinguistic variable of gender.

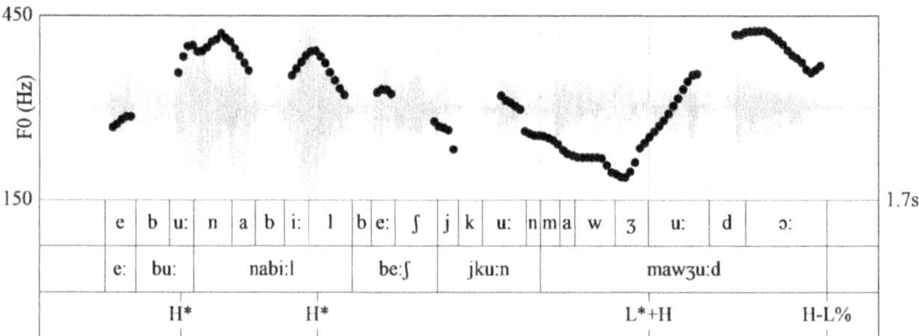

**Figure 1.1.** Yes–no question from read speech produced with vowel epenthesis [tuns-ynq6-f4].

| e: | bu: | na'bi:l | be:ʃ | jku:n | /maw'ʒu:d/ [maw'ʒu:də:] |
|---|---|---|---|---|---|
| um | father-of Nabil | PART | he will be | present |

*Will Nabil's father be there?*

Overall then, the goal here is to explore to what extent the patterns of text–tune adjustment observed in Tunisian Arabic resemble those observed in Romance languages across the Mediterranean; could the pattern be explained solely in terms of 'north–south' language contact, or should we look elsewhere for explanations?

We start by providing an overview of what is known so far about the prosodic phonology of Tunisian Arabic, and about tune–text adjustment phenomena in other languages, as motivation for the research questions of this chapter. The methods employed in the study are then outlined, including details of the corpus data and analysis techniques. The results of the analysis are presented, taking each potential conditioning factor in turn culminating in a statistical analysis which seeks to clarify the relative contribution of each factor to the observed variation in the data. The implications of the findings are then discussed in the light of intonational phonology and intonational typology, as well as our understanding to date of patterns of language contact known to influence Arabic varieties, and our knowledge of potentially comparable patterns in other dialects. A brief conclusion closes this chapter, with suggestions for potentially fruitful avenues of further research.

# 2 Background

## 2.1 The prosodic phonology of Tunisian Arabic

Tunisian Arabic, defined here as the urban (sedentary) variety spoken in Tunis, has received less attention in the phonological literature than some other dialects of Arabic. In terms of syllable structure, TA permits complex onsets and codas, with geminates permitted in syllable initial and syllable final position (Bouchhioua, 2008), but, as in all Arabic dialects, onsets are obligatory. A wide range of syllable types is thus observed (CV, CVV, CVC, CCV, CCVV, CCVC, CVCC, CCVCC). The distinction between phonological 'long'/'short' vowels in TA is primarily a matter of quality, not duration; nevertheless, in our phonetic transcriptions, 'long' vowels are marked as long (i.e. with [:]) as they would be in cognate words in other varieties of Arabic, for ease of comparison, but without postulating phonemic vowel length in TA.

TA displays a typical, rule-governed stress assignment pattern for Arabic dialects, characterised by the following algorithm: stress falls on a final superheavy syllable if present, else on the penultimate syllable (Ghazali, 1973; cited in Bouchhioua, 2008). The phonetic correlates of stress in TA have been investigated in some detail by Bouchhioua (2008) who found word-level lexical stress to be marked primarily by means of spectral balance and F1 lowering, and phrase-level, post-lexical stress (pitch accent) marked primarily by duration.

There has been little prior work on the intonation of Tunisian Arabic, limited to several Masters dissertations carried out in Tunisia (Aloulou, 2003; Knis, 2004; Saadi, 2014). According to Aloulou (2003, cited in Bouchhioua, 2008) discourse-non-final declaratives bear a rising tone, whereas discourse-final declaratives bear a falling tone; yes–no questions bear a rising tone, but wh-questions generally bear a falling tone (a subset show a complex rise–fall or fall–rise). Knis (2004; summarised in Ghazali, Hamidi, & Knis, 2007) presents sample utterances from two speakers each of a range of Arabic dialects, including TA, but the dataset is too small to permit meaningful generalisations. The most recent study of these, Saadi (2014), describes the contour in yes–no questions as a rise–fall contour with a final H-L% boundary, partially resembling the findings in our study here.

However, none of these previous small-scale studies of TA intonation mention any pattern of vowel epenthesis associated either with yes–no questions or with an interrogative rise–fall contour. To the best of our knowledge, therefore, the present study is the first description of this pattern, which is however robustly observed in the dataset examined. It is possible that the pattern is a relatively recent innovation in TA; alternatively, it may be the case that the small sample sizes used in prior studies failed to capture the full range of intonational expression in TA, which we are now able to explore with the aid of the present, somewhat larger corpus.

## 2.2  A typology of tune–text alignment

One of the first studies to explore tune–text alignment phenomena in detail was Grabe (1998), who observed a difference between English and German in resolving the problem of how to realise a complex intonational contour, in contexts of tonal crowding. A typical tonal crowding context would be a monosyllabic word in utterance-final position, such that all and any tonal targets in the nuclear pitch accent and following edge tones must be realised on a single syllable. Grabe noticed that, in general, in Southern Standard British English (SSBE) in such contexts, the slope of the intonational contour is increased, resulting in a steeper fall or rise than is observed when the same prosodic contour is realised on a polysyllabic word or with non-final stress; this strategy is described as *compression* of the contour. In contrast, in parallel contexts, in Standard German, the slope of the intonational contour is unchanged, and instead the rise or fall fails to be fully realised, but is cut off before the fall or rise is complete; this alternative strategy is described as *truncation* of the contour. In subsequent work, on varieties of British English spoken in different cities in the UK, Grabe and colleagues observed variation across dialects. Some British dialects display truncation of the contour (e.g. Leeds), and others show compression of the contour (e.g. Newcastle), in parallel contexts. A stylised example is shown in Figure 1.2 below, based on Grabe (2004:11).

A logical alternative to the problem of tonal crowding – instead of adjusting the intonational 'tune' to fit the available segmental 'text' – is to increase the amount of segmental material available, so as to be able to realise the full intonational contour, without either compression or truncation. Adjustment of the segmental material could in principle take the form either of lengthening of existing segments or insertion of additional segments. Both types of text–tune adjustment have been reported in Standard European Portuguese (SEP), but we focus here on reported cases of word-final vowel insertion, which may provide clues to the factors conditioning utterance-final vowel epenthesis in TA, which is the focus of the present study.

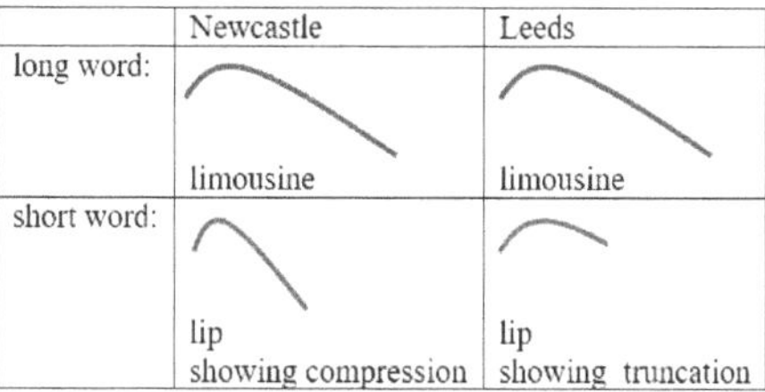

**Figure 1.2.** Stylised representation of compression vs. truncation, as observed in varieties of British English spoken in Newcastle vs. Leeds (based on examples in Grabe, 2004:11).

Word-final vowel 'insertion' (i.e. epenthesis), in the form of blocking of a more general rule of final-vowel deletion, is observed in SEP in yes–no questions and in vocative chants (Frota et al., 2015), and is restricted to cases where the word in question has a final sonorant consonant (examples show [r], [l] and [n]). This contrasts with observations of the same phenomenon in the variety of Portuguese spoken in the Alentejo region of central-southern Portugal, which displays word-final epenthesis after a sonorant consonant in all sentence types. Epenthesis is thus analysed as a general marker of the right-edge of the intonational phrase in that variety (Cruz, 2013), mirroring a similar pattern reported for Galician (Martínez-Gil, 1997). Word-final vowel epenthesis is seen in SEP in contexts with the nuclear contours listed in (1) below:

(1)   yes–no questions         H+L* LH%

      greeting vocative call    H* !H%

      insistent vocative call    H* L%

The yes–no question contour has a complex bitonal boundary tone (see arguments against analysis of this as L-H% in (Frota, 2002)), which it could be argued requires additional segmental material to be realised. Frota et al. (2015) also note that the !H% boundary tone in SEP greeting vocatives displays 'spreading qualities', and that such spreading might plausibly be seen as a hallmark of both types of vocatives, suggesting that the relative 'weight' or complexity of the edge tones is a potential unifying factor across the contours and contexts in (1). Most of the cited examples in the work on SEP are taken from read speech, but there is at least one example reported from spontaneous speech Map Task data (Frota et al., 2015:256, Figure 7.13), suggesting that the phenomenon is not confined to read speech in SEP.

A similar pattern of tune–text adjustment, depending in part on the shape of the prosodic contour, has also been reported in an experimental study of loanwords into Bari Italian (Grice, Savino, Caffo, & Roettger, 2015). Amid a general picture of considerable variation by speaker and by item, the authors report that vowel insertion was conditioned by a number of factors including 'prosodic contour' (defined as question vs. statement), number of syllables in the word, and voicing of the final consonant in the phrase-final word. The incidence of word-final vowel epenthesis was higher in read speech than in spontaneous speech (Grice p.c.).

In summary therefore, utterance-final vowel epenthesis (or blocking of final vowel deletion) has been observed in certain varieties of two Romance languages spoken in southern Europe (Table 1.1).

**Table 1.1.**  Summary of factors reported to condition utterance-final vowel epenthesis.

| *Language* | *Discourse function* | *Segmental and metrical context* | *Prosodic contour* |
| --- | --- | --- | --- |
| Standard European Portuguese | yes–no questions vocatives | if final consonant is sonorant | H+L* LH% <br> H* !H% <br> H* L% |
| Alentejo European Portuguese | all sentence types | if final consonant is sonorant | H+L* L% <br> L* L% |
| Bari Italian | yes–no questions | more common on monosyllables | L+H* L-H% <br><br> L* L-H% |
|  | continuation rises | more common if final consonant is voiced | H* H-^H% |

## 2.3   Research questions

This chapter seeks to determine whether or not the factors which have been shown to condition word-final epenthesis in varieties of European Portuguese and Italian also condition word-final epenthesis in TA. The study thus investigates a range of internal and external factors which might explain the observed patterns of word-final epenthesis in TA, in a small dataset extracted from a larger corpus of TA speech.

The key factors explored are variation due to individual speaker or lexical item, alongside discourse function (e.g. question, vocative, continuation), tonal contour (choice of nuclear accent and/or boundary tones), segmental and metrical context (number of syllables in the word, position of stress in the word, type of final segment) and speech style (spontaneous vs. read/scripted speech). Speech style is included due to the observation by

Ng (2013) that word-final vowel epenthesis (or, *paragoge*, to use her term) is frequently observed in language contact scenarios, such as second language acquisition or loanword adaptation; Ng thus ascribes word-final epenthesis to hyperarticulation ('reduced gestural overlap') in effortful speech. If this characterisation is correct, then the incidence of word-final vowel epenthesis in TA is predicted to be higher in read speech than in spontaneous speech, as is indeed reported for Bari Italian (Grice, p.c.). Furthermore, if Ng's (2013) hypothesis that paragoge is a diagnostic of language change is correct, then we might reasonably expect that change to follow typical patterns observed in diffusion of linguistic innovations, and to be led by women (Eckert & McConnell-Ginet, 2003; Labov, 2001), resulting in a potential effect of gender as a conditioning factor. An additional factor explored here, therefore, which was not discussed in prior parallel studies on Italian or European Portuguese, is a potential role of gender, as a sociolinguistic factor.

## 2.4  Methods

The study exploits data from the Intonational Variation in Arabic (IVAr) corpus (Hellmuth & Almbark, 2019), rather than from an experiment designed specifically to target this construction; not all potentially relevant variables are systematically varied in the dataset under investigation therefore. The key potential conditioning factors can be investigated, however, and use of corpus data allows us to explore the extent to which vowel epenthesis is observed in both read and semi-spontaneous speech, as well as the degree of variation across speakers.

The data in the Tunisian Arabic portion of the IVAr corpus (which bears the short code 'tuns') was collected in Tunis, Tunisia, in April 2014. Recordings were made with 12 speakers (6 female, 6 male). They were aged between 20–24 at the time of recording, and all were born and raised in Tunisia, to parents who were both born and raised in Tunisia. All were first language speakers of TA, though all were also fluent in French, which is taught in schools in Tunisia from the age of 10 (Grade 5). Two speakers (f2 and f3) were born to parents who were born in the south of Tunisia; the remainder were born to parents born in the north of Tunisia.

Declarative statements with varying information structure, together with a range of different question types, were embedded in a scripted dialogue which was read aloud as a role play by all 12 speakers, working in pairs. The metrical structure of the last lexical item in each target sentence was systematically varied, with stress on the antepenult, penult or final syllable. We extracted from these dialogues a set of read speech yes–no questions (*ynq*, N=68) and a set of control sentences (N=58) of other types (including declaratives and wh-questions) in which the last lexical item is the same as in one or more of the *ynqs*. We also extracted from the scripted dialogue a set of read speech vocatives (N=12). In addition, a search was made for tokens of vowel epenthesis in list items (N=24) elicited in a Discourse Completion Task (cf. Frota & Prieto, 2015) and for yes–no questions in spontaneous speech (N=40) collected using a Map Task (Anderson et al., 1991). All of the data are from the IVAr corpus and details of the data elicitation materials are available from the IVAr database webpage.[1]

The extracted subsets of data provide 202 tokens which were submitted to qualitative impressionistic auditory analysis to identify various phenomena of interest, including the presence/absence of an utterance-final vowel and the shape of the prosodic contour. All data analysis was performed by the author, with qualitative analysis based on auditory impression with reference to the spectrogram and fundamental frequency contour using Praat (Boersma & Weenink, 2015). Criteria used for identification of an epenthetic vowel were the presence of periodic vibration and/or formant structure after the consonantal release, or a visible change in the formant structure and/or intensity after a word-final lexical vowel (following Grice et al., 2015). Acoustic measurements of the epenthetic vowels were performed using a Praat script written by the author, to extract the duration, mean intensity and F1/F2 values (at the midpoint) of each labelled vowel.

For annotation of TA prosodic contours, the Autosegmental-Metrical framework is adopted (Ladd, 2008), in which intonational tunes are comprised of phonological tonal targets which are phonologically associated with certain positions in the metrical structure of the utterance. Like most – though not all – Arabic dialects described so far (Hellmuth, 2013), TA displays postlexical intonational marking of both the heads and edges of prosodic domains. An intonational tune in TA is thus formed of one or more pitch accents (tones associated with prominent syllables) and boundary tones (associated with the right edge of phrases). For the present study, relevant portions of the data were prosodically annotated by the author using a prototype annotation system for Arabic which is currently under development (Hellmuth, in preparation), but which is based on the ToBI annotation system proposed for American English (Beckman & Elam, 1997; Beckman, Hirschberg, & Shattuck-Hufnagel, 2005). A key difference between the original ToBI system and the transcription system used here, is that in the original ToBI system, the high phrase accent (H-) in a final H-L% boundary combination (phrase accent + boundary tone) is assumed to have an effect of upstep on the following low boundary tone (L%) such

---

[1]  http://ivar.york.ac.uk/

that the H-L% sequence is realised with level pitch. In the transcription system used here, instead, a H-L% boundary combination is realised as a slight fall at the boundary (as seen in the example illustrated in Figure 1.1 above). This analysis is motivated by the fact that, in this contour, the final H peak is aligned quite consistently at short distance before the phrase boundary, and is thus analysed as a phrase accent (H-). In contrast, the position of the elbow at the start of the rise towards this peak does vary according to prosodic structure of the utterance, with a somewhat earlier start to the rise in cases where the stressed syllable in the target word is earlier in the word (i.e. on the antepenult or penult syllable), but without showing tight alignment to the start of the accentual syllable, which is generally realised with low pitch; the post-accentual rise is thus analysed as a trailing tone which is part of a bitonal pitch accent associated with the accented syllable (L*+H). The specific detail of the labels used in annotation is not critical to the investigation here, though identification of the presence or absence of a complex rise–fall (L*+H H-L%) contour, as opposed to a plain rise (L* H-H%) is important, as will be seen. Additional quantitative analysis of the fundamental frequency contour was performed, therefore, in a subset of the data (the read speech data only), using a Praat script written by the author, to support the qualitative analysis. Descriptive statistics were produced using Excel or R (R Development Core Team, 2008) and a Classification by Regression Trees (CART) analysis (Baayen, 2008) was carried out using R.

# 3    Results

The vowel epenthesis pattern was initially observed during prosodic annotation of yes–no questions in read speech. Our goal in this chapter is to establish the distribution of the pattern, by inspecting a wider range of available corpus data, in both read and semi-spontaneous speech, and exploring a range of potentially relevant factors which we treat in turn.

## 3.1    Discourse function and speech style

The first task is to determine whether vowel epenthesis is primarily conditioned by discourse function; that is, whether vowel epenthesis in TA marks yes–no questions only, or not. Table 1.2, below, shows the results of auditory analysis carried out to determine the presence or absence of a word-final vowel, in read speech yes–no questions. Just over half (54%) were produced with vowel epenthesis, suggesting that, although vowel epenthesis

**Table 1.2.** Incidence of vowel epenthesis in read speech yes–no questions, by target utterance.

| *Target* | *Last lexical item* | | *Number of tokens in which vowel epenthesis was observed* | |
| --- | --- | --- | --- | --- |
| ynq1 | [ˈja.ma.ni] | 'Yemeni' | 6 (N=12) | 50% |
| ynq2 | [ˈba.la.di] | 'traditional' | 7 (N=11) | 64% |
| ynq3 | [ˈzeː.na] | 'Zena' | 7 (N=12) | 58% |
| ynq4 | [la.ˈjaː.li] | 'nights' | 4 (N=11) | 36% |
| ynq5 | [ʔa.ˈmiːn] | 'Amin' | 6 (N=10) | 60% |
| ynq6 | [maw.ˈʒuːd] | 'present' | 7 (N=12) | 58% |
| Total | | | 37 (N=68) | 54% |

is common in yes–no questions, it is not a necessary or consistent cue to yes–no question status.

In contrast, when the set of control utterances from read speech was inspected, containing the same lexical item in utterance-final position as in one or more of the yes–no questions, but with a different discourse function (including focus statements and wh-questions), no cases of vowel epenthesis were observed, as shown in Table 1.3. This contrasts with the pattern observed in the Alentejo variety of European Portuguese, in which utterance-final vowel epenthesis is observed across a range of sentence types (Cruz, 2013).

Since vowel epenthesis was reported in vocatives in SEP, a set of read speech vocative utterances, extracted from the scripted dialogue were inspected also. Of the 12 vocatives inspected, only one was produced with utterance-final vowel epenthesis (tuns-voc-f3, see Figure 1.5 below), which we assume would be interpreted with interrogative force, as well as vocative function, and which we will discuss further in the next section. Similarly, since vowel epenthesis was reported in continuation rises in Bari Italian, we inspected examples of semi-spontaneously produced lists, elicited using a Discourse Continuation Task (DCT, see Methods). In one task, speakers were asked to list the days of the week, and in a second task, to list what they had eaten so far that day. DCT data was collected with all 12 speakers in our sample, but no instances of vowel epenthesis were observed in any of the (N=24) lists produced.

Finally, to determine whether speech style conditions vowel epenthesis in TA (as was observed in Bari Italian, Grice, p.c.), we identified a set of yes–no questions produced in semi-spontaneous speech, in Map Task data. In total, 40 yes–no questions were identified in the Map Task data, and of

**Table 1.3.** Incidence of vowel epenthesis in read speech control sentences, by target utterance.

| Target | Last lexical item | | Number of tokens in which vowel epenthesis was observed | |
|---|---|---|---|---|
| coo1 | [ˈja.ma.ni] | 'Yemeni' | 0 (N=11) | 0% |
| idf1 | [ˈja.ma.ni] | 'Yemeni' | 0 (N=12) | 0% |
| whq1 | [ˈja.ma.ni] | 'Yemeni' | 0 (N=11) | 0% |
| con4 | [ˈzeː.na] | 'Zena' | 0 (N=12) | 0% |
| con6 | [maw.ˈʒuːd] | 'present' | 0 (N=12) | 0% |
| Total | | | 0 (N=58) | 0% |

these, 25 were produced with utterance-final vowel epenthesis (63%). This suggests that utterance-final vowel epenthesis in TA is not restricted to read speech. The incidence of vowel epenthesis is slightly higher in the spontaneous speech sample than in the read speech data, however, more of the tokens in the spontaneous speech sample were produced by female speakers (N=27) than by male speakers (N=13), and, as we shall see below, in the read speech sample female speakers tended to use vowel epenthesis more than male speakers. A sample token of vowel epenthesis in spontaneous speech is illustrated in Figure 1.3 below. The response of the interlocutor in this instance was 'yes' [ʔeː], which provides independent 'next-turn proof' (Hutchby & Wooffitt, 2008) of our auditory impression that the opening utterance can be classified as a yes–no question, since it was treated as such by the interlocutor in the original conversation.

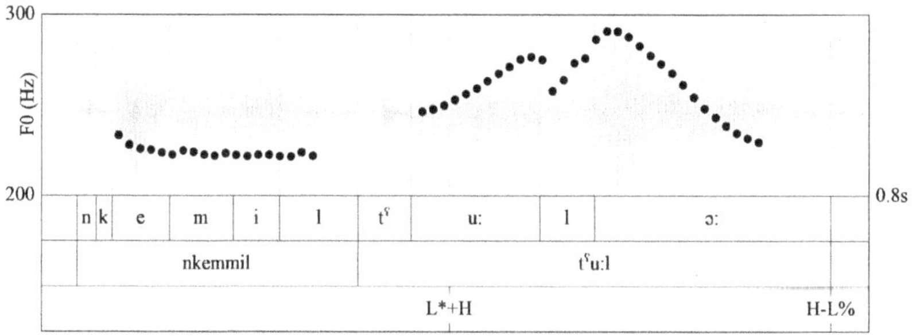


**Figure 1.3.** Yes–no question from Map Task data produced with vowel epenthesis [tuns-mp1-f3.109-110].

ˈnkem.mil   /tˤuːl/ [ˈtˤuːləː]
I-continue   straight ahead
*Should I go straight ahead?*

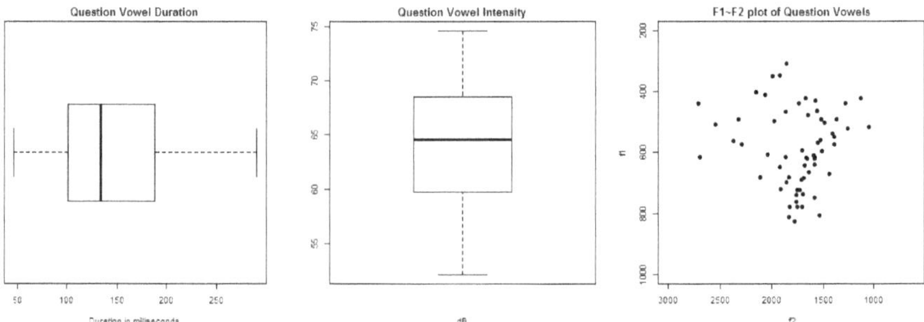

**Figure 1.4.** All epenthetic vowels: boxplots of duration (left) and intensity (centre), and F1/F2 plot (right).

Figure 1.4 shows the spread of values of measures of vowel duration and mean intensity in the labelled epenthetic vowels, as well as a plot of F1/F2 taken at the midpoint of each labelled vowel. Duration and intensity are normally distributed, but there is considerable variation in the quality of the inserted vowel, an issue to which we return below.

In summary, although the vowel epenthesis pattern is only observed consistently in yes–no questions, it is not a necessary cue to yes–no question status, since epenthesis is observed in roughly half of *ynq* tokens only. Other potentially relevant contexts did not yield a similar proportion of vowel epenthesis tokens, but instead only isolated examples, with one case observed in a wh-question (tuns-whq1-f5) and one in a vocative (tuns-voc-f3). In each case, these outlier tokens were produced with a different prosodic contour than that observed in all other parallel utterances (which typically ended in a fall H* L-L% or rise L* H-H%). In the next section therefore we turn to the detail of the prosodic contour, to see whether this is the primary determiner of utterance-final vowel epenthesis in TA.

## 3.2   Prosodic contour

To determine the extent to which utterance-final vowel epenthesis in TA is conditioned by prosodic context, firstly, the read speech yes–no questions were prosodically annotated. Figure A in the Appendix sets out in full the incidence of vowel epenthesis according to nuclear contour (last pitch accent + boundary tones) and by speaker. The most common prosodic contour observed on the last lexical item in read speech yes–no questions was a complex rise–fall pitch contour comprised of a rising nuclear pitch accent L*+H followed by a complex falling edge tone, analysed here as H-L%. There were no instances of vowel epenthesis in utterances produced with a simple

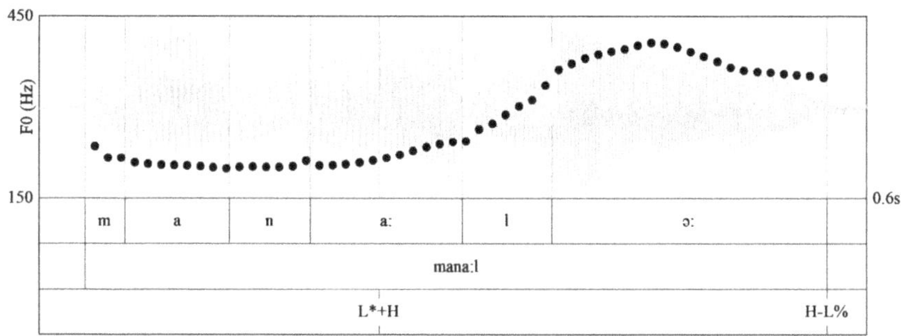


**Figure 1.5.** Vocative from read speech data produced with vowel epenthesis [tuns-voc-f3].

/maˈnaːl/ [maˈnaːləː]
(name.f)
*Manal!?*

pitch contour with no change of direction, such as a rise (L*+H H-H%) or fall (H* L-L%). Among the vocatives, the only instance of a complex pitch contour was found in the one token in which vowel epenthesis was also observed (tuns-voc-f3), illustrated in Figure 1.5.

It seems therefore that vowel epenthesis is primarily conditioned by prosodic contour shape, since no instances at all of vowel epenthesis are observed on utterances which bear a simple rising (L* H-H%) or falling (H* L-L%) contour.

Nevertheless, it is not the case that a complex pitch contour necessarily triggers the presence of vowel epenthesis. Figure 1.6 below shows plots of mean F0 for female and male speakers and for tokens produced with or without vowel epenthesis, measured at ten points through the last lexical item, in all read speech utterances transcribed with a L*+H H-L% contour (N=54). The plots show a clear rise to a peak (analysed here as a L*+H accent) following by a small fall at the right edge of the word (analysed here as H-L%), regardless of whether or not an epenthetic vowel is produced. Note that the position of the H peak relative to the stressed syllable of the accented word does not vary according to the prosodic structure of the target word (here, varied in terms of the position of stress in the word), hence analysis of that peak as a H- phrase accent. In contrast, the position of the elbow at the start of the rise towards that peak does shift somewhat earlier as the position of the stressed syllable moves earlier in the word, so that the rise extends onto the postaccentual syllable, whenever present; this rising movement is thus analysed as due to a trailing H tone which is part of a bitonal pitch accent associated with the accented syllable (L*+H).

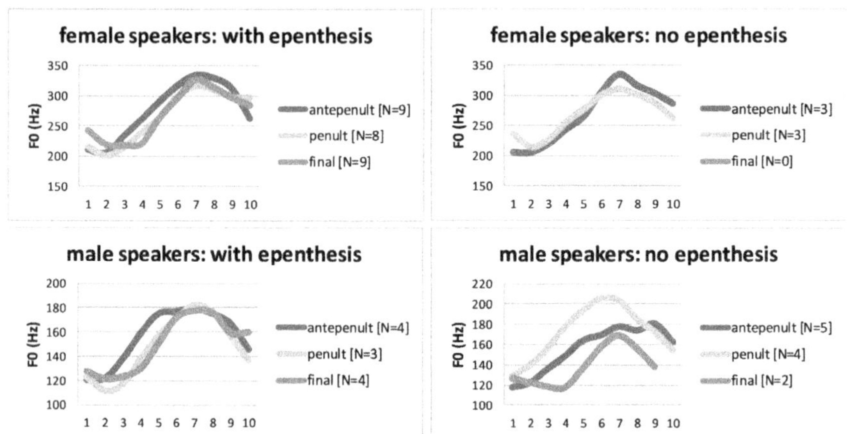

**Figure 1.6.** Mean values of F0, at ten measuring points through the last lexical item, in read speech yes–no questions produced with L*+H H-L% contour by female and male speakers, by presence of vowel epenthesis or not, and by position of the stressed syllable in the word.

To summarise, a key conditioning factor for vowel epenthesis in TA yes–no questions appears to be the presence of the complex rise–fall nuclear pitch contour (here, L*+H H-L%), as no epenthesis was observed in tokens bearing other contour types. However, not all utterances produced with the complex pitch contour show vowel epenthesis. In the next two sections we explore other factors which may further influence the occurrence of vowel epenthesis.

## 3.3   Segmental and metrical context

A number of factors are reported to constrain the incidence of vowel epenthesis, in the prior literature on text–tune adjustment in southern European languages (as summarised in Table 1.1 above). These include the metrical structure of the target word (with more epenthesis observed on monosyllables) and the segmental content of the target word (with more epenthesis after a sonorant and/or voiced consonant). An exhaustive list was created of all lexical items found in utterance-final position in all yes–no questions analysed (N=108), including data from read speech (N=68) and spontaneous speech (N=40). A count was then made of the incidence of vowel epenthesis in these lexical items, by different relevant factors.

The only instances of monosyllables in the dataset are from spontaneous speech (e.g. as in Figure 1.3 on the words [tˤuːl] 'straight ahead'), as no utterance-final monosyllables were elicited in the read speech scripted dialogue task. This results in a small number of tokens (N=5) for analysis here, but the majority of these monosyllables (4 out of 5) show vowel epenthesis. Nevertheless, vowel epenthesis is frequently observed on polysyllabic words, as shown in Figure 1.7. If vowel epenthesis in TA were a pure case of tune–text adjustment, serving to provide sufficient segmental material for realisation of all intonational tones, we might expect vowel epenthesis to be much less common at the end of polysyllabic words, where plentiful segmental material is available, and this is not the case. The incidence of vowel epenthesis also seems not to be conditioned by the position of stress in the word, as shown in Figure 1.8 below, and as can also be seen in the left hand plots in Figure 1.6 above (among the tokens in which vowel epenthesis was observed, there is a roughly equal incidence of vowel epenthesis in tokens

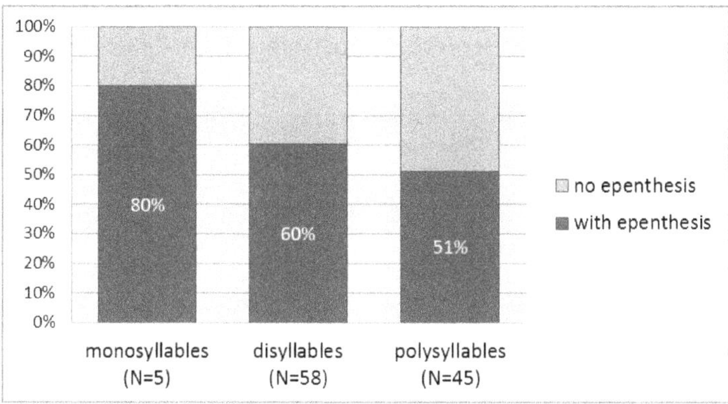


**Figure 1.7.** Vowel epenthesis by number of syllables in the word, in all yes–no questions (N=108).

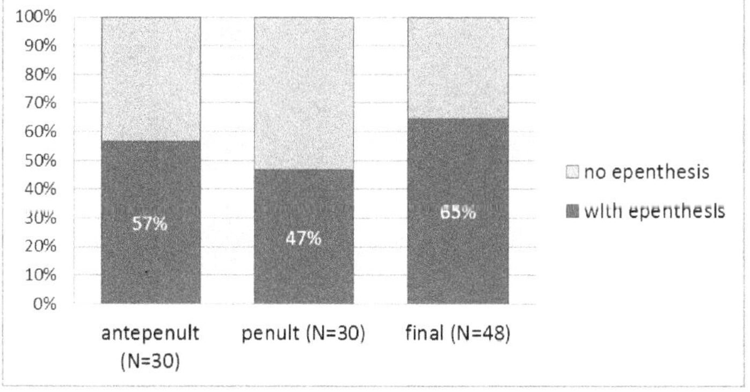


**Figure 1.8.** Vowel epenthesis by position of stress in the word, in all yes–no questions (N=108).

regardless of the position of stress in the utterance-final word). Again, if tonal crowding were the motivation for text–tune adjustment, we might expect more vowel epenthesis in words with final stress, and this is not the case. Finally, there appears also to be no categorical effect of final segment type (that is, the type of segment appearing at the end of the utterance final word). Vowel epenthesis is seen just as frequently in tokens in which the utterance-final word ends in an obstruent (whether voiced or voiceless e.g. [maw.ˈʒuːd] 'present' or [ʕliːk] 'to you') as in words ending in a sonorant or vowel, as shown in Figure 1.9 below.

There is, however, an effect of final segment type on acoustic properties of the epenthesised vowel, as shown in Figure 1.10. Epenthetic vowels following a consonant tend to be longer and louder than those following a vowel. Following a vowel, the quality of the epenthetic vowel is also highly variable, tracking the quality of the vowel it follows (though in all cases some change in formant structure must have been detected for it to be

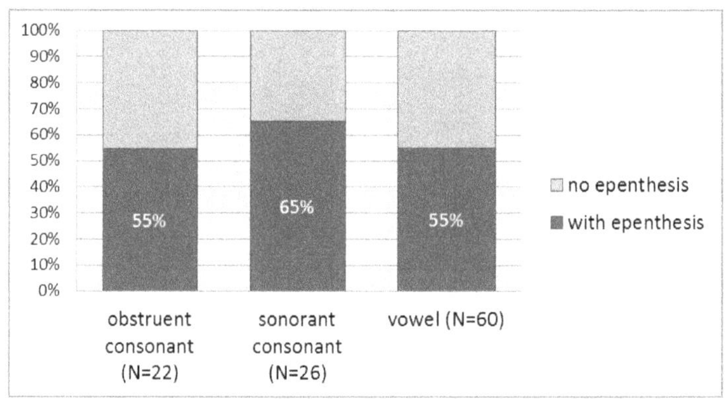



**Figure 1.9.** Vowel epenthesis by final segment type, in all yes–no questions (N=108).

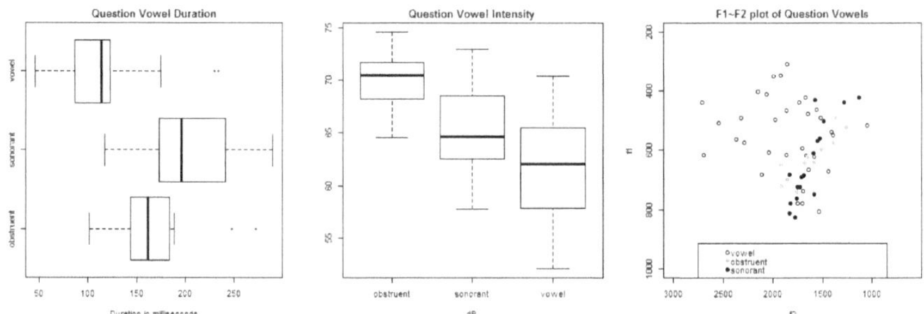



**Figure 1.10.** All epenthetic vowels, split by preceding utterance-final segment type: boxplots of vowel duration (left) and mean intensity (centre), and F1/F2 at vowel midpoint (right).

labelled); there is more limited variation in the quality of vowels along an [a]~ [ə]~[u] continuum after a final sonorant, which overlaps fully in distribution with that of vowels after a final obstruent.

We explore below whether there are probabilistic effects of these factors on the incidence of vowel epenthesis, as was observed in Bari Italian (Grice et al., 2015), but from these descriptive results there is no indication that vowel epenthesis in TA is a categorical tonal crowding effect, since there is no obvious conditioning due to segmental or metrical context.

## 3.4   Speaker variation

The incidence of vowel epenthesis appears to vary according to gender in TA, as illustrated in Figure 1.11 below, with female speakers (f1–f6) displaying on average more epenthesis (76%) than male speakers (m1–m6) (32%). A full breakdown by item and speaker is provided in Figure B in the Appendix. In this read speech data, one female speaker (f4) produces an utterance-final vowel in all of her yes–no questions, whereas there are two male speakers (m2, m6) who never produce any utterance-final vowels. Variation by gender has not been reported in other studies of utterance-final vowel epenthesis.

This pattern is mirrored in the set of yes–no questions extracted from spontaneous speech, as shown in Figure 1.12 below. Although there is an uneven number of tokens produced across speakers, due to the spontaneous nature of the elicitation task, nevertheless, the same two male speakers (m2, m6) produce no vowel epenthesis, and there is in general a higher incidence of vowel epenthesis in spontaneous speech produced by female speakers (78%) compared to male speakers (38%).

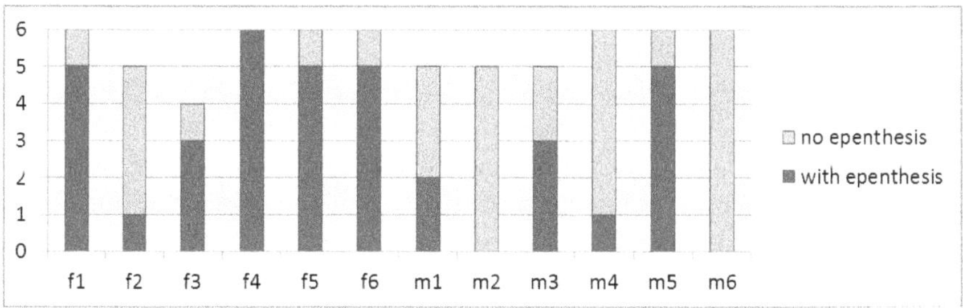


**Figure 1.11.** Number of read speech yes–no questions in which vowel epenthesis was observed or not, by speaker. Female speakers = f1-f6; male speakers = m1-m6.

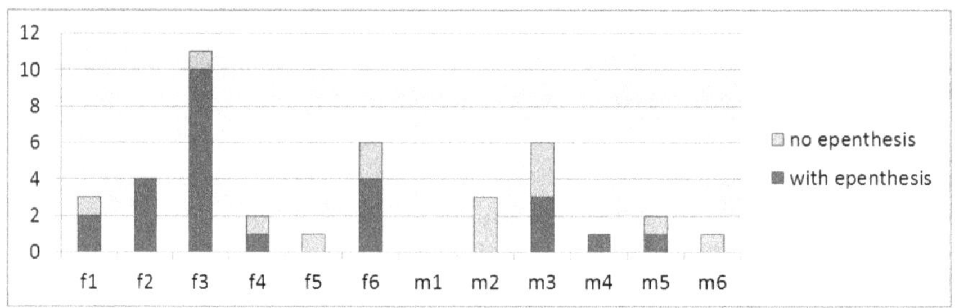

**Figure 1.12** Number of spontaneous speech yes–no questions in which vowel epenthesis was observed or not, by speaker. Female speakers = f1-f6; male speakers = m1-m6.

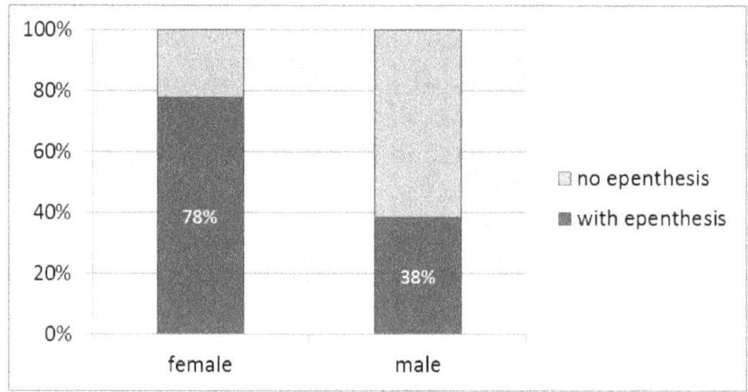

**Figure 1.13.** Incidence of vowel epenthesis in all yes–no questions (N=108), by gender.

Overall, in all yes–no questions, female speakers produce vowels in 77% of tokens and male speakers produce vowels in 32% of tokens, as shown in Figure 1.13.

As well as producing more vowel epenthesis overall, female speakers produced epenthetic vowels which tended to be longer and louder than those produced by male speakers, and with fronter, lower vowel quality (closer to [a] than [u]), as shown in Figure 1.14.

Since the quality of the epenthetic vowel after a word-final vowel is highly variable across all speakers, Figure 1.15 shows F1/F2 for epenthetic vowels after a final consonant only, split by gender of the speaker, and by region of birth of speaker's parents (north or south). From the present limited sample it is not possible to tease apart fully the effects of gender vs. region on epenthetic vowel quality, and we highlight this as a topic ripe for further investigation.

Finally, recall, from Figure A (in the Appendix), that male speakers tend to use simple pitch contours, and in particular rises, more than female speakers, as illustrated in Figure 1.16.

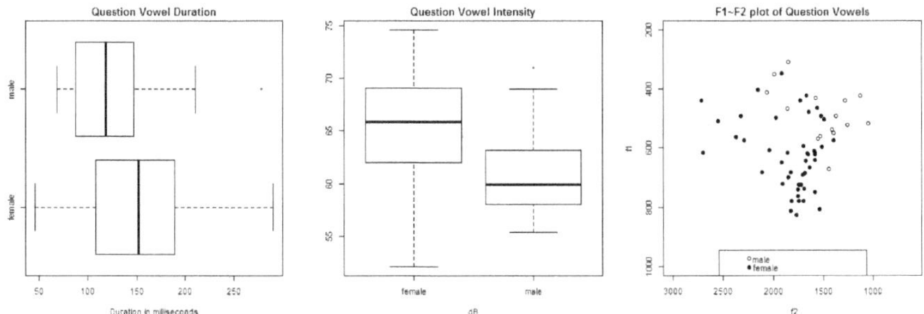

**Figure 1.14.** All epenthetic vowels, split by gender of speaker: boxplots of vowel duration (left) and mean intensity (centre), and F1/F2 at vowel midpoint (right).

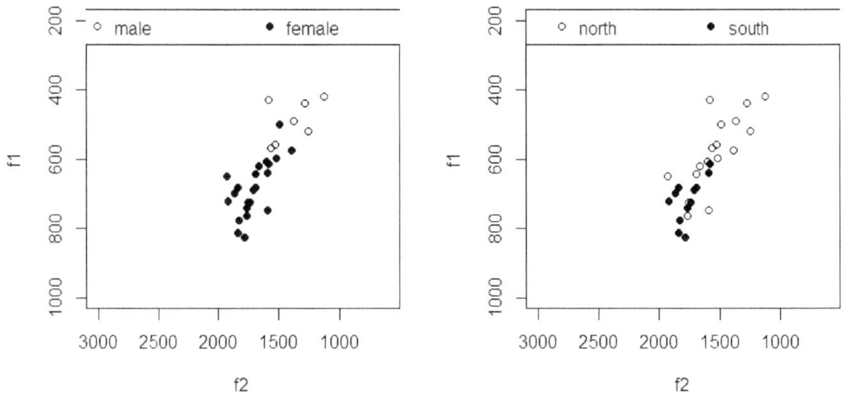

**Figure 1.15.** Measures of F1/F2 at vowel midpoint of epenthetic vowels following a final consonant, split by gender (left) and region of birth of speaker's parents (right).

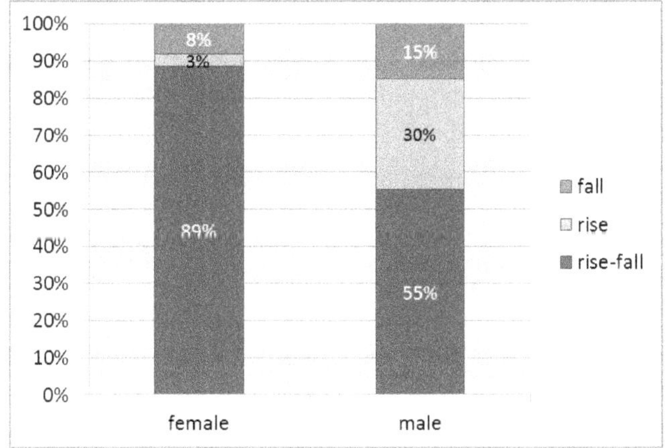

**Figure 1.16.** Incidence of different contour types in all yes–no questions (N=108), by gender.

Some of the variation in the data could thus perhaps be explained in terms of a trading relation between the choice to produce an epenthetic vowel and the choice to produce a complex pitch contour L*+H H-L% vs. a simple rise H-H%. Indeed, it may be that male speakers are producing truncated forms of the rise–fall contour, neutralising the contrast between L*+H H-L% and L* H-H%. However, the observed co-variation between choice of contour shape and vowel epenthesis is not total, since male speakers produce complex pitch contours in 55% of tokens (Figure 1.16) but produce a vowel in only 38% of tokens (Figure 1.13). This is seen also in Figure 1.6, which includes tokens (on the left hand side) which bear a complex pitch contour but are realised without a vowel, by male as well as female speakers.

Overall then, within the subset of the data which bears a complex pitch contour, there is still some residual variation. A Classification by Regression Trees (CART) analysis was used to determine whether this residual variation was significant (Baayen, 2008; cf. Grice et al., 2015), taking all factors into account (contour shape, final segment, position of stress, number of syllables, speech style and gender). A cost complexity pruned CART tree showed only marginal improvement (13% misclassification) over a baseline model (17% misclassification) in which only choice of contour is used as a predictor. The only statistically significant predictor of utterance-final vowel epenthesis in the present sample of yes–no questions in TA is thus the choice of prosodic contour.

## 3.5  Summary

Utterance-final vowel epenthesis in Tunisian Arabic (TA) yes–no questions was found to be variable across both speakers and items. The primary conditioning factor (present in all observed cases) is a complex pitch contour (analysed here as L*+H H-L%). However, not all utterances bearing a complex pitch contour are realised with a final epenthetic vowel. An important secondary conditioning factor appears, on the surface, to be gender, with female speakers more likely to produce an epenthetic vowel than male speakers, though this effect is not statistically significant, in the present dataset. The epenthetic vowels produced by females tend also to be longer, louder and more peripheral in vowel quality. A potential trading relation between vowel epenthesis and boundary is observed which opens up the possibility that the gender-driven variation in TA may in fact be between a truncation strategy and an epenthesis strategy. Nevertheless, these two 'strategies' are observed only in yes–no questions, and only in utterances which bear no obvious evidence of tonal crowding (such as polysyllables with non-final stress), in contrast to patterns observed in other languages.

# 4  Discussion

Analysis of data in Tunisian Arabic (TA) from a corpus of both read and spontaneous speech indicates that utterance-final vowel epenthesis is frequently observed in yes–no questions, but only in exceptional cases in other sentence types. All instances of vowel epenthesis in the present data are found in tokens bearing a complex pitch contour (here, L*+H H-L%), and the presence of this complex pitch contour is a primary conditioning factor. This pattern is thus different from that observed in Alentejo Portuguese, for example, in which vowel epenthesis co-occurs with a variety of different tonal contours.

There are tokens in the present dataset bearing a complex pitch contour which are realised without vowel epenthesis however (N=18), but none of the constraining factors observed in SEP and Bari Italian – such as sonority of the final segment or the number of syllables in the word, nor an equivalent factor of position of stress in the word – are robust predictors of the presence or absence of vowel epenthesis in TA.

It is puzzling that utterance-final vowel epenthesis is observed in TA in contexts which appear to provide sufficient segmental material on which to realise a complex pitch contour. Under a standard AM framework phonological account, it is hard to characterise this as a pure case of 'text–tune adjustment'. There are some indications of a trading relation between truncation (somewhat preferred by male speakers) and vowel epenthesis (preferred by female speakers), which, if confirmed in further data in future, might still suggest that an element of tonal crowding is nevertheless at work.

A potential alternative explanation as to the origins of this TA epenthetic vowel pattern would be historical migration patterns into North Africa from the Arabian Peninsula, resembling similarly discontinuous patterns of syntactic variation across Arabic dialects (Lucas & Lash, 2010). Holes (2016) reports the existence of a clitic suffix [-ə] which attaches to a word or sentence to create a yes–no question, in the Baħarna dialect of Bahrain (BBA), and in sedentary dialects in Oman. In BBA, the /-ə/ clitic is realised as [-hə] or [-jə] after a vowel or glide, and there are parallel cases in the present dataset, in that the utterance-final word ['jamani] is realised by some speakers as

[ˈjamanijə].[2] Holes notes that rising intonation is used in BBA in tag questions, which mirror the vowel clitic in meaning, and confirms that the /-ə/ clitic is also accompanied by a characteristic rise–fall tune (Holes, p.c.). In TA, we have assumed thus far that it is the complex boundary which conditions vowel epenthesis, rather than the reverse, but it is tempting to consider the possibility of treating the TA epenthetic vowel as a question particle, by analogy with the BBA case. Another potential source of such a particle would be from contact with Tamazight, since an interrogative clitic [a] polar question particle is reported for Zwara Tamazight (Gussenhoven, 2018), a variety of Tamazight spoken in western Libya close to the border with Tunisia. However, in Zwara Tamazight, this particle is expressly reported to be accompanied only and always by a final falling intonational contour, so the match with the TA pattern is only partial.

A further puzzle is that, if we treat these TA epenthetic vowels as question particles, arising in a historical contact scenario, adoption of vowel epenthesis is quite clearly not a case of linguistic innovation, since the BBA phenomenon is reported by Holes only in the speech of an older generation of speakers, and we can assume that any Tamazight substrate influence pre-dates the arrival of Arabic to Tunisia. If vowel epenthesis is, then, a conservative feature of TA we might expect it to be used more by male speakers than female, rather than the reverse as observed here. Indeed, we note that the one male speaker (m5) who produces rather more epenthetic vowels than other male speakers, also displays consistent palatalisation in his speech, which is a known innovative feature in Egyptian Arabic, initially adopted by female speakers (Haeri, 1996) but which we now also observe in the speech of young male EA speakers, for example in IVAr corpus data, (cf. also Youssef, 2016). A similar *sociolinguistic* distribution of schwa epenthesis has been reported for Parisian French (Hansen, 1997) – that is, used more frequently by young female speakers – and we might thus entertain the possibility that French is the source of the pattern observed in our data here, since French is spoken bilingually alongside TA by most educated Tunisians, and indeed by all of the participants in our study. However, although utterance final vowel epenthesis is accompanied by a rise–fall contour more frequently than other contours, in Hansen's (1997) Parisian data, the pattern is not confined to yes–no questions, but is instead used more often to express emphasis or indignation, or in a non-final position in the speaker's turn; and, in addition, the incidence of schwa epenthesis

---

[2]   For one speaker (f4), there is accompanying shift of stress to the penult yielding [jamaˈnijə], showing that for this speaker the appended vowel is integrated into the phonological word, for purposes of stress assignment.

varied according to the type of final segment. This contrasts with the TA pattern observed in our data whereby an epenthetic vowel is appended only in utterances bearing the rise–fall contour, and almost exclusively in yes–no questions, and showed no categorical variation dependent on the utterance-final segment.

# 5    Conclusion

This chapter highlights, for the first time, the existence of a phonological pattern of prosodically conditioned vowel epenthesis in TA yes–no questions. Our exploration here of the conditioning factors governing the incidence of utterance-final vowel epenthesis in TA suggests, firstly, that this is not a case of 'text–tune' adjustment at all, but rather a 'question vowel' particle of some type. This in turn suggests, secondly, that we should set aside the possibility that the pattern arises due to contact from languages across the Mediterranean (Portuguese or Italian), and instead focus on older contact scenarios via historical migrations and/or substrate influence from varieties of Tamazight. We hope that investigation of the intonation patterns of neighbouring dialects of Arabic along the coast of North Africa might yield further insights as to the spread of the phenomenon and its origins. Similarly, a perceptual study might determine whether yes–no questions produced with a 'truncated' boundary rise are perceptually equivalent to those produced with a complex pitch contour, and what role the presence or absence of an appended vowel plays in the interpretation of utterances. Lastly, but by no means least, our findings suggest that vowel epenthesis in yes–no questions would be a useful variable for inclusion alongside others in sociolinguistic analysis of TA, to determine what other sociolinguistic factors may be relevant, how widespread the pattern is in Tunisia and whether the incidence of the pattern is changing.

# Acknowledgements

The IVAr database project was funded by a grant to the author from the UK Economic and Social Research Council (ES/I010106/1). The IVAr project is indebted to the TA speakers who participated in data collection and gave generously of their time and language expertise. I am grateful to: Rana Almbark who carried out data collection in Tunis for the IVAr project; to Nadia Bouchhioua who hosted our visit to Tunis; to Zaineb Chihi who, as a native speaker of TA, ran all of the data elicitation sessions; and to Sihem Saadi who transcribed the data. Pitch trace figures were produced using a script kindly shared by Francesco Cangemi. Thanks are due to the editors, and to three anonymous reviewers, for their very helpful suggestions.

# Appendix

|     | ynq1 | ynq2 | ynq3 | ynq4 | ynq5 | ynq6 |
|-----|------|------|------|------|------|------|
| f1  | complex | complex | complex | complex | complex | complex |
| f2  | complex | complex | complex | complex |         | complex |
| f3  | complex | complex | complex |         | complex | complex |
| f4  | complex | complex | complex | complex | complex | complex |
| f5  | complex | complex | complex | complex | complex | *rise* |
| f6  | complex | complex | complex | complex | **fall** | complex |
| m1  | complex | complex | complex | complex |         | complex |
| m2  | *rise*  |         | *rise*  | *rise*  | *rise*  | *rise*  |
| m3  | complex | complex | complex | *rise*  | complex | *rise*  |
| m4  | complex | complex | complex | *rise*  | **fall** | *rise* |
| m5  | complex | complex | complex | complex | complex | complex |
| m6  | complex | **fall** | complex | complex | **fall** | complex |

**Figure A.**  Prosodic contour on last lexical item in read speech *ynqs*, by target utterance and speaker (dark shaded cells: with vowel epenthesis; light shaded cells: no vowel epenthesis; empty cells: missing token; Key: complex = L*+H H-L%; *rise* = L*+H H-H%; fall = H* L-L%).

|       | f1 | f2 | f3 | f4 | f5 | f6 | m1 | m2 | m3 | m4 | m5 | m6 | *Total* |
|-------|----|----|----|----|----|----|----|----|----|----|----|----|---------|
| ynq1  | ✓ | ✗ | ✗ | ✓ | ✓ | ✓ | ✓ | ✗ | ✗ | ✗ | ✓ | ✗ | 6 |
| ynq2  | ✓ | ✗ | ✓ | ✓ | ✓ | ✓ | ✗ | -- | ✓ | ✗ | ✓ | ✗ | 7 |
| ynq3  | ✗ | ✗ | ✓ | ✓ | ✓ | ✓ | ✗ | ✗ | ✓ | ✓ | ✓ | ✗ | 7 |
| ynq4  | ✓ | ✗ | -- | ✓ | ✓ | ✓ | ✗ | ✗ | ✗ | ✗ | ✗ | ✗ | 4 |
| ynq5  | ✓ | -- | ✓ | ✓ | ✓ | ✗ | -- | ✗ | ✓ | ✗ | ✓ | ✗ | 6 |
| ynq6  | ✓ | ✓ | ✓ | ✓ | ✗ | ✓ | ✓ | ✗ | ✗ | ✗ | ✓ | ✗ | 7 |
| *Total* | 5 | 1 | 4 | 6 | 5 | 5 | 2 | 0 | 3 | 1 | 5 | 0 | |

**Figure B.**  Incidence of vowel epenthesis in read speech *ynqs*, by target utterance and speaker (Key: ✓ vowel observed; ✗ no vowel observed; -- denotes a missing token due to disfluency).

# References

Aloulou, M. (2003). *The Intonation Patterns of Tunisian Arabic and English: A Comparative Study* (Unpublished master's thesis). Institut Supérieur des Langues de Tunis, University of Carthage, Tunis.

Anderson, A., Bader, M., Bard, E. G., Boyle, E., Doherty, G., Garrod, S, Isard, S., Kowtko, J., McAllister, J., Miller, J., Sotillo, C., Thompson, H., & Weinert, R. (1991). The HCRC Map Task Corpus. *Language and Speech, 34*(4), 351–366. https://10.1177/002383099103400404

Baayen, R. H. (2008). *Analyzing Linguistic Data: A Practical Introduction to Statistics Using R.* UK: Cambridge University Press.

Beckman, M., & Elam, G. A. (1997). *Guidelines for TOBI Labelling (version 3.0 1997).* USA: The Ohio State University Research Foundation.

Beckman, M., Hirschberg, J., & Shattuck-Hufnagel, S. (2005). The original ToBI system and the evolution of the ToBI framework. In S.-A. Jun (Ed.), *Prosodic Typology: The Phonology of Intonation and Phrasing* (pp. 9–54). Oxford: Oxford University Press.

Boersma, P., & Weenink, D. (2015). *Praat: Doing Phonetics by Computer (Version 5.4.09).* Retrieved from http://www.praat.org

Bouchhioua, N. (2008). *The Acoustic Correlates of Stress and Accent in TunisianArabic: A Comparative Study with English* (Unpublished doctoral dissertation). University of Carthage, Tunis.

Cruz, M. (2013). *Prosodic Variation in European Portuguese: Phrasing, Intonation and Rhythm in Central-Southern Varieties* (Unpublished doctoral dissertation). Universidade de Lisboa, Portugal.

Eckert, P., & McConnell-Ginet, S. (2003). *Language and Gender.* Cambridge: Cambridge University Press.

Frota, S. (2002). Nuclear falls and rises in European Portuguese: A phonological analysis of declarative and question intonation. *Probus, 14*(1), 113–146. https://10.1515/prbs.2002.001

Frota, S., & Prieto, P. (2015). *Intonation in Romance.* Oxford: Oxford University Press.

Frota, S., Cruz, M., Fernandes-Svartman, F., Collischonn, G., Fonseca, A., Serra, C., Oliveira, P., & Vigário, M. (2015). Intonational variation in Portuguese: European and Brazilian varieties. In P. Prieto & S. Frota (Eds.), *Intonation in Romance* (pp. 235–283). Oxford: Oxford University Press.

Ghazali, S. (1973). *Tunisian Arabic and French Interference with English: Word Stress and the Phoneme* (Unpublished master's thesis). University of Texas at Austin, U.S.A.

Ghazali, S., Hamidi, R., & Knis, K. (2007). Intonation and rhythmic patterns across the Arabic dialects continuum. In E. Benmamoun (Ed.), *Perspectives on Arabic Linguistics: Papers from the Annual Symposium on Arabic Linguistics Volume XIX: Urbana, Illinois April 2005* (pp. 97–122). Amsterdam: John Benjamins.

Grabe, E. (1998). Pitch accent realization in English and German. *Journal of Phonetics, 26*(2), 129–143. https://10.1006/jpho.1997.0072

Grabe, E. (2004). Intonational variation in urban dialects of English spoken in the British Isles. In P. Gilles & J. Peters (Eds.), *Regional Variation in Intonation* (pp. 9–31). Linguistische Arbeiten. Tuebingen: Niemeyer.

Grice, M., Savino, M., Caffo, A., & Roettger, T. B. (2015). The tune drives the text: Schwa in consonant-final loan words in Italian. In The Scottish Consortium for ICPhS (Ed.), *Proceedings of the 20th ICPhS* (paper 0381). Glasgow.

Gussenhoven, C. (2018). Zwara (Zuwārah) Berber. *Journal of the International Phonetic Association, 48*(3), 371–387. doi:10.1017/S0025100317000135

Haeri, N. (1996). *The Sociolinguistic Market of Cairo: Gender, Class and Education.* London: Keegan Paul International.

Hansen, A. B. (1997). Le nouveau [ə] prépausal dans le français parlé à Paris. In *Polyphonie pour Ivan Fonagy* (pp. 173–198). Paris-Montréal: L'Harmattan.

Hellmuth, S. (2013). Phonology. In J. Owens (Ed.), *The Oxford Handbook of Arabic Linguistics* (pp. 45–70). Oxford: Oxford University Press.

Hellmuth, S., & Almbark, R. (2019). *Intonational Variation in Arabic Corpus 2011–2017.* [Data Collection]. Colchester, Essex: UK Data Archive. https://dx.doi.org/10.5255/UKDA-SN-852878

Hellmuth, S. (in preparation). *Intonation in spoken Arabic dialects.* Oxford: Oxford University Press.

Holes, C. (2016). *Dialect, Culture, and Society in Eastern Arabia: Phonology, Morphology, Syntax, Style.* Leiden, The Netherlands: BRILL.

Hutchby, I., & Wooffitt, R. (2008). *Conversation Analysis* (2nd edition). UK, USA: Polity Press.

Knis, K. (2004). *ʔatharu ʔallahajaat ʔalʔarabiyya fi tanghiim ʔal-fuSHaa* [The effects of colloquial dialects on the intonation of Formal Arabic] (Unpublished master's thesis). Institut Supérieur des Langues de Tunis, University of Carthage, Tunis.

Labov, W. (2001). *Principles of Linguistic Change. Volume 2: Social factors.* Oxford: Blackwell.

Ladd, D. R. (2008). *Intonational Phonology* (2nd edition). Cambridge: Cambridge University Press.

Lucas, C., & Lash, E. (2010). Contact as catalyst: The case for Coptic influence in the development of Arabic negation. *Journal of Linguistics, 46*(2), 379–413. https://10.1017/S0022226709990235

Martínez-Gil, F. (1997). Word-final epenthesis in Galician. In F. Martínez-Gil & A. Morales-Front (Eds.), *Issues in the Phonology and Morphology of the Major Iberian Languages* (pp. 270–340). Whashington D. C.: George Town University Press.

Ng, E.-C. (2013). *Paragoge as an Indicator of Language Contact*. Poster presented at *LSA 2013* (Linguistic Society of America), Boston, 3–6 January 2013.

R Development Core Team. (2008). *R: A Language and Environment for Statistical Computing*. Vienna, Austria: R Foundation for Statistical Computing. Retrieved from http://www.R-project.org

Saadi, S. (2014). *Regional Effects on the Intonation Patterns of Three Different Groups of Tunisian EFL Learners* (Unpublished master's thesis). University de la Manouba, Tunis.

Youssef, I. (2016). Palatalization in educated Cairene Arabic. *Nordlyd: Tromsø University Working Papers on Language & Linguistics, 42*, 21–31. https://10.7557/12.3739

**Sam Hellmuth** is Professor of Linguistics in the Department of Language and Linguistic Science at the University of York. Sam was Director and Principal Investigator of the UK Economic and Social Research Council-funded project Intonational Variation in Arabic. Her research seeks to understand the scope of variation observed in the intonational systems of spoken Arabic dialects, and the interaction of intonation in these languages with segmental and metrical phonology, syntax, semantics, and information structure. Sam also works on second language acquisition of prosody, and the prosodic properties of regional dialects of British Englishes and World Englishes.

# 2
# Asking questions across Portuguese varieties

Marisa Cruz, Verònica Crespo-Sendra, Joelma Castelo &
Sónia Frota

## 1    Introduction

Recent research on yes–no question intonation in European and Brazilian Portuguese suggests that there is a high variability of nuclear patterns in yes–no questions, not only between European and Brazilian varieties but also across European Portuguese varieties (Castelo & Frota, 2017; Cruz et al., 2017; Frota, Cruz, et al. 2015, among others). However, there is a lack of studies that include a detailed description and comparison of yes–no questions across different varieties of Portuguese. Therefore, the first goal of the current study is to describe the intonation of yes–no questions in European and Brazilian Portuguese (hereafter EP and BP, respectively) by analysing a wide range of regions covered within the project *Interactive Atlas of the Prosody of Portuguese* (Frota, coord., 2012–2015). Freely accessed online (http://labfon.letras.ulisboa.pt/InAPoP/), this atlas is a central output of research on prosodic, intonational, and rhythmic variation in Portuguese developed so far. It provides users with maps showing the distribution of varieties as to the observed phrasing preferences, tonal density, intonational typology, and rhythmic properties. It offers prototypical examples, methodological information, as well as training materials.

It is well known that questions can have different pragmatic meanings. We analysed two types of yes–no questions: neutral yes–no questions and counterexpectational yes–no questions (these have also been called incredulity, presumptive, etc.). Neutral yes–no questions are those in which the speaker does not know the answer and asks without any prior knowledge. For this reason, they are also called information-seeking yes–no questions. Counterexpectational yes–no questions are those in which the speaker asks about something that, given prior knowledge, is strange or surprising to him/her. In such sentences, the speaker does not seek information but expresses incredulity, surprise, disbelief, or disgust at something that was not expected (Frota, Cruz et al., 2015).

Several studies have shown that speakers can signal the difference between neutral and counterexpectational questions intonationally, in various languages and language varieties, such as Brazilian Portuguese, European Portuguese, Bari Italian, Buenos Aires Spanish, or Catalan (Crespo-Sendra, 2011; Frota, 2002, 2014; Lee, Martínez-Gil & Beckman, 2008; Savino & Grice, 2007; Truckenbrodt, 2009). Some studies found a gradient (phonetic) contrast between the two types of questions (cf. Hirschberg and Ward, 1992, for American English, or Crespo-Sendra, 2011, for Catalan, among others), while other studies indicate that the contrast is expressed categorically (cf. Savino and Grice, 2007, 2008, for Bari Italian; Truckenbrodt, Sandalo, and Abaurre, 2009, for Brazilian Portuguese).

Hirschberg and Ward (1992) showed that in American English a compression in pitch range with the nuclear configuration L*+H LH% changes the interpretation of the incredulity meaning into the uncertainty one. Listeners interpreted stimuli with larger pitch ranges as conveying incredulity and those with smaller pitch ranges as conveying uncertainty. The authors even suggest that the association of greater pitch range with incredulity can be accounted for by the well-known tendency to associate larger pitch ranges with a greater degree of speaker involvement (Hirschberg & Ward, 1992, p. 241). Similarly, Lee et al. (2008) reported that the difference between information-seeking and counterexpectational yes–no questions in Buenos Aires Spanish lies in the use of a wider overall pitch range in questions of the latter sort. The same was observed in Catalan. Crespo-Sendra, Vanrell, and Prieto (2010) demonstrated that the main cue in distinguishing information-seeking from counterexpectational yes–no questions for Central Catalan listeners was the pitch range difference at the prenuclear and nuclear levels. In this study, pitch range is a gradient cue to distinguish the two types of questions.

However, other studies found a categorical contrast between questions conveying the two pragmatic meanings. Savino and Grice (2007) investigated the difference between unbiased (neutral) and negative-polarity biased (counterexpectational) yes–no questions in Bari Italian. The results showed that pitch range differences determine whether a sentence is unbiased or biased, and that this feature is perceived in a categorical way. In Brazilian Portuguese, besides the higher pitch height of counterexpectational yes–no questions, Truckenbrodt et al. (2009) showed that they also differ from neutral yes–no questions in tonal alignment (L+H* L% and L*+H L%, respectively).

Given this background, the aims of this research are: (i) to compare and phonologically analyse the nuclear configuration of neutral and counterexpectational yes–no questions across Portuguese varieties; (ii) to investigate the strategies that EP and BP speakers use to convey incredulity, and (iii) to perform a phonetic analysis that addresses the phonological account.

This chapter is organised as follows. Section 2 summarises previous research on yes–no questions intonation in European and Brazilian Portuguese, highlighting findings with respect to different pragmatic meanings of this sentence type. In section 3 we describe the methodology used in this research. Section 4 is divided into three parts: the first one presents the results of neutral yes–no question intonation in EP and BP varieties; the second one presents the main strategies used to convey incredulity in yes–no questions in EP and BP; and the third one complements the phonological analysis with a phonetic analysis, exploring different phonetic cues. Finally, in the conclusion (section 5), we summarise the most important outcomes of this study and discuss the main tonal configurations of neutral and counterexpectational yes–no questions in EP and BP.

# 2    Background

## 2.1    Neutral yes–no questions

### 2.1.1    European Portuguese

In contrast with statements and wh-questions, yes–no questions are considered as the sentence type showing more intonational variation in European Portuguese (Frota, Cruz, et al. 2015) and in several other languages (and their varieties), such as Italian, Occitan or Romanian (Frota & Prieto, 2015; Gili Fivela et al., 2015; Jitca, Apopei, Paduraru & Marusca, 2015; Savino, 2012; Sichel-Bazin, Meisenburg & Prieto 2015).

According to previous studies, most EP varieties (Braga and Porto in the North; Alentejo and Algarve in the South) present an all-rising nuclear contour in neutral yes–no questions (L* H% or L*+H H%). The standard variety (Lisbon), by contrast, exhibits a falling–rising nuclear configuration (Cruz, 2013; Frota, 2002, 2014; Frota, Cruz et al., 2015; Vigário & Frota, 2003). In all varieties studied so far neutral yes–no questions in EP are characterised by a high/rising boundary tone, which is not observed in Brazilian varieties of Portuguese (Frota, Cruz et al., 2015; Frota & Moraes, 2016).

Importantly, interrogativity in EP varieties is mainly conveyed by the whole nuclear configuration that contrasts between sentence types:

statements are produced with a low/falling nuclear contour, and neutral yes–no questions are mainly produced with an all-rising nuclear contour instead. The exception is the standard variety, where the nuclear pitch accent is the same for statements and yes–no questions (H+L*) and the difference between these sentence types lies on the tonal boundary marking (low in statements, but rising in yes–no questions; Frota, 2002). Although not being the dominant contour, a low/falling nuclear configuration may also be used to convey interrogativity in some EP varieties, thus being intonationally similar to statements. Such cases were reported in the northern variety of Braga (Vigário & Frota, 2003), as well as in the Central-Southern varieties of Alentejo and Algarve (Cruz, 2013; Cruz & Frota, 2011; Cruz et al., 2017). Since this is not the common nuclear contour of neutral yes–no questions in those varieties, it has not yet been phonetically analysed in detail. However, it would be interesting to find out whether these two sentence types are distinguished by native (and also non-native) speakers of those varieties and what are the implications (if any) for the intonational grammar of EP.

In the present study, an analysis of the intonation of neutral yes–no questions in 9 regions of continental and non-continental Portugal (4 analysed for the first time) was performed to extend and deepen the current knowledge on intonational variation in Portuguese.

### 2.1.2  Brazilian Portuguese

In Brazilian Portuguese, neutral yes–no questions also display differences across varieties. The melodic shape in Northern varieties is characterised by a rising configuration, whereas the Central-Southern varieties display a rising–falling contour (Castelo & Frota, 2017; Frota, Cruz, et al., 2015; Frota & Moraes, 2016; Lira, 2009; Nunes, 2011; Silva, 2011). In fact, Northern varieties seem to exhibit two types of rising nuclear contour. The first consists in a rising contour that begins in the second half of the stressed syllable and is extended to the post-stressed syllable(s) (L*+H H%), whereas the second displays a low tone in the stressed syllable, followed by a rise to the post-stressed syllable(s) (L* H%). In the Central-Southern varieties, the rising–falling nuclear contour also seems to show two possibilities: (i) a rising contour in the stressed syllable, followed by a low boundary tone (L*+H L%), more typical of Central varieties, or (ii) a low nuclear pitch accent associated with the stressed syllable, followed by a complex high–low boundary (L* HL%), more typical of Southern varieties (Castelo, 2016). A rising nuclear contour was also found in semi-spontaneous speech in Southern varieties, but with a different distribution from the Northern ones, i.e., it was found as an alternative contour in the South (Frota, Cruz et al., 2015; Nunes, 2011; Silva, 2011). These production patterns were found to be reflected in the perception of yes–no questions across BP varieties, with speakers from the Centre and South showing similar perception patterns, which differ from those exhibited by speakers from the North (Silva et al., 2018).

The differences in peak alignment in Central-Southern varieties motivate the varying tonal association of the rising–falling nuclear contour in this region (Castelo & Frota, 2017). L*+H L% displays an earlier alignment of the high tone compared to L* HL%. This fact can be explained by a difference in the tonal association of the high tone: in Central varieties, the high tone is associated with the nucleus, as part of the nuclear pitch accent,  whereas in the Southern varieties it is associated with the boundary. Indeed, the tonal association of the high tone has been long discussed in the literature. Some authors consider that the high tone is the nucleus of the rising pitch accent (L+H*), thus providing more relevance to the rising stressed syllable and the alignment of the high tone on its right limit (Moraes, 2008; Moraes & Colamarco, 2007; Truckenbrodt et al., 2009). Other authors consider that the low tone is the nucleus of the rising pitch accent, therefore giving more importance to the anchor of the low tone, which is realised at the beginning of the stressed syllable, than to the rising contour or the point of the stressed syllable where the high tone is attained (Frota, Cruz et al., 2015). More recently, Frota and Moraes (2016) propose an uncompromising annotation (L+H) for the cases under discussion, thus leaving the rising pitch accent unspecified as to the starred tone.

Similarly to Brazilian Portuguese, where the rising–falling pattern is predominantly used for neutral yes–no questions, other languages such as Italian (Gili Fivela et al., 2015; Grice, D'Imperio, Savino & Avesani, 2005; Savino, 2012) or languages from Eastern Europe (Grice, Ladd & Arvaniti, 2000) also exhibit a preference for the LHL melodic shape in several dialectal areas and also present tonal alignment differences which distinguish among regions (e.g., in Bari Italian the LHL melody displays early alignment of the peak when compared to other varieties from the South).

In the current study, the analysis of neutral yes–no questions was extended to other regions along the Brazilian Atlantic coast. In addition, phonetic details were also inspected to check for empirical support for the proposed phonological analyses.


## 2.2   Counterexpectational yes–no questions

In this chapter, only counterexpectational yes–no questions with a late nucleus will be examined. Therefore, we will only consider descriptions of these kinds of questions and exclude those with an early nucleus.

### 2.2.1   European Portuguese

Differently from statements in EP, where a specific pitch accent type is consistently used across varieties to convey contrastive focus (Frota, 2000, 2014; Frota, Cruz et al., 2015), for yes–no questions different strategies were observed: (i) the whole nuclear configuration changes; (ii) only the boundary tone changes; or (iii) the phonological shape is the same, but the phonetic realisation is different.

In the standard variety, the whole nuclear configuration changes from a falling–rising shape (H+L* LH%) in neutral yes–no questions to a rising–falling pitch movement (L*+H HL%) in counterexpectational yes–no questions with a late nucleus (Frota, 2002, 2014; Frota, Cruz et al., 2015).

For Alentejo, one of the central-southern varieties of EP, the falling boundary tone (HL%) is considered as the distinguishing feature of counterexpectational yes–no questions, in contrast with the rising boundary found in neutral yes–no questions (Frota, Cruz et al., 2015). In the variety of Porto, in the North, and Algarve, in the extreme South, counterexpectational yes–no questions exhibit the same rising tune as neutral yes–no questions (Cruz, 2013; Cruz & Frota, 2012; Frota, Cruz et al., 2015). Given that the varieties of the North (Porto included) show truncation in tonal crowding contexts (Frota et al., 2016), it is important to examine the counterexpectational question contour in contexts that allow the full realisation of the nuclear contour, as it was done in the present study. For Algarve, an exploratory study on the phonetic implementation of the rising tune (Cruz & Frota, 2012) showed that counterexpectational yes–no questions present higher rises when compared to neutral yes–no questions. However, a detailed inspection of this potential realisational difference is needed. This is explored in the current study, together with a systematic analysis of the nuclear contours of counterexpectational yes–no questions in European Portuguese varieties.

### 2.2.2   Brazilian Portuguese

Differently from neutral yes–no questions, studies on counterexpectational yes–no questions in Brazilian Portuguese are still scarce. Frota, Cruz et al. (2015) showed that although a rising nuclear contour (L*+H) can be used to convey both neutral and counterexpectational yes–no questions, the boundary tone signals the pragmatic meaning. Results from semi-spontaneous corpora show that Bahia, a Northern variety with final rising in neutral yes–no questions (L*+H H%), displays a falling boundary tone to convey incredulity (L*+H HL%). In the central-southern varieties of Minas

Gerais, São Paulo and Rio Grande do Sul, a high boundary tone (L*+H H%) is used to convey incredulity instead of the final low boundary tone (L%) found in neutral yes–no questions. Previous studies also showed that contrastive focus may be expressed in yes–no questions by means of phonetic cues, like peak height or lengthening in the Rio de Janeiro variety (Moraes, 2008). Similarly to the Northern varieties of EP, in BP the melody predominantly truncates when the text is too short to accommodate the tune (Frota et al., 2016). Thus, it is crucial to examine the counterexpectational question contour in contexts that allow the full realisation of the nuclear contour, as in the present study.

In this chapter, we aim to add to the knowledge of counterexpectational yes–no questions in Brazilian Portuguese, by extending the phonological analysis to cover new varieties, together with the inspection of phonetic cues.

# 3    Methodology

## 3.1   Participants

Three female native speakers from 9 urban regions in Portugal and 8 urban regions in Brazil participated in the study, in a total of 51 speakers (see section 3.3 for further details on the data collection points). Since gender differences in the prosody of questions have been reported for other languages (e.g., Niebuhr, 2015), we decided to control for gender. Moreover, the choice of female voices was motivated by their acoustic properties, which generally enable a better computation of F0 utterance finally, i.e., in nuclear position.

## 3.2   Materials

In order to investigate the phonological structure of yes–no question intonation we used a Reading task, comprising pre-existing corpora (Frota, 2002) that were also used within the *Interactive Atlas of the Prosody of Portuguese* project (Frota, coord., 2012–2015). The materials were elicited through the presentation of written contexts, leading to a neutral or counterexpectational reading. In the latter case, the context explicitly states that the speaker has contradictory information on a given subject, and thus has to ask about a specific piece of information (see example 1).

(1)    Neutral meaning: Os rapazes compraram **lâ**minas? *Did the boys buy slides?*

Counterexpectational meaning: [C: Gostaria de saber se foram mesmo lâminas que eles compraram e não outro objeto qualquer.] Os rapazes compraram **LÂ**MINAS? *[C: I would like to know whether the boys really bought slides (and not any other object).] Did the boys buy SLIDES?*

Each sentence was produced twice by each speaker. For analysis we selected 10 neutral and 9 counterexpectational yes–no questions with varying stress position in the nuclear word (final, penult and antepenult stress) as illustrated in (2). Stressed syllables are shown in boldface.

(2)    Ela foi ver o **mar**? *Did she go to see the sea?*

Ela foi ver a Ma**ri**na? *Did she go to visit Marina?*

Os rapazes compraram **lâ**minas? *Did the boys buy slides?*

A total of 540 neutral yes–no questions (10 sentences × 3 speakers × 2 renditions × 9 regions) and of 486 counterexpectational yes–no questions (9 × 3 × 2 × 9) for EP, and a total of 480 neutral yes–no questions (10 × 3 × 2 × 8) and of 432 counterexpectational yes–no questions (9 × 3 × 2 × 8) for BP were analysed (see Appendix I).

Additionally, data collected by means of a Discourse Completion Task (DCT – Billmyer & Varghese, 2000; Félix-Brasdefer, 2010) were also analysed. The survey of situations was orally presented by an interviewer, leading to neutral or counterexpectational productions by the speaker. In the latter case, the interviewer presents a given shared context and explicitly states that the speaker has contradictory information on this subject, and has to express it (see example 3).

(3)    [C: Um amigo teu diz-te que um colega vosso, o Mário, vai concorrer para Presidente do clube da terra. Ficas muito surpreendido e voltas a perguntar ao teu amigo, sem acreditar, se ele está a dizer que o Mário vai concorrer para Presidente.] Estás a dizer que o Mário vai concorrer para PRESIDENTE?![1] *[C: Your friend told you that Mário, a friend in common, is running for President of the local club. You didn't know this*

---

[1]    This context can actually lead to the production of the contrastive focus either in the target words 'Presidente' (late focus) or 'Mário' (early focus). However, only the late focus productions were considered for analysis.

> *and it is hard to believe it, thus you ask your friend if he is saying that*
> *Mário really is running for President.] (Are you saying that) Mário is*
> *running for PRESIDENT?*

A total of 162 neutral yes–no questions (3 sentences × 3 speakers × 2 renditions × 9 regions) and of 108 counterexpectational yes–no questions (2 × 3 × 2 × 9) for EP and a total of 144 neutral yes–no questions (3 × 3 × 2 × 8) and of 96 counterexpectational yes–no questions (2 × 3 × 2 × 8) for BP were analysed (see Appendix I). However, the DCT corpus only includes nuclear words with final and penult stress, as illustrated in (4). Importantly, some nuclear words with penult stress end with a schwa vowel, which, in EP, may undergo a deletion process (Ellison & Viana, 1996; Frota, 2000; Vigário, 1998, 2003) and result in the production of a nuclear word with final stress instead, as illustrated in (5).

(4)    Cho**veu**? *Did it rain?*

Tem com**po**ta? *Do you have jam?*

(5)    O Manel vai ser presi**den**t<u>e</u>? *Manel is going to be president?*

This might impact on the intonational contour produced, possibly leading to a truncation strategy in some varieties (Frota et al., 2016). For this reason, the results reported in section 4 are mainly (but not exclusively) based on the analysis of the reading task, and examples with antepenult and penult stress were preferred.

Pitch measurements were performed and extracted using *Praat* software (Boersma & Weenink, 2012) and intonation contours were annotated using the ToBI labelling system for Portuguese (Frota, 2014; Frota, Oliveira, Cruz & Vigário, 2015). Annotation and analysis were independently performed by three researchers, experts in intonation analysis: a native speaker of European Portuguese, a native speaker of Brazilian Portuguese, and a non-native speaker of Portuguese. This was performed in two stages. In a first round, the native speaker of European Portuguese (standard variety – SEP) annotated data from all the European Portuguese varieties, the native speaker from Brazilian Portuguese (Rio de Janeiro variety) annotated data from all the Brazilian varieties, and the non-native speaker annotated data from both Portuguese varieties. In a second round, data annotation and analysis were cross-checked among the three coders. Disagreement among the coders has only arisen for cases involving pitch alignment (not for nuclear configuration types), which were addressed by the phonetic analysis implemented (see section 4.3 for further details).

## 3.3    Data collection points

In the present study, we analysed data from 7 localities in continental Portugal – Braga, Porto, Castelo Branco, Lisboa, Évora, Beja, and Faro – and 2 localities in the islands of Madeira (Funchal) and Azores (Ponta Delgada), all of them urban places. The choice of these data collection points was driven by previous studies on segmental variation in EP (Figure 2.1). The idea was to cover, throughout the country, the major linguistic areas identified by Cintra (1971), Segura and Saramago (2001) and Segura (2013): the Northern varieties (in light and dark gray), the Central-Southern varieties (in medium gray and white), all at the right side of the figure, and the insular varieties (in gray, at the left side of the figure).

For Brazil, we followed a similar criterion in the choice of the regions covered, i.e., we aimed to cover the two main linguistic areas defined by Nascentes (1953) – the North and the South (Figure 2.2). However, we only selected urban regions along the Atlantic coast: Paraíba, Sergipe, and Bahia in the North; Minas Gerais, Rio de Janeiro, São Paulo, Santa Catarina, and Rio Grande do Sul, in the Centre-South.

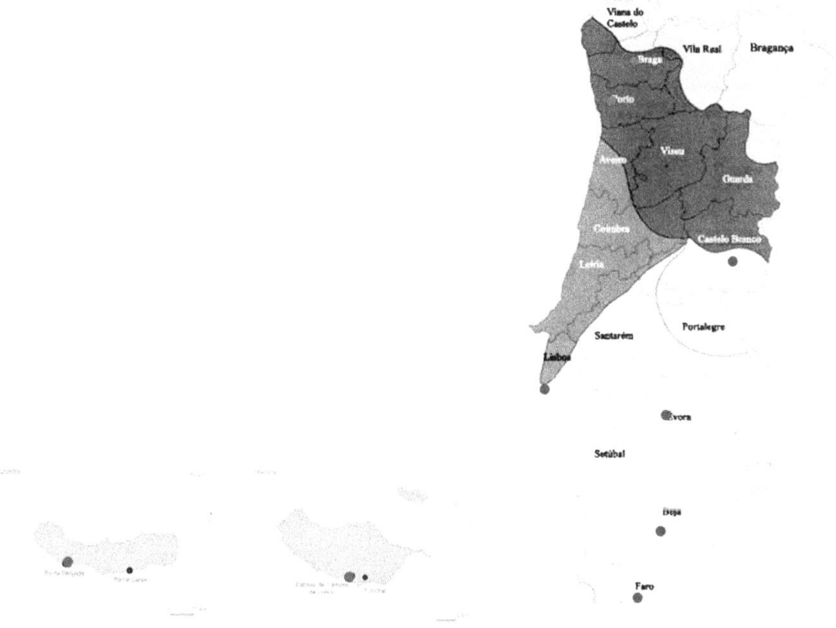


**Figure 2.1.** Data collection points (bullets) covering European Portuguese varieties based on phonetic and phonological segmental phenomena according to Cintra (1971). Map adapted from Segura and Saramago (2001). Maps of the islands (on the left side) extracted from the *InAPoP* webplatform (Frota & Cruz, coords., 2012–2015).

**Figure 2.2.** Data collection points (bullets) covering the two main linguistic areas defined by Nascentes (1953): North (Amazonico and Nordestino) and South (Baiano, Sulista, Mineiro and Fluminense).

# 4   Results

In this section we present the results of the phonological analyses of the nuclear configurations of neutral and counterexpectational yes–no questions in European and Brazilian Portuguese. Although nuclear words with three stress patterns were included in the analysis (cf. section 3.2), the figures presented in this section mostly illustrate nuclear configurations with the antepenult stress pattern, so that the full contour is realised. Additionally, and because the melody is often truncated in the Northern varieties of EP and in BP varieties when the text is too short to bear the tune, especially in cases of complex tunes realised in monosyllabic nuclear words or nuclear words with final stress (Frota et al., 2016), the descriptive quantitative analysis presented refers to the frequency of occurrence of the dominant nuclear contour observed in words with penult and antepenult stress only. The frequency of occurrence of the dominant nuclear contour corresponds to the average frequency across the reading task and the DCT, based on the contours rates for each task. Importantly, and because inter-speaker variability was also found in our data, the criterion followed in order to determine that a given contour is the dominant one was its production by all speakers of the region under analysis even though it may not be the dominant contour for one out of the three speakers.

Section 4.1 describes the results for neutral yes–no questions in both varieties. Counterexpectational yes–no questions are described in section 4.2, and the main strategies used in each variety to convey incredulity are pointed out. Finally, in section 4.3 we explore the difference between neutral and counterexpectational yes–no questions in varieties that exhibit the same tune in both pragmatic meanings. We thus complement the phonological analysis with the inspection of phonetic cues, such as duration, alignment, and pitch range.

## 4.1 Neutral yes–no questions

Results for neutral yes–no questions divide EP into four groups: Lisbon stands by itself in the first group; Braga, Porto, Beja and Faro constitute the second group; the third group includes Castelo Branco; and Évora together with the islands form the fourth group.

In Lisbon the nuclear configuration of neutral yes–no questions is mainly (88%) characterised by a low tone associated with the last stressed syllable and preceded by a high pretonic syllable (H+L*), that is followed by a rising boundary tone (LH%) (Figure 2.3).

A different nuclear configuration was found in Braga, Porto, Beja and Faro, namely, a low tone followed by a rise. In Beja, the stressed syllable is low and the boundary syllable is high, i.e., the tune L* H% predominates (77%) (Figure 2.4). Another instance of the rising configuration is the low tone followed by a high tone still within the stressed syllable (L*+H H%), as in Porto (55%) and Faro (67%). Finally, the rising contour may be preceded by a high tone associated with the pre-stressed syllable ((H+)L* H%), as in Braga (52%).

Unlike in the previous regions, in Castelo Branco a low boundary tone was found, after a nuclear rise or a nuclear fall. In this region, we found a

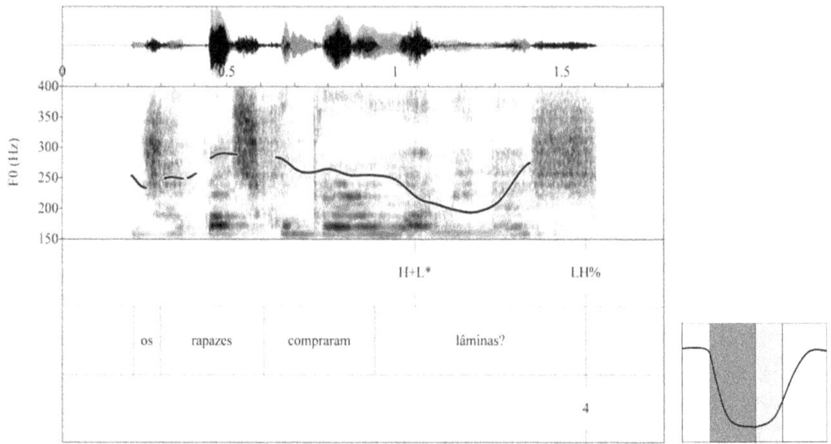

**Figure 2.3.**   Neutral yes–no question produced by a speaker from Lisbon: 'Os rapazes compra-ram lâminas?' (*Did the boys buy slides?*). Tonal representation of the nuclear configuration H+L* LH% (from Frota, Oliveira et al., 2015).[2]

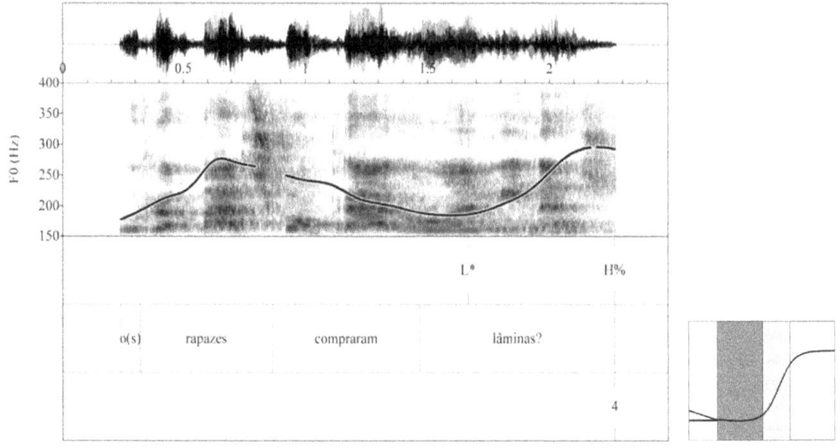

**Figure 2.4.**   Neutral yes–no question produced by a speaker from Beja: 'Os rapazes comprar-am lâminas?' (*Did the boys buy slides?*). Tonal representation of the nuclear configuration L* H% (Frota, Oliveira et al., 2015).

different dominant contour depending on the task performed, as it was already observed by Cruz et al. (2017). In the reading task, a low tone on the stressed syllable followed by a rise until the post-stressed syllable and a low boundary tone (L*+H L%) predominates (69%), as illustrated in Figure 2.5.

---

[2]   The schematic representation accompanying Figures 2.3–2.15 corresponds to a stylized contour based on the underlying contours empirically observed. The stressed syllable is in dark gray and the boundary syllable is in white.

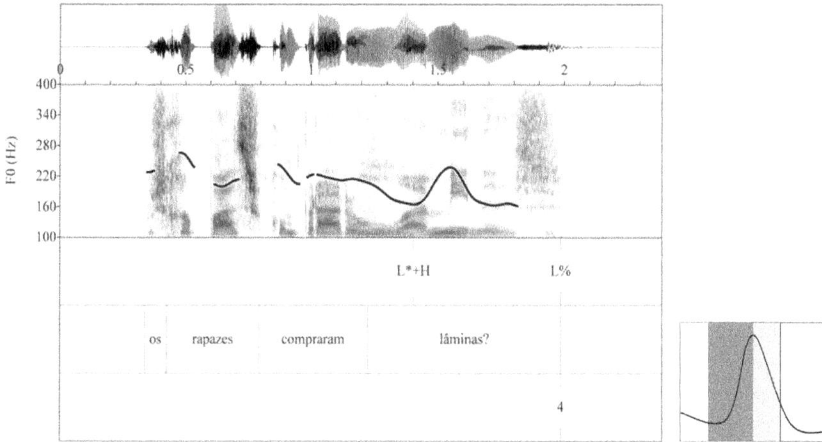

**Figure 2.5.** Neutral yes–no question produced by a speaker from Castelo Branco: 'Os rapazes compraram lâminas?' (*Did the boys buy slides?*). Tonal representation of the nuclear configuration L*+H L% (Frota, Oliveira et al., 2015).

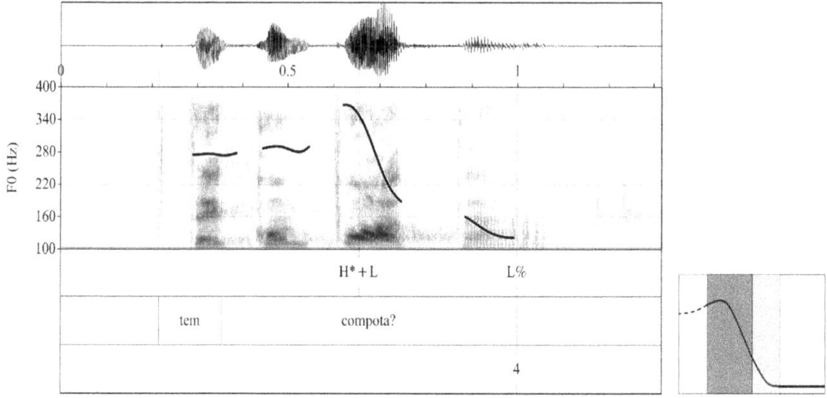

**Figure 2.6.** Neutral yes–no question produced by a speaker from Castelo Branco: 'Tem compota?' (*Do you have jam?*). Tonal representation of the nuclear configuration H*+L L% (Frota, Oliveira et al., 2015).

By contrast, a high tone on the stressed syllable followed by a fall until the post-stressed syllable and a low boundary tone (H*+L L%) was predominantly (58%) observed in the DCT, as illustrated in Figure 2.6.

Finally, the last group includes Évora and the islands (Azores and Madeira) and is characterised by an all-falling nuclear configuration (Figure 2.7). In these 3 regions neutral yes–no questions were mainly produced

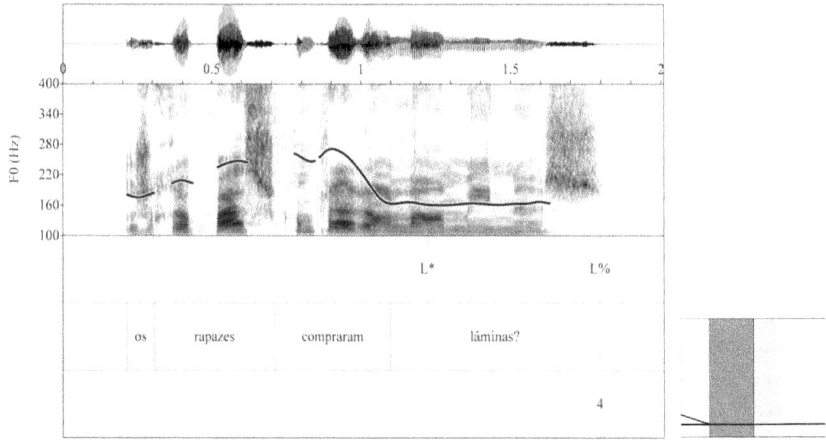

**Figure 2.7.** Neutral yes–no question produced by a speaker from Azores: 'Os rapazes compraram lâminas?' (*Did the boys buy slides?*). Tonal representation of the nuclear configuration L* L% (Frota, Oliveira et al., 2015).

(36%[3], 95% and 51% respectively) with a low tone that can be preceded by a high tone on the pre-stressed syllable, followed by a low boundary tone ((H+)L* L%).

Results for neutral yes–no questions in Brazilian Portuguese varieties show two different groups, as it was also reported in Castelo (2016) and Castelo and Frota (2017). The first group includes the three regions of the North (Paraíba, Sergipe, Bahia), where neutral yes–no questions are produced with a rising pattern: L* H% or L*+H H%. The first configuration, with a low pitch accent followed by a high boundary tone, is predominantly used in Paraíba (64%) and Sergipe (54%) (Figure 2.8, top panel); the second one, characterised by a rising pitch accent followed by a high boundary tone, is the most common nuclear pattern in Bahia (49%) (Figure 2.8, bottom panel).

Although Brazilian Northern varieties are generally characterised by a rising pattern, the two nuclear configurations are phonologically different. The main difference is the starting point of the rise in the nuclear pitch accent: in the most northern localities the nucleus is totally low (L*), and the rise starts after the stressed syllable; by contrast, in Bahia, a complex nuclear

---

[3]   In Évora, the all-falling nuclear contour was systematically produced by all speakers. However, two of them alternate between this melody and the one mainly found in SEP (H+L* LH%), with a final rising (28%), which is more evident in the DCT than in the reading task. We believe this alternation is due to prosodic entrainment (Giles, Mulac, Bradac & Johnson, 1987), i.e., the less dominant speaker (the participant) adapts her intonation to the interviewers', who were SEP speakers.

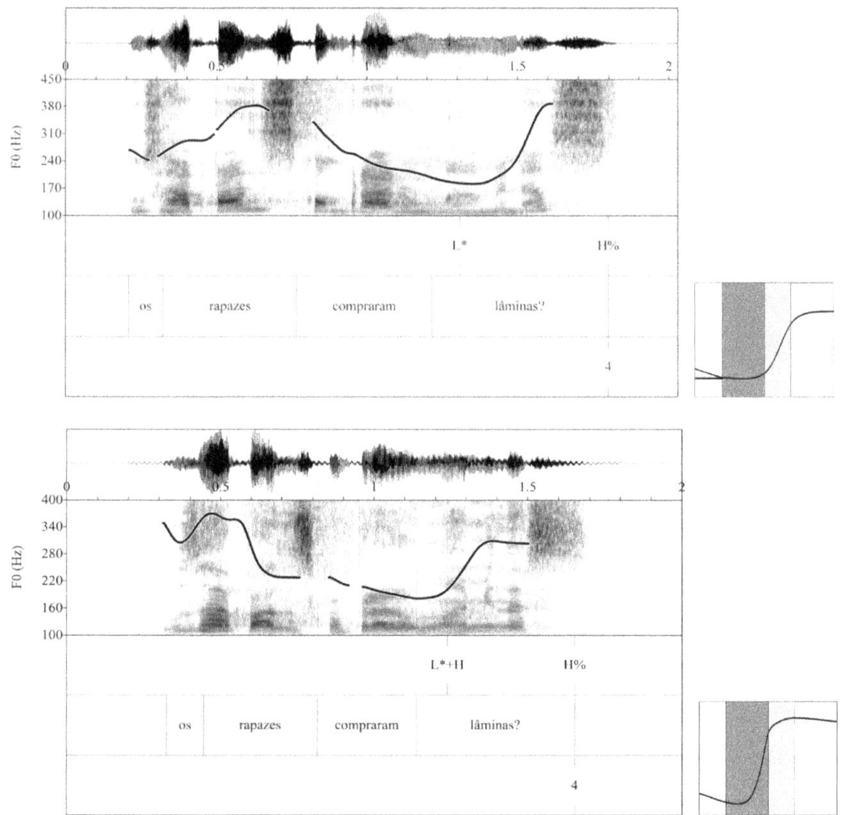

**Figure 2.8.** Neutral yes–no questions produced by a speaker from Sergipe (top panel) and a speaker from Bahia (bottom panel): 'Os rapazes compraram lâminas?' (*Did the boys buy slides?*). Tonal representation of the nuclear configurations L* H% (top panel) and L*+H H% (bottom panel) (Frota, Oliveira et al., 2015).

pitch accent (L*+H) is found, characterised by a rising movement beginning at the middle of the stressed vowel.

The other group in Brazilian Portuguese is formed by the 5 regions of the Centre-South (Minas Gerais, Rio de Janeiro, São Paulo, Santa Catarina and Rio Grande do Sul). In these regions we found the same basic rising–falling melody (LHL) with differences related to the alignment of the high tone. Two different nuclear configurations were found depending on whether the high tone is associated with the pitch accent or with the boundary. The first one is characterised by a rising pitch accent and a low boundary tone, L*+H L% (Figure 2.9, top panel), and it is the most common pattern in Minas Gerais and Rio de Janeiro (94% for both regions) and in São Paulo (70%). The second nuclear configuration consists of a simple low pitch accent (L*) and

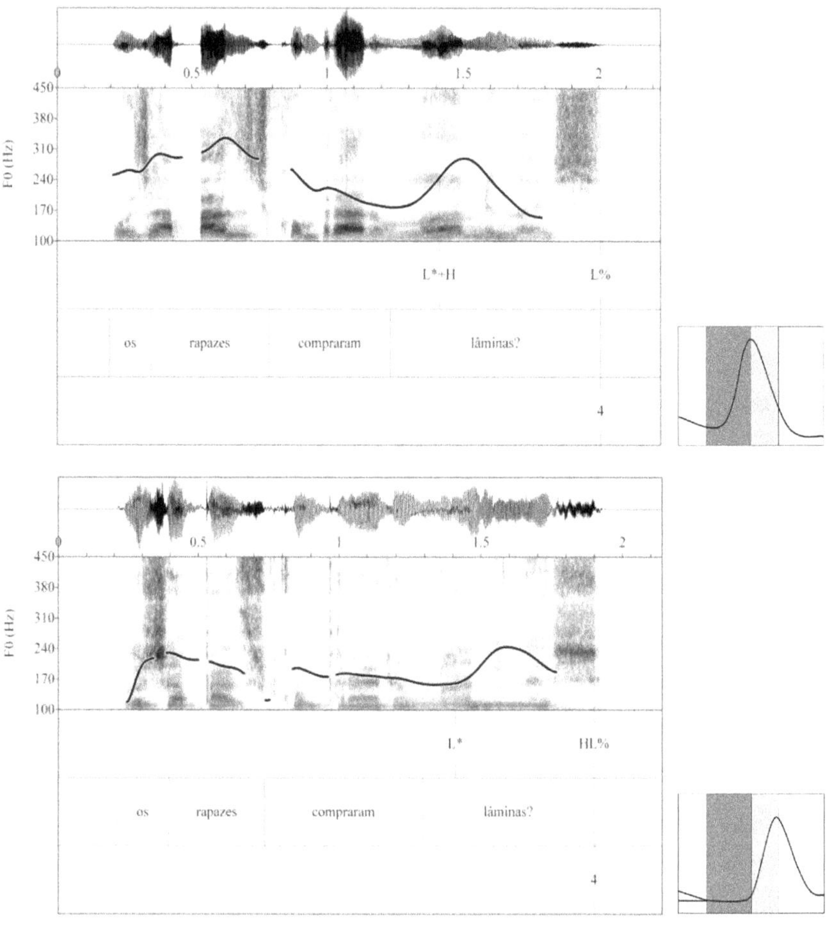

**Figure 2.9.** Neutral yes–no questions produced by a speaker from Rio de Janeiro (top panel) and a speaker from Santa Catarina (bottom panel): 'Os rapazes compraram lâminas?' (*Did the boys buy slides?*). Tonal representation of the nuclear configurations L*+H L% (top panel) and L* HL% (bottom panel) (Frota, Oliveira et al., 2015).

a complex boundary tone HL% (Figure 2.9, bottom panel), dominant in the Southern regions (Santa Catarina and Rio Grande do Sul – 83% and 94%, respectively).

## 4.2  Counterexpectational yes–no questions

The intonational analysis of counterexpectational yes–no questions in European Portuguese reveals two different strategies. In general, speakers change the nuclear configuration in almost all the regions, by using a different pitch accent and/or boundary tone, except for Castelo Branco, Faro and Azores.

In Braga, Porto, Lisbon, Évora, Beja and Madeira the nuclear configuration of neutral questions is changed into a rising–falling tune (L*+H (H)L%) to convey an incredulity pragmatic meaning. Two different realisations were observed: in Braga (72%), Évora (61%) and Madeira (79%) the L*+H L% configuration (Figure 2.10, top panel) was found, whereas in Porto (61%), Lisbon (82%) and Beja (60%) counterexpectational yes–no questions were produced with the L*+H HL% nuclear configuration (Figure 2.10, bottom panel). The main difference between both configurations is the boundary tone. In the first contour, the last syllable is totally low; by contrast, in the second contour, the last syllable shows a falling melody.

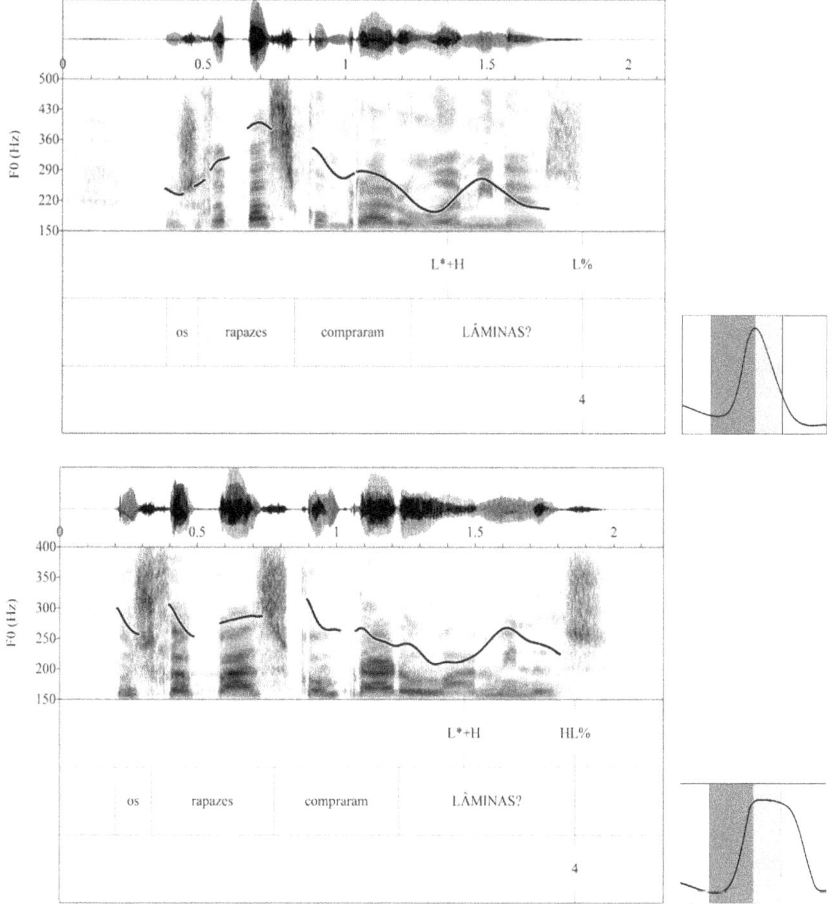


**Figure 2.10.** Counterexpectational yes–no question produced by a speaker from Évora (top panel) and a speaker from Porto (bottom panel): 'Os rapazes compraram lâminas?' (*Did the boys buy slides?*). Tonal representation of the nuclear configurations L*+H L% (top panel) and L*+H HL% (bottom panel) (Frota, Oliveira et al., 2015).

Interestingly, the regions exhibiting a rising–falling contour in counter-expectational yes–no questions present different contours in neutral yes–no questions (see section 4.1). Thus, there is variation in the strategies used to convey incredulity across regions. In Braga, a region where neutral yes–no questions are produced with a falling–rising nuclear configuration (H+L* H%), the whole nuclear configuration is changed in order to convey incredulity. Differently, in Évora and Madeira only the nuclear pitch accent changes (from low into a rising accent) in order to convey incredulity. In the regions presenting the rising–falling nuclear configuration with a complex boundary tone in counterexpectational yes–no questions (Porto, Lisbon and Beja), two different strategies were also found: in Porto and Beja, the main difference lies on the boundary tone, which changes from a high boundary tone in neutral yes–no questions to a falling boundary tone in the counterexpectational yes–no questions. In Lisbon, the whole configuration changes from a falling–rising nuclear configuration in neutral yes–no questions into a rising–falling one in counterexpectational yes–no questions. In short, the strategies to convey incredulity may involve a change in the nuclear pitch accent only, a change in the boundary tone only, or a change in the whole nuclear contour.

In Castelo Branco, the same rising–falling contour (L*+H L%) found in neutral yes–no questions produced in the reading task is also used to convey incredulity (50%) (Figure 2.11). However, in the DCT, speakers change the neutral falling melody (H*+L L%) into a rising–falling one (L*+H L%) to convey incredulity (100%). Since in Castelo Branco there are differences across the speech styles analysed, we decided not to inspect these contours from a phonetic perspective.

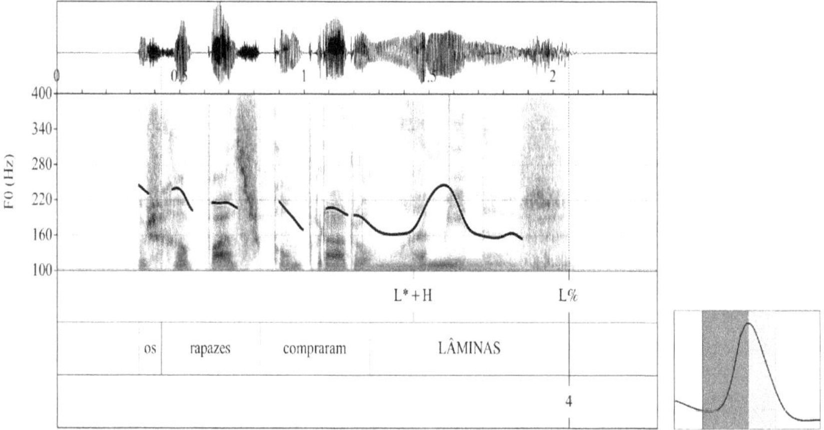


**Figure 2.11.** Counterexpectational yes–no question produced by a speaker from Castelo Branco: 'Os rapazes compraram LÂMINAS?' (*Did the boys buy slides?*). Tonal representation of the nuclear configuration L*+H L% (Frota, Oliveira et al., 2015).

Finally, in Faro and Azores the same phonological nuclear configuration for neutral and counterexpectational yes–no questions was consistently found in both speech styles. In Faro, both pragmatic meanings are produced with a rising nuclear pitch accent followed by a high boundary tone (L*+H H%). Figure 2.12 illustrates the contour for the incredulity meaning (82%) (top panel), which is very similar to the neutral one (bottom panel). In Azores counterexpectational yes–no questions are produced with a low pitch accent followed by a low boundary tone (L* L% – 89%), a similar all-falling tune to that found for neutral yes–no questions (see Figure 2.13 below and Figure 2.7 in section 4.1). Potential phonetic differences between neutral and counterexpectational nuclear contours in these two regions are explored in section 4.3.

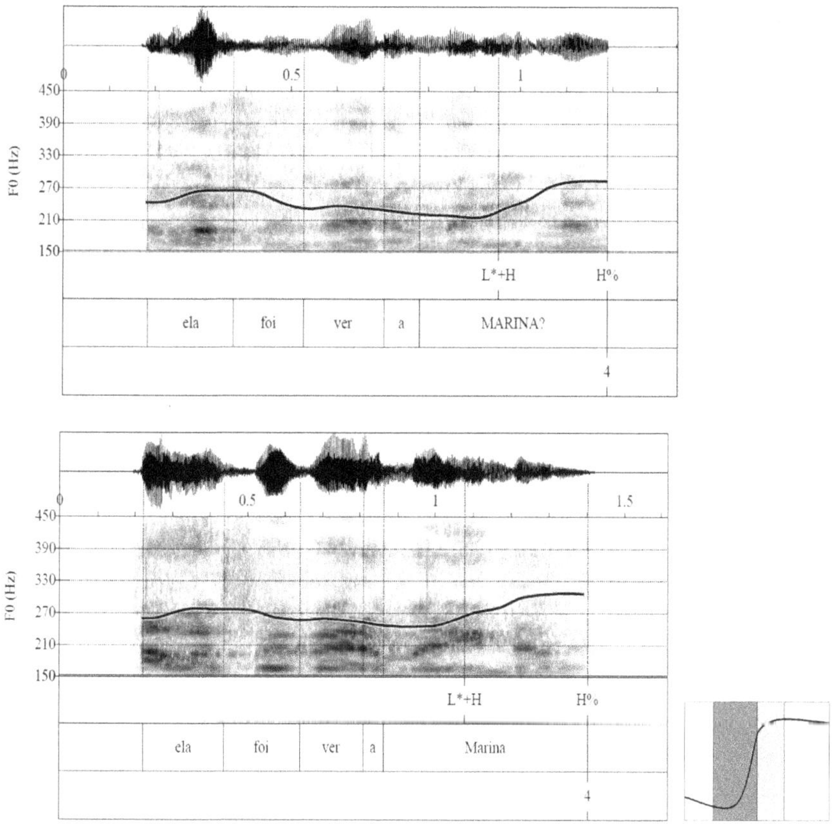



**Figure 2.12.** Counterexpectational yes–no question (top panel) and neutral yes–no question (bottom panel) produced by a speaker from Faro: 'Ela foi ver a Marina?' (*Did she go to visit Marina?*). Tonal representation of the nuclear configuration L*+H H% (Frota, Oliveira et al., 2015).

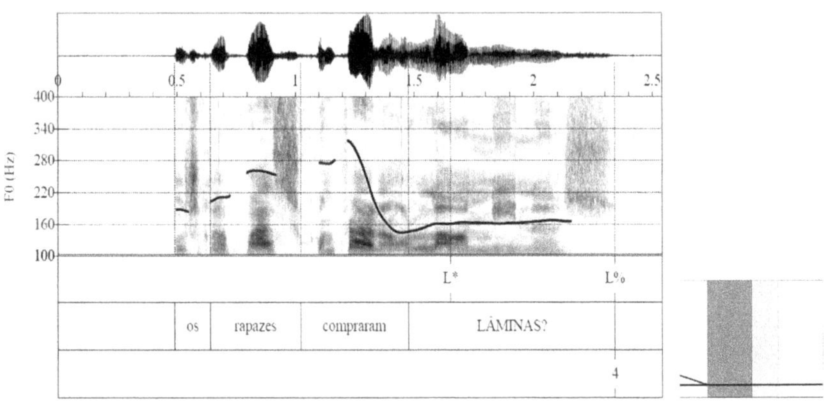

**Figure 2.13.** Counterexpectational yes–no question produced by a speaker from Azores: 'Os rapazes compraram lâminas?' (*Did the boys buy slides?*). Tonal representation of the nuclear configuration L* L% (Frota, Oliveira et al., 2015).

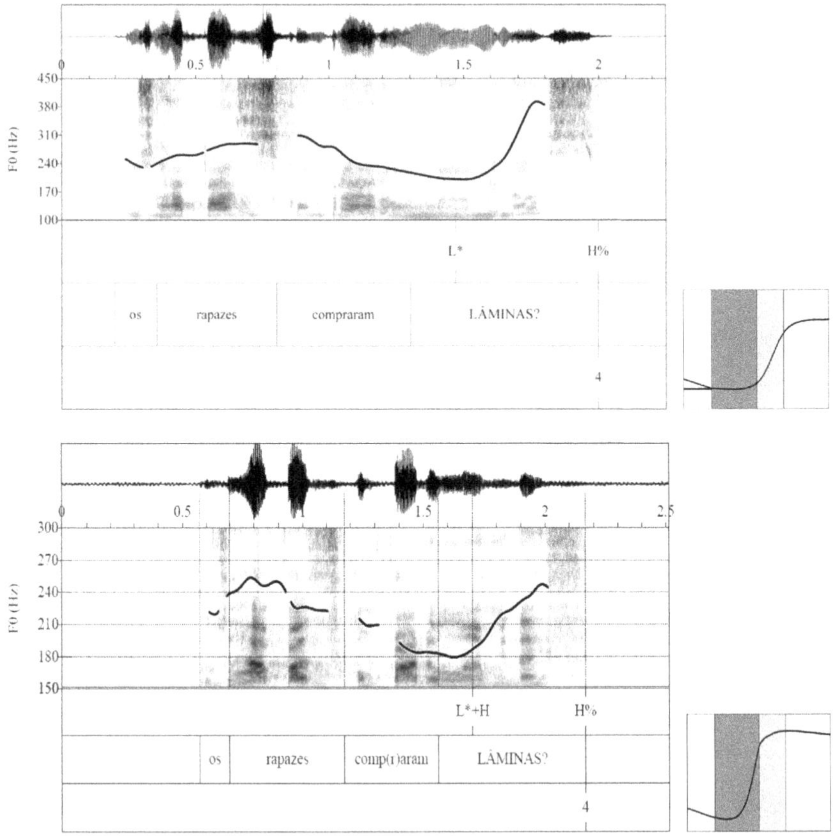

**Figure 2.14.** Counterexpectational yes–no questions produced by a speaker from Sergipe (top panel) and by a speaker from Bahia (bottom panel): 'Os rapazes compraram lâminas?' (*Did the boys buy slides?*). Tonal representation of the nuclear configurations L* H% and L*+H H% (Frota, Oliveira et al., 2015).

Similarly to Faro and Azores in EP, BP varieties also show the same nuclear contour for both pragmatic meanings, in both speech styles. Therefore, we can divide Brazilian varieties in the same two groups: Northern regions, and Centre-Southern regions.

In the Northern regions (Paraíba, Sergipe, Bahia) speakers also produce counterexpectational yes–no questions with a rising pattern: L* H% in Paraíba (64%) and Sergipe (68%) (Figure 2.14, top panel), and L*+H H% in Bahia (49%) (Figure 2.14, bottom panel).

In the Centre-Southern regions (Minas Gerais, Rio de Janeiro, São Paulo, Santa Catarina, and Rio Grande do Sul), the same rising–falling nuclear configuration used for neutral questions was also found to express counterexpectational yes–no questions: L*+H L% in Minas Gerais (97%), Rio de Janeiro (98%) and São Paulo (73%) (Figure 2.15, top panel); and L* HL% in Santa Catarina (100%) and Rio Grande do Sul (100%) (Figure 2.15, bottom panel).

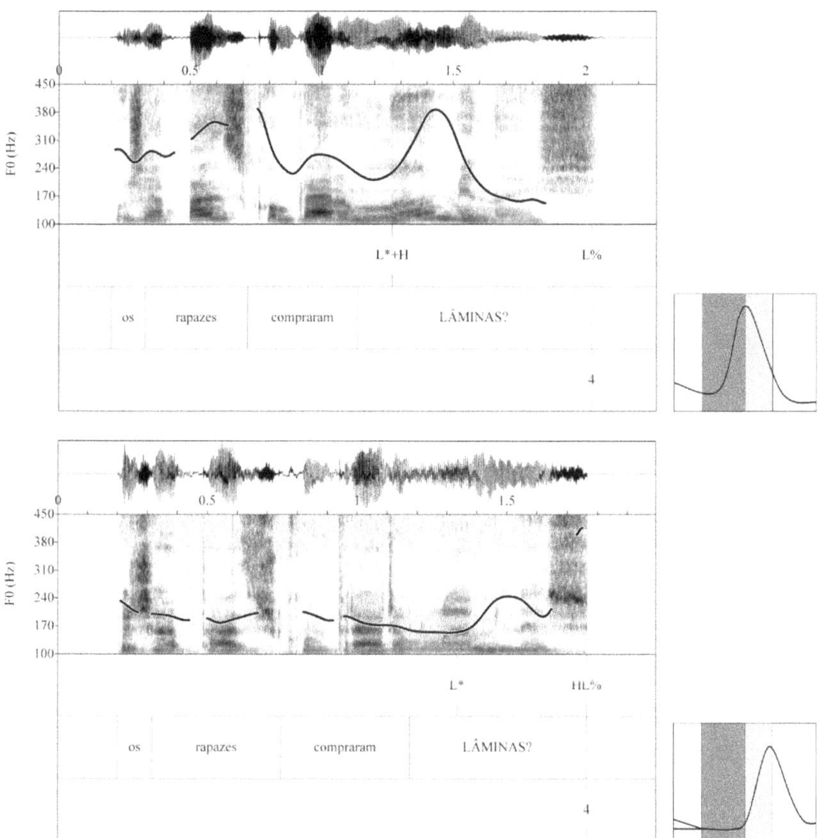


**Figure 2.15.** Counterexpectational yes–no questions produced by a speaker from Rio de Janeiro (top panel) and by a speaker from Santa Catarina (bottom panel): 'Os rapazes compraram lâminas?' (*Did the boys buy slides?*). Tonal representation of the nuclear configurations L*+H L% and L* HL% (Frota, Oliveira et al., 2015).

Potential phonetic differences between neutral and counterexpectational configurations in all these regions are explored in section 4.3.

## 4.3 Phonetic differences between pragmatic meanings

In this section we examine potential phonetic differences between neutral and counterexpectational yes–no questions for all the regions where the same tune was consistently used to convey both pragmatic meanings. This is the case of Faro and Azores, two European Portuguese varieties, and of all Brazilian Portuguese varieties. In order to avoid variability possibly caused by pragmatic differences between the speech styles analysed, only read materials with nuclear words with penult and antepenult stress were considered for phonetic inspection. This corresponds to 27 yes–no questions (neutral and counterexpectational) for the European Portuguese regions of Faro and Azores), and to 105 yes–no questions (neutral and counterexpectational) for Brazilian Portuguese (all regions). Importantly, stressed syllables of the nuclear words are all CV syllables (see Appendix I).

The following phonetic cues were analysed: (i) the duration of the low pitch stretch (i.e., the duration of low pitch in the stressed syllable until the elbow of the L tone is reached); (ii) the alignment of the L tone of the nuclear pitch accent relative to the onset of the stressed syllable, a landmark widely used in previous studies on segmental anchoring (Atterer & Ladd, 2004; Grice et al., 2005; Ladd, Faulkner, Faulkner & Schepman, 1999; Prieto & Torreira, 2007); and (iii) global pitch range.

Figure 2.16 shows the duration of the low pitch stretch relative to the duration of the stressed syllable in neutral (light gray) and counterexpectational (dark gray) yes–no questions in Faro and Azores. As no distinction was found between neutral and counterexpectational yes–no questions, the difference between the two pragmatic meanings is not cued by the duration of the low pitch stretch.

By inspecting the duration of the segmental string corresponding to the low pitch stretch within the nuclear stressed syllable, we may also get relevant information on the alignment pattern. Indeed, in Faro both pragmatic meanings are conveyed by a rising nuclear pitch accent where the rise starts before the middle of the stressed syllable, as only 25–30% of the stressed syllable is low; by contrast, in Azores the stressed syllable is completely low. Furthermore, differences in alignment of the low tone between the two pragmatic meanings are not expected in Faro. The alignment of the low tone is shown in Figure 2.17. Although alignment is not an important cue for the difference between neutral and counterexpectational yes–no

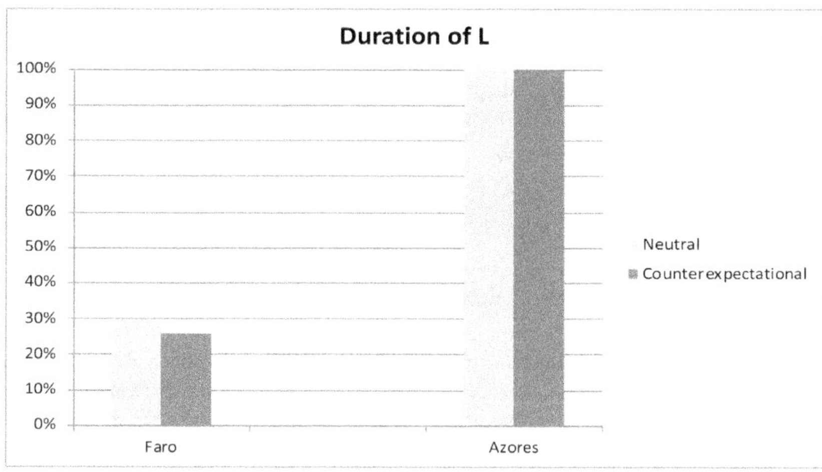


**Figure 2.16.**  Duration of the low pitch stretch in neutral yes–no questions (light gray) and in counterexpectational yes–no questions (dark gray) in EP regions. The y-axis represents the proportional duration of the low pitch stretch relative to the total duration of the nuclear stressed syllable.

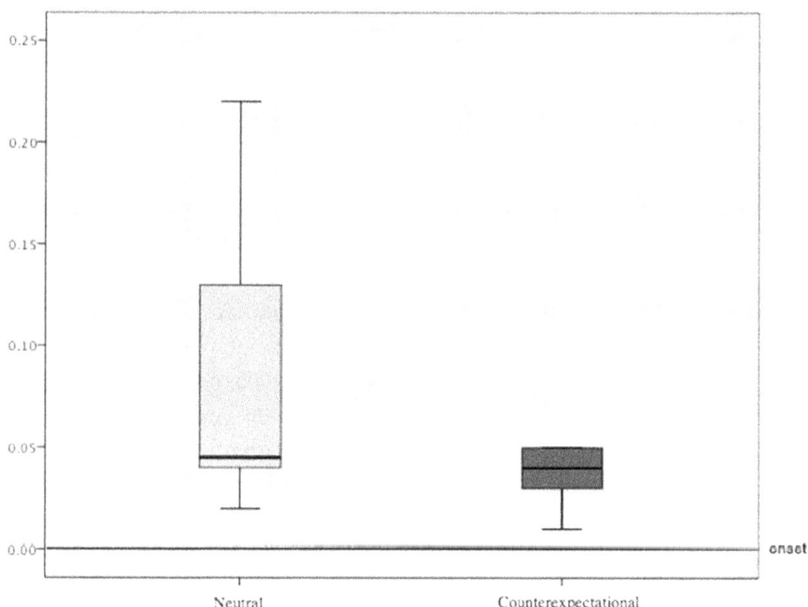


**Figure 2.17.**  Boxplot representing the alignment of the low tone in neutral (light gray) and counterexpectational (dark gray) yes–no questions in Faro. The horizontal line marking the 0-point in the y axis signals the onset of the stressed syllable.

questions, it can be seen that the alignment of the low tone is more stable (or less variable) in counterexpectational than in neutral yes–no questions.

Since both duration and alignment did not provide evidence for a phonetic difference between the two pragmatic meanings under study, we decided to inspect pitch range. For this purpose, we measured the pitch height of the lowest F0 point (F0 min) that is aligned with the stressed syllable, and the pitch height of the highest F0 point (F0 max), i.e., the edge of the utterance in the case of Faro, and the pre-nuclear syllable in the case of Azores. Mean values of F0 max and min are presented in Table 2.1.

**Table 2.1.**  Mean values of F0 max and min, and pitch range (Hz) for neutral and counterexpectational yes–no questions produced in Faro and Azores. Standard errors are given in parentheses.

| Pragmatic meaning | Faro | | | Azores | | |
|---|---|---|---|---|---|---|
| | *F0max* | *F0min* | *Pitch range* | *F0max* | *F0min* | *Pitch range* |
| Neutral y–n | 276.00 | 197.33 | 78.67 | 317.24 | 185.20 | 132.04 |
| | (19.64) | (18.31) | (9.33) | (20.47) | (11.44) | (11.38) |
| Counter-expectational y–n | 274.10 | 185.38 | 88.72 | 319.15 | 133.35 | 185.80 |
| | (11.35) | (13.17) | (5.31) | (20.71) | (13.16) | (11.99) |

Pitch range seems to play a role in conveying incredulity, especially in Azores, where counterexpectational yes–no questions are produced with a wider pitch range (53,76Hz more) than neutral yes–no questions. In Faro, neutral and counterexpectational yes–no questions also show different pitch ranges, thus confirming the exploratory findings in Cruz and Frota (2012). Although in the same direction, the difference is smaller in Faro than in Azores. Further research and more data are needed in order to examine whether the small difference found is enough for native speakers to distinguish between the two pragmatic meanings. We leave this topic for future research. Importantly, since phonetic analysis was implemented in a partial data set of our corpus, the recommended criteria for running statistical inferential analysis were not met.

When F0 max and min values are compared between pragmatic meanings in Faro and Azores, we conclude that the difference in range is explained by the F0 min values only, i.e., F0 max is similar in both pragmatic meanings, but F0 min is lower in counterexpectational yes–no questions than in their neutral counterpart (Figure 2.18).

Let us turn to Brazilian Portuguese varieties. Figure 2.19 shows the duration of the low pitch stretch relative to the duration of the stressed syllable in neutral (light gray) and counterexpectational (dark gray) yes–no

**Figure 2.18.** Schematic representation of mean values of F0 max and min (Hz) for neutral (light gray) and counterexpectational yes–no questions (dark gray) produced in Faro (left) and Azores (right).

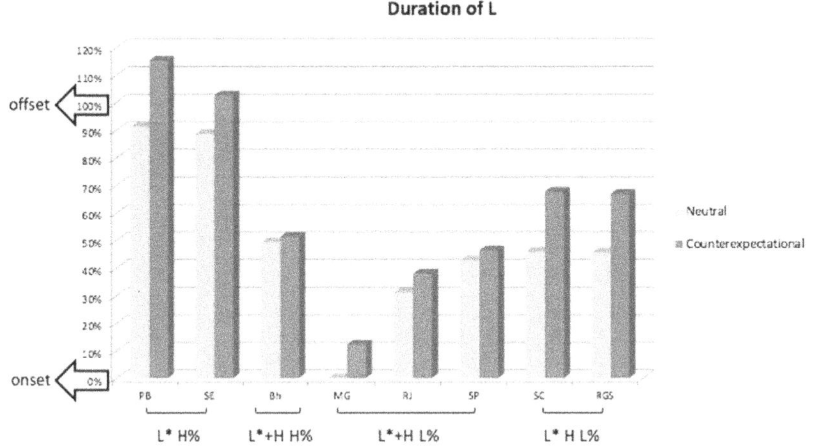



**Figure 2.19.** Duration of the low pitch stretch in neutral yes–no questions (light gray) and in counterexpectational yes–no questions (dark gray) in BP regions. The y-axis represents the proportional duration of the low pitch stretch taking into account the total duration of the nuclear stressed syllable.

questions. In counterexpectational yes–no questions the low pitch stretch is longer than in neutral yes–no questions, which suggests that duration plays a role in conveying incredulity. Furthermore, the duration results provide relevant information on the alignment patterns.

Indeed, the longer duration of the low pitch stretch relative to the stressed syllable underpins the presence of a simple low pitch accent (L*), as in the two northern varieties (Paraíba and Sergipe). By contrast, the shorter duration of the low pitch stretch underpins the presence of a bitonal pitch accent (L*+H), as we may observe in Minas Gerais, Rio de Janeiro and São Paulo. Bahia and the two southern regions (Santa Catarina and Rio Grande

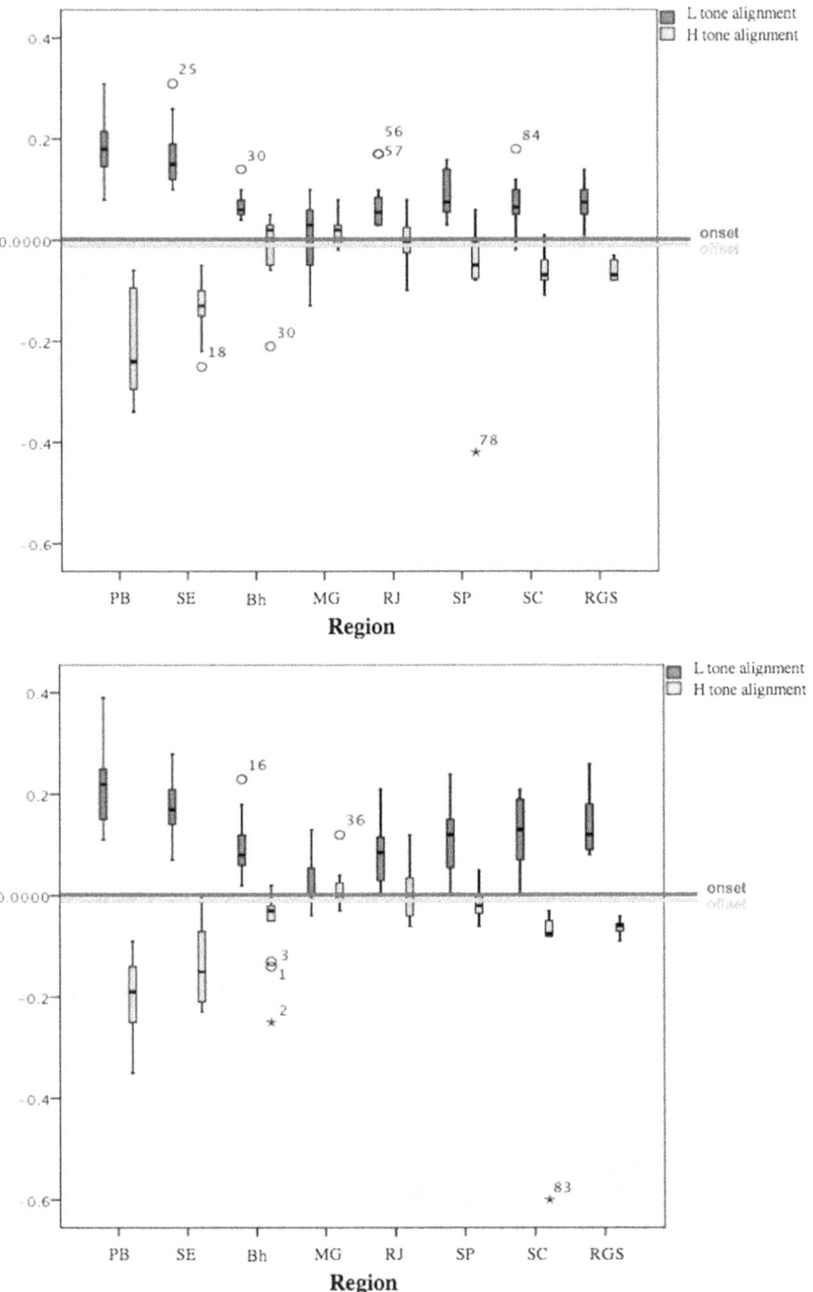

**Figure 2.20.**  Boxplots representing the alignment of the low tone (dark gray) and the alignment of the high tone (light gray) in BP varieties, for neutral yes–no questions (top panel) and counterexpectational yes–no questions (bottom panel). The horizontal lines marking the 0-point in the y axis signal the onset (in dark gray) and the offset (in light gray) of the stressed syllable.

do Sul) show intermediate values. These patterns call for a further inspection of the alignment of the low tone and of the high tone that immediately follows the low tone.

The boxplots in Figure 2.20 show the alignment differences across BP varieties for both pragmatic meanings: neutral yes–no questions in the top panel and counterexpectational yes–no questions in the bottom panel. Dark gray boxplots represent the alignment patterns of the low tone, measured from the onset of the stressed syllable until the end of the low target; light gray boxplots represent the alignment patterns of the high tone, measured from the offset of the stressed syllable until the high target. Thus, light gray boxplots close to the offset point are representative of a trailing high tone (L*+H), whereas light gray boxplots below the offset point (negative values) are representative of a high tone associated with the boundary.

The alignment results show that the high tone clearly belongs to the boundary in Paraíba and Sergipe (L* H%), for both pragmatic meanings. In Bahia and the Central varieties, the high tone belongs to the pitch accent (respectively, L*+H H% and L*+H L%), for both pragmatic meanings. In the Southern varieties, the alignment of the high tone is less clear, but consistent with the phonological analysis L* HL% (see Castelo & Frota, 2017 on a phonological interpretation of high tone alignment in Southern varieties). In short, the phonetic findings on alignment provide support for our phonological analysis.

In conclusion, alignment did not provide evidence for a phonetic difference between the two pragmatic meanings under study, unlike the duration of the low pitch stretch.

# 5    Conclusion

We have investigated the phonology and phonetics of neutral and counterexpectational yes–no questions across Portuguese varieties, by analysing a wide range of utterances and regions from Portugal and Brazil.

The intonation of yes–no questions divides EP varieties into four groups: (i) Lisbon (H∣L* LH%); (ii) Castelo Branco (L*∣H L% or H*+L L%); (iii) Braga, Porto, Beja and Faro ((H+)L* H%; L*+H H%), and (iv) Évora and the islands ((H+)L* L%). BP varieties are divided into two groups: (i) the Northern varieties, that use a rising pattern (L* (+H) H%) and (ii) the Central and Southern varieties, that show a rising–falling pattern (L*(+) H L%).

As for counterexpectational yes–no questions, EP varieties are divided into three different groups: (i) those varieties that use a phonological contour different from the one for neutral yes–no questions, namely Lisbon,

Braga, Évora, Madeira, Porto and Beja (L*+H (H)L%), (ii) those that show an unsystematic behaviour, namely Castelo Branco (H*+L L%), and (iii) those that use the same phonological contour for neutral yes–no questions and counterexpectional yes–no questions, namely Faro and Azores (L*+H H% and L* L%, respectively). All BP varieties use the same phonological contour for both pragmatic meanings. The results and nuclear configurations for both pragmatic meanings are summarised in Table 2.2 for European Portuguese and in Table 2.3 for Brazilian Portuguese.

**Table 2.2.** Summary of the nuclear configurations for neutral and counterexpectational yes–no questions observed in European Portuguese. Gray cells represent differences between the two pragmatic meanings.

| Region | Neutral | Counterexpectational |
| --- | --- | --- |
| Lisbon | H+L* LH% | L*+H HL% |
| Braga | (H+)L* H% | L*+H L% |
| Porto | L*+H H% | L*+H HL% |
| Beja | L* H% | L*+H HL% |
| Faro | L*+H H% | L*+H H% |
| Castelo Branco | L*+H L%[†] | L*+H L% |
| Évora | H+L* L% | L*+H L% |
| Madeira | (H+)L* L% | L*+H L% |
| Azores | L* L% | L* L% |

[†] This contour is the dominant one in the reading task. However, in the DCT, H*+L L% predominates instead.

**Table 2.3.** Summary of the nuclear configurations for neutral and counterexpectational yes–no questions observed in Brazilian Portuguese varieties.

| Region | Neutral | Counterexpectational |
| --- | --- | --- |
| Paraíba | L* H% | L* H% |
| Sergipe | L* H% | L* H% |
| Bahia | L*+H H% | L*+H H% |
| Minas Gerais | L*+H L% | L*+H L% |
| Rio de Janeiro | L*+H L% | L*+H L% |
| São Paulo | L*+H L% | L*+H L% |
| Santa Catarina | L* H L% | L* H L% |
| Rio Grande do Sul | L* H L% | L* H L% |

Overall, the results show a clear asymmetry between European and Brazilian Portuguese varieties in the realisation of the two pragmatic meanings, with more phonological variation in EP than in BP. Moreover, the results of the present study show that varieties of the same language may express counterexpectational yes–no questions in different ways: by means of a categorical (i.e., phonological) distinction in most EP varieties, and by gradual (i.e., phonetic) distinctions in BP varieties and a few EP varieties. More precisely, European Portuguese speakers, in general, change the nuclear configuration to convey incredulity, by using a different pitch accent and/or boundary tone (except in Faro and Azores, where the same nuclear configuration is used for both pragmatic meanings, but with differences in the pitch range). By contrast, Brazilian Portuguese speakers produce counterexpectational yes–no questions with the neutral pattern but with phonetic differences cued by the duration of the low pitch stretch in the stressed syllable. By exploring different speech styles, the current findings also show that intonational patterns are generally consistent independently of the communicative context.

The present study offers, to the best of our knowledge, the first detailed phonological and phonetic analysis of neutral and counterexpectational yes–no questions across European and Brazilian Portuguese varieties. Additionally, it expands and deepens our knowledge of intonational variation in Portuguese, strengthening the P-ToBI proposal of prosodic annotation and analysis (Frota, Oliveira et al., 2015) with new empirical evidence related to rising(–falling) contours and tonal alignment in Portuguese.

# References


Atterer, M., & Ladd, D. R. (2004). On the phonetics and phonology of "segmental anchoring" of F0: Evidence from German. *Journal of Phonetics, 32*(2), 177–197. https://doi.org/10.1016/S0095-4470(03)00039-1

Billmyer, K., & Varghese, M. (2000). Investigating instrument-based pragmatic variability: Effects of enhancing discourse completion tests. *Applied Linguistics, 21*(4), 517–552. https://doi.org/10.1093/applin/21.4.517

Boersma, P., & Weenink, D. (2012). *Praat: Doing phonetics by computer* [Version 5.3.10]. Retrieved from http://www.fon.hum.uva.nl/praat/.

Castelo, J. (2016). *A entoação dos enunciados declarativos e interrogativos no Português do Brasil: Uma análise fonológica em variedades ao longo da Costa Atlântica* [The intonation of declarative and interrogative utterances in Brazilian Portuguese: A phonological analysis in varieties along the Atlantic Coast] (Unpublished doctoral dissertation). Faculdade de Letras, University of Lisbon, Lisbon, Portugal.

Castelo, J., & Frota, S. (2017). The yes–no question contour in Brazilian Portuguese: A geographical continuum. In P. Barbosa, M. C. Paiva & C. Rodrigues (Eds.), *Studies on variation in Portuguese*. Issues in Hispanic and Lusophone Linguistics, 14 (pp. 111–133). Amsterdam/Philadelphia: John Benjamins Publishing. https://doi.org/10.1075/ihll.14.04cas

Cintra, L. (1971). Nova proposta de classificação dos dialectos galego-portugueses [New proposal for the classification of galician-portuguese dialects]. *Boletim de Filologia, 22,* 81–116. Lisboa: Centro de Estudos Filológicos.

Crespo-Sendra, V. (2011). *Aspectes de l'entonació del valencià* [Intonational aspects of Valencian] (Unpublished doctoral dissertation). Universitat Pompeu Fabra, Catalunya, Spain.

Crespo-Sendra, V., Vanrell, M. M., & Prieto, P. (2010). Information-seeking questions and incredulity questions: Gradient or categorical contrast? *Proceedings of Speech Prosody 2010,* paper 164.

Cruz, M. (2013). *Prosodic variation in European Portuguese: Phrasing, intonation and rhythm in central-southern varieties* (Unpublished doctoral dissertation). Faculdade de Letras, University of Lisbon, Lisbon, Portugal.

Cruz, M., & Frota, S. (2011). Prosódia dos tipos frásicos em variedades do Português Europeu: Produção e percepção [Prosody of sentence types in European Portuguese varieties: Production and perception]. In M. A. Costa, I. Falé & P. Barbosa (Eds.), *Textos Seleccionados do XXVI Encontro Nacional da Associação Portuguesa de Linguística* (pp. 208–222). Lisboa: APL.

Cruz, M., & Frota, S. (2012). Para a prosódia do foco em variedades do Português Europeu [On the prosody of focus in European Portuguese varieties]. In A. Costa, C. Flores & N. Alexandre (Eds.), *Textos Seleccionados do XXVII Encontro Nacional da Associação Portuguesa de Linguística* (pp. 196–216). Lisboa: APL.

Cruz, M., Oliveira, P., Palma, P., Neto, B., & Frota, S. (2017). Building a prosodic profile of European Portuguese varieties: The challenge of mapping intonation and rhythm. In P. Barbosa, M. C. Paiva & C. Rodrigues (Eds.), *Studies on variation in Portuguese*. Issues in Hispanic and Lusophone Linguistics, 14 (pp. 81–110). Amsterdam/Philadelphia: John Benjamins Publishing. DOI: 10.1075/ihll.14.03cru.

Ellison, M., & Viana, M. C. (1996). Antagonismo e elisão de vogais átonas finais em Português Europeu [Clash and deletion of unstressed final vowels in European Portuguese]. In I. Duarte & M. Miguel (Orgs.), *Actas do XI Encontro Nacional da Associação Portuguesa de Linguística* (pp. 261–281). Lisboa: APL.

Félix-Brasdefer, J. C. (2010). Data collection methods in speech act performance: DCTs, role plays, and verbal reports. In E. Usó Juán & A. Martinéz-Flor (Eds.), *Speech act performance: Theoretical, Empirical, and Methodological Issues* (pp. 41–56). Amsterdam: John Benjamins Publishing. https://doi.org/10.1075/lllt.26.03fel

Frota, S. (2000). *Prosody and focus in European Portuguese. Phonological phrasing and intonation.* New York: Garland Publishing.

Frota, S. (2002). Nuclear falls and rises in European Portuguese: A phonological analysis of declarative and question intonation. *Probus, 14*(1), (Special Issue on Intonation in Romance, edited by J. I. Hualde), 113–146. https://doi.org/10.1515/prbs.2002.001

Frota, S. (2014). The intonational phonology of European Portuguese. In S.-A. Jun (Ed.), *Prosodic Typology II* (pp. 6–42). Oxford: Oxford University Press. DOI:10.1093/acprof:oso/9780199567300.001.0001

Frota, S. (Coord.) (2012–2015). *Interactive Atlas of the Prosody of Portuguese Project* (PTDC/CLE-LIN/119787/2010). Funded by FCT – Fundação para a Ciência e a Tecnologia, Portugal.

Frota, S., & Cruz, M. (Coords.) (2012–2015). *Interactive Atlas of the Prosody of Portuguese Webplatform.* ISLRN 596-167-619-923-0. Available online at http://labfon.letras.ulisboa.pt/InAPoP/

Frota, S., & Prieto, P. (2015). Intonation in Romance: Systemic similarities and differences. In S. Frota & P. Prieto (Eds.), *Intonation in Romance* (pp. 392–418). Oxford: Oxford University Press.

Frota, S., Cruz, M., Fernandes-Svartman, F., Collischonn, G., Fonseca, A., Serra, C., Oliveira, P., & Vigário, M. (2015). Intonational variation in Portuguese: European and Brazilian varieties. In S. Frota & P. Prieto (Eds.), *Intonation in Romance* (pp. 235–283). Oxford: Oxford University Press.

Frota, S., Oliveira, P., Cruz, M., & Vigário, M. (2015) *P-ToBI: Tools for the transcription of Portuguese prosody.* Lisboa: Laboratório de Fonética, CLUL/FLUL. ISBN: 978-989-95713-9-6. http://labfon.letras.ulisboa.pt/InAPoP/P-ToBI/

Frota, S., & Moraes, J. (2016). Intonation of European and Brazilian Portuguese. In W. L. Wetzels, J. Costa & S. Menuzzi (Eds.), *The Handbook of Portuguese Linguistics* (pp. 141–166). John Wiley & Sons, Inc. DOI: 10.1002/9781118791844.ch9.

Frota, S., Cruz, M., Castelo, J., Barros, N., Crespo-Sendra, V., & Vigário, M. (2016). Tune or Text? Tune-text accommodation strategies in Portuguese. *Proceedings of the Speech Prosody 2016.* Boston: Boston University.

Giles, H., Mulac, A., Bradac, J., & Johnson, P. (1987). *Speech accommodation theory: The first decade and beyond.* Beverly Hills, CA: Sage.

Gili-Fivela, B., Avesani, C., Barone, M., Bocci, G., Crocco, C., D'Imperio, M., Giordano, R., Marotta, G., Savino, M., & Sorianello, P. (2015). Intonational phonology of the regional varieties of Italian. In S. Frota & P. Prieto (Eds.), *Intonation in Romance* (pp. 140–197). Oxford: Oxford University Press.

Grice, M., Ladd, D. R., & Arvaniti, A. (2000). On the place of phrase accents in intonational phonology. *Phonology, 17*(2), 143–185. https://doi.org/10.1017/S0952675700003924

Grice, M, D' Imperio, M., Savino, M., & Avesani, C. (2005). Strategies for intonation labelling varieties of Italian. In S.-A. Jun (Ed.), *Prosodic Typology. The Phonology of Intonation and Phrasing* (pp. 362–389). Oxford: Oxford University Press. DOI:10.1093/acprof:oso/9780199249633.003.0013

Hirschberg, J., & Ward, G. (1992). The influence of pitch range, duration, amplitude and spectral features on the interpretation of the rise-fall-rise intonation contour in English. *Journal of Phonetics, 20*, 241–251. https://doi.org/10.1016/S0095-4470(19)30625-4

Jitca, D., Apopei, V., Paduraru, O., & Marusca, S. (2015). Transcription of Romanian intonation. In S. Frota & P. Prieto (Eds.), *Intonation in Romance* (pp. 284–316). Oxford: Oxford University Press.

Ladd, D. R., Faulkner, D., Faulkner, H., & Schepman, A. (1999). Constant "segmental anchoring" of F0 movements under changes in speech rate. *The Journal of the Acoustical Society of America, 106*(3), 1543–1554. https://doi.org/10.1121/1.427151

Lee, S. A., Martínez-Gil, F., & Beckman, M. E. (2008, September). The intonational expression of incredulity in absolute interrogatives in Buenos Aires Spanish. Paper presented at the *Laboratory Approaches to Spanish Phonology (LASP 4)*. University of Texas Austin, USA.

Lira, Z. (2009). *A entoação modal em cinco falares do nordeste brasileiro* [Modal intonation in five ways of speaking of Northeastern Brazilian] (Unpublished doctoral dissertation). Universidade Federal da Paraíba, João Pessoa, Brazil.

Moraes, J. (2008). The pitch accents in Brazilian Portuguese: Analysis by synthesis. In P. Barbosa, S. Madureira & C. Reis (Eds.), *Proceedings of Speech Prosody 2008* (pp. 389–397).

Moraes, J., & Colamarco, M. (2007). Você está pedindo ou perguntando? Uma análise entonacional de pedidos e perguntas no Português do Brasil [Are you requesting or asking? An intonational analysis of requests and questions in Brazilian Portuguese]. *Revista de Estudos da Linguagem, 15*(2), 113–126. http://dx.doi.org/10.17851/2237-2083.15.2.113-126

Nascentes, A. (1953). *O linguajar carioca* [Carioca's way of speaking]. Rio de Janeiro: Organização Simões.

Niebuhr, O. (2015). Gender differences in the prosody of German questions. *Proceedings of the 18th International Congress of Phonetic Sciences* (ICPhS 2015), Glasgow, Scotland.

Nunes, V. (2011). *Análises entoacionais de sentenças declarativas e interrogativas totais nos falares florianopolitano e lageano* [Intonational analyses of declarative sentences and yes–no questions from Florianópolis and Lages] (Unpublished master dissertation). Universidade Federal de Santa Catarina, Florianópolis, Brazil.

Prieto, P., & Torreira, F. (2007). The segmental anchoring hypothesis revisited: Syllable structure and speech rate effects on peak timing in Spanish. *Journal of Phonetics, 35*(4), 473–500.

Savino, M. (2012). The intonation of polar questions in Italian: Where is the rise? *Journal of the International Phonetic Association, 42*(1), 23–48. https://doi.org/10.1017/S002510031100048X

Savino, M., & Grice, M. (2007). The role of pitch range in realising pragmatic contrasts: The case of two question types in Italian. *Proceedings of the XVI International Congress of Phonetic Sciences (ICPhS 2007)* (pp. 1037–1040).

Savino, M., & Grice, M. (2008, September). Reaction time in the perception of intonational contrasts in Italian. Paper presented at the *Third TIE Conference on Tone and Intonation (TIE3)*. University of Lisbon, Lisbon, Portugal.

Segura, L. (2013). Variedades dialectais do Português Europeu [European Portuguese dialects]. In E. Paiva Raposo, M. F. Bacelar do Nascimento, M. A. Mota, L. Segura & A. Mendes (Orgs.), *Gramática do Português*, Vol. I (pp. 85–142). Lisboa: Fundação Calouste Gulbenkian.

Segura, L., & Saramago, J. (2001). Variedades dialectais portuguesas [Portuguese dialects]. In M. H. M. Mateus (Ed.), *Caminhos do Português: Exposição Comemorativa do Ano Europeu das Línguas* (pp. 221–237). Lisboa: Biblioteca Nacional.

Sichel-Bazin, R., Meisenburg, T., & Prieto, P. (2015). Intonational phonology of Occitan: Towards a prosodic transcription system. In S. Frota & P. Prieto (Eds.), *Intonation in Romance* (pp. 198–233). Oxford: Oxford University Press.

Silva, J. (2011). A prosódia regional em enunciados interrogativos espontâneos do Português do Brasil [Regional prosody of Brazilian Portuguese spontaneous interrogatives]. *Revista Gatilho, 13*, 1–13.

Silva, J. C. B. da, Fonseca, A., Collischonn, G., Henrique, P., & Frota, S. (2018). The Perception of yes–no questions across varieties of Brazilian Portuguese. *Filologia E Linguística Portuguesa, 20*(esp.), 11–25. https://doi.org/10.11606/issn.2176-9419.v20iEspecialp11-25

Truckenbrodt, H. (2009, September). Question intonation: For the layman and results on Brazilian Portuguese for the expert. Poster presented at the *Workshop on Prosody and Meaning*. Universitat Pompeu Fabra, Barcelona, Spain.

Truckenbrodt, H., Sandalo, F., & Abaurre, M. B. (2009). Elements of Brazilian Portuguese intonation. *Journal of Portuguese Linguistics, 8*(1), 75–114. https://doi.org/10.5334/jpl.122

Vigário, M. (1998). *Aspectos da Prosódia do Português Europeu: Estruturas com Advérbios de Exclusão e Negação Frásica* [Aspects of the Prosody of European Portuguese: Structures with Adverbs of Exclusion and Sentence Negation] Colecção Hespérides / Linguística 2. Braga: Universidade do Minho.

Vigário, M. (2003). *The prosodic word in European Portuguese*. Berlin: Mouton de Gruyter.

Vigário, M., & Frota, S. (2003). The intonation of standard and northern European Portuguese: A comparative intonational phonology approach. *Journal of Portuguese Linguistics, 2*(2) (Special issue on Portuguese phonology, ed. W. L. Wetzels), 115–137. https://doi.org/10.5334/jpl.31

**Marisa Cruz** is Assistant Professor at University of Lisbon. She obtained a PhD on prosodic variation in European Portuguese (phrasing, intonation and rhythm) in 2013, in the same institution. She is currently member of the Direction Board of Center of Linguistics of the University of Lisbon, where she investigates visual prosody in European Portuguese, by comparing the prosodic role of gestures in spoken language with the prosody of Portuguese Sign Language. Her research interests also cover language acquisition and language disorders.

**Verònica Crespo-Sendra** is Teacher at the Institut Rovira-Forns, Santa Perpètua de Mogoda, Barcelona, since 2015. She obtained her PhD on the intonational phonology of Catalan dialects in 2011, at Universitat Pompeu Fabra, Barcelona, and had a postdoctoral fellowship within the *Interactive Atlas of the Prosody of Portuguese* project (2012–2015) at the Phonetics and Phonology Lab, University of Lisbon, in 2014–2015.

**Joelma Castelo** is Lecturer at the Center of Human Sciences and Education of Universidade Estadual do Paraná, Brazil, and postdoctoral researcher at the University of São Paulo, Brazil. Her research focuses on the phonetics and phonology of intonational variation in Portuguese. Her most relevant publications are *Variação entoacional dos enunciados interrogativos, The yes–no question contour in Brazilian Portuguese* (Castelo & Frota, 2017), and *The perception of yes–no questions across varieties of Brazilian Portuguese* (Castelo et al., 2018).

**Sónia Frota** is Full Professor of Experimental Linguistics at the University of Lisbon. Her research seeks to understand the properties of prosodic systems (phrasing, intonation, and rhythm), the extent to which they vary across and within languages, and how they are acquired by infants and help to bootstrap the learning of language. She is the editor in chief of the *Journal of Portuguese Linguistics* (since 2002), Associate Editor of *Phonetica* (since 2015) and the Director of the Center of Linguistics at the University of Lisbon (since 2020).

# 3
# High pre-tonic falls in Northeastern Brazilian varieties: may a prenuclear high target spreading rightward re-categorize as a nuclear leading tone?

Marco Barone & Joelma Castelo

## 1    Introduction

The goal of this study is to present an interpretation of an instance of phonological variation in the intonation of northeastern Brazilian Portuguese statements with broad focus as the possible result of an ongoing process of reanalysis, or oversimplification by analogy. According to our hypothesis, a complex rule of context-conditioned phonetic implementation of the intonational contour is being replaced over time by a simpler rule, aided by the fact that in a certain context, with a high frequency of occurrence, both rules produce the same surface outcome.

After reviewing the literature on Brazilian Portuguese intonation, especially those analyses carried out under the autosegmental-metrical framework, we introduce data on the intonation of broad focus statements in a different language, the southern variety of Italian spoken in Pescara (see Figure 3.1, left panel, for location). Although unrelated as a language, the analysis of Pescara Italian helps to simplify the interpretation of the variation in Brazilian Portuguese (BP, henceforth): the nuclear contours of Pescara Italian statements with broad focus exhibit two out of the three possible phonetic implementations found in northeastern Brazil; in Pescara Italian the only rule applying, in a perfectly systematic way, to decide which of the two phonetic contours must be used, is a rather complicated rule of

**Figure 3.1.** The Italian city of Pescara (left panel) and Brazilian cities of João Pessoa and Recife (right panel).

context-conditioned contour implementation: the outcome of the surface pattern only depends on whether the postverbal stretch has one or more than one tone-bearing units (TBU henceforth).

Next, we present data from two sociolinguistic surveys on BP broad focus statements, carried out in the northeastern Brazilian cities of Recife, in the state of Pernambuco and João Pessoa, in the state of Paraíba, about the use of these patterns and, in the case of Recife, its dependence on gender (see Figure 3.1, right panel, for locations). We show how the variation found in Brazilian male subjects is similar to the Italian variation and we posit that, assuming the Italian rule was the original one applied to BP, this rule is being lost over time, and would therefore explain the variation found in BP.

We can describe the contours involved in the variation under analysis as follows: a falling nuclear pitch accent was found in BP statements, preceded by a salient pretonic rise from a low target before the pretonic syllable to a high target on the pretonic syllable (Castelo, 2016; Cunha & Colamarco, 2005; Lira, 2009; Silvestre, 2012). For some Brazilian varieties, the statements showing this pattern were identified as narrow focus statements, and the contour was labeled as ¡H+L*[1] (Dabkowski, 2012; Moraes, 2008). The authors of the present study have documented this contour for broad focus

---

[1] In line with the Autosegmental-Metrical principle that no pitch accent can be associated with a syllable which is not stressed at the word level, and the convention that Portuguese ToBI labelling system (Frota, Oliveira, Cruz & Vigário, 2015) avoids tritonal combinations such as L+H+L*, the labeling ¡H+L* carries the understanding that the change of slope far away from a stressed position (a rise from the pre-pretonic syllable to the pretonic syllable) could be justified by an extra-high target.

statements in Recife and João Pessoa through different elicitation tasks.[2] A minority of occurrences shows a simple falling pitch accent from a mid-high pretonic target to a low level in the tonic syllable, with no rising movement preceding it, but the present study will exclude these renditions and only focus on the broad focus statements uttered with a saliently high tone on the pretonic nuclear syllable, trying to explain the origin of the pretonic rise in terms of a phonological reanalysis of the rule for phonetic implementation. This chapter is organized as follows: in Section 2 we review the previous work on the intonational phonology of statements in BP. In Section 3 we introduce an analysis of statements in Pescara Italian, whose contour variation is a subset of the Brazilian variation for the same sentence type and strictly complies with a specific rule for phonetic implementation. We explain how this apparently complex rule is actually a reasonable consequence of a phenomenon of tonal repulsion, in a situation of tonal crowding, and how the same rule accounts for simplifying part of the analysis proposed for Brazilian statements. In Section 4, we describe the methodology of the study, including the analysis of one existing set of data, the building of a new elicitation task, specific to the study, and the analysis of the new set of data: materials, procedures and speakers. The results are presented in Sections 5 and 6, with a first discussion of the data from Recife. In Section 7 we introduce the concept of reanalysis, providing examples from different modules of linguistics, and a model of language change is discussed, which extends such a notion to the domain of intonation. Finally, in Section 8, the model is applied to BP, the results are analyzed and a conclusion ends the chapter.

# 2    Background on the intonation of statements in Brazilian Portuguese

Studies on modal intonation have particularly focused on comparing linguistic systems. The universalist approach, according to which languages have an overall tendency to display a falling contour for complete statements and a rising contour for incomplete statements (Bolinger, 1978), has been overcome, since it is known that the relationships of prominence at the sentence level are governed by a set of specific rules for each system (Ladd,

---

[2]  In order to ensure that the pretonic rise–falling accent does not correspond to a narrow focus on the rightmost nuclear element exhibiting the salient movement, as in the studies mentioned, compound words with non-transparent semantics have been used by the authors, where such a narrow focus interpretation would be meaningless.

2008). Studies on the intonational phonology of an increasing number of languages have revealed that there are languages, such as Chicasaw and English (Gordon, 2005 for Chicasaw; Britain, 1992; Guy, Horvath, Vonwiller, Daisley & Rogers, 1986; Warren, 2005; Warren & Britain, 2000; among others, for English), that may use final rising contours for complete statements.

Recent research on BP has begun to apply the Autosegmental-Metrical model to intonational phonology (Pierrehumbert, 1980). Differently from preceding studies, which were based on configuration patterns (Hirst & Di Cristo, 1998; 't Hart, Collier & Cohen, 1990), this approach analyzes the melodic contours as implemented by interpolation of strings of phonological units composed of only two levels (Low and High), according to specific phonological rules based on a prosodic hierarchy (Frota & Vigário, 2000; Moraes, 2008).

This section reviews studies on the intonational system of BP, focusing on findings related to the declarative sentence type. We selected studies by Frota and Vigário (2000), Moraes (2008) and Truckenbrodt, Sandalo and Abaurre (2009) for the analyses of several sentence types based on the main urban varieties, as well as studies by Cunha (2000) and Frota et al. (2015) based on dialectal corpora, in order to account for the geographic variation of the intonation of statements in BP. In addition, we also reviewed more specific works on BP intonation at the word level, distinguishing simple and compound words (Vigário & Fernandes-Svartman, 2010).

Frota & Vigário (2000) provide a comparative study of the intonational phonology of Portuguese spoken in São Paulo (one of the main urban varieties of BP) and in Lisbon (Standard European Portuguese – SEP), which describes the similarities and differences between them in terms of prosodic, rhythmic and intonational structure. BP shows a higher density of pitch accents for statements than SEP. This indicates a difference in terms of the prosodic structure (a lower prosodic level – the phonological phrase – is more relevant for BP; and a higher prosodic level – the intonational phrase, for SEP. In terms of rhythm BP has a more strongly alternating rhythmic pattern than SEP, which can also be captured by the sequences of LH contours). As for the similarities, both varieties share the same intonational contour for statements with broad focus, mainly described by Frota & Vigário (2000) as a falling contour along the stressed syllable (H+L*) followed by a low boundary tone (L%).

The study by Moraes (2008) provides an overview of the intonational lexicon of the nuclear and prenuclear pitch accents of a wide range of sentence types produced by the speakers of the Rio de Janeiro variety of BP. The contours found are described as bitonal pitch accents with a leading tone (T+T*) that mainly convey the pragmatics in a nuclear position. The melodic contours are classified, as in traditional studies on intonational phonology, into falling and rising contours, and are further analyzed according to other acoustic parameters such as scaling, alignment and lengthening that mark, at the surface, relevant phonological units conveying the pragmatics of the sentences.

Truckenbrodt et al. (2009) provide a phonological description for broad and narrow focus statements and for interrogative sentences, with specific predictions about the distinctive elements in the intonational system of BP. Similarly to the results of Moraes (2008), they find a falling contour described as H+L* L% for statements. In addition, they present a detailed description of the alignment of the L tone, which may be not completely realized on the stressed sylable. The alignment of statements is also discussed in Castelo & Frota (2016).

The two studies mentioned above and other works on the intonation of the main urban Brazilian varieties (Frota & Moraes, 2016; Serra, 2009; Fernandes-Svartman, 2007; Tenani, 2002) describe a uniform phonological nuclear contour H+L* L% for statements. Studies focusing on intonational variation (Castelo & Frota, 2016; Silvestre, 2012) confirm the analysis as a unique H+L* L% contour at the phonological level. However, they point out phonetic differences in terms of the alignment of the high peak of the H+L* pitch accent: Northern (Paraíba, Sergipe, and Bahia) and Central (Rio de Janeiro and Minas Gerais) varieties tend to show the peak of the nuclear contour at the beginning of the last pretonic syllable whereas in Southern varieties (Santa Catarina and Rio Grande do Sul) the whole falling movement is contained in the tonic syllable.

Scaling is another important parameter for expressing variation in Southern varieties. Broad focus statements, also referred to as "neutral" declarative sentences, are characterized by a simple fall, starting from a medium pitch level in the pretonic (H+L* L%). Narrow focus statements, in turn, are characterized by a fall from an extra high pretonic peak (¡H+L* L%), differently from the broad focus pattern (Moraes, 2008; Truckenbrodt et al., 2009). In addition to the increase of F0, narrow focus statements also show higher values of intensity and duration, which concur with the perception of a different pragmatic meaning (Moraes, 2008). The involvement of the speaker is also recognized by phonetic cues in this sentence type, namely the expansion of the pitch range (Truckenbrodt et al., 2009). The latter study proposes a new phonological pattern (L H+L* L%), with a preceding low target, justified as an optional part of the H+L* L% declarative contour. Studies based on dialectal data show that salient scaling features can also be found in the neutral declarative pattern. In the Recife variety, the pretonic syllables of statements were originally described as salient in terms of frequency, duration and intensity (Cunha, 2000).

Regarding the intonational phonology of statements at the word level, Vigário (2010) proposes a non-recursive level for a prosodic domain composed of two prosodic words, which has been confirmed by recent studies on BP (Vigário & Fernandes-Svartman, 2010; Toneli, 2014). This domain, the "prosodic word group" (PWG, henceforth) is identified as a unit of a hierarchical level between prosodic word and phonological phrase. The main argument that justifies its existence in the prosodic hierarchy of Portuguese is the application of phonological rules different to those that apply to prosodic words. In terms of tone association, it is expected that only one pitch accent is associated to the PWG.

Considering the rich tonal density of BP spoken in São Paulo, Vigário and Fernandes-Svartman (2010) explore the intonational properties of the PWG in BP, by analyzing short (*guarda-costas*, "bodyguard") and long (*macro-endividamento*, "macro-indebtedness") compound words, as branching and non-branching subjects and objects. The authors show that there is a mandatory pitch accent associated with the head of the PWG and an optional pitch accent associated with the non-head element. In short branching PWGs (6 syllables), there is no pitch accent associated with the non-head element, except in the case of a non-branching object. In long branching compounds (9 syllables), in contrast, both objects and subjects have an optional pitch accent associated with the non-head element of the PWG in more than half of the cases. An initial H(+L) accent may be found at the beginning of the PWG, whose probability of occurrence seems to be sensitive to whether the PWG is composed of only one prosodic word: at the level of the PW, H(+L) association mainly occurs if the stress is on the fifth syllable or later. In the case of a compound word spanning the entire PWG, however, this accent is mainly produced if the stress is on the fourth syllable or later. Regarding tonal constituency of the PWG and its pitch accents, an L+H* accent associated with both words was frequently found in subject compounds and an L+H* followed by an H+L* in objects compounds (Fernandes-Svartman, 2007). The last contour will be the object of investigation in the present study.

## 3   The motivation for the study: the analysis of the pretonic rise in Pescara

In this section, we introduce a different language where two of the three Northeastern BP contours for broad focus statements are also found, and an analysis is provided for this variation, which will help to simplify the analysis of BP variation as well. A recent study comparing the intonation of the Italian variety of Pescara (Barone, in preparation, data also present in Gili Fivela et al., 2015) with its substratum language, Pescarese, using the Discourse Completion Task methodology (Blum-Kulka, House & Kasper, 1989), shows that a falling accent preceded by a pretonic rise is the unique pattern found, for both languages, on narrow noncontrastive focus affirmative SVO statements with no branching object, as well as on broad focus statements of Pescarese, by virtue of a rule of mandatory default position for non-informational focalization[3]. We will refer to this implementation as "pretonic rise–fall pattern," understanding that this is a phonetic definition. For broad focus statements of Pescara Italian, the pretonic rise–fall pattern is also found, together with another one: a nonsalient mid-to-low nuclear fall, without a pretonic rise. Through a survey by age groups and considerations on intonational bilingualism, Barone (in preparation) explains how young "speakers" of Pescara Italian (mainly able only to understand Pescarese but unable to speak it) have inherited from their parents (mainly able to speak Pescarese) a Pescarese-like intonation and transferred it onto Italian, so that Pescara Italian presents a complex intonational system, in which for many sentence types there exists one Pescarese-like intonational contour (corresponding to, roughly, "speaking with an accent") and a Standard-like contour (corresponding to "speaking without an accent"). For Italian broad focus statements, the Pescarese rule of mandatory default position may or may not apply, depending on whether the speakers choose to speak with a Pescarese-like intonation (in which a focus-like salient prominence is mandatory somewhere in the sentence, and in the absence of informational focus, in the "default" position) or with a more standard intonation (in which utterances with no focus-like salient prominence are

---

[3]  The justification suggested for the peculiar distribution of contours according to focus type is that in Pescarese the pattern used for marking narrow focus at the last position of statements remains identical in broad focus statements, because the typical salient prosodic prominence found in focused positions in Pescarese is mandatory and must appear somewhere in the sentence, even in the absence of a specific phrase with an informational focus value, in which case it will appear on a specific "default" position for mandatory "non-informational focalization". The element occupying the default position may show a kind of prominence or saliency with respect to the others, equal to the prominence that a focused element would have, but which is not necessarily corresponding to an informational focus value, in the sense of Selkirk (1984), and that default position would be in the case of Pescarese the postverbal stretch coinciding, for non-branching objects, with its rightmost element, the nucleus.

allowed)[4]. The author then focused only on those contours displaying a prominence: that is, the contour with a pretonic rise–falling (right panels in Figure 3.2) pattern, be it corresponding to an informative narrow focus or a default prominence on a broad focus, and realized that all sentences from the DCT survey contained a non-branching, or "simple", object: that is, a postverbal stretch (or postverbal PWG, according to the terminology introduced by Vigário for BP) composed of just one tone-bearing unit. In view of this fact, and as the pretonic rise–fall pattern seems to show a complex inner structure, the author added to the DCT survey of Pescara Italian a number of statements with a postverbal object phrase, which corresponds to a prosodic word group containing more than one tone-bearing unit. Surprisingly, in none of the sentences added was the rise–fall pattern present, and instead a "hat" plateau pattern was found in all of them, with a prenuclear rise to the first TBU of the postverbal object, followed by a nuclear fall on the last TBU (left panels in Figure 3.2). Between the rising and falling accent a plateau joining the two high peaks was visible, a result of right spreading of the high prenuclear target until the nucleus (see Gussenhoven, 2004 for spreading).

For other sentence modalities and pragmatic types (such as yes–no questions, contrastive statements, statements of the obvious, items in a list), the prenuclear rising accent is maintained, as well as its rightward spreading for postverbal objects with more than one TBU, whereas the nuclear accent may vary according to the pragmatics. The left panels of Figure 3.3 show the implementation of a hat pattern ending with an H*+L nuclear accent (L+H*+high plateau+H*+L: contrastive focus statement) and one ending with an L*+H nuclear accent (L+H*+high plateau+L*+H: statement of the obvious), on sentences with an object formed either by more than one PWG or by PWG with a compound. The whole postverbal object, enclosed between the two accents, receives a prosodic prominence and the first (rising) pitch accent can be thought of as an initial marker of such an event of prominence. However, for non-branching objects corresponding to a PWG with only one PW, the same nuclear accents are preceded by a pretonic rise, instead of a high plateau (right panels of Figure 3.3).

---

[4] This makes distinguishing broad focus from narrow focus in final position difficult, in those cases in which the participants opt for speaking "with an accent," and implies a risk of circularity: the author can only define as broad focus statements those elicited sentences that are a reaction to neutral contexts, where speakers are asked to just answer general questions such as "What's happening?," relying on the correct execution of the elicitation and hoping that, for the majority of the cases, the speakers would limit themselves to perform the required tasks without adding extra informational values.

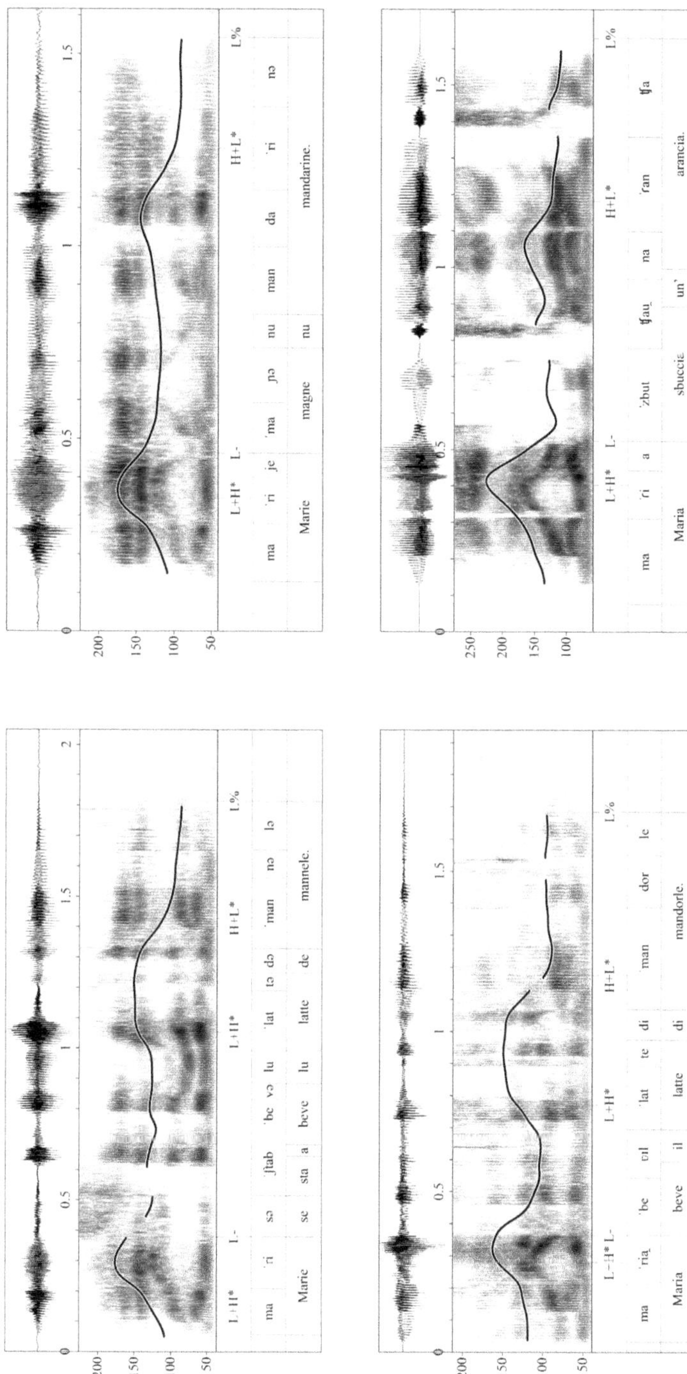

**Figure 3.2.** The implementation of the "hat" pattern on postverbal objects with more than one PWG (left panels: Maria beve [il latte di mandorle] 'Maria is drinking [almond milk]') and that of the pretonic rise-fall patterns on postverbal objects with a PWG corresponding to only one PW (top right panel: Marie magne [nu mandarine] 'Maria is eating a tangerine'; bottom right panel: Maria sbuccia [un'arancia] 'Maria is skinning [an orange]') as transferred from Pescarese (top panels) to Pescara Italian (bottom panels). The speakers were asked to look at a picture and answer "What is Maria doing?" (discouraging informational focalization on the object).

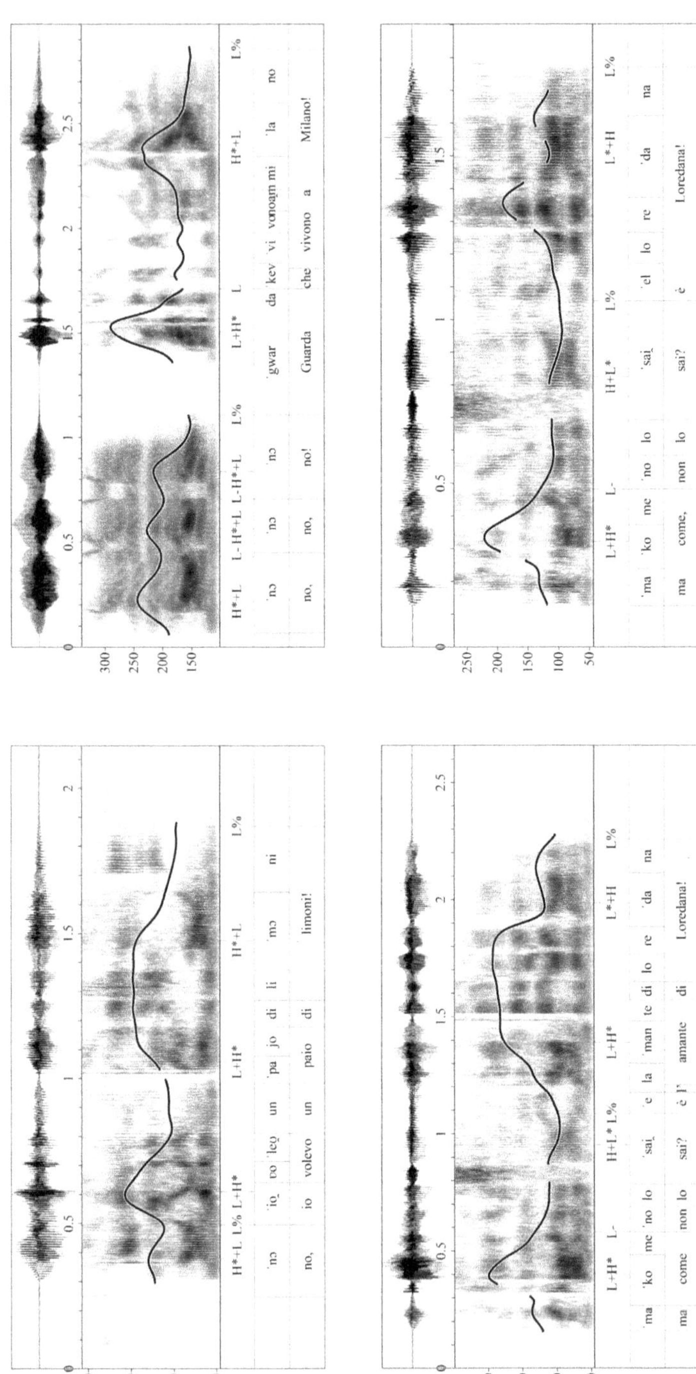

**Figure 3.3.** The nuclear pitch accent H*+L (top panels: contrastive statements, with contrastive focus on the postverbal PWG) and L*+H (bottom panels: statements of the obvious), both preceded by the rise+high spreading plateau pattern for postverbal objects with more than one PWG (left panels: *Vorrei [un paio di limoni]* 'I would like [a couple of lemons]' and *È [l'amante di Loredana]!* 'He is [Loredana's lover]!') and by the pretonic rise for postverbal objects with a PWG corresponding to only one PW (right panels: *Guarda che vivono [a Milano]* 'Mind that they live [in Milan]' and *È Loredana!* 'It's [Loredana]!'). Sentences produced by Pescara Italian speakers.

This evidence suggests that the first rising accent L+H*, which is shared by all pragmatic sentence types presented, is an initial structural marker of the presence of a PWG, in the sense that it only marks the beginning of a prosodic unit, intermediate between prosodic word and phonological phrase, formed by the whole postverbal PWG, and does not matter for pragmatics. However, the author finds other sentence types in which the rising accent and the plateau in the first TBU of the postverbal PWGs (or, respectively, the pretonic rise of the PWG with only one PW) are absent and even minimal pairs in which the presence of this pattern is the only distinctive element[5]. So we will restrict our attention to a fixed sentence type (broad focus or narrow focus statements) that exhibit these rising patterns. Unlike other initial structural accents found in the literature, such as the French *arc accentuel* (Di Cristo, 1999) marking the left boundary of a constituent (which usually occur on the first syllable of its first word and are classified as phrase accents), this accent always occurs on the stressed syllable of the first prosodic word of the phrase with more than one TBU, behaving like a prenuclear L+H* pitch accent instead of a phrase accent. The rule for implementation of this prominence is therefore very simple: a prenuclear L+H* accent is found on the stressed syllable of the first word (or first TBU) of the postverbal object, and a nuclear pitch accent (depending on pragmatics) on the stressed syllable of the last word, with a high plateau connecting the two. However, when the postverbal object only has one stressed syllable, that is, the first and last stressed syllables coincide (right panels in the Figure 3.3), according to this rule this unique syllable should receive both an L+H* accent (for being the first TBU) and the nuclear accent (for being the last one), which depends on pragmatics and is possibly different from L+H*. Tonal crowding is therefore resolved, as the figures above show, by moving back the L+H* rise by one entire syllable, mapping it to the pretonic syllable.

Table 3.1 tries to explain this type of tonal repulsion, which we may refer to as the rule of (possibly degenerated) plateau. Postverbal objects with more than one TBU (that is, objects with more than one PWG and objects with one PWG formed by compounds) have to be considered as the unmarked case; and PWGs with just one TBU (non-branching objects corresponding to a PWG with only one PW) as marked, degenerating case, with plateaus of length zero. In the bottom line of Table 3.1, the first tone-bearing unit "LAT" of the postverbal object receives the initial pitch accent L+H* and the last TBU, "MAN," receives the nuclear pitch accent, which is H+L*

---

[5]    For instance, uttering the sentence in the bottom left panel without an L+H*+plateau (respectively, without a pretonic rise, for the bottom right panel), one would hear a counterexpectational yes–no question instead of a statement of the obvious.

**Table 3.1.** Pescarese and Pescara Italian rule for implementation of prominence on a postverbal PWG in the case of broad focus statements (nuclear accent = H+L*). The letter N after brackets stands for 'nucleus' and "PWG" is the type pf prosodic phrase (between prosodic word and phonological phrase) that the postverbal stretch forms. Word-stressed syllables are underlined.

| *Maria sbuccia [[un'arancia]$_N$]$_{PWG}$* 'Maria is skinning an orange' | | | | | | ↗⇐↘↗ | |
|---|---|---|---|---|---|---|---|
| | MA | <u>RIA</u> | SBUC | CIA-U | NA | <u>RAN</u> | CIA |
| *...beve [il latte [di mandorle]$_N$]$_{PWG}$* '(Maria) drinks almond milk' | | ↗ | → | → | ↘ | | |
| <u>BE</u> | VE-IL | <u>LAT</u> | TE | DI | <u>MAN</u> | DOR | LE |

because the sentence is a broad focus statement. But in the top sentence of Table 3.1 the postverbal PWG *un'arancia* only has one TBU, its tonic syllable "RAN," which is at the same time the first and last TBU of the object. Therefore, it should take both L+H* (dotted arrow) and H+L* pitch accents. In order to avoid crowding, the rising is anticipated to the pretonic syllable, as the thick backward arrow points out. We can summarize the rule for (possibly degenerated) plateau, which we label as RULE-1, as:

RULE-1: Put an L+H* rise on the first TBU of the object and H+L* on its last TBU (nucleus) unless these TBUs coincide (in that case, move the rise back one syllable.)

A configuration with a rising accent followed by a plateau and a falling accent was observed in a number of languages and called "suspension bridge contour" (Bolinger, 1961, for English) or "(flat) hat pattern" (Cohen & 't Hart, 1967, for Dutch; Wunderlich, 1991, for German) across intermediate phrase boundaries. Other studies (Grabe, 2004; Gussenhoven, 1984) have found hat patterns in English and Duch also within noun phrases[6]. Nguyễn, Ingram & Pensalfini (2008), in their elicitation of postverbal English two-syllable compounds, also found a plateau pattern, used by native English speakers for broad focus, and referred to it as H*__H*L%. Brazilian Portuguese may also show this type of prominence for postverbal PWGs formed by compounds, with one rising and one falling accent, although they do not always show the typically sustained plateau that is found in Pescara but a slight sag is generally observed instead, depending on the distance between the two positions. Vigário & Fernandes-Svartman (2010) use the label L*+H__H+L* for some of these configurations for compound words with two TBUs. It is reasonable to think that both accents play two different

---

[6]   The pattern H*__H*(L) is considered as the result of a process of "tone complete linking" in Gussenhoven (1984).

functions in determining the structure/focus/pragmatics of the compound and they are not dispensable.

Clearly, when the constituent is simple, there is no way to observe the same strategy, as two distinct accents cannot be simultaneously implemented on the same syllable. Therefore our question is: how is it possible to render phonetically the same phonological value of the double accent contour in BP in the case of simple constituents, where the first and last tonic syllable coincide? What would the result be? Would we find an event of tonal repulsion, leading to a high pretonic peak, like in Pescara?

It is a fact that Northeastern BP shows, for simple constituents, the high pretonic peak pattern in broad focus statements and it is reasonable to believe that this is not a coincidence. Figure 3.4 shows an instance of a double accent for a compound constituent and a pretonic rise for a non-branching object corresponding to a PWG with only one PW in Northeastern BP. This is compatible with the hypothesis that the same rule that was observed in Pescara applies to Northeastern BP broad focus statements.

Contours like these, corresponding to those observed in Pescara, may be also found in Castelo (2016) and among the data elicited for the InAPoP project (Frota, coord., 2012–2015), for the varieties of Recife and João Pessoa. The InAPoP database only includes data elicited from female speakers, and most of the BP participants were young speakers. However, unlike in Pescara, both in João Pessoa and Recife a pretonic rise–fall strategy was also found for constituents with either more than one PWG or a PWG formed by a compound (i.e. for constituents with more than one TBU), especially for the elicitations of young women, with a deaccentuation of the first TBU of the object and just a pretonic rise–falling pattern on its last TBU, that is, in nuclear position. This intonational strategy is forbidden in Pescara Italian and in Pescarese. The pattern is shown in Figure 3.5.

Hence, Recife Portuguese displays two prominence strategies for constituents with more than one TBU, corresponding to the same strategy for constituents with only one TBU. Table 3.2 provides a comparative picture of the possible realizations in Pescara and Recife.

At the level of the phonological analysis, in Pescara the only rule for phonetic implementation of the intonation of broad focus statements is the rule for (possibly degenerated) plateau, yielding plateaus for postverbal objects with more than one PWG or with PWGs formed by compounds and pretonic rise–fall contours for non-branching objects, which correspond to a PWG with only one PW, with no exception. In the Recife variety of BP, the presence of two different contours for objects formed either by more than one PWG or by a PWG formed by a compound is compatible with the hypothesis that two distinct rules for phonetic implementation are applicable,

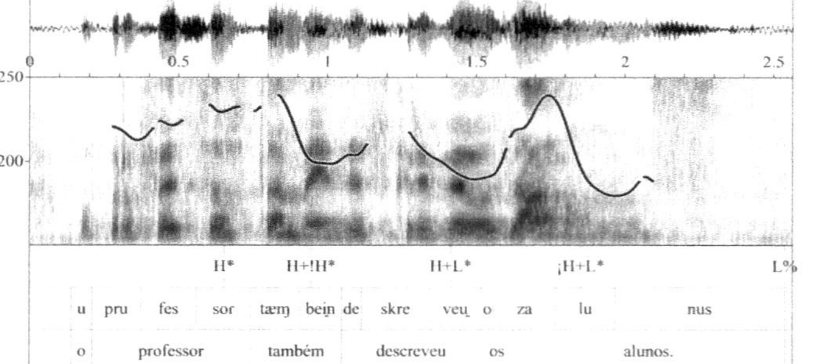 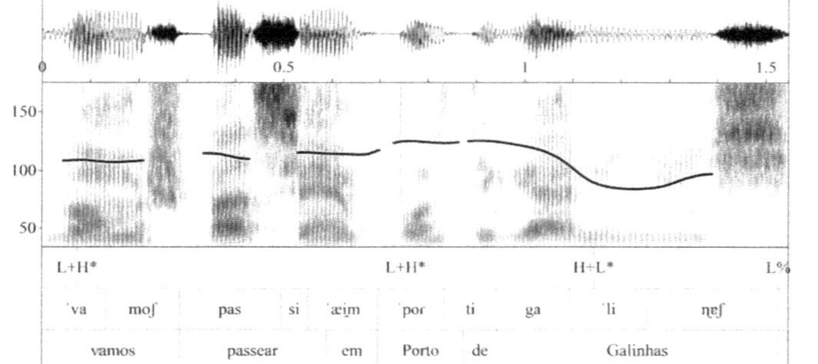

Figure 3.4. Northeastern Brazilian Portuguese broad focus statements: a hat pattern on the postverbal PWG formed by a compound (left panel: *vamos passear em* [*Porto de Galinhas*] 'we are taking a stroll in [Porto de Galinhas]' uttered by a speaker from Recife) and a pretonic rise-fall pattern on the postverbal PWG with only one PW (right panel: *o professor também descreveu* [*os alunos*] 'The teacher also described [the students]' uttered by a speaker from João Pessoa).

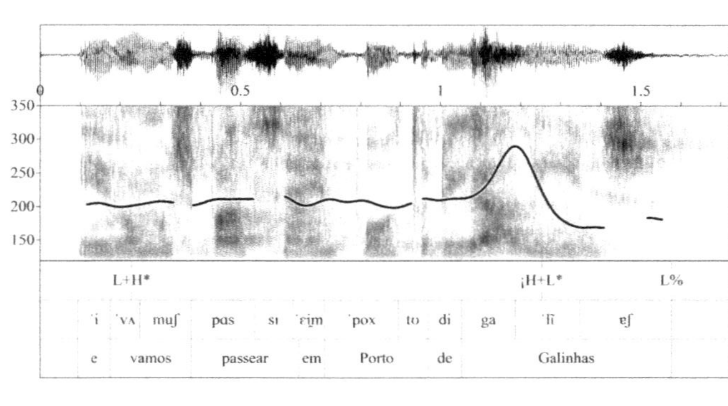

Figure 3.5. The pretonic rise implementation of a PWG formed by a compound (*vamos passear em* [*Porto de Galinhas*] 'we are taking a stroll [in Porto de Galinhas]'). This is the same sentence as in the left panel of Figure 3.4 but does not follow RULE-1. Unlike on constituents with only one TBU, on a constituent with more than one TBU RULE-1 and a simple "pretonic rise" rule yield different surface outcomes.

**Table 3.2.** The phonetic contours in Pescara (left side) and Brazilian Northeast (right side).

| Pescara | | | | | | | | | Brazilian Northeast | | | | | | | | |
|---|---|---|---|---|---|---|---|---|---|---|---|---|---|---|---|---|---|
| *Maria sbuccia [[un'arancia]$_N$]$_{PWG}$<br>'Maria is skinning an orange'<br>(ALLOWED) | | MA | RIA | SBUC | CIA-U | NA | RAN | CIA | ...*descreveu [[os alunos]$_N$]$_{PWG}$<br>'(The teacher) described the students' (ALLOWED) | | DES | CRE | VEU | OS | A | LU | NOS |
| ...*beve [il latte [di mandorle]$_N$]$_{PWG}$<br>'(Maria) drinks almond milk'<br>(ALLOWED) | BE | VE-IL | LAT | TE | DI | MAN | DOR | LE | ..*pra [Porto [de Galinhas]$_N$]$_{PWG}$<br>'(We go) to Porto de Galinhas'<br>(ALLOWED) | ... | PRA | POR | TO | DE | GA | LI | NHAS |
| *(NOT ALLOWED) | | | | | | | | | (ALLOWED) | | | | | | | | |
| | BE | VE-IL | LAT | TE | DI | MAN | DOR | LE | | ... | PRA | POR | TO | DE | GA | LI | NHAS |

resulting in different outcomes: the rule of (possibly degenerated) plateau found in Pescara (RULE-1) and a much simpler rule, namely the realization of a pretonic rise–fall contour in any case, independently of the number of TBUs of the postverbal stretch (RULE-2). Below is the set of rules that may apply in Recife for the realization of the intonational contour of statements:

> RULE-1: "Put an L+H* rise on the first TBU of the object and H+L* on its last TBU (nucleus) unless these TBUs coincide (in that case, move the rise one syllable back)".

> RULE-2: Put a pretonic rise and an H+L* on the nucleus.

Unlike Pescara, where only RULE-1 is at work, in Recife intonation both rules are active. Observing non-branching objects corresponding to a PWG with only one PW, which represent the majority of postverbal PWGs in everyday speech, it is impossible to tell whether RULE-1 or RULE-2 is being applied, as they yield the same outcome. However, for objects with more than one PWG and with PWGs formed by compounds, the two rules give different results and RULE-2 seems to be easier to learn. We propose that, if the observation of the variation in objects with more than one PWG and with PWGs formed by compounds provides a clue for a change trend, this is likely to reflect an overall drift from RULE-1 to RULE-2.

Based on this evidence, we have decided to analyze the sentences with postverbal PWGs from João Pessoa, included in the InAPoP database, as previous analyses on this variety (Castelo, 2016) points to similarities between João Pessoa and Recife. We have also carried out a new production study in Recife.

# 4   Methods of the study

Two sets of data were considered. One existing data set (from the InAPoP corpus) was selected and analyzed, consisting of speakers from João Pessoa. A specific study was run in Recife and the resulting data set was analyzed. Table 3.3 and Table 3.4 provide general information about the two corpora.

For the set of data from the InAPoP corpus, the sentences analyzed were statements with postverbal stretches, all of them with more than one TBU, corresponding to a direct or indirect object of the main verb. It was either made of (i) a morphological compound word (e.g., *mini-torneio*, "mini competition"), or of (ii) a noun phrase head plus a modifier, corresponding to

**Table 3.3.** General information on the two corpora analyzed.

| | *Number of speakers* | | | *Number of sentences analyzed* | | *Number of tokens analyzed* | |
|---|---|---|---|---|---|---|---|
| | Female | Male | Total | Postverbal objects with more than one PWG or a compound (one) PWG | Postverbal objects with one-PW PWG | Postverbal objects with more than one PWG or a compound (one) PWG | Postverbal objects with one-PW PWG |
| João Pessoa | 3 | 0 | 3 | 19 | 0 | 45 | 0 |
| Recife | 4 | 3 | 7 | 19 | 4 | 220 | 28 |

two PWGs (e.g., *melodia maravilhosa*, "marvelous melody"). They were uttered by three female speakers (aged 20 to 40) from João Pessoa, during a reading task.

After analyzing the corpus, the authors decided to check whether the variation found was sensitive to sociolinguistic parameters, and possibly reflecting a change in time. Both authors have directly taken part in the InAPoP project and the first author has applied reading tasks on elderly speakers from Recife, finding the recording phase quite problematic, especially for controlling pragmatics and spontaneity. More specifically, for various sentence types, a correct spontaneous rendition would be uttered only after several attempts, not only according to the researcher (who despite being neutral had some expectations about the outcome) but the speakers themselves would often judge themselves to have "overperformed", adding a special emphasis or a certain nuance and asked to repeat the recording. Under these conditions, sentence types like broad focus statements, whose range of possible contours overlaps with that of narrow focus statements, could be mistaken for final narrow focus interpretation beyond reasonable statistical acceptance and pragmatics would then be difficult to control.

Therefore, instead of opting to test specific age groups, we decided to take a different route and compare young female and young male speakers from another Northeastern capital, Recife. This is in line with the hypothesis that women show a tendency to lead processes of language change (Eckert & McConnell-Ginet, 2003; Labov, 2001), and more specifically with Labov's claim that "in the good majority of linguistic changes, women are a full generation ahead of men." (Labov, 2001). If this expectation applies to

**Table 3.4.** The João Pessoa corpus (left panel) and the Recife corpus (right panel). Gray shade highlights the utterances including one-PW PWGs, only collected in Recife.

| *Elicited target sentences (João Pessoa corpus)* | *Elicited target sentences (Recife corpus)* |
|---|---|
| | Ele trouxe uma sombrinha. |
| | Faz frio aqui no interior, acho que eu vou pra Recife. |
| | Pois é, ele tava cansado e voltou pra casa. |
| | Pois tu sabe que ela é pesada. |
| As jovens abriram o porta-malas. | Tu ta passando mal, mía filha, eu vou lhe fazer um chá preto. |
| As lojas inauguravam na quarta-feira. | Tu ta passando mal, mía filha, eu vou lhe fazer um chá de boldo. |
| O governador geria agro-negócios. | Essa posição chama Flor de Lótus. Eu fazia a Flor de Lótus. |
| O governador inaugurava auto-estradas. | Eu fazia a posição da Flor de Lótus. |
| O vice-reitor promove mini-torneios. | Ele trouxe um guarda-chuva. |
| O belgo-inglês examinava os beija-flores. | Não, olha, ele trouxe um porta-objetos. |
| Os homens temiam o macro-endividamento. | Pois tu sabe que ela é superpesada. |
| As uruguaias elogiavam os ibero-americanos. | Esse ano to lisa/o demais pra sair do Brasil, acho que eu vou pro Rio de Janeiro. |
| Os roubos amedrontavam os germano-italianos. | Ele veio pra comprar cadeira de rodas. |
| A libanesa falava do macro-endividamento. | Ele mora em Foz do Iguaçu. |
| O hispano-iraniano saía do macro-endividamento. | Pois é, ele é muito cara de pau. |
| Os recém-aprisionados ludibriaram as ibero-italianas. | Pois é, ele é cara de pau. |
| A libanesa rememorava a melodia maravilhosa. | Dia 28 vai tocar Caetano Veloso. |
| A jovem rememorava a melodia maravilhosa. | Ele trouxe uma espécie de sombrinha. |
| A libanesa levava a marmelada maravilhosa. | Tu ta molhando tudo, você precisaria de um "porta-guarda-chuva". |
| A jovem levava a marmelada de Borborema. | E vamos passear em Porto de Galinhas. |
| A libanesa rememorava a melodia da Madalena. | Isso tem gosto de morango. |
| A jovem rememorava a melodia da Madalena. | Devia ter visto a casa de Vanessa. |
| A libanesa levava a marmelada da Madalena. | Eu falei com o filho da irmã de Vanessa. |

Recife, and if there is an ongoing change, then the distribution of the two implementations of the prominence for compound phrases should be sensitive to gender.

Therefore a second study was carried out in Recife. Participants of this study were seven young speakers (3 male and 4 female) from the metropolitan area of Recife, aged 23 to 31, and had completed high school. A list was prepared containing 23 affirmative sentences (to be uttered as broad focus statements), with one verb and postverbal prosodic word groups ending the sentence, five negative statements and two negative imperatives. Affirmative sentences were analyzed: four of them had a non-branching object corresponding to a PWG with only one PW coinciding with the nucleus and 19 had a postverbal object with a PWG formed by a compound or with more than one PWG, containing the nucleus as its rightmost and sentence-final element. Compound postverbal phrases with nontransparent meanings were chosen, such as *Rio de Janeiro*[7], in order to prevent an informational narrow focus interpretation on the rightmost element.

For each trial, the speaker was given a paper strip with the exact sentence that had to be uttered. However, they should not produce it straight away. The researcher and an assistant (from Recife) began a 30-second to 1-minute dialogue that would at some point naturally require the speaker to enter the conversation and produce the target sentence exactly. By the time it was "called for," the speaker had learnt the sentence by heart and was no longer looking at the paper strip. This method aimed to ensure that the desired sentence be uttered in a spontaneous fashion, based on the intuition that the distraction offered by the live interaction would prevent the speaker from producing mentally "pre-rehearsed" intonation and visual stimulation would help retain the memory of the sentence no further than at the segmental level. Young and local slang words were often added to ensure empathy, ease off the pressure of the task, and help spontaneous productions. Two examples of such interactions are provided below:

---

[7]   *Rio de Janeiro* is a prosodic word group formed by two prosodic words (*Rio* + *de Janeiro*, as the word *de* is a clitic). Therefore it contains two tone-bearing units, namely syllable "RI" (first TBU) and syllable "NEI" (second and last TBU). It literally means "river of January" but it semantically refers to the Brazilian city Rio de Janeiro, that is, its meaning is non-compositional and it is impossible to utter it with a narrow informational focus value on the nucleus *de Janeiro* ("of January"), that is answering question "which river?" (narrow noncontrastive focus) or as opposed to "river of February" (narrow contrastive focus).

Example 1

Researcher: Did you tell Fernanda about Kaline?

Assistant: No way, Fernanda, you gotta listen to this. Kaline called up last night, she kept complaining the whole freaking time, that she couldn't read the scores properly, and she'd not been warned about the schedule change and this and that. She kept me more than one hour, nothing but whining... I mean, holy cow, what a bore, man!

Fernanda (speaker): *Pois é, tu sabe que ela é* [*super-pesada*]*!*

"Well, you know she's a sadsack!"

Example 2

Researcher: Holiday tomorrow, folks! What are we up to?

Assistant: Kaline, how about you?

Kaline (speaker):  I don't know.

Researcher: I mean, if the sun is out we can go to the beach.

Assistant: Yeah, but I want to have a great breakfast tomorrow. Then we can take a shower, get ready, jump into the car, heading South...[8]

Kaline (speaker): *E vamos passear em Porto de Galinhas.*

"And we'll take a stroll in Porto de Galinhas."

---

[8]  Porto de Galinhas, literally "Harbour of hans," is the name of a Southern Pernambuco beach. Here, besides the impossibility of narrow focus on *de Galinhas*, as was explained in the previous footnote, in order to discourage narrow focus on *em Porto de Galinhas* and favor broad focus on the whole sentence, the main action *passear* "to take a stroll" was presented after a list of other actions, "take a shower," "get into the car" and not, for example, after a list of other places to go to.

# 5　Results and discussion (João Pessoa)

The contours of the three female speakers from João Pessoa included in the read corpus of the InAPoP database were analyzed as to whether the PWG would receive prominence and, in this case, whether it would be a double accent (rise+fall), a pretonic rise, or another type of prominence. For one speaker we only have data for morphological compounds. ToBI labels have been used for annotating the pitch accents. Table 3.5 summarizes the results.

**Table 3.5.** The distribution of contour types on postverbal objects with either a PWG formed by a compound or more than one PWG, for statements (data from InAPoP database). Utterances produced by three female speakers (KS, AS and JP are their initials) from João Pessoa, northeastern Brazil.

| *Types of pattern by speaker* | *Morphological compounds* | | | *Objects with more than 1 PWG* | |
|---|---|---|---|---|---|
| | KS | AS | JP | KS | AS |
| L+H(*) H+L* (double accent) | 0% (0) | 57% (4) | 50% (9) | 0% (0) | 0% (0) |
| upstep (pretonic rise) | 88% (7) | 43% (3) | 33% (6) | 67% (4) | 67% (4) |
| H+L* L% (no prominence marking) | 0% (0) | 0% (0) | 6% (1) | 0% (0) | 33% (2) |
| H+L* H+L* L% (other prominence) | 13% (1) | 0% (0) | 11% (2) | 33% (2) | 0% (0) |

The results show that it is possible to have a double accent for a morphological compound[9], with the first rise on the first TBU of the PWG, but that this rise can also be delayed onto the nuclear pretonic syllable, as in Figure 3.5. However, the bare analysis of a wide and heterogeneous corpus of statements contains some inherent limitations, and testing a specific variable requires that an appropriate methodology of elicitation be set in order to obtain statistically significant results. More specifically, firstly, the data only include young female speakers and say little about variation and its possible connection with change. Secondly, it is very hard to ensure, in a reading task, spontaneous speech, which is key to restrict our corpus. Finally, it is almost impossible to control whether the speakers are uttering a broad focus or a narrow focus on the PWG: indeed, for compounds with a compositional meaning, it makes sense to focus informationally on the last

---

[9]　The reader should keep in mind that, as explained in the introduction, compounds are semantically transparent within this dataset. We introduced instead compounds with non-compositional meaning in the study run in Recife.

PW of the PWG, that is, the nucleus, and even speakers accidentally producing such occurrences of narrow focus may bias the tally in favor of pretonic rises. The findings from the InAPoP database, as well as these considerations, motivate a more thorough investigation of this variation and the social parameters that can affect it. For these reasons, and those presented in the methodology section, a second study was carried out in Recife, whose results are presented in the next section.

# 6    Results and a first discussion (Recife)

The research question to be tested was whether the presence of a pretonic rise or a double accent, on compound constituents, are sensitive to gender.

Table 3.6 summarizes the realizations of simple falls (no prominence), falls from a pretonic rise, double accents on first and last TBUs (these ones only in the case of objects with more than one PWG and with PWGs formed by compounds) or other contours, for non-branching objects corresponding to a PWG with only one PW or branching objects corresponding to more than one PWG, according to gender.

In the three blocks of Table 3.6, the relevant lines are the first two, showing the number of sentences with either of the two types of marking, pretonic rise and double accent, and the last line showing percentages of pretonic rise occurrences out of the total of marked contours (pretonic rise occurrences + double accent occurrences), after excluding from the tally a minority of cases with no prominence marking (a nonsalient mid-to-low fall) and a few different unidentified types. In the case of non-branching objects corresponding to a PWG with only one PW, the only way of marking prominence is a pretonic rise–falling contour (indicated by ¡H+L* in the table), whereas in the case of objects with more than one PWG and with PWGs formed by compounds it could be either a pretonic rise or a double accent. However, men use a pretonic rise in 37% of the objects formed either by more than one PWG or by a PWG formed by compounds (and a double accent in the remaining 63%), whereas women use a pretonic rise in 79% of such objects (and use a double accent to mark prominence in the remaining 21% of the cases).

In other words, men strongly prefer an implementation of the prominence on objects formed either by more than one PWG or by a PWG formed by compounds which is only compatible with RULE-1, as mentioned in the previous section, whereas women seem mostly to apply a contour which is only compatible with RULE-2. We may infer that these

**Table 3.6.** The distribution of contour types on postverbal constituents corresponding to a PWG with only one PW (i.e., constituents with only one TBU), and to either more than one PWG or to a PWG formed by a compound (i.e., constituents with more than one TBU) for broad focus statements. Utterances produced by four female and three male speakers from Recife, northeastern Brazil.

| | | *One-PW PWG* | *Objects with more than one PWG or with a PWG formed by a compound* |
|---|---|---|---|
| MEN | ¡H+L* (Pretonic rise) | 10 | 34 |
| | L+H* H+L* (Double accent) | | 57 |
| | H+L* (No prominence marking) | 5 | 10 |
| | Other | 2 | 5 |
| | Marked contours/Total contours (M) | 10/17 (59%) | 91/106 (86%) |
| | Pretonic rise/Marked contours (M) | 10/10 (100%) | 34/91 (37%) |
| WOMEN | ¡H+L* (Pretonic rise) | 23 | 94 |
| | L+H* H+L* (Double accent) | | 25 |
| | H+L* (No prominence marking) | | 12 |
| | Other | 1 | 11 |
| | Marked contours/Total contours (F) | 23/24 (96%) | 119/142 (83%) |
| | Pretonic rise/Marked contours (F) | 23/23 (100%) | 94/119 (79%) |
| TOTAL | ¡H+L* (Pretonic rise) | 33 | 128 |
| | L+H* H+L* (Double accent) | | 82 |
| | H+L* (No prominence marking) | 5 | 22 |
| | Other | 3 | 16 |
| | Marked contours/Total contours | 33/41 (80%) | 210/248 (85%) |
| | Pretonic rise/Marked contours | 33/33 (100%) | 128/210 (61%) |

percentages actually reflect the percentages of applications of the two rules, even in the case of simple constituents, where variation cannot be observed. A Chi-square test was performed and a significant relationship was found between female gender and occurrence of pretonic rise, $\chi^2$ (1, N=210) = 37.547, p < .01. In the following section we provide a schematic picture of the process of reanalysis behind these results.

# 7    Further discussion: the reanalysis phenomenon and a model of language change

The goal of this section is to recall the concept of reanalysis, defined for several linguistic modules (morphology, syntax, semantics), provide a logical, module-independent definition of it and extend this definition to the domain of intonation. Reanalysis has often been observed to be a powerful trigger of language change and, together with analogy, it is mainly responsible for the processes of grammaticalization and grammatical change. In syntax, reanalysis has been defined as "a mechanism which changes the underlying structure of a syntactic pattern and which does not involve any immediate or intrinsic modification of its surface manifestation" (Harris & Campbell, 1995).

This definition is easily adaptable to other linguistic modules (morphological, semantic reanalysis) and may be thought of as the coexistence of two underlying structures or grammatical rules, one conservative and one innovative, both compatible with the same surface manifestation. Such surface manifestation usually has few or no variants, or is the most frequent of a number of variants, generally corresponding to an unmarked environment. This allows interchangeability of the underlying grammatical rules in the speaker's mind, with a possible silent change, impossible to observe on the surface, from one ("conservative rule," or "conservative analysis") to another ("innovative rule," or "innovative analysis"). However, when an exceptional or unfrequent variant emerges, on which the two underlying analyses do not give the same result, reanalysis can be measured concretely.

This can also be achieved if the researcher is able to methodologically create *ad hoc* constructions, prompting differences to surface. The innovative analysis often arises, so to say, "by mistake" or "by misinterpretation," meaning that the only reason for its emergence is that it is compatible with the surface structure.

A simpler way of saying this is that an unperceivable, gradual shift takes place, from the conservative to the innovative analysis, which is not directly observable because of the ambiguous unique surface phonetic form. However, by analogy, the new rule may spread to more marked (and statistically less frequent) environments, where it gives rise to new surface formations and only in this moment will reanalysis be revealed and become overt.

A very simple example – and one of the most typical – of morphological reanalysis in English, cited more than once in literature and even in schoolbooks (Ottenheimer, 2008; Shukra & Connor-Linton, 2006; among others), is the reanalysis of the derived noun "hamburg-er" as "ham-burger," which (supposedly after a period of latency) only becomes overt by licensing, by analogy, forms like "cheese-burger." According to this model of change, both rules of analysis (derived "hamburg-er" and compound "ham-burger") are available and able to coexist in the mind of speakers but the relevance and the frequency of the second analysis is not experimentally observable or measurable on the common surface form "hamburger," until new forms like "cheeseburger" arise[10].

As for semantic reanalysis, a typical example is the French adverb of negation *pas* (see Van Trijp, 2016, among others), originally meaning "step" and used in expressions like *je ne marche pas* (lit. "I don't walk (a single) step") only after verbs of motion and later extended, by analogy, to all postverbal environments with a meaning of "at all," until it became a mandatory part of the negative sentence. The first analysis is impossible for most negative sentences nowadays, however it is possible that, during a certain period of the evolution of modern French in time, a phrase like *ce n'est pas* could gradually switch from the rather awkward and unlikely interpretation "it's not (a) step" to just "it's not."

In a nutshell, we may say that reanalysis is the covert phase of grammatical change, only becoming overt and observable on the innovations it licenses. Reanalysis causes rule change, whereas analogy causes rule spread (Hopper & Traugott, 1993; Lindström, 2004). Tables 3.7 and 3.8 provide a schematic picture.

The reasons for reanalysis have been widely investigated. Rather than asking why a second rule emerges in the first place (as, in some sense, the rule "is always there", as a latent possibility of analysis), one may wonder why such an innovative rule ends up prevailing and which conditions favor it. Many types of mechanisms have been alleged to "feed" reanalysis, such as previous ongoing change, speaker–hearer asymmetries, processes of

---

[10]   This kind of morphological reanalysis is called resegmentation (Langacker, 1977).

**Table 3.7.** An example of grammatical change by reanalysis: the morphological resegmentation of "hamburg-er" as "ham-burger." Boldface and full lines indicate the prevailing rule analysis at each moment, dotted lines indicate the less frequent (incipient or obsolescent) rule. Here "underlying structures" are rules of morphological segmentations.

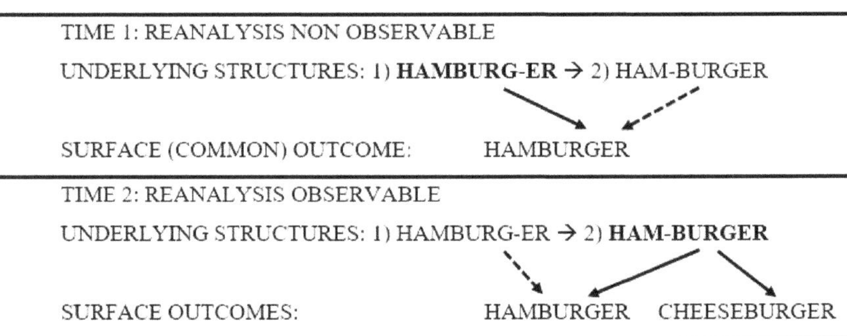



**Table 3.8.** An example of grammatical change by reanalysis: the semantic reanalysis (re-association between form and meaning) of the word *pas* from its original meaning 'step' to the current meaning 'not.' Boldface and full lines indicate the prevailing rule analysis at each moment, dotted lines indicate the less frequent (incipient or obsolescent) rule. The small dotted lines indicate that the interpretation is almost impossible. Here "underlying structures" are rules of meaning association. The meaning was unequivocally encoded in its English translation.

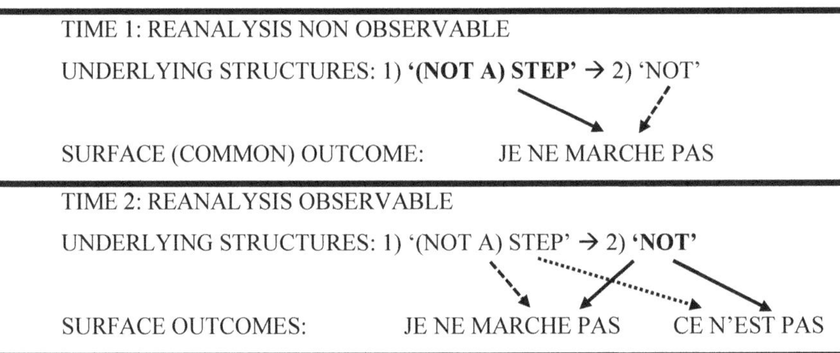



inferencing and language acquisition with subsequent transmission (Hopper & Traugott, 1993). It seems that a certain amount of ambiguity is needed for reanalysis, in the least marked (and statistically more frequent) environment (Timberlake, 1977). It is also reasonable to believe that a universal tendency to simplification (the innovative rule being simpler than the original one) may speed up reanalysis.

The model proposed extends the concept of reanalysis to the suprasegmental level and will be able to describe the variation between two rules, in a context in which both the unmarked and the marked environments allow the two analyses, but reanalysis is covert on the unmarked environment (non-branching objects corresponding to a PWG with only one PW, the most frequent environment) and overt on the marked environment (objects with more than one PWG and with a PWG formed by compounds). What we will try to prove is that the variation observable on the marked environment shows a direction of change, by analyzing its dependency on gender and assuming Labov's hypothesis.

# 8 The model applied to Brazilian Portuguese

Data from Recife are analyzed according to the model proposed: two competing underlying phonological analyses are assumed to be available for the BP speaker, each of which will produce a specific surface phonetic implementation. The implementations produced by the two analyses coincide on non-branching objects corresponding to a PWG with only one PW, and this lack of surface conflict between the two analyses licenses a silent and gradual shift from one to another (Table 3.9).

As the two rules represent different phonological analyses, we may choose ToBI labellings for identifying them: (L+H*)_H+L* for RULE-1, the parentheses meaning that the plateau can be degenerated, and ¡H+L* for RULE-2. Figure 3.6 explains how the process of reanalysis proceeds in time and how it is revealed.

Figure 3.6 can be interpreted as follows: the left panels show the intonation contours of the statement with a postverbal PWG formed by a compound *pois tu sabe que ela é* [*super-*[*pesada*]] "Well, you know she is [super-heavy]," uttered twice, once according to RULE-1 (top left panel) and once according to RULE-2 (bottom left panel). The right panels show the intonation contours of the sentence with a non-branching object corresponding to a PWG with only one PW *pois tu sabe que ela é* ⌊*pesada*⌋ "Well, you know she is [heavy]" uttered twice, with the same phonetic surface implementation, but analyzed according to RULE-1 in the top right panel and according to RULE-2 in the bottom right panel, as the differences in the corresponding tone layers for phonological analysis reveal. The fact that the surface

**Table 3.9.** A model for prosodic reanalysis: while in a first stage only the rule of (possibly degenerated) plateau applies and pretonic rises are only allowed on non-branching objects corresponding to a PWG with only one PW, as degenerated plateaus, the emergence of a pretonic rise on objects with more than one PWG or with a PWG formed by a compound with deaccentuation of the first TBU, at a later time, is a sign that pretonic rises on non-branching objects corresponding to a PWG with only one PW are starting to be analyzed according to a different rule. Boldface and full lines indicate the prevailing rule analysis at each moment, dotted lines indicate the less frequent (incipient or obsolescent) rule. Here "underlying structures" are phonological analyses.

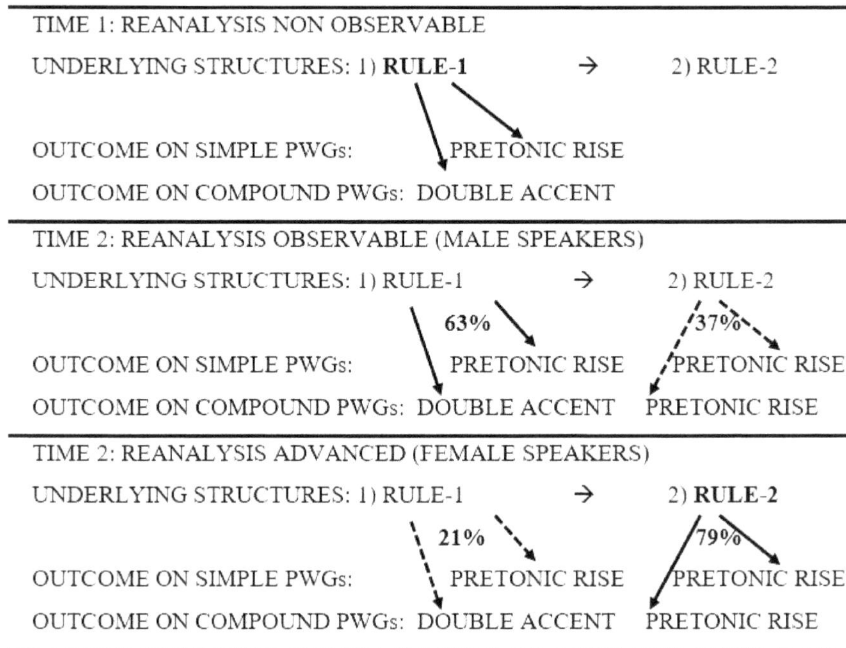


form is the same allows the silent reanalysis to proceed during language transmission, gradually moving from a (L+H*)H+L* L% analysis, with one prenuclear accent and one nuclear accent (both bound to the same syllable and an application of tonal repulsion rule to avoid crowding), to a new, and more simple, analysis as ¡H+L* L%. A simpler model can be schematized as in Table 3.10, as change would apply to a sentence with a postverbal PWG formed by a compound, *Vou pra Porto de Galinhas* "I'm going to Porto de Galinhas", through covert reanalysis (from double accent to pretonic rise) on a sentence with a non-branching object corresponding to a PWG with

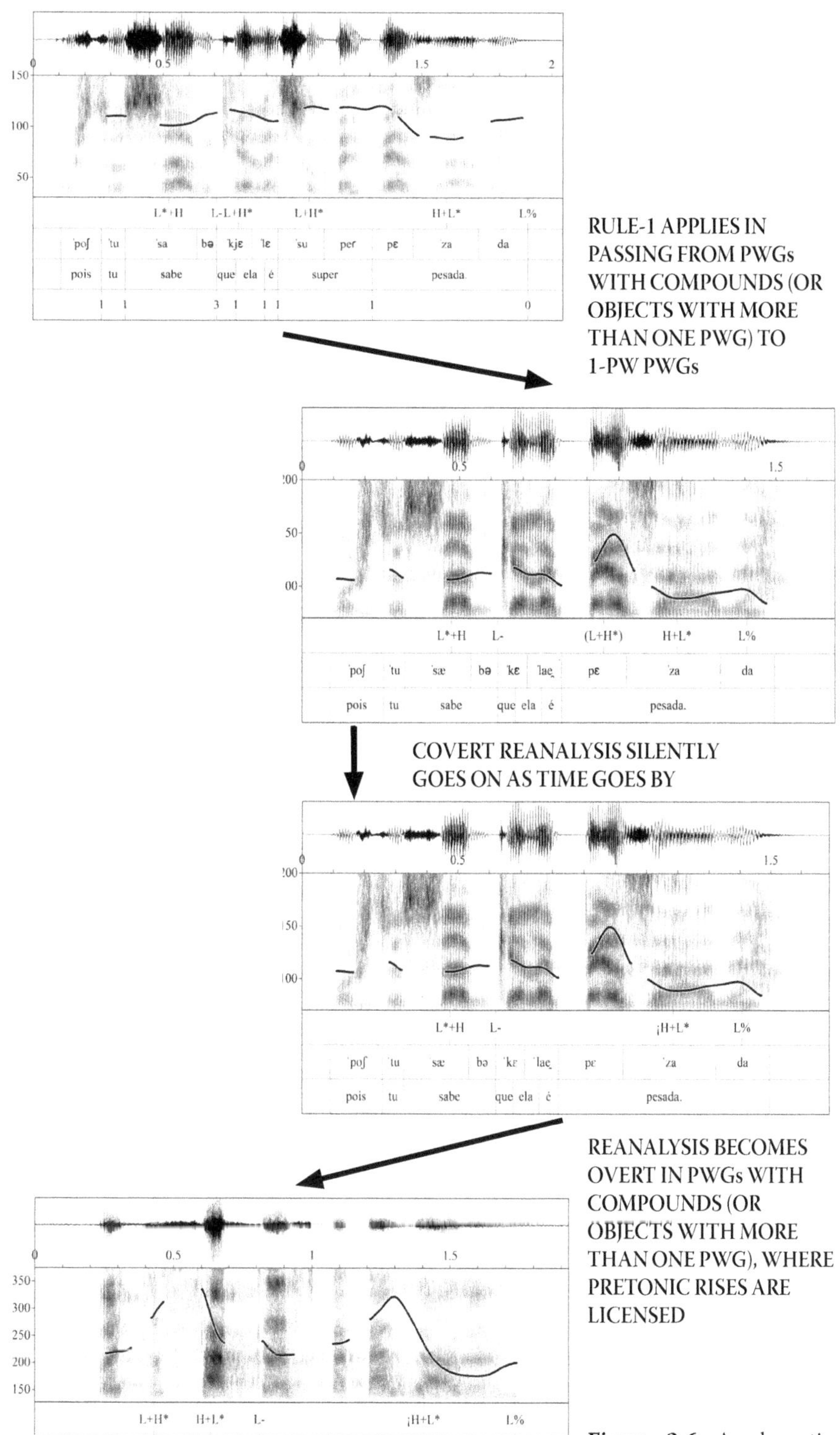


**Figure 3.6.** A schematic explanation of the process of reanalysis.

**Table 3.10.** A schematic representation of the process of reanalysis.

| | | L+H* | | | | H+L* | |
|---|---|---|---|---|---|---|---|
| | | | | | | | |
| VOU | PRA | POR | TO | DE | GA | LI | NHAS |

RULE-1

| | | (L+H*) | H+L* | |
|---|---|---|---|---|
| | | | | |
| VOU | PRA | RE | CI | FE |

REANALYSIS

| | | | ¡H+L* | |
|---|---|---|---|---|
| | | | | |
| VOU | PRA | RE | CI | FE |

**REANALYSIS
BECOMING OVERT**

| | | | | | | ¡H+L* | |
|---|---|---|---|---|---|---|---|
| | | | | | | | |
| VOU | PRA | POR | TO | DE | GA | LI | NHAS |

only one PW, such as *Vou pra Recife* "I am going to Recife" on which the two analyses yield the same surface outcome.

# 9 Conclusion

By looking at the analysis of an Italian variety, we have identified that languages displaying a hat pattern on postverbal objects with more than one TBU may show nuclear falls preceded by a pretonic salient rise for the corresponding utterances with simple postverbal phrases (one word-stressed syllable), as a result of a tonal repulsion between the rising and the falling accents comprising the hat contour, as a degenerated plateau of length zero. We have postulated a rule (RULE-1) for phonetic implementation of hat-type contours that may apply cross-linguistically, fitting perfectly the Italian variety observed. We have observed that the same contours are found in two northeastern Brazilian varieties, but that postverbal objects with either more than one PWG or a PWG formed by a compound have also started to be uttered with a pretonic rise, independently of the length of the postverbal stretch. By looking at gender variation, we have provided some evidence that this is a recent innovation, introduced by northeastern young female speakers and posited that a new, simpler rule is replacing RULE-1. We have interpreted this result in light of the theory of reanalysis and grammatical change, providing an example of ongoing change in the grammar of intonation. The main goal of the chapter was to describe a complex phenomenon of covert change, that of prosodic phonological reanalysis: on the one hand this is a warning for researchers on prosodic change to always take into account possible occurrences of prosodic reanalysis, however on the other hand the chapter should provide evidence that it is possible to disentangle and present reanalysis in an explanatory manner. The final hypothesis about the existence of a change and a specific direction encoded in the variation observed strongly depends on Labov's hypothesis and therefore the study is not conclusive: further investigation into different age groups is needed to confirm that there is an ongoing change.

# References

Barone, M. (in preparation). *Intonation in Pescara: The Case of Two Languages in Contact* (Unpublished doctoral dissertation), Department of Translation and Language Studies, Pompeu Fabra University, Barcelona, Spain.

Blum-Kulka, S., House, J., & Kasper, G. (1989). *Cross-Cultural Pragmatics: Requests and Apologies.* Norwood, NJ: Ablex.

Bolinger, D. L. (1961). Contrastive accent and contrastive stress. *Language, 37,* 87–96. https://doi.org/10.2307/411252

Bolinger, D. L. (1978). Intonation across languages. In J. Greenberg (Ed.), *Universals of Human Language* (pp. 471– 524). Stanford, CA: Stanford University Press.

Britain, D. (1992). Linguistic change in intonation: The use of high rising terminals in New Zealand English. *Language Variation and Change, 4,* 77–104. https://doi.org/10.1017/S0954394500000661

Castelo, J. (2016). *A Entoação dos Enunciados Declarativos e Interrogativos no Português do Brasil: Uma Análise Fonológica em Variedades ao Longo da Costa Atlântica* (Unpublished doctoral dissertation). Universidade de Lisboa, Portugal. Retrieved from http://repositorio.ul.pt/bitstream/10451/26298/1/ulfl218789_td.pdf

Castelo, J., & Frota, S. (2016). Variação entoacional no Português do Brasil: Uma análise fonológica do contorno nuclear em enunciados declarativos e interrogativos. *Revista da Associação Portuguesa de Linguística, 1*, 143–168. https://doi.org/10.21747/2183-9077/rapla6

Cohen, A., & 't Hart, J. (1967). On the anatomy of intonation. *Lingua, 19*, 177–192. https://doi.org/10.1016/0024-3841(69)90118-1

Cunha, C. S. (2000). *Entoação Regional no Português do Brasil* (Unpublished doctoral dissertation). Federal University of Rio de Janeiro, Brazil.

Cunha, C. S., & Colamarco, C. P. M. (2005). Do Recife aos Pampas: Um experimento prosódico. *Anais do IV Congresso Internacional da ABRALIN* (pp. 851–862). Brasília, Brazil: ABRALIN/ UNB.

Dabkowski, M. (2012). *Transcription of the Intonation of Northeastern Brazilian Portuguese* (Master's thesis). Retrieved from http://d-scholarship.pitt.edu/11637/

Di Cristo, A. (1999). Vers une modélisation de l'accentuation en français (première partie). *Journal of French Language Studies, 9*(2), 143–179. https://doi.org/10.1017/S0959269500004671

Eckert, P., & McConnell-Ginet, S. (2003). *Language and Gender.* Cambridge, England: Cambridge University Press. https://doi.org/10.1017/CBO9781139245883

Fernandes-Svartman, F. R. (2007). Tonal association in neutral and subject-narrow-focus sentences of Brazilian Portuguese: A comparison with European Portuguese. *Journal of Portuguese Linguistics, 6*(1), 91–115. https://doi.org/10.5334/jpl.146

Frota, S. (Coord.) (2012–2015). *InAPoP - Interactive Atlas of the Prosody of Portuguese.* (Funded by Fundação para a Ciência e a Tecnologia – FCT, PTDC/CLE-LIN/119787/2010). http://labfon.letras.ulisboa.pt/InAPoP/

Frota, S., & Moraes, J. (2016). Intonation of European and Brazilian Portuguese. In W. L. Wetzels, S. Menuzzi & J. Costa (Eds.), *The Handbook of Portuguese Linguistics* (1st edition, pp. 141–166). Hoboken, NJ: John Wiley & Sons, Inc. https://doi.org/10.1002/9781118791844.ch9

Frota, S., & Vigário, M. (2000). Aspectos de prosódia comparada: Ritmo e entoação no PE e no PB. In R. V. Castro & P. Barbosa (Eds.), *Actas do XV Encontro da Associação Portuguesa de Linguística* (pp. 533–555). Coimbra, Portugal: Associação Portuguesa de Linguística. Retrieved from http://labfon.letras.ulisboa.pt/SonseMelodias/APLPEPB.pdf

Frota, S., Oliveira, P., Cruz, M., & Vigário, M. (2015). *P-ToBI: Tools for the Transcription of Portuguese Prosody.* Lisboa: Laboratório de Fonética, CLUL/FLUL. ISBN: 978-989-95713-9-6. http://labfon.letras.ulisboa.pt/InAPoP/P-ToBI/

Frota, S., Cruz, M., Fernandes-Svartman, F., Collischonn, G., Fonseca, A., Serra, C., Oliveira, P., & Vigário, M. (2015). Intonational variation in Portuguese: European and Brazilian varieties. In S. Frota & P. Prieto (Eds.), *Intonation in Romance* (pp. 235–283). Oxford, England: Oxford University Press. https://doi.org/10.1093/acprof:oso/9780199685332.003.0007

Gili Fivela, B., Avesani, C., Barone, M., Bocci, G., Crocco, C., D'Imperio, M., Giordano, R., Marotta, G., Savino, M., & Sorianello, P. (2015). Intonational phonology of regional varieties of Italian. In S. Frota & P. Prieto (Eds.), *Intonation in Romance* (pp. 140–197). Oxford, England: Oxford University Press. https://doi.org/10.1093/acprof:oso/9780199685332.003.0005

Gordon, M. (2005). An autosegmental/metrical model of Chickasaw intonation. In S-A. Jun (Ed.), *Prosodic Typology: The Phonology of Intonation and Phrasing* (pp. 301–330). Oxford, England: Oxford University Press. Retrieved from http://www.linguistics.ucsb.edu/faculty/gordon/Chickasawintonation.pdf

Grabe, E. (2004). Intonational variation in urban dialects of English spoken in the British Isles. In P. Gilles & J. Peters (Eds.), *Regional Variation in Intonation* (pp. 9–31). Tuebingen, Germany: Niemeyer. Retrieved from http://www.phon.ox.ac.uk/files/people/grabe/Grabe_Niemeyer.pdf

Gussenhoven, C. (1984). *On the Grammar and Semantics of Sentence Accents.* Dordrecht, Holland: Foris. https://doi.org/10.1515/9783110859263

Gussenhoven, C. (2004). *The Phonology of Tone and Intonation.* Cambridge, England: Cambridge University Press. https://doi.org/10.1017/CBO9780511616983

Guy, G., Horvath, B., Vonwiller, J., Daisley, E., & Rogers, I. (1986). An Intonational Change in Progress in Australian English. *Language in Society, 15,* 23–52. https://doi.org/10.1017/S0047404500011635

Harris, A. C., & Campbell, L. (1995). *Historical Syntax in Crosslinguistic Perspective.* Cambridge, England: Cambridge University Press. https://doi.org/10.1017/CBO9780511620553

Hirst, D., & Di Cristo, A. (1998). A survey of intonation systems. In D. Hirst & A. Di Cristo (Eds.), *Intonation Systems: A Survey of Twenty Languages* (pp. 1–43). Cambridge, England: Cambridge University Press.

Hopper, P. J., & Traugott, E. C. (1993). *Grammaticalization.* Cambridge, England: Cambridge University Press. https://doi.org/10.1017/CBO9781139165525

Labov, W. (2001). *Principles of Linguistic Change. Social Factors.* Oxford, England: Blackwell.

Ladd, D. R. (2008). *Intonational Phonology* (2nd edition). Cambridge, England: Cambridge University Press. https://doi.org/10.1017/CBO9780511808814

Langacker, R. (1977). Syntactic reanalysis. In C. N. Li (Ed.), *Mechanisms of Syntactic Change* (pp. 57–139). Austin, TX: University of Texas Press.

Lindström, T. Å. M. (2004). *The History of the Concept of Grammaticalisation* (Unpublished doctoral dissertation). Sheffield University, Sheffield, England. Retrieved from http://etheses.whiterose.ac.uk/1437/2/Lindstrom_Tiedemann%2C_Therese.pdf

Lira, Z. S. (2009). *A Entoação Modal em Cinco Falares do Nordeste Brasileiro* (Unpublished doctoral dissertation). Federal University of Paraíba, João Pessoa, Brazil.

Moraes, J. A. (2008). The pitch accents in Brazilian Portuguese. *Proceedings of Speech Prosody 2008* (pp. 389–397). Campinas, Brazil: Editora RG/ CNPq.

Nguyễn, T. A.-T., Ingram, C. L. J., & Pensalfini, J. R. (2008). Prosodic transfer in Vietnamese acquisition of English contrastive stress patterns. *Journal of Phonetics, 36*, 158–190. https://doi.org/10.1016/j.wocn.2007.09.001

Ottenheimer, H. J. (2008). *The Antropology of Language: An Introduction to Linguistic Antropology.* Stamford, CT: Cengage Learning.

Pierrehumbert, J. B. (1980). *The Phonology and Phonetics of English Intonation* (Unpublished doctoral dissertation). Massachusetts Institute of Technology, USA. Retrieved from http://dspace.mit.edu/handle/1721.1/16065

Selkirk, E. (1984). *Phonology and Syntax. The Relation between Sound and Structure.* Cambridge, MS: MIT Press.

Serra, C. R. (2009). *Realização e Percepção de Fronteiras Prosódicas no Português do Brasil: Fala Espontânea e Leitura* (Unpublished doctoral dissertation). Federal University of Rio de Janeiro, Brazil.

Shukra, S., & Connor-Linton, J. (2006). Language change. In R. W. Fasold & J. Connor-Linton (Eds.), *An Introduction to Language and Linguistics* (pp. 274–310). Cambridge, England: Cambridge University Press.

Silvestre, A. (2012). *A Entoação Regional dos Enunciados Assertivos nos Falares das Capitais Brasileiras* (Master's thesis). Federal University of Rio de Janeiro, Brazil.

Tenani, L. E. (2002). *Domínios Prosódicos no Português* (Unpublished doctoral dissertation). State University of Campinas, Campinas, Brazil.

't Hart, J. R. Collier, & Cohen, A. (1990). *A Perceptual Study of Intonation. An Experimental-Phonetic Approach to Speech Melody.* Cambridge, England: Cambridge University Press. https://doi.org/10.1017/CBO9780511627743

Timberlake, A. (1977). Reanalysis and actualization in syntactic change. In C. N. Li (Ed.), *Mechanisms of Syntactic Change* (pp. 141–177). Austin, TX: University of Texas Press.

Toneli, P. (2014). *A Palavra Prosódica no Português Brasileiro.* (Unpublished doctoral dissertation). State University of Campinas, Campinas, Brazil. Retrieved from http://labfon.letras.ulisboa.pt/texts/Toneli_2014.pdf

Truckenbrodt, H., Sandalo, F., & Abaurre, M. (2009). Elements of Brazilian Portuguese Intonation. *Journal of Portuguese Linguistics, 8*, 75–114. https://doi.org/10.5334/jpl.122

Van Trijp, R. (2016). *The Evolution of Case Grammar.* Berlin, Germany: Language Science Press. http://library.oapen.org/handle/20.500.12657/32371

Vigário, M. (2010). Prosodic structure between the Prosodic Word and the Phonological Phrase: Recursive nodes or an independent domain? *The Linguistic Review 27*(4): 485–530. https://doi.org/10.1515/tlir.2010.017

Vigário, M., & Fernandes-Svartman, F. R. (2010). A atribuição de acentos tonais em compostos no Português do Brasil. In A. M. Brito, F. Silva, J. Veloso & A. Fiéis (Eds.), *XXV Encontro da Associação Portuguesa de Linguística – Textos Seleccionados* (Vol. 1, pp. 769–786) Porto, Portugal: Nunes. Retreived from: http://repositorio.ul.pt/bitstream/10451/26461/1/50-Marina Vigario.pdf

Warren, P. (2005). Patterns of late rising in New Zealand: intonational variation or intonational change? *Language Variation and Change, 17*(2), 209–230. https://doi.org/10.1017/S095439450505009X

Warren, P., & Britain, D. (2000). Intonation and prosody in New Zealand English. In A. Bell & K. Kuiper (Eds.), *New Zealand English* (pp.146–172). Wellington, New Zealand: Victoria University Press. https://doi.org/10.1075/veaw.g25.10war

Wunderlich, D. (1991). Intonation and contrast. *Journal of Semantics, 8*(3), 239–251. https://doi.org/10.1093/jos/8.3.239

**Marco Barone** is Assistant Professor at the Department of Languages of the Federal University of Pernambuco, Brazil. He is an Italian-Brazilian sociolinguist, phonologist and former mathematician. His research area is intonation change, especially focused on the intonational phonology of varieties of Portuguese and Italian in contact. Currently, he coordinates the Committee for Endangered Languages of the Brazilian Association for Linguistics (ABRALIN).

**Joelma Castelo** is Lecturer at the Center of Human Sciences and Education of Universidade Estadual do Paraná, Brazil, and postdoctoral researcher at the University of São Paulo, Brazil. Her research focuses on the phonetics and phonology of intonational variation in Portuguese. Her most relevant publications are *Variação entoacional dos enunciados interrogativos, The yes–no question contour in Brazilian Portuguese* (Castelo & Frota, 2017), and *The perception of yes–no questions across varieties of Brazilian Portuguese* (Castelo et al., 2018).

# 4
# From ToBI phonological events to functional melodic forms at the communicative level

Doina Jitcă

## 1    Introduction

### 1.1    Aim of this chapter

This chapter proposes a communicative perspective in intonational analysis which aims to explain utterance organization as a hierarchy of communicative units (CUs) to which Information Structure (IS) partitions can be related. Some aspects of earlier IS models are reviewed in order to explain the new proposal based on a communication act perspective. In this view the functional constituents of IS partitions have roles firstly at the neuro-linguistic level for building speech communication and then they may bear linguistic meaning. The chapter explains how IS functions are conveyed at the pragmatic level by intonational forms with different acoustical features. Various Romanian intonational contour types have been selected to illustrate how the IS model presented in this chapter can add more clarity to phonological analyses, shedding light on issues related to nuclear accent assignment within intonational contour analysis.

This chapter is structured as follows: the first part introduces the notion of communicative unit (CU) as a contrast unit between two IS functional elements and the second part provides a context for the current functional approach within various texts on IS. Section 2 tackles the idea of a two-level model of IS. The intonational analysis based on CU partitioning and phonological and IS annotation is used in the third section to present several Romanian intonational contour types with their issues related to nucleus position. The last section explores the consequences of decoding and partitioning intonational contours on the basis of a communicative and IS perspective.

## 1.2   Communicative unit hierarchy

Utterance organization models define units in which an IS partition can be analyzed. Halliday (1967) defines this as an informational unit and relates it to a tonal group. The model presented in this chapter works with the notion of communicative unit as a contrast unit of two pitch contour segments which have complementary functions at the IS level. CUs may correspond to prosodic phrases or may be lower level units. For instance, in SVO sentences the intonational phrase is usually structured as a right embedded CU related to the verbal phrase. As is described in (1), the subject is a simple constituent with a generic F function which is paired at the global CU level with the complex constituent of the verbal phrase having the NF contrasted function. Within the embedded CU the verb bears the F function and the object the NF function. The object projects its NF function to the whole embedded CU. The intonational phrase of an SVO sentence is structured by two nested CUs with their IS partitions.

$$(1) \quad \{(F)^{Subject}/[(F)^{Verb}/(NF)^{Object}]_{NF}\}$$

CUs are units which reflect cognitive associations between conceptual elements. Intonational phrases (IPs) and intermediate phrases (ips) are information packages which generally correspond to nested CU hierarchies. In certain cases CUs cannot be related to one of the traditional prosodic domain types. For these cases Ladd (1996, 2008) proposes the notion of compound prosodic domain (CPD) to denote derived prosodic domains which, as constituents, are realized as traditional prosodic domains. CPD may be a compound of prosodic words, of intermediate phrases or of intonational phrases that are equivalent to prosodic phrases, ips or IPs, respectively. CPD introduces a limited type of recursion in the prosodic hierarchy.

Wagner (2005) introduces full recursion in the syntax–prosody interface and analyzes information structure at the level of word groups corresponding to any association of two prosodic constituents, taken as prosodic phrases.

By introducing recursion at the level of CU hierarchies and their related IS partition hierarchies, we bypass recursivity at the prosodic hierarchy level. Prosodic phrases (intonational and intermediate phrases) mark information packages within the utterance and at the same time they may be related to higher level CUs within the recursive CU hierarchy of utterance. Thus, recursion does not come into play at the level of prosodic phrases. However, defining prosodic phrases as CU realizations implies that these will be equivalent at any level in the prosodic hierarchy.

This chapter proposes a framework for intonation analysis that combines the functional perspective of our IS analysis with the phonological view given by the AM model and the ToBI annotation system (Beckman, Hirschberg & Shattuck-Hufnagel, 2005; Gussenhoven, 2004; Pierrehumbert, 1980; among others). Consequently, the intonational contours presented in this chapter are described at the phonological level using the ToBI labels. The model proposed here is an analysis at the pragmatic level rather than a mapping of the abstract phonological level. Our intonation analysis adds other shapes and tonal features to pitch events in order to explain IS marking of corresponding CU constituents. The original aspect of our IS approach consists in keeping IS comprehension at the pragmatic level that does not involve a semantic model as that of Alternatives (Rooth, 1992) for justifying the IS functions of CU constituents. This chapter brings data that suggests that IS functions can be deduced only by using the F0 contour form interpretation. It is not always a straightforward task to perform an IS analysis by using linguistic arguments where there is no discourse context. IS utterance organization is firstly a consequence of how speech processing is organized at the neuro-linguistic level – neurolinguistic realization driven in certain cases by different linguistic determinations of syntactic, semantic or discourse features.

## 1.3    Previous work within Information Structure

This section presents a review of the literature on information structure models aiming to bring into focus two terms used by the earlier IS description. Our analysis stems from the IS model evolution presentation of von Heusinger (2002). The earliest models in this presentation are those of Paul (1880) and von der Gabelentz (1869). We single out the following definitions: i. Paul's (1880) definition of the sentence "as the linguistic expression that connects several (psychological) concepts or groups of concepts produced in the mind of the speaker"; ii. von der Gabelentz's (1869) definitions of psychological subject (PS) and psychological predicate (PP). The PS is defined as "that to which the speaker directs the hearer's attention" and PP as "that which the speaker makes the hearer think about."

We need to return to these earlier stages in the history of the IS modelling to introduce a psychological or neurolinguistic view in defining IS functions of word concepts at the brain level. These functions transform all word concepts into CU constituents and they are in relation to the cortical organization of speech processing. More recent IS studies than those of Gabelentz and Paul, analyze IS at the linguistic level and they transform PP and PS into theme and rheme constituents. Thus, PP and PS lose their initial significance as psychological concepts at the pre-linguistic level of expression. Although there is considerable variation in terminology and approaches, most studies accept that IS is a sentence-level structure that encodes two semantic/discourse aspects: givenness (given/old information-topic) vs. new (information- focus), and aboutness (topic/theme and comment/rheme). Most analyses tackle issues about the relation between IS and syntax and discourse, such as Kuno (1972), Firbas (1966), Halliday (1967), Prince (1981), Chafe (1976, 1993), Lambrecht (1986, 1994), Rooth (1985), Vallduvi (1990), Erteschik-Shir (1997, 2007), Zimmerman & Féry (2009), Krifka (2006), Krifka & Musan (2012), Büring (2005, 2006), Steedman (1991, 2000, 2014), and Pană-Dindelegan (2013), among others.

Halliday's (1967) approach defines the theme–rheme structure at the sentence level but the second IS level of old–new information is related to intonation. Topic/focus elements are marked by intonation with respect to their discourse anchoring within informational units (IU). He relates tonal groups (prosodic phrases) to IUs and treats IU as topic or focus domain realization. The most prominent intonational feature, the pitch accent, is correlated with the most informative part, while the rest of the IU is considered as less informative. The IU structuring is often described as background–focus or background–Kontrast partitions. Steedman (2000) uses information structure along the lines of Halliday (1967) and proposes two dimensions of IS that are both related to intonational forms. Theme–rheme and background–focus are the two levels of Steedman's IS model. His approach is an important contribution in relating intonational forms to IS functions. The focus/topic–background structure of IUs and theme–rheme structures of sentence are not independent IS levels (e.g. topic is usually related to theme part of sentence) and other semantic devices are added in Steedman (2000, 2014) in order to describe all intonational variations. Theme–rheme and topic–focus structures need to be redefined and overlapped at any level of utterance tree in order to become two independent structures.

IS in Romanian is treated in Pană-Dindelegan (2013) at a linguistic and semantic level by presenting structures in canonic word order within the discourse to generate certain IS events as: e.g. rhematization by focalization, topicalization, contrastive topic, hanging topic. The IS model proposed here can be applied to corresponding intonational contours to explain in detail how exactly functional elements of intonational contours generate respective discourse events.

Romanian intonational contours are presented in Dascălu-Jinga (1998, 2001) by using phonetic descriptions without any relation to IS functions. In Jitcă, Apopei, Păduraru & Maruşcă (2015) several types of Romanian contours are described at the phonological level by using the RO_ToBI annotation system but no IS functional perspective was applied. In the present chapter intonational forms are discussed in relation to CU constituents and their functions of a two level IS model.

# 2 A two dimensional model of information structure

This chapter defines an IS model with two independent levels which is applied to utterance IS partitioning in order to relate intonational forms of CU constituents to IS descriptions. CUs are binary units that have functionally contrasted elements. One element bears two overlapped IS functions. This overlapping is possible because pitch variations encode these functions and involve two acoustic cue categories: tonal target level and pitch excursion shape or slope (temporal features).

Another new aspect of our modelling consists in relating the IS functions firstly to the word packaging within utterances. Thus, IS elements are not discussed only in relation to semantic/discourse categories. The relation of IS functions with semantic/discourse categories is analyzed when a discourse context of the analyzed utterance exists. This model introduces neurolinguistic aspects related to speech communication in the analysis of intonational contours.

The block diagram in Figure 4.1 illustrates CU realizations which are determined by both pragmatic/communicative and linguistic aspects. The functions of CU constituents at both IS levels are reflected by intonational contours.

In our model "topic–focus" structure conveys at the pragmatic level a relation between two elements that have contrasted functional marking within the cortical organization of information packaging. The communicative and linguistic aspects of an utterance are embedded into CUs which show that the "topic–focus" structure conveys a qualitative difference between functional constituents. The qualitative difference consists of different temporal characteristics of pitch excursion during their pitch accents or prosodic words.

In concrete discourse contexts "topic" and "focus" constituents can be related to givenness and newness categories of discourse modelling. Thus pragmatic "topic" and "focus" functions are also defined as topic and focus in our intonational analyses even in certain cases where there is no discourse context for the analyzed utterances. Both focus and topic constituents modulated by the second IS level may be marked by tonal prominence (e.g. when they bear emphasis).

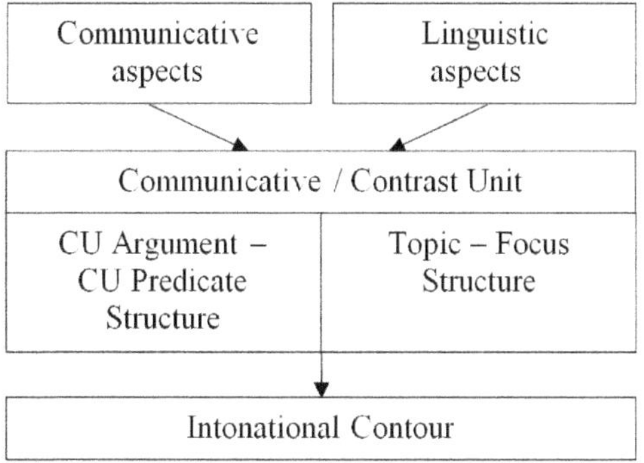


**Figure 4.1.** A view on the communicative unit structure.

The second level of our model results by reformulating the PP-PS structure of Gabelentz's model in terms of a general predicate–argument structure, which is also used at the syntactic and semantic levels. We introduced *CU_ predicate* function, which refers to the constituent which bears the "first or general reference" of the object of communication unit. Constituents with CU_predicate function always have a thematic role at the related CU level, which may be significant or not at the semantic level. CU-predicate elements correspond to PS in the Gabelentz's model. *CU_argument* function defined by our model is associated to the "added reference" of the object of communication unit. CU-argument elements correspond to PP in the Gabelentz's model and to rhematic constituents within all CUs. "Rheme" at the communicative level may be significant or not at the semantic level. CU_predicate–CU_argument structure introduces the "aboutness"-principle at any CU level. The relation between these two functional constituents conveys the essence of communication unit.

In Romanian CU_predicate element is called *predicat enunţiv* (*utterance predicate* in English) by Pană-Dindelegan (2008). This notion is introduced in Pană-Dindelegan (2008) in discussing different levels of predications in Romanian: syntactic, semantic and enouncement levels. It is not defined in the context of IS modelling. CU-predicate element may be prominent when it is a relevant referential topic at the discourse level.

The topic–focus and CU_predicate–CU_argument contrasts are conveyed by two types of acoustic features: i. temporal features – pitch excursion shape or slope of pitch accents or prosodic words; ii. F0 frequency target level. ToBI pitch accent categories have F0 patterns with specific acoustic features for marking CU_predicate vs. CU_argument and topic vs. focus constituents: e.g. F0 pattern of H+L* pitch accent have abrupt falling pitch movement for focus elements and slow variation in pitch movement for topic elements during the accented syllable or the following non-accented syllables. The H* pitch accent patterns have lower target tone for CU_predicate constituents and higher target tone for CU_argument constituents, comparatively to their paired constituents.

The IS model presented in this chapter organizes any simple or complex utterance into a hierarchy of local CUs with their own IS partitioning. The IS partitioning description consists of pairs of functional labels separated by slash that correspond to CU constituents. Each constituent has two functions at the CU_Predicate–CU_Argument and topic–focus IS levels.

At the CU description level the CU_Predicate and CU_Argument constituents are labelled by P and A, respectively, while at the topic–focus structure level, CU constituents are annotated by T and F labels. The two functional labels of one constituent are linked by "+" and enclosed between round parentheses.

In (2) all four possible variants of IS partitions, based on a two level IS model, are presented. CU_predicate and CU_argument can change their positions within a CU, independently of its topic–focus structure but depending on speaker-dependent text representations at the brain level or semantic/discourse contexts.

(2)   a. (A+T)/(P+F)   b. (A+F)/(P+T)   c. (P+T)/(A+F)   d. (P+F)/(A+T)

The chapter aims to demonstrate that the CU_argument, CU_predicate, topic and focus functions can be viewed as a minimal set of functions that can describe IS partitioning at any level of utterance tree. The IS functions of CU constituents can be deduced at the pragmatic level by analyzing intonational forms of prosodic words (prominent tones and temporal features). The IS categories defined at the pragmatic level may be added to the phonological categories within intonational analysis which can be used in future studies on prosodic variation. Thus, we can explain differences between contours of the same type that differ at the IS organization level.

# 3    Nuclear accent placement in Romanian

This section presents several Romanian intonational contours adding new arguments for the nuclear accent assignment from the IS modelling point of view. We choose to analyze several Romanian contour types already discussed elsewhere in order to demonstrate how the IS model presented in this chapter can improve the existing phonological analysis of intonation. The contours correspond to the following categories of sentences: statements, information seeking yes–no questions and information seeking wh-questions. We discuss statements with non-emphasized declarative contours because they are also discussed in Dascălu-Jinga (1998, 2001), but there is no indication about nuclear accent position. Regarding Romanian non-emphasized contour statements, in Göbbel (2003) and Jitcă et al. (2015), only statements with sentence-final nuclear configuration are presented. Given that Romanian is a syllable-timed language, word stress can also grade the load of information in an utterance and can function as a cue to features such as "length of sentence" making some syntactic features or words that bear new or important information predictable.

We selected Romanian information-seeking interrogatives to discuss the nucleus position aspect because the phonological analysis of these types of contours raised various issues discussed in Ladd (1996, 2008). The lack of acoustical salience of the nuclear element in yes–no questions with a sentence-initial nucleus and the presence of an additional prominence towards the end of long wh-question contours shows that it is difficult to understand how nucleus is assigned in these types of utterances. The nucleus in Romanian wh-questions is related to the main prominence of the wh-word in sentence-initial position (Dascălu-Jinga, 2001; Jitcă et al., 2015). Also Ladd (2008:228) observed the presence of a post-focal prominence in Romanian long wh-questions. In this section we explain what the function of this prominence is by describing the utterance partitioning of long wh-question used in Ladd (2008:228). Our model is also able to provide a straightforward analysis of yes–no questions in line with Ladd (2008:228), which, as the author points out, should not be controversial.

## 3.1 Methodology

This chapter is theoretical in its approach, however several utterances were selected and analyzed in order to show how our model can shed some light in contexts that raised previous difficulties particular to Romanian with regards to nucleus accent placement, such as long wh-questions and declarative and yes–no questions. We recorded several utterances for illustrating changes of nucleus positions in non-emphasized declarative and yes–no question contours.

We devised a questionnaire that includes two wh-questions of different length which were selected in order to explain the presence of final small prominence in long wh-questions comparatively to short wh-questions. The short sentence is original and for the long wh-question we used one of the two sentences used in Ladd (1996, 2008).

A single sentence was introduced in the questionnaire for yes–no question contour elicitation but two different contexts were assigned in order to change the word to which the question refers.

In statements with non-emphasized contour, an emotional context was built for the sentence because the emotional utterances can move the nucleus on different words which are more related to emotion cause, depending on the speaker's feeling.

The recording procedures were conducted by the authors of the chapter. The discourse context was presented to the speaker and then the speaker uttered the sentence keeping in mind the requirements formulated in the questionnaire. The recordings were made at 11 KHz and were obtained using GoldWave, a piece of sound recording and editing software. Only two files for each type of contour were selected. The corresponding F0 contours were computed and labeled by a speech analysis PRAAT program.

## 3.2    Non-emphasized declarative contours

Short non-emphasized declarative contours are described at the phonetic level in Dascălu-Jinga (1998, 2001). The contour has a rising–falling pattern in an asymmetrical form with a lower level boundary tone at the end compared to the tone at the beginning of the intonational phrase. In this section we explain the role of a lower boundary tone in non-emphasized declarative contours by using IS analysis.

This type of contour is exemplified by using two utterances of the sentence ALIna măNÂNcă ciocoLAta. "Alina is eating the chocolate" having a SVO syntactic structure. The sentence is a clause embedded within a larger sentence presented in (3). In the discourse context the speaker has a sister, Alina. The children have only one chocolate for each. The boy (the speaker) is upset because his sister eats the chocolate and he tells his mother.

> (3)    *(Mamă,) ALIna măNÂNcă ciocoLAta.*
>        [(Mummy,) Alina is eating the chocolate.]

In the first variant presented in Figure 4.2 and described in (4) the three prosodic words of the intonational phrase are structured by two nested CUs. The low level CU has the verb and the object as contrastive constituents.

The subject is a focus constituent having a rising pitch movement (L+H*) followed by a constant high level pitch movement during the last non-accented syllable. The high target tone gives the subject the CU_argument function and it is annotated by the A+F label in (4).

At the embedded CU level the verb is a focus element having a high pitch accent within a prosodic word with equal levels for its beginning and end tones. We annotate by ~H* label the high pitch accent within a prosodic word with this acoustic feature. This prosodic word has a rising–falling F0 contour pattern. The high target tone of the verb comparatively to the low target tone of the object gives the CU_argument function to the verb and we annotate it by the A+F label.

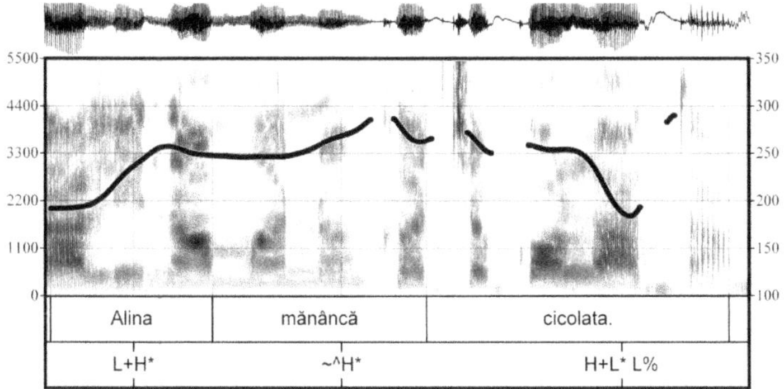


**Figure 4.2.** The F0 contour and the spectrogram of the non-emphasized statement *ALIna măNÂNcă ciocoLAtă*. 'Alina is eating the chocolate.' in the case of the sentence-final position of the global CU_predicate element.

$$(4) \quad \{\, (A+F)^{Alina}{}_{L+H^*} / \{(A+F)^{mănâncă}{}_{\sim H^*} / (P+T)^{ciocolata}{}_{H+L^*\,L\%} \,\}_{P+T} \,\}$$

The object is the contrasted P+T element of the verb because it has the lowest target tone and slow falling pitch movement during the accented syllable. The constituent of the object is acoustically prominent due to the longer duration of the accented syllable and it projects its functions to the embedded phrase at the higher level of the CU hierarchy.

At the global level, the embedded CU inherits CU_predicate and topic functions from the object. The subject is the contrastive element of the embedded CU and this explains its CU_argument and focus functions.

In conclusion, the sentence-final word bears the global CU_predicate function (the global "theme"). Thus, it is the word which the sentence refers to. In non-emphasized declarative contours, the nuclear accent is related to the word with global CU_predicate function conveyed by a tonal minimum of its prosodic word. This explains the sentence-final position of the nucleus in broad focus statements because final pitch accent and boundary tone are prominent marks of global CU_predicate element. The sentence-final position of nuclear accent in Romanian broad focus statements is also discussed in a similar vein in Göbbel (2003) and Jitcă et al. (2015).

In this chapter we illustrate the case of statements with non-emphasized contours but with a non-final position of its global CU_predicate element. We illustrate this case by another utterance of the same sentence where the subject becomes the thematic element. The F0 contour is presented in Figure 4.3 and is described in (5).

The three prosodic words of the contour in Figure 4.3 are also structured by two nested CUs. The low level CU has the verb and the object as constituents. The verb is a focus element because the rising pitch movement is stopped during the last non-accented syllable and it continues with a very short falling pitch movement. The verb is paired with the object which bears topic function due to the large slow pitch fall during the H+L* pitch accent.

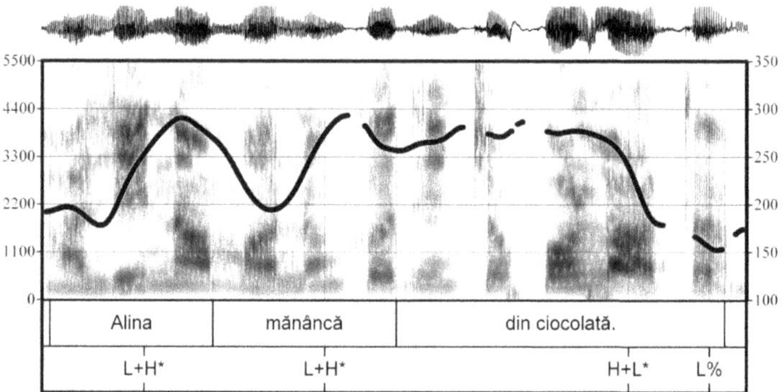


**Figure 4.3.** The F0 contour and the spectrogram of the non-emphasized statement *ALIna măNÂNcă din ciocoLAtă* 'Alina is eating the chocolate.' in the case of a sentence-initial position of the global CU_predicate element.

$$(5) \quad \{\ (P+F)^{Alina}{}_{H*}/\{\ (P+F)^{mănâncă}{}_{H*}/(A+T)^{din\ ciocolată}{}_{H+L*\ L\%}\}_{A+T}\ \}$$

The last pitch accent (H+L*) during the most part of the accented syllable keeps high tones much longer than the second L+H* pitch accent during the stressed syllable of the verb and this marks the object for CU_argument function and the verb as CU_predicate element. The object projects its topic and CU_argument function to the whole embedded CU because the longer duration of the accented syllable gives it an acoustical salience. The embedded CU is in contrast at the global CU level with the subject which is intonationally marked by an L+H* pitch accent having a lower target tone comparatively to those of the verb and the object. Thus, the subject bears the global CU-predicate function. This sentence-initial word also bears focus function because its rising pitch movement during the accented syllable changes into a slow falling pitch movement during the last non-accented syllable. The final pitch accent and boundary tones do not have enough duration at the low tonal level during the last accented syllable, compared to the sentence-initial pitch accent.

The F0 contour presented in Figure 4.3 results from the production of a non-emphasized utterance where a particular cognitive representation moves the global "theme" on the subject. Consequently, the nuclear accent has the sentence-initial position because it corresponds to the global CU_ predicate element.

The first intonational variant presented in Figure 4.2 corresponds to a non-emphasized contour statement with an implicit final thematic element while the second variant presented in Figure 4.3 may be considered a non-emphasized contour statement with an (explicit) non-final thematic element. In the former instance the speaker is saying something about chocolate (it is eaten by Alina and, in the latter, the speaker is saying something about the subject Alina – she is eating the chocolate).

## 3.3    Romanian information-seeking and confirmation-seeking yes–no questions

The contour of an information-seeking yes–no question in Romanian and other Eastern languages, such as Greek and Russian, are treated in Ladd (1996, 2008). Referring to the nuclear accent in this type of contour Ladd agrees that the nuclear accent position is on the low-pitched syllable of the sentence-initial word (the verb) even if it is not related to any acoustic salience. He presents Xu & Xu's (2005) opposite opinion claiming that the authors "equate the pragmatic prominence with acoustic salience" and do not accept a pragmatic prominence on the low-pitched syllable of the verb.

Xu & Xu's (2005) Parallel Encoding & Target Approximation (PENTA) model organizes intonational components in terms of communicative functions which do not start at the Information Structure level. Thus, focus is considered as a communicative function at the discourse level which serves to highlight a particular piece of information and not as a function within IS partition in relation to a speech unit. Within the PENTA model it is difficult to see the particular IS context where focus elements also bear "theme" and nucleus functions within the respective unit.

For Dascălu-Jinga (2001) this particular IS context of "theme" and nucleus overlapping within Romanian yes–no question contours is described by using the notion of "negative" prominence of the "interrogative emphasis" related to the word referred in the question ("theme"). In this case "interrogative emphasis" is marked by the "negative" prominence of a low pitch event. In this section we propose a nucleus assignment rule using an analysis of yes–no questions from an IS perspective.

This type of Romanian yes–no question contour is illustrated in Figure 4.4 by the F0 contour of the sentence *Ai văZUT aCEAStă fotograFIe?* "Did you see this photo?" The F0 contour has a low level stretch until the last stressed syllable. During the last accented syllable a rising pitch movement occurs up to very high level and then the contour has a slow falling pitch movement during the last non-accented syllable.

The first two prosodic words have small variations at low level by keeping the same level for their beginning and end low tones. This acoustic mark which applies focus function to the related words is annotated in Figure 4.4 by an ~L* pitch accent. Example (6) shows how IS is partitioned. The three prosodic words of the contour are structured by two nested CUs.

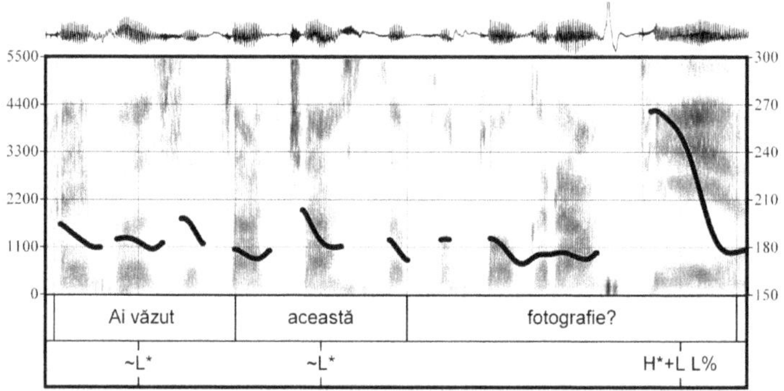


**Figure 4.4.** The F0 contour and the spectrogram of the information-seeking yes–no question *Ai văZUT aCEAStă fotograFIe?* ' Did you see this photo?', with a non-final nucleus.

$$(6) \quad \{ (P+F)^{\text{Ai văzut}}{}_{\sim L^*}/\{ (P+F)^{\text{această}}{}_{\sim L^*}/(A+T)^{\text{fotografie}}{}_{H^*+L\ L\%} \}_{A+T} \}$$

The embedded CU pairs the two syntactic constituents of the noun phrase *această fotografie.* The first constituent *această* bears focus and CU_ predicate functions justified by the ~L* pitch accent. It is annotated in (6) by the P+F label.

The third prosodic word has a step up to a very high level during the accented syllable (H*+L pitch accent) followed by a slow falling pitch movement during the last non-accented syllable. The slow falling pitch movement from a very high level gives topic and CU_argument functions to the sentence-final word annotated by the A+T label in (6). The pitch excursion within the A+T element does not fall below the tonal level of the P+F element of the embedded CU and thus the tonal spaces of the two prosodic words are separated. This leads to a local emphasis on the last word and the A+T element projects its topic and CU_argument functions to the higher node of the CU hierarchy.

At the global level CU the constituent of the verb is a P+F element having the same acoustic marks as the P+F element of the embedded CU. It is paired with the A+T constituent of the embedded CU. The pitch excursion of the embedded CU falls below the tonal level of the first accented syllable of the verb (198 Hz). In this case the tonal spaces of the two CU constituents are not separated and the nucleus is related to the lowest target tone. This explains why the sentence-initial P+F element bears the global CU_predicate function. Dascălu-Jinga defines this type of contour as a contour with non-final "interrogative emphasis." In fact it is a yes–no question contour with a sentence-non-final nucleus. The acoustical salience of the last pitch accent does not mark an emphasis on the last word at the global level of the utterance because the first accented syllable is a little higher (198 Hz) than the bottom level (180 Hz) of the tonal space of the last pitch accent. The tonal level of the second accented syllable is also at this level of 180 Hz.

Another category of yes–no question contours refers to contours with a final nuclear accent. We illustrate this type of contour in Figure 4.5 by using another utterance of the sentence *Ai văZUT aCEAStă fotograFIfie?* "Did you see this photo?" The last word shows a genuine emphasis with low prominence conveyed by an L*+H H% pitch event sequence and a "valley" pitch contour of the last prosodic word. The minimum low tone is reached during the last accented syllable and then a large rising pitch movement occurs during the last non-accented syllable.

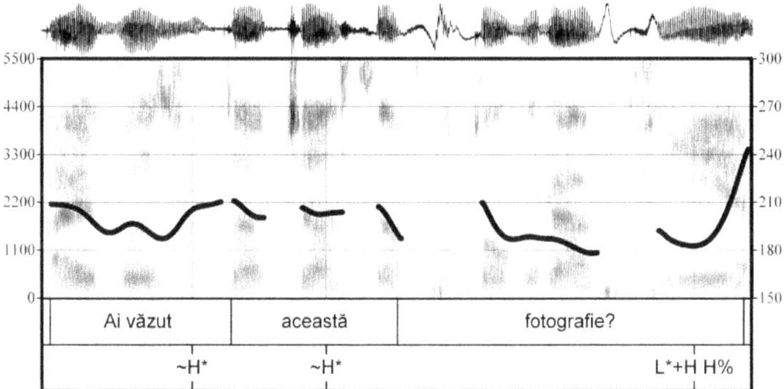


**Figure 4.5.**  The F0 contour and the spectrogram of the confirmation-seeking yes–no question *Ai văZUT aCEAStă fotograFIe?* ' Did you see this photo?' with sentence-final nucleus.

This acoustic marking of the sentence-final word produces an emphasis. The first two prosodic words have contours with medium tonal levels that we annotate by an ~H* pitch accent because it keeps the same relative high levels for the beginning and end tones compared to the last target tone of the F0 contour. The F0 contour is described in (7).

(7)    { (A+F)^{Ai văzut}_{~H*}/{ (A+F)^{această}_{~H*}/(P+T)^{fotografie}_{L*+H H%} }_{P+T} }

In the embedded CU the ~H* pitch accent gives focus and CU_argument functions to the adjective *această* (labeled by A+F). It is paired with the word *fotografie* which has CU_predicate and topic functions. These functions are produced by the minimum low tone reached during its accented syllable and the following slow rising pitch movement. The presence of emphasis on the P+T constituent gives it a prominence and thus it projects its functions to the whole embedded CU.

The constituent of the embedded CU is the A+F constituent of the global CU and the verb is the P+T element in the same CU. The sentence-final word bears the global CU_predicate function and it also bears emphasis with "negative" prominence. In this case of a yes–no question contour there are two causes for the sentence-final position of the nucleus: the global CU_predicate function of the last word and the presence of the emphasis on this word.

In conclusion the rule for nucleus assigning in yes–no questions with non-emphasized contours is the same as in statements with non-emphasized contours. It states that the nucleus is related to the word with a global CU_predicate function. In emphasized yes–no question contours, nucleus is related to an emphasis produced during a prosodic word which reaches the lowest tonal level during the accented syllable and then rises the pitch contour to very high levels.

The possibility of identifying the nucleus with the global thematic element within non-emphasized ascending contours may be studied in other languages, too. Further studies in prosodic typology are needed to confirm whether or not the low level nuclear accent of these types of contours are a characteristic of Eastern European languages and whether this interpretation is also available to other European languages.

## 3.4   Romanian information-seeking wh-question

We treat Romanian wh-question contours in this chapter firstly because they are an emphasized type of descending contours and secondly because there is an issue referring the nucleus position in long wh-question contours. In Romanian wh-question contours the wh-word bears an emphasis (Dascălu-Jinga, 2001). Its high pitch accent followed by a large falling pitch movement marks it as the most important word which bears the nucleus (Jitcă et al., 2015). Ladd (2008) accepts that in the short Romanian wh-question contours, the major prominence is on the left but for long contours he observes that an additional prominence may occur further to the right.

We illustrate the short wh-question contour by using the sentence *CÂT duREAză FILmul?* "How long is the movie?" The F0 contour of this utterance is presented in Figure 4.6 and described in (8). The three prosodic words of the short wh-question are structured by two nested CUs. The left embedded CU has a CU-argument constituent of the wh-word (high target tone) and a local CU_predicate constituent of the verb (low target tone). At local level a CU_argument constituent of a wh-word is the most acoustically prominent element. Its prominence is due to the emphasis produced by the contrast between a high-pitched syllable of the wh-word and the low target tone of the following word.

In the embedded CU the wh-word has a focus function (high level ~H* pitch accent) and the verb has topic function due to the slow falling pitch movement during the accented syllable (H+L* pitch accent). The wh-word (labeled A+F) projects its functions at the global level where the embedded CU is paired with the last word (labeled P+T). The last prosodic word continues the falling tendency of the contour at a small pitch range (30 Hz). The last word bears the global CU_predicate function having the lowest target tone. It also bears topic function due to the slow pitch movement during the accented syllable.

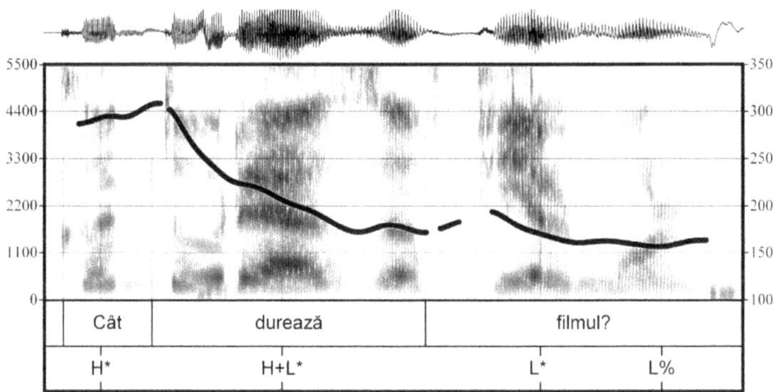


**Figure 4.6.** The F0 contour and the spectrogram of the short wh-question *CÂT duREAză FIL-mul?* ' How long is the movie?'.

$$(8) \quad \{\,\{(A+F)^{Cât}{}_{H*}/(P+T)^{durează}{}_{H+L*}\}_{A+F}/(P+T)^{filmul?}{}_{L*L\%}\,\}$$

Final pitch movements during the sentence-final word produce a small acoustical salience of the last pitch event in a case of long wh-question as Ladd observes in analyzing Romanian wh-question contours. We illustrate this case by using the sentence *De UNde ai cumpăRAT craVAta aCEASta?* "Where did you buy the necktie?" The F0 contour of the utterance is presented in Figure 4.7 and described in (9). The F0 contour of the global CU is structured by two sequential CUs. In the left CU the wh-word bears the focus function due to its rising/abrupt falling pitch movement. The verb bears the topic function produced by the slow down-stepping tendency of its F0 contour (the end tone is lower than the beginning tone).

In the right CU the noun *cravata* "the necktie" has focus function by keeping a constant low level during its prosodic word. The constituent *aceasta* is an element with an L* pitch accent on a slow down-stepping tendency of its F0 contour. Its prosodic word steps "up" the tonal level in the beginning of the last two syllables and then falls until their end producing an acoustical salient element within a small pitch range (15–20 Hz).

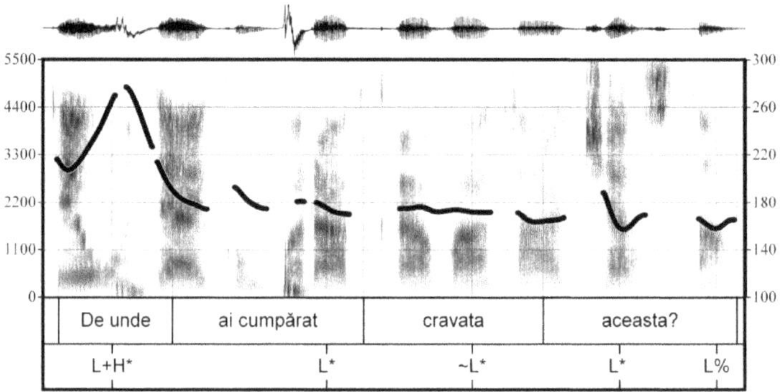


**Figure 4.7.** The F0 contour and the spectrogram of the long wh-question *De UNde ai cumpăRAT craVAta aCEASta?* 'Where did you buy the necktie?'.

(9)  $\{ \{(A+F)^{\text{De unde}}_{\text{H*}}/(P+T)^{\text{ai cumpărat}}_{\text{H+L*}}\}_{\text{A+F}} \{(A+F)^{\text{cravata}}_{\text{~L*}}/(P+T)^{\text{aceasta}}_{\text{L* L\%}} \}_{\text{P+T}}\}$

The last word has an acoustical salience compared to its paired constituent. This final acoustical salience is necessary in the case of a long wh-question in order to project the functions of the final constituent to the global level where the right CU becomes a P+T element. This can explain the presence of an additional prominence on the last word in Romanian long wh-question contours that is observed by Ladd (1996, 2008).

In the ToBI annotation of emphasized descending contours the post-emphasis part of the utterance associated with compressed pitch range remains outside the intermediate phrase which includes the emphasized word. IS partitioning improves F0 contour understanding by relating all pitch events to IS functions whether they have a significant pitch range or not. Wh-question contour interpretation is useful in comprehension emphasized Romanian descending contours of statements where the nucleus moves to the left on non-final emphasized words.

**Table 4.1.** Nucleus assignment rules based on IS view.

| Sentence type | Contour Type | Nuclear element function |
| --- | --- | --- |
| Statement | Non-emphasized descending | global CU_predicate |
| Yes–No Question | Non-emphasized ascending | global CU_predicate |
| Statement | emphasized descending | global CU_argument |
| Information-seeking wh-question | emphasized descending | global CU_argument |

We summarize in Table 4.1 the conclusions about the nucleus position within different types of Romanian intonational contours related to different types of sentences.

We conclude arguing that it is necessary to take into account emphasis when it is present within intonational contour in order to select the correct rule for nucleus identification. Emphasis partially overlaps the narrow focus category but it also includes other pitch events as that presented in Romanian wh-question contour. These claims are arguments for introducing emphasis in the phonological analysis not only as a paralinguistic aspect.

# 4  Conclusions

The chapter aims to present an IS model in order to introduce IS partitioning in intonational contour analysis. We introduce the notion of CU and relate it to any pair of pitch contour segments which have complementary functions at the IS level. CU corresponds to one IS partition while prosodic phrase may contain more than one IS partition.

This chapter demonstrates that all intonational variations of a sentence can be explained by applying IS partitioning of their contours in direct relation with the phonetic and phonological events. This leads to an improved intonational contour comprehension.

The IS model is a two-dimensional one having two structures: CU predicate–CU argument and topic–focus structures. The IS functional constituents have roles firstly at the neurolinguistic level for building speech communication and then at the level of bearing linguistic meaning.

At the cognitive level, topic and focus elements correspond to two conceptual elements, which are paired within one CU by marking them with different temporal features at pragmatic level. At the semantic level they may correspond to givenness and newness categories. We transformed the psychological subject and predicate elements of Gabelentz's elements into CU_predicate and CU_argument elements, respectively, at the CU level.

Then we overlapped both CU_predicate–CU_argument and topic–focus contrasts at any CU level. In this manner we defined a pragmatic IS model with two independent structural levels.

Based on the IS model, we formulate important nuclear accent assignment rules in Romanian statements. We can distinguish between broad focus statements with an implicit sentence-final nucleus and the type of statements with explicit non-final nucleus.

We explain why the lack of acoustical salience of the low-pitched syllable event in a yes–no question contour is not incompatible with the nucleus function of the corresponding word. The rule for this type of contour states that nucleus is related to the global CU_predicate constituent. Intonational analysis has only to demonstrate that the low-pitched event occurs at the minimum low level of the F0 contour and that this acoustical mark gives it the nuclear accent function. It is not necessary to compare its acoustical salience with that of the last pitch accent because they support complementary IS functions at the global CU level and they do not compete for the nuclear position. This competition exists at the local CU level because only one of the two constituents projects their IS functions at the higher level of CU hierarchy.

Short and long wh-questions are illustrated in the chapter for explaining the role of small prominence in the end of long wh-questions contours. The small prominence of the last constituent transfers its functions to the last CU which contrasts with the utterance-intial CU. The initial CU includes wh-word which carries the global nucleus conveyed by emphasis.

Lastly, utterance partitioning consisting of identifying CU hierarchy and its related IS partition hierarchy should be a target of any intonational contour analysis. Utterance partitioning says something about word packaging within utterances.

# References

Beckman, M. E., Hirschberg, J., & Shattuck-Hufnagel, S. (2005). The original ToBI system and the evolution of the ToBI framework. In S-A. Jun (Ed.), *Prosodic Typology. The Phonology of Intonation and Phrasing* (pp. 9–54). Oxford: Oxford University Press.

Büring, D. (2005). *Semantics, Intonation and Information Structure*. MS. UCLA.

Büring, D. (2006). Focus projection and default prominence. In *V. Molnár*, S. Winkler (Eds.), *The Architecture of Focus* (pp. 321–346). Berlin: Mouton de Gruyter.

Chafe, W. L. (1976). Givenness, contrastiveness, definiteness, subjects, topics and point of view. In Charles N. Li (Eds.), *Subject and Topic* (pp. 27–55). New York: Academic Press.

Chafe, W. L. (1993). Prosodic and Functional Units of Language. In J. Edwards & M. D. Lampert (Eds.), *Talking Data: Transcription and Coding in Discourse Research*. New Jersey: Laurence Erlbaum Associates.

Dascălu-Jinga, L. (1998). Intonation in Romanian. In D. Hirst & A. Di Cristo (Eds.), *Intonation Systems: A Survey of Twenty Languages* (pp. 239–261). Cambridge: Cambridge University Press.

Dascălu-Jinga, L. (2001). *Melodia Vorbirii* în *Limba Română*. Bucureşti: Univers Enciclopedic.

Erteschik-Shir, N. (1997). *The Dynamics of Focus Structure*. Cambridge: Cambridge University Press.

Erteschik-Shir, N. (2007). *Information Structure. The Syntax-Discourse Interface*. Oxford: Oxford University Press.

Firbas, J. (1966). On defining the theme in functional sentence analysis. *Philologica Pragensia*, 8, 170–176.

*von der Gabelentz, G. (1869). Ideen zu einer vergleichenden Syntax. Wort und Satzstellung Zeitschrift für Völkerpsychologie und Sprachwissenschaft, 6, 376–384.*

*Göbbel, E. (2003).* On the Relation between Focus, Prosody and Word Order in Romanian. In J. Quer, J. Schroten, M. Scorretti, P. Sleeman & E. Verheugd-Daatzelaar (Eds.), *Romance Languages and Linguistic Theory* 2001. *Selected papers from 'Going Romance', Amsterdam, 6–8 December 2001* (pp. 75–92). Amsterdam/Philadelphia: John Benjamins.

Gussenhoven, C. (2004). *The Phonology of Tone* and *Intonation*. Cambridge: Cambridge University Press.

Halliday, M. A. K. (1967). *Intonation and Grammar in British English*. The Hague: Mouton.

von Heusinger, K. (2002). Information Structure and the partition of sentence. In E. Hajičová, P. Sgall, J. Hana & T. Hoskovec (Eds.), *Prague Linguistic Circle Papers/Travaux du Cercle Linguistique de Prague Nouvelle* Série, 4, 275–305.

Jitcă, D., Apopei, V., Păduraru, O., & Maruşcă, S. (2015). Transcription of Romanian Intonation. In S. Frota & P. Prieto (Eds.), *Intonation in Romance* (pp. 284–316). Oxford: Oxford University Press.

Krifka, M. (2006). Association with focus phrases. In V. Molnár & S. Winkler (Eds.), *The Architecture of Focus* (pp. 105–136). Berlin: Mouton de Gruyter.

Krifka, M., & Musan, R. (2012). Information Structure: Overview and Linguistic Issues. In M. Krifka & R. Musan (Eds.), *The Expression of Information Structure* (pp. 1–44). The *Expression of Cognitive Categories (ECC)*, 5. Berlin: Mouton de Gruyter.

Kuno, S. (1972). Functional Sentence Perspective: A Case Study from Japanese and English. *Linguistic Inquiry, 3*(3), 269–320.

Ladd, D. R. (1996). *Intonational Phonology* (1st edition). Cambridge: Cambridge University Press.

Ladd, D. R. (2008). *Intonational Phonology* (2nd edition). Cambridge: Cambridge University Press.

Lambrecht, K. (1986). *Topic, Focus, and the Grammar of Spoken French*. PhD dissertation, University of California, Berkeley.

Lambrecht, K. (1994). *Information Structure and Sentence Form. Topic, Focus, and the Mental Representation of Discourse Referents*. Cambridge: Cambridge University Press.

Pană-Dindelegan, G. (2008). Predicatul. In V. Guţu Romalo (Coord.), *Gramatica Limbii Române II: Enunţul* (pp. 241–266). Bucureşti: Editura Academiei Române.

Pană-Dindelegan, G. (2013). *The Grammar of Romanian*. Oxford: Oxford University Press.

Paul, H. (1880). *Prinzipien der Sprachgeschichte* (5th edition). Halle: Niemeyer, Peregrin, Jaroslav 1995.

Pierrehumbert, J. (1980). *The Phonetics and Phonology of English Intonation*. Ph.D. Dissertation, Massachussets Institute of Technology.

Prince, E. (1981). Toward a taxonomy of given-new information. In P. Cole (Ed.), *Radical Pragmatics* (pp. 223–256). New York: Academic Press.

Rooth, M. (1985). *Association With Focus*. PhD dissertation, University of Massachusetts at Amherst.

Rooth, M. (1992). A Theory of Focus Interpretation. *Natural language semantics, 1*(1), 75–116. https://doi.org/10.1007/BF02342617

Steedman, M. (1991). Structure and intonation. *Language, 68*, 260–296.

Steedman, M. (2000). Information structure and the syntax-phonology interface. *Linguistic Inquiry, 34*, 649–689. https://doi.org/10.1162/002438900554505

Steedman, M. (2014). The Surface-Compositional Semantics of the English Intonation. *Language, 90*, 2–57. https://doi.org/10.1353/lan.2014.0010

Vallduvi, E. (1990). *The informational component*. PhD Dissertation, University of Pennsylvania, Philadelphia.

Wagner, M. (2005). Prosody and recursion. Unpublished doctoral dissertation, Massachusetts Institute of Technology, Cambridge, MA.

Xu, Y., & Xu, C. X. (2005). Phonetic realization of focus in English declarative intonation. *Journal of Phonetics, 33*(2), 159–197. https://doi.org/10.1016/j.wocn.2004.11.001

Zimmerman, M., & Féry, C. (2009). *Information Structure: Theoretical, Typological and Experimental perspectives*. Oxford: Oxford University Press.

**Doina Jitcă** is a Scientific Researcher at the Speech Processing Department of the Institute of Computer Science of Romanian Academy – Iasi Branch, Romania. Intonation modeling is her domain of interest, having recently published the following contributions for this research field: *Information Packaging correlates of Semantic Information Structure Categories* (Jitca, 2020), and *A Cognitive View on Romance Yes–No Question Contours* (Jitca, 2022).

# PART II: PROSODIC PHRASING AND SEGMENTS

# 5
# Prosody of contrastive focus in two varieties of Assamese

Asim. I. Twaha & Shakuntala Mahanta

## 1    Introduction

Assamese, spoken by 13,168,484 speakers in India as per Census of India 2001 (Census Report, 2001), belongs to the Eastern Indo-Aryan language area of the Indo-European language family (Dutta Baruah, 2007; Goswami, 1982; Goswami & Tamuli, 2003). The dialectal variation of Assamese can be categorised into four groups: 1) the eastern Assamese group, 2) the central Assamese group, 3) the Kamrupi group and 4) the Goalparia group (Moral, 1992). In the present study we compare the phonology of contrastive focus marking in two varieties of Assamese, namely Standard Colloquial Assamese (henceforth SCA) and Nalbariya variety of Assamese (henceforth NVA). SCA belongs to the eastern group of dialects, spoken mainly in the districts of Sivasagar and Lakhimpur (Goswami & Tamuli, 2003), whereas NVA is a variety from the Kamrupi group spoken mainly in Nalbari district (Moral, 1992).

The speech communities speaking SCA and NVA are geographically cut off from each other by the region where the central group of Assamese dialects are spoken. The two varieties demonstrate segmental, intonational, morphological, and lexical differences, which at times cause mutual incomprehensibility across the speech communities (Goswami, 1982; Goswami & Tamuli, 2003). Since the thrust of the present study is on post-lexical prosody and its role in highlighting contrastive focus (henceforth CF) in SCA and NVA, we will concentrate on the intonational aspect only, without going into morphological and vocabulary differences. Goswami and Tamuli (2003) very briefly state that intonational patterns across Assamese dialectal groups are different. In the present study, we have investigated the intonational differences between the two dialectal groups with specific reference to CF realisation in SCA and NVA.

Assamese as a head final language falls into the prosodic typology of most other South Asian languages like Bengali (Hayes & Lahiri, 1991; Khan, 2008), Hindi (Genzel & Kügler, 2010; Patil et al., 2008), Tamil (Keane, 2014), etc. where a declarative utterance culminates with a verb.

In this chapter, we will start with a rudimentary introduction to the prosodic structure and intonational pattern in SCA and NVA (section 2). The next section (section 3) discusses the various aspects of contrastive focus in general and the sense in which the term has been used in this work. In the next section (section 4) we describe the methodology of data collection, analysis and interpretation. Then we move on to the next section (section 5) that deals with contrastive focus realisation in SCA and NVA respectively. After a brief discussion (section 6) on the findings related to contrastive focus marking in the two varieties, the chapter ends with concluding remarks on the intonational phonology and focus marking in the studied varieties vis-à-vis other South Asian Languages (section 7).

# 2     Prosodic structure of SCA and NVA

The present chapter aims at describing the intonational phonology of SCA and NVA, and the prosodic manifestation of contrastive focus in the varieties. In order to do so, we have adopted the ToBI framework (Beckman & Ayers Elam, 1997), which is based on the Autosegmental-Metrical theory of tonal representations developed in the works by Liberman (1975), Bruce (1977), Pierrehumbert (1980), Beckman and Pierrehumbert (1986), and Pierrehumbert and Beckman (1988). Following this framework, we have considered the turning points in the fundamental frequency contour as a reliable cue to the underlying prosodic structure in the two studied varieties. While describing the intonational patterns in the concerned varieties, adopting Nespor and Vogel (1986) and Selkirk (1978, 1984, 1986) among others, we assume that both varieties obey a hierarchical structure of the prosodic constituents: Intonational Phrase (henceforth IP) > Phonological phrase (henceforth P-phrase) > Prosodic word (henceforth P-word). Since the domains below the P-word are not within the scope of the present study, we will consider P-word to be the lowest node in the hierarchy of the prosodic phrasing. These constituents in the hierarchy are discussed below from the lowest to the highest node.

## 2.1 Prosodic word

A P-word in SCA and NVA phonologically maps a syntactic word, and it creates a phonological domain parallel to the syntactic word. We assume that a minimal P-word must contain at least one foot, which being always bimoraic, maintains a strong–weak rhythmic profile both in SCA (Mahanta, 2001) and NVA. As such, each foot maintains a trochaic meter among the morae, retaining the rhythm at the level of morae not at the level of syllables. A morpheme qualifies minimally for a P-word if it is prosodically independent and morphologically free (Fitzpatrick-Cole, 1991; Inkelas, 1990). As such, P-words in Assamese are identical to those in Bengali (Hayes & Lahiri, 1991; Lahiri & Fitzpatrick-Cole, 1999). Unlike Genzel & Kügler's (2010) proposal regarding Hindi P-words which considers P-word as the domain of tonal association, we hold that SCA and NVA P-words get tonally specified only when they constitute P-phrases.

## 2.2 P-phrase

In Assamese, we will consider P-phrases to be the smallest of tonally marked phonological domains. P-phrases in Assamese behave similarly to P-phrases or Accentual Phrases (henceforth APs) in Bengali (Hayes & Lahiri, 1991; Khan, 2008, 2014), Hindi (Patil et al., 2008), Tamil (Keane, 2014), etc. Similar to these languages, in Assamese, P-phrases are the minimal units of tonal specification which are characterised by initial pitch accent ($T^*$) and final boundary tone $(T_p)$[1]. However, we maintain a difference between SCA P-phrases and Bengali or Tamil APs; in SCA, P-phrases constitute phonological domains, and are not always characterised by pitch accents and P-phrase boundary tones (Hayes and Lahiri's work, 1991, also implies that, in Kolkata Bengali, pitch accents are not obligatory for P-phrases). We propose that though the final constituent of SCA declarative IPs forms a P-phrase, it lacks intonational prominence. Due to a lack of phonological prominence, the concluding P-phrase is not assigned any pitch accent. This claim will further be explained in section 4.1.6, where we will

---

[1] As per the Autosegmental-Metrical model, pitch accents are prominence-lending tones which get associated with the metrically prominent syllable in a P-phrase, and boundary tones are edge marking tones which associate with the boundary of a prosodic domain (P-phrase/ IP).

see that under contrastive focus (henceforth CF) conditions, the post-focus sequence undergoes complete pitch compression. This post-focal compression (henceforth PFC) of pitch (Xu, 2011), however, does not mandatorily influence the prosodic phrasing within the sequence. NVA P-phrases on the other hand, similar to Bengali and Tamil APs, are obligatorily characterised by pitch accents.

Féry (2010) proposes an alternative intonational modelling of P-phrases, which is uniform for South Asian Languages. Instead of a combination of pitch accent and boundary tone, she characterises each P-phrase in Bengali, Hindi, Malayalam, and Tamil with two sets of boundary tones: $L_pH_p$ and $H_pL_p$ designating non-final and final P-phrases respectively. These languages have been analysed and claimed by Féry (2010) as phrase languages, where the beginning and the end of P-phrases are demarcated by boundary tones: low P-phrase boundary tone ($L_p$) demarcates the left edge and high P-phrase boundary tone ($H_p$) demarcates the right edge of non-final P-phrases, whereas a high P-phrase boundary tone ($H_p$) marks the left edge of the final P-phrase and a low IP boundary tone ($L_I$) gets associated with its right edge. While it seems like an appealing idea to analyse languages such as Bengali, Hindi, Malayalam, and Tamil with a different pitch and prominence system than European languages, both the authors of this chapter as native speakers of Assamese could perceive a prominence on the left edge of a phonological phrase. Perception experiments may show how pitch peaks and prominence are perceived by speakers of these languages.

Apart from the intonational characteristics of pitch accent and boundary tone, P-phrases in SCA and NVA serve as phonological domains and, as such, they accommodate various segmental processes within their periphery. A few of them have been discussed below with reference to both varieties. Though the examples are schematic in nature in the following two sections (section 2.2.1 and section 2.2.2), they will be further substantiated with the help of spectrograms in due course.

### 2.2.1 SCA P-phrase domain

An SCA P-phrase serves as a phonological domain which licenses segmental processes like /r/ deletion and intervocalic spirantisation of aspirated plosives to take place within the P-phrase domain internally. These processes are blocked across prosodic boundaries.

In SCA, word internal /r/ is not pronounced when preceded by a vowel (Moral, 1992), instead it is compensated with vowel lengthening. In (1a) few words have been listed, for example, where word internal /r/ gets deleted, whereas it is maintained word finally (1b).

1)　　a. dʰɔrmɔ　　→　dʰɔ:mɔ　　'religion'

　　　　　dɔrza　　　→　dɔ:za　　　'door'

　　　　　xɔmpurnɔ　→　xɔmpu:nɔ　'complete'

　　　b. daŋɔr　　　→　daŋɔr　　　'big'

　　　　　xar　　　　→　xar　　　　'manure'

　　　　　nibir　　　→　nibir　　　'intimate'

This kind of assimilation is not always limited to the lexical domain; when a P-word from (1b) forms P-phrase with another word, the final /r/ undergoes deletion leaving a compensatory lengthening in the preceding vowel. For instance, in (2) and (3), the word final /r/ of *daŋɔr* and *dɔrzar* undergoes deletion and is compensated by a longer preceding vowel /ɔ/ and /a/ respectively.

2)　　　[[rɔmɛn]$_P$　[daŋɔr　manuh]$_P$　[ho-l]$_P$]$_I$

　　　　　　　　　　　　　[ɔ:]

　　　Ramen　　　big　　　man　　　happen-PST3[2]

　　　Ramen became a great man.

3)　　　[[rɔmɛn-ɛ]$_P$　[dɔrza-r　sabi-pat]$_P$　[milɔn-ɔk]$_P$　[di-l-ɛ]$_P$]$_I$

　　　　　　　　　　　　　[a:]

　　　Ramen-NOM　door-GEN　key-CLS　Milan-ACC　give-PST-3

　　　Ramen gave the door-key to Milan.

In SCA there is another word internal segmental process called intervocalic spirantisation of aspirated plosives[3]. When placed between two vowels, an SCA aspirated plosive is pronounced as its fricative counterpart. In (4a)

---

[2]　The glossing of the examples has been done according to the Leipzig convention format (2016).

[3]　In Assamese, aspirated plosives such as [pʰ, bʰ, tʰ, dʰ, kʰ, gʰ], which are otherwise pronounced as fortis, undergo lenition in intervocalic environment (Goswami, 1982).

two words are presented where spirantisation takes place word internally, whereas they are produced as aspirated plosives word initially (4b).

4)  a. xɔgʰɔn          →  xɔɣɔn            'frequent'

   xopʰura         →  xoɸura           'small box'

b. kʰa-bo-loi       →  kʰa-bo-loi       'eat-FUT-DAT'

   gʰɔtɔna         →  gʰɔtɔna          'incident'

c. kɔmɔla kʰa-bo-loi  →  kɔmɔla xa-bo-loi  'orange eat-FUT-DAT'

In (4c), we further see how such spirantisation is accommodated across P-words forming a P-phrase. For example in (5), [kʰ] spirantisation (loss of aspiration as well as the stop occlusion) is accommodated within and blocked at the left edge of P-phrase domains.

5)  [[madʰɔb]$_P$ [kɔmɔla  kʰa-boloi]$_P$ [kʰɔgɛn-ɔr  gʰɔr-ɔloi]$_P$ [go-is-ɛ]$_P$]$_I$

   [ð]          [x]      [kʰ]    [ɔː] [ɣ]

   Madhab    oranges   eat-to        Khagen-GEN house-DAT  go-PRF-3

   Madhab went to Khagen's house to eat oranges

In (5), *kɔmɔla kʰaboloi* constitutes a P-phrase and, as a result, the word initial [kʰ] of *kʰaboloi* gets an intervocalic environment across P-word boundaries, and consequently spirantises to [x] or [χ]. The same is true for [gʰ] → [ɣ] spirantisation in the P-phrase *kʰɔgɛnɔr gʰɔrɔloi*. However, the intervocalic context (across P-phrases) of the word initial [kʰ] in *kʰɔgɛnɔr* does not spirantise [kʰ] because spirantisation is blocked across (but not within) P-phrases.

### 2.2.2  NVA P-phrase domain

Identical to SCA, NVA accommodates various segmental lenition processes P-phrase domain internally. These segmental processes include /r/ assimilation, voicing assimilation, flapping, spirantisation and debuccalisation, which are robust within a phonological domain and not obligatory across it. Although we have referred to different segmental processes, our discussion will mostly concentrate on /r/ assimilation, and velar spirantisation and debuccalisation; other lenition processes will be mentioned whenever appropriate.

In NVA, when /r/ is followed by a coronal consonant P-word internally, it may regressively assimilate to the following coronal consonant and form a geminate (Goswami, 1958).

6) /dɔr-dam/ → /dɔ**dd**am/ 'bargain'

/dɔrza/ → /dɔ**zz**a/ 'door'

/kɔr-s-i/ → /kɔ**ss**i/ 'do-PRF-3'

This assimilation is also seen across P-words when they form a P-phrase. Similar findings regarding /r/ assimilation have been reported for Bengali (Hayes & Lahiri, 1991; Lahiri & Fitzpatrick-Cole, 1999). For instance, in (7) *dɔrzar* and *sabipat* constitute a P-phrase where both occurrences of /r/ assimilate with /z/ and /s/ within and across P-word boundary respectively. Thus we get two geminates within the P-phrase *dɔzzas sabipat*.

7) /dɔrzar sabipat/ → /dɔ**zz**as sabipat/ 'the door key'

In the present NVA data, it has been observed that the underlying aspirated stops are produced as aspirated stops when in word initial position (8a), and as their fricative counterparts in word internal position, if in an intervocalic environment (8b).

8) a) /gʰɔr/ → [gʰɔr] 'house'

   b) /agʰɔn/ → [aɣɔn] 'name of a month'

   c) /makʰɔn/ → [maxɔn] 'butter'

   [mafiɔn] (in post-focus position)

The intervocalic spirantisation may further undergo optional debuccalisation ([maxɔn] > [mafiɔn]) in post-focus position (8c).

These intervocalic lenition processes of spirantisation and debuccalisation seem to be cues to NVA P-phrase domain when they occur across two P-words. In (9a), two P-words *kɔmla* 'orange' and *kʰa-ba* 'eat-DAT' constitute the P-phrase *kɔmla kʰaba*, which accommodates /kʰ/→[x] intervocalic spirantisation, while there is no word initial /kʰ/→[x] spirantisation in *kʰaba* (9b). This intervocalic spirantisation may undergo further lenition and result in loss of place of articulation ([x] → [ɦ] debuccalisation) in post-focus position (9c).

9)    a)   /kɔmla kʰaba/  →    [qɔmla xaba]  'to eat oranges'

       b)   /kʰa-ba/      →    [kʰa-ba]      'eat-PRF'

       c)   /kɔmla kʰaba/  →    [qɔmla ɦaba] (in post focus positon)

       d)   /raŋa gʰɔr/    →    [raŋa ɣɔr]    'red house' (police station)

Similarly, as it is observed in (8b), /gʰ/→[ɣ] spirantisation is allowed within the word domain *agʰɔn* and optionally blocked word initially in *gʰɔr* (8a). Accommodation of /gʰ/ spirantisation in *raŋa gʰɔr* in (9d) across word boundaries testifies *raŋa gʰɔr* as a phonological domain. Here, we see how spirantisation is optionally blocked word initially (8a), although allowed within the word domain (8b) and phrase domains (9d).

## 2.3   **Intonational Phrase (IP)**

It has already been mentioned that the top-most node in the prosodic hierarchy tree is that of IP. It is 'a concatenation of one or more P-phrases' (Hayes, 1989). Normally, in Assamese, an IP phonologically represents a prosodic phrase which corresponds to 'a clause in syntactic constituent structure'. Similar to IPs in other South Asian Languages mentioned above, an IP in Assamese is characterised by non-final LH melody (corresponding to non-final P-phrases), a subsequent pause and IP final boundary tones. Non-final P-phrases are designated by L* $H_p$ or L*+H $H_p$ pitch pattern, which prosodically highlights their non-finality, and the final P-phrase shows an $F_0$ fall marking its final position in the IP. As far as declarative IPs are concerned, we propose that SCA and NVA differ from each other vis-à-vis nuclear accent[4] assignment. In SCA, the penultimate (mostly the

---

[4]   The term 'nuclear accent' has been used in the present work to refer to the last accent in an IP (see Ladd, 2008; Pierrehumbert, 1980; and Xu, 2011). Although British tradition (Cruttenden, 1997) upheld nuclear accent as the last and the most prominent accent in the IP domain, in the present chapter we will stick to the Autosegmental-Metrical model (Beckman & Pierrehumbert, 1986), and consider nuclear accent as the last pitch accent in an IP.

immediate pre-verbal) constituent and, in NVA, the final constituent are assigned the nuclear accent on the leftmost prominent syllable. In SCA, the penultimate constituent is designated by L*H$_p$ pitch pattern: L* and H$_p$ are realised on the first and the last syllables of the constituent respectively. After the constituent, pitch drops smoothly under the influence of the IP final low boundary tone L$_I$. On the other hand, NVA assigns nuclear accent H* on the final constituent in wide focus declarative utterances. Previous research on South Asian Languages shows that the IP final constituent has been assigned either a H* pitch accent as in Kolkata Bengali (Hayes & Lahiri, 1991; Lahiri & Fitzpatrick-Cole, 1999) or L* pitch accent as in Bangladeshi Bengali (Khan, 2008) and Tamil (Keane, 2014).

In the following section, SCA and NVA declarative IPs will be discussed with reference to the lower prosodic categories of P-word and P-phrase.

## 2.3.1   SCA IP

In the IP given in (10), already given in (3), each syntactic word can be analysed as a P-word, which is intonationally underspecified. They get tonal specification only when they form P-phrases. In (10), *rɔmɛnɛ* and *milɔnɔk* are both designated by L*H$_p$ pitch specification since they constitute two separate P-phrases. On the other hand, *dɔrzar* and *sabipat* lack the boundary tone H$_p$ and pitch accent L* respectively, since they contribute to a single P-phrase *dɔrzar sabipat*, which is characterised by L*+H H$_p$ pitch structure. L*+H associates with the first syllable of the P-phrase i.e. *dɔr* of *dɔrzar* and boundary tone H$_p$ with the final syllable of the phrase *pat* of *sabipat*.

|  | L* | H$_p$ | L*+H |  | H$_p$ | L* | H$_p$ |  | L$_I$ |
|---|---|---|---|---|---|---|---|---|---|

10)  [[rɔmɛn-ɛ]$_P$     [dɔrza-r      sabi-pat]$_P$   [milɔn-ɔk]$_P$  [di-l-ɛ]$_P$]$_I$

                [ɔː] [aː]

Ramen-NOM   door-GEN   key-CLS   Milan-ACC   give-PST-3

Ramen gave the door-key to Milan

The prosodic phrasing pattern of (10) is demonstrated in Figure 5.1 in the form of a prosodic hierarchy tree.

The prosodic tree demonstrates that P-words are dominated by P-phrase nodes, and how one or more P-words constitute P-phrases. It further shows that P-phrases must minimally contain one P-word. The pitch contour of utterance (10) is displayed in Figure 5.2 (see section 5.1.1) which shows how

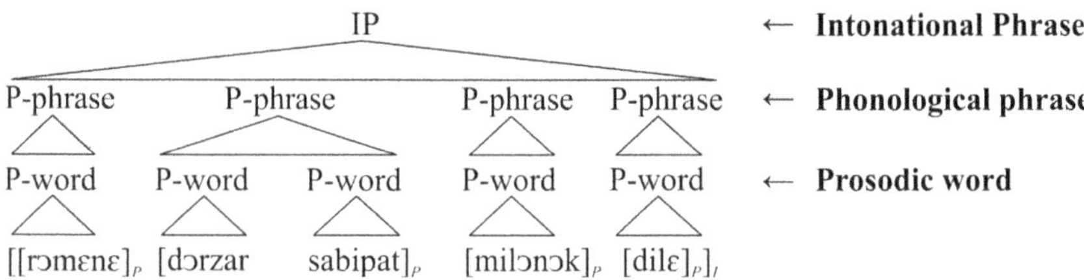

**Figure 5.1.** Prosodic hierarchy demonstrated with the sentence *rɔmɛnɛ dɔrzar sabipat milɔnɔk dilɛ* 'Ramen gave the door-key to Milan.'

each non-final P-phrase designated by either L* or L*+H pitch accent and $H_p$ boundary tone demonstrates rising contour.

SCA always maintains a downstepped order of P-phrases within declarative IPs, where each succeeding P-phrase maintains lower pitch rise in comparison with the previous P-phrase (Twaha & Mahanta, 2016a). Such IP internal downstepping has also been reported by Patil et al. (2008) in their study of Hindi. In a sequence of two rises belonging to two different P-phrases, the rise in the second phrase is downstepped. As a consequence, we see a gradual decline in the pitch peak on each of the succeeding P-phrases (Figure 5.2). Though the IP final constituent *dilɛ* has been assumed to constitute a P-phrase, it lacks post-lexical prosodic prominence. Hence, it is not assigned any pitch accent. The motivation for this assumption is derived from both intonational and segmental evidence. Intonationally, the $F_0$ contour does not show any turning point on *dilɛ* (Figure 5.2) in particular and SCA IP final constituents in general (for example Figure 5.9 and Figure 5.11). The $F_0$ track demonstrates a smooth fall through declarative IP final constituents. Further, when voiceless /k/ is followed by voiced /d, b, bʰ, dʰ, z, g/ within a phonological domain, the former undergoes voicing assimilation, such as in *bak debi* (goddess Saraswati) > /bag debi/ (Dutta, 2010, p. 92). However, in Figure 5.2 such assimilation is blocked suggesting the presence of a prosodic boundary between /k/ of *milɔnɔk* and /d/ of *dilɛ*.

### 2.3.2   *NVA IP*

As far as arrangement of P-words into P-phrases and P-phrases into IP is concerned, NVA is identical to SCA. The IP given in (11), which is an NVA replica of IP (10), highlights this affinity at the level of prosodic structure.

$$\text{L*} \qquad \text{H}_P \qquad \text{L*+H} \qquad\qquad \text{H}_P \qquad \text{L*} \qquad \text{H}_P \qquad \text{H*} \qquad \text{L}_I$$

11)  [[rɔmɛn-ɛ]$_P$  [dɔrza-r   sabi-pat]$_P$  [milɔn-ɔk]$_P$  [di-l-ak]$_{P}$]$_I$

[z] [s]

Ramen-NOM  door-GEN  key-CLS   Milan-ACC  give-PST-3

Ramen gave the door-key to Milan.

The phrasing pattern of (11) demonstrates a prosodic hierarchy tree identical to the one given in Figure 5.1 for SCA. Similar to the SCA phrasing pattern seen in (10), we have five P-words which are arranged into four P-phrases: *rɔmɛnɛ*, *dɔrzar sabipat*, *milɔnɔk* and *dilak*[5]. In shorter P-phrases (*rɔmɛnɛ* and *milɔnɔk*), we see low pitch accent L*, whereas with longer strings (*dɔrzar sabipat*) we get a bitonal pitch accent L*+H. If we look at the intonational realisation of the IP given in Figure 5.13, it can be seen that the non-final P-phrases show rising contours, while the final constituent displays falling contour.

In the above discussion, it is seen that NVA and SCA share commonalities as far as arrangement of P-words to P-phrases and P-phrases to IP is concerned. However, the two varieties differ vis-à-vis nuclear accent assignment: in SCA the nuclear accent falls on the penultimate constituent and in NVA the final constituent bears the nuclear accent. When we move towards CF marking in these varieties, we see that they have specific ways of highlighting CF constituents, and handling pre-focus constituents and post-focus compression. The next section gives a brief introduction to CF and the different prosodic ways it is marked cross-linguistically.

# 3    Contrastive Focus (CF)

CF has been considered the strongest type of focus 'as the speaker asserts something which may contradict the expectations of the hearer' (Féry, 2013). Féry (2013) proposed that focus has a tendency to align with a phonological domain such as P-phrase, IP etc. It has been described variously as identificational focus (Kiss, 1998), alternative focus (Rooth, 1992) and contrastive focus (Kratzer, 2004; Selkirk, 2002; Zimmermann, 2008; Zubizarreta, 1998). Although CF has been differentiated from the instances of

---

[5]  Although the final /k/ of *di-l-ak* 'give-PST-3' has been used in the NVA IPs, it remains mostly unrealised. The fourth tier of the diagrams representing ToBI transcriptions contain the information regarding the realisation of /k/ in *dilak*.

focus created out of correction (Tomioka, 2009; Zimmermann & Onea, 2011), in this chapter both types of foci will be treated interchangeably as both of them generate a set of alternatives out of which the focused alternant receives contrastive focus (Kiss, 1998; Rooth, 1992; Vallduvi & Vilkuna, 1998). In the examples cited in this chapter, focused constituents are highlighted in bold face.

Rooth (1992) defines CF in terms of a set of alternatives. According to the author, when a constituent receives CF it generates a set of alternatives which constitutes its focused meaning. This alternatives set includes the ordinary meaning of the focused constituent within its focused meaning.

12)   A.   Ram killed the cat.

   B.   No, **Ramen** killed the cat.

In (12) when *Ramen* is focused it creates an alternatives set of ordinary meanings: [Ramen killed the cat, Ram killed the cat, Shyam killed the cat, etc.] of which the focused meaning is also a part. It is this set of alternatives which differentiates a focused constituent from non-focused ones: constituents which are not focused do not generate an alternative set of meanings (Rooth, 1992, 1997).

According to Zubizarreta (1998), CF makes its realisation in relation to the context; it is the preceding statement that provides the context for CF. Zubizarreta describes the two-fold function of CF: apart from negating 'the value assigned to a variable' in the preceding statement, CF provides an alternate value for the variable. In the following example, the context for CF is created by (13A), and (13B), which bears CF on *red*, performs two simultaneous functions: first it negates *John is wearing a blue shirt today* i.e. John is not wearing a blue shirt today, and second it induces an alternate value for the constituent which has been negated, i.e, *red*, which is introduced in contrast to *blue* in the previous context statement: *John is wearing a red shirt today.*

13)   A.   John is wearing a blue shirt today.

   B.   John is wearing a **red** shirt today (not a blue shirt).

Languages employ phonological and phonetic cues in order to mark focus. Languages like English (Silverman & Pierrehumbert, 1990), Dutch (Gussenhoven, 1983), Bengali (Hayes & Lahiri, 1991) and Korean (Jun & Lee, 1998) phonologically distinguish contrastive focus from broad or wide focus (henceforth WF). In these languages, CF is marked by either placing a nuclear accent on the focused constituent or by demarcating a prosodic boundary after focus or both. For example, in English, the tonal pattern of a sentence changes with focus change: the nuclear stress falls on the most prominent word or constituent within the IP and the post-focus constituents undergo deaccentuation. There are other languages like French (Féry, Hörnig, & Pahaut, 2010) and Bengali (Hayes & Lahiri, 1991) where focus prosodically demarcates the focused constituent. These languages employ pitch accents and phrasing in a phonologically significant way in order to highlight the focused status of a constituent. In Hindi (Genzel & Kügler, 2010), CF does not change the tonal configuration though the focused constituent is characterised by increased pitch span. Further, in the case of Tamil (Keane, 2014), CF constituents are characterised by a rising pitch contour, which may (or may not) maintain a scaling difference from their WF realisations.

In section 5, we see how SCA demarcates CF constituents asserting its similarity to Kolkata Bengali (Hayes & Lahiri, 1991), whereas NVA shows its affinity to Bangladeshi Bengali (Khan, 2008) and Korean (Jun & Lee, 1998) when it allows the focused constituent to form a P-phrase with the succeeding constituents.

# 4    Methodology

In order to see how CF interacts with prosody in SCA and NVA declarative sentences, we recorded single IP sentences of different lengths. The methodology involved here is correction of sentences. Data was collected in a dialogic format; the speaker utters the WF variant of a sentence in response to the question *ki hol?* (What happened?). His/her rendering is followed by the same utterance said by the recordist as a question with a difference of one constituent, which s/he needs to correct by uttering the previously uttered sentence once again. His/her second rendering bears CF on the corrected word. The material was presented to the speaker with the help of a laptop. A randomly selected example from SCA has been demonstrated below which only explains the schema of data collection. In the illustration below, the speaker first produces *rɔmɛnɛ dɔrzar sabipat milɔnɔk dilɛ* (Ramen gave the door key to Milan) in WF condition as a response to the question *ki hol?* When the listener reproduces the same sentence with a question intonation and by replacing *dɔrzar* 'door-GEN' by *kʰirikir* 'window-GEN', the speaker clarifies the mistake by re-uttering the sentence with CF on *dɔrzar*.

Question: ki  ho-l?

 what  happen-PST3

 What happened?

Speaker: rɔmɛn-ɛ  dɔrza-r  sabi-pat milɔn-ɔk di-l-ɛ

 Ramen-NOM door-GEN key-CLS Milan-ACC give-PST-3

 Ramen gave the door key to Milan.

Question: rɔmɛn-ɛ  *kʰiriki-r*  sabi-pat milɔn-ɔk di-l-ɛ?

 Ramen-NOM window-GEN key-CLS Milan-ACC give-PST-3

 Did Ramen give the window key to Milan?

Speaker: nai nai rɔmɛn-ɛ  **dɔrza-r** sabi-pat milɔn-ɔk di-l-ɛ

 No no Ramen-NOM **door-GEN** key-CLS Milan-ACC give-PST-3

 No no, Ramen gave the **door** key to Milan.

A total number of 44 (forty four) sentences of varying length constituted the core WF data corpus for the present chapter, 22 (twenty two) each from SCA and NVA. Following the above illustrated dialogue format and depending upon the length, each sentence generates as many CF utterances as there are words; for instance, if a sentence contains four words/phrases, it generates at least four variants with CF on different words/phrases in each of the variants. As against the WF variant of *rɔmɛnɛ dɔrzar sabipat milɔnɔk dilɛ*, we get five other CF variants of the utterance with CF on *rɔmɛnɛ, dɔrzar, sabipat, dɔrzar sabipat, milɔnɔk* and *dilɛ*. Since sentence length was variable, the number of CF variants against each sentence varied with the number of constituents. As such, we have a total of 147 responses from each speaker, out of which 22 were WF utterances and 125 their CF variants.


## 4.1 Subjects and recording setting

For the SCA data, 3 (three) male and 2 (two) female speakers (20 to 30 years old) from Sivasagar district of Assam were recorded in the recording booth of the Phonetics and Phonology Lab, Indian Institute of Technology Guwahati. For the NVA data, five male speakers, belonging to the age group of 22 to 28 years, from Nalbari district were recorded in a quiet environment. The recording was done using a Tascam, D-100 PCM recorder in wav format at the sampling rate of 44.1 kHz with 16-bit resolution with the help of a Shure SM10A head-worn microphone.

Whenever there was any hesitation on the part of the speaker, s/he was asked the same question once again to derive an accurate response, and each response was followed by a pause. We followed a randomised order of questions so that the speaker could not anticipate a question. This was done in order to avoid pre-meditated responses from the speakers. They were allowed to read the core sentences to be recorded, but, other than the question, no explicit instruction was provided on which constituent to focus. The entire recording was conducted by the first author of this chapter who has a good command of both SCA and NVA.

## 4.2    Data analysis

The collected data was segmented following ToBI conventions (Beckman & Ayers Elam, 1997). The sound files were annotated in 4-tier TextGrid files in PRAAT (Boersma & Weenink, 2015). The first tier is the Tone tier containing information regarding tonal alignment and tone levels, the second tier contains orthographic representation of the sentences recorded. In the third tier, which is the break index tier, word and phrase level boundaries are demarcated where 1, 2 and 3 refer to P-word, P-phrase and IP boundary respectively. The lowest tier (miscellaneous) contains information regarding the prosodic phrasing of corresponding IPs and segmental changes accommodated within P-phrases in them. The $F_0$ contour used for display in the images has been smoothed in PRAAT at the bandwidth of 10 Hz.

## 4.3    Interpretation of the data

In this chapter, our claims regarding CF manifestation do not rely merely upon the trends of intonational contours, we have further considered various phonological processes which are blocked across prosodic boundaries. These phonological processes include phrase internal /r/ deletion and intervocalic spirantisation which have been discussed already in section 2.2.1 and section 2.2.2. Before going into these processes characterising the string with CF as a phonological domain, the various contours generated by CF are discussed below.

The pitch tracks illustrated in this chapter are not produced by a single speaker. Contours from different speakers have been demonstrated here in order to show the intonational consistency the speakers maintain in spite of their inter-personal differences. The major difference in IPs could be seen in respect of overall pitch range, which can be attributed to gender differences among speakers: female speakers demonstrated greater overall pitch range compared to their male counterparts.

In this chapter, an 'f' diacritic is assigned to the high boundary tone linked to CF in SCA, and a high trailing tone in NVA. It has been used here to mark the focus induced high tones. The 'f' diacritic has been used extensively by Khan (2008, 2014) in his work on focus realisation in Bangladeshi Standard Bengali. He pointed out three motivations for assigning the diacritic (Khan, 2008, 2014): 1) 'f' marked high tones exercise a complete pitch compression on the post-focus constituents, 2) 'f' marked high tones are not susceptible to other tones, and 3) 'f' marked constituents block IP internal downstep among succeeding APs. In the present work, our use of the 'f' diacritic is slightly different from Khan's third motivation. In Assamese, though 'f' marked high tones are characterised by greater pitch value, they do not obligatorily block downstepping. In Assamese, an 'f' marked high tone either triggers complete PFC of pitch (in SCA) or dephrases (in NVA) the post-focus constituents, and it is not overridden by any co-occurring tones.

# 5    CF realisation in SCA and NVA

In this section, we discuss how a contrastively focused constituent is prosodically highlighted in SCA and NVA. The first section explains CF phonology of SCA supported by intonational and segmental evidence.

## 5.1   CF phonology in SCA

### 5.1.1   *CF phrasing (L*fH$_p$/L*+H fH$_p$)*

When a constituent receives CF, it is marked by a rising pitch contour characterised by a low pitch accent, which is also the IP nuclear accent and high focus boundary tone[6] (Twaha & Mahanta, 2016a). After the nucleus is real-

---

[6]   Existence of a focus high boundary tone associated to the right edge of a focused constituent leads to a durational increase in the final syllable of the focused constituent (Twaha & Mahanta, 2016a).

ised on the focused constituent, all the following constituents, if there are any, undergo PFC (see section 5.1.4). Here we can consider the same sentence given in (10) but produced with CF on *milɔn-ɔk* 'Milan-ACC' *sabi-pat* 'key-CLS', *dɔrza-r* 'door-GEN', *rɔmɛn-ɛ* 'Ramen-NOM', di-l-ɛ 'give-PST-3'and *dɔrza-r sabi-pat* 'door-GEN key-CLS' as given in (15), (16), (17), (18), (19) and (20) respectively. The WF IP (10) has been reproduced below in (14) for ready reference.

       L*        H$_P$   L*+H          H$_P$    L*   H$_P$    L$_I$

14)   [[rɔmɛn-ɛ]$_P$  [dɔrza-r   sabi-pat]$_P$  [milɔn-ɔk]$_P$  [di-l-ɛ]$_P$]$_I$  ←WF

       L*        H$_P$   L*+H          H$_P$    L*   fH$_P$    L$_I$

15)   [[rɔmɛn-ɛ]$_P$  [dɔrza-r   sabi-pat]$_P$  **[milɔn-ɔk]**$_P$  [di-l-ɛ]$_P$]$_I$

       L*        H$_P$   L*   H$_P$   L*   fH$_P$            L$_I$

16)   [[rɔmɛn-ɛ]$_P$  [dɔrza-r]$_P$  **[sabi-pat]**$_P$  [milɔn-ɔk]$_P$  [di-l-ɛ]$_P$]$_I$

       L*        H$_P$   L*   fH$_P$                   L$_I$

17)   [[rɔmɛn-ɛ]$_P$  **[dɔrza-r]**$_P$  [sabi-pat]$_P$  [milɔn-ɔk]$_P$  [di-l-ɛ]$_{P]I}$        ← CF

       L*        H$_P$   L$_I$

18)   [[**rɔmɛn-ɛ**]$_P$  [dɔrza-r   sabi-pat]$_P$  [milɔn-ɔk]$_P$  [di-l-ɛ]$_P$]$_I$

       L*        H$_P$   L*+H          H$_P$    L*   H$_P$    L* fH$_P$ L$_I$

19)   [[rɔmɛn-ɛ]$_P$  [dɔrza-r   sabi-pat]$_P$  [milɔn-ɔk]$_P$  **[di-l-ɛ]**$_P$]$_I$

       L*        H$_P$   L*+H          fH$_P$              L$_I$

20)   [[rɔmɛn-ɛ]$_P$  **[dɔrza-r   sabi-pat]**$_P$  [milɔn-ɔk]$_P$  [di-l-ɛ]$_P$]$_I$

The pitch contour of (14) has been demonstrated in Figure 5.2, which shows intonational manifestation of the prosodic phrasing.

Out of the three non-final P-phrases *rɔmɛnɛ*, *dɔrzar sabipat* and *milɔnɔk*, the third P-phrase *milɔnɔk* bears the nuclear pitch accent of the IP (14) since in SCA, IP final P-phrases lack pitch accent. The contour seen in Figure 5.2 will be served as the baseline against which the CF manifestations (15–20) will be compared.

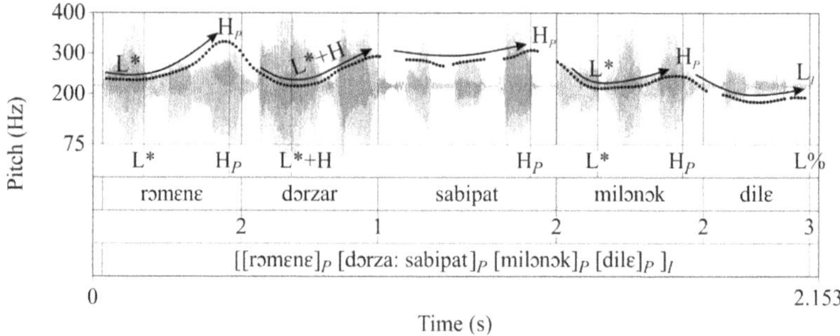

**Figure 5.2.** Wide focus rendering of the sentence *rɔmɛnɛ dɔrzar sabipat milɔnɔk dilɛ* 'Ramen gave the door key to Milan' [Speaker-3; Sex: Female; Variety: SCA].

The intonational contour of IP (15) has been demonstrated in Figure 5.3, which illustrates how the focused constituent *milɔnɔk* is demarcated by low pitch accent L* and focus boundary tone fH$_p$. Here, the pitch contour on the focused constituent, apart from higher scaling on the right edge, does not seem to be different from the contour of WF IP (14) seen in Figure 5.2. We assume that the similarity between these two realisations is caused because the position of the constituent receiving CF pitch accent in (15) and that of the constituent bearing default WF nuclear pitch accent in (14) is identical. In both instances, the right edge is demarcated by high prosodic boundary tone (H$_p$/ fH$_p$), which is not followed by another pitch accent.

In (16), which bears CF on *sabipat*, the focused word forms a P-phrase overriding the default phrasing *dɔrzar sabipat* seen in (14); it becomes apparent when we compare Figure 5.4 with Figure 5.2. The focused word bears the nuclear accent (L*) of the IP on its first syllable, and it is demarcated by a focus high boundary tone (fH$_p$) on the last syllable. The L* pitch accent and the P-phrase high boundary tone (H$_p$) seen on the last syllable of *milɔnɔk*

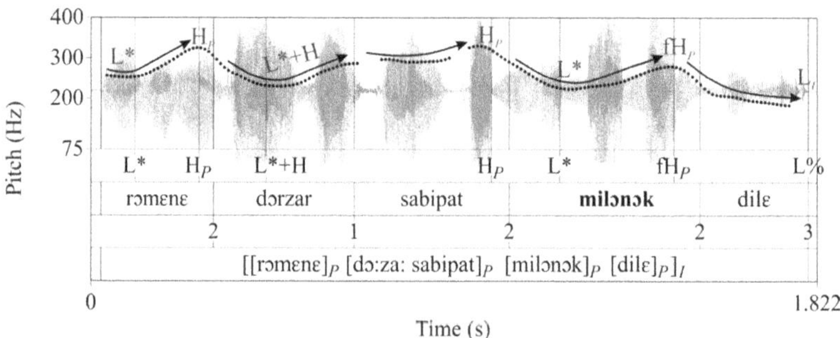

**Figure 5.3.** Here the sentence *rɔmɛnɛ dɔrzar sabipat milɔnɔk dilɛ* 'Ramen gave the door key to Milan' is uttered with CF on *milɔnɔk*. [Speaker-3; Sex: Female; Variety: SCA].

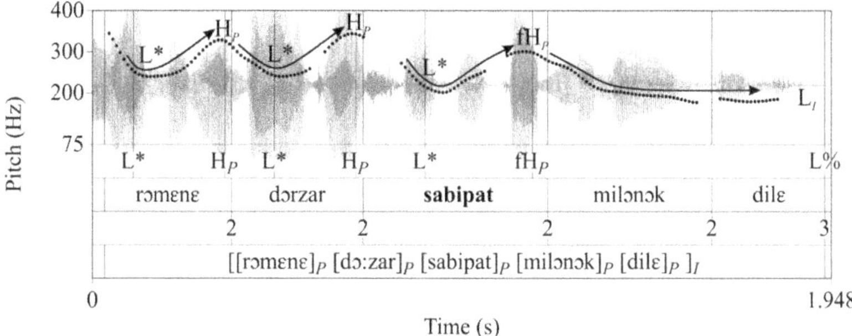

**Figure 5.4.**  Here the sentence *rɔmɛnɛ dɔrzar sabipat milɔnɔk dilɛ* (Ramen gave the door key to Milan) is uttered with CF on *sabipat*. [Speaker-3; Sex: Female; Variety: SCA].

in Figure 5.2 is not realised in Figure 5.4. Since in (16), *milɔnɔk* occurs in a post-focus environment, it undergoes PFC (see section 5.1.4) and has to compromise its tonal specifications. As such, we get a smooth fall through the post-focus sequence until the IP boundary, which is specified for $L_I$ IP boundary tone.

When CF falls on *dɔrzar*, as is the case in (17), it forms a P-phrase with $L^*fH_P$ pitch contour, while in WF context (14), the same word forms a P-phrase together with *sabipat* parallel to a Noun Phrase at the syntactic level. Succeeding the focus, all potential P-phrases (which are otherwise intonationally realised in WF condition (14)) are tonally compromised. It is only the low IP boundary tone ($L_I$) that remains intact. As can be seen in Figure 5.5, in the post-focus sequence, the $F_0$ curve shows a smooth fall until the IP boundary. Though all the constituents in this sequence undergo PFC of pitch, they retain their prosodic phrasing (see section 5.1.4 for details).

In the next IP (18), CF is on the IP initial constituent *rɔmɛnɛ*, which is assigned $L^*fH_P$ pitch specifications. The intonational realisation of (18),

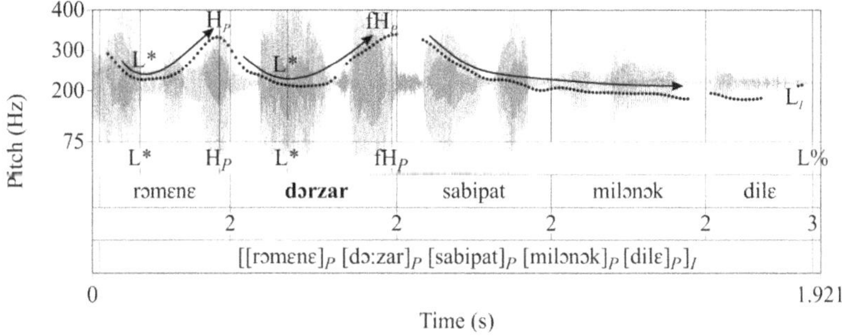

**Figure 5.5.**  Here the sentence *rɔmɛnɛ dɔrzar sabipat milɔnɔk dilɛ* (Ramen gave the door key to Milan) is uttered with CF on *dɔrzar*. [Speaker-3; Sex: Female; Variety: SCA].

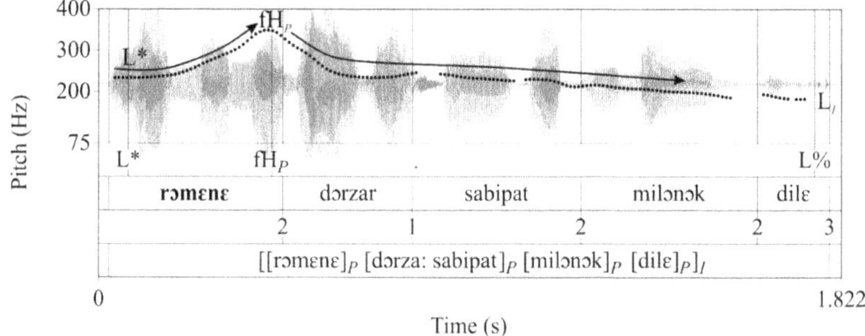

**Figure 5.6.** Intonational contour of the IP *rɔmɛnɛ dɔrzar sabipat milɔnɔk dilɛ* 'Ramen gave the door key to Milan' uttered with CF on *rɔmɛnɛ*. [Speaker-3; Sex: Female; Variety: SCA].

displayed in Figure 5.6, shows how *rɔmɛnɛ* is characterised by a rising contour.

In Figure 5.6, the low pitch accent is realised on the first syllable and the focus high boundary tone fH$_p$ is manifested on the final syllable of the focused constituent *rɔmɛnɛ*. The entire post-focus string *dɔrzar sabipat milɔnɔk dilɛ* displays a smooth fall demonstrating a tonally under-specified prosodic sequence. In the next IP (19), the IP final constituent *dilɛ* receiving CF forms a P-phrase, and it is also designated by L*fH$_p$ pitch specification. The intonational contour is illustrated in Figure 5.7.

In Figure 5.7, the focused constituent *dilɛ* shows a rising contour on it. The final syllable of the constituent right aligns with two prosodic boundaries, CF P-phrase boundary and IP final boundary, and it exhibits the tones associated with both boundaries: fH$_p$ and L$_I$ respectively. As such, we get a high-fall on the final syllable of *dilɛ* buttressing our claim that in SCA, CF triggers the insertion of P-phrase boundaries associated with both left and

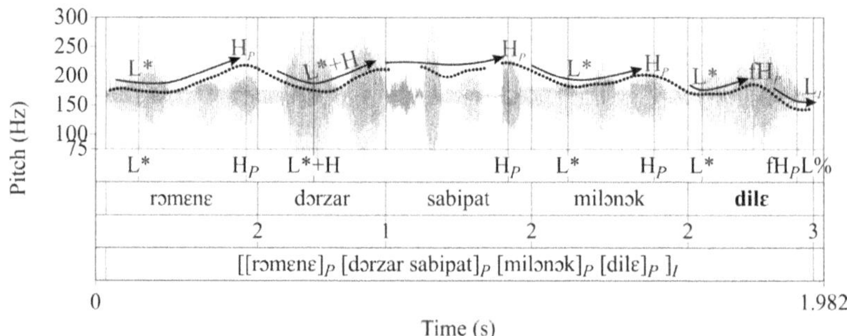

**Figure 5.7.** Intonational contour of the IP *rɔmɛnɛ dɔrzar sabipat milɔnɔk dilɛ* 'Ramen gave the door key to Milan' uttered with CF on *dilɛ*. [Speaker-2; Sex: Male; Variety: SCA].

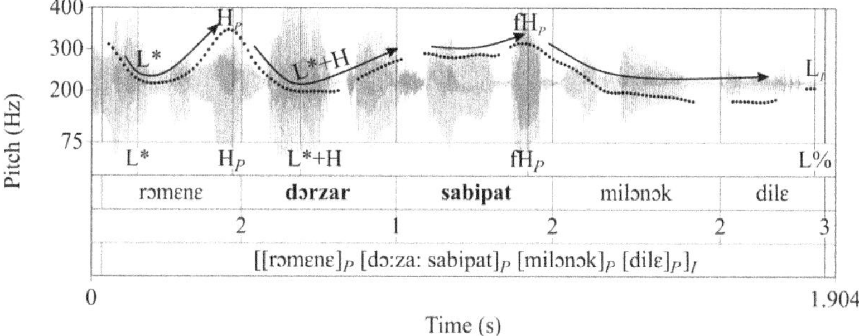


**Figure 5.8.** Here the sentence *rɔmɛnɛ dɔrzar sabipat milɔnɔk dilɛ* (Ramen gave the door key to Milan) is uttered with CF on *dɔrzar sabipat*. [Speaker-3; Sex: Female; Variety: SCA].

right edges of the focused constituent, which is characterised by L*fH$_p$ pitch contour. It further validates our claim that 'f' marked tones are resilient to tonal compromise.

However, with longer strings of focused constituents, the CF pitch contour may be produced with a steeper rise. In sentence (20), *dɔrzar sabipat* is in focus and, as a result, the two P-words *dɔrzar* and *sabipat* form the nuclear P-phrase.

In Figure 5.8, the nuclear pitch accent is realised on the first syllable *dɔr* of *dɔrzar*. After a swift rise on the second syllable, the $F_0$ track maintains a plateau until the final syllable *pat* of *sabipat* where the focus domain is demarcated by a focus high boundary tone fH$_p$. In such cases, where focus is on a longer sequence, CF smooth rise (L*fH$_p$) may be realised as L*+H fH$_p$[7]. The post-focus constituents *milɔnɔk* and *dilɛ* display a fall.

---

[7] One of the reviewers inquired why the trailing tone of L*+H pitch accent should not be an H$_p$, and whether L*+HH$_p$ is different from the sequence L*H$_p$L*H$_p$ only in terms of the presence or absence of L* between two H$_p$s in the latter. In our study, the motivation for proposing the first high tone as a trailing tone is derived from the segmental processes taking place within the domain with L*+HH$_p$ tonal specification. If L*+HH$_p$ is replaced by L*H$_p$L*H$_p$ pitch pattern, the latter will insert a prosodic boundary between the two rises and thus block any of the segmental processes discussed in section 2.2.1 and section 5.1.2. For instance, in Figure 5.10, /kʰ/ → [χ] spirantisation is accommodated between *rɔmɛnɛ* and *kʰɔgɛnɔk* since they together form a single phonological domain *rɔmɛnɛ kʰɔgɛnɔk* with L*+HH$_p$ specification. If they are assigned L*H$_p$L*H$_p$, both P-words will form separate phonological domains, and this will block /kʰ/ → [χ] spirantisation across P-phrase boundaries as is the case in Figure 5.9.

### 5.1.2 Segmental evidence

Apart from intonational characteristics, a constituent with CF serves as a phonological domain which licenses segmental processes like /r/ deletion and intervocalic spirantisation of aspirated plosives to take place focus domain internally. These processes are blocked across prosodic boundaries (see section 2.2.1).

The sentences given in (15) to (20) bear evidence that the focus domain initiates a separate phonological domain from the rest of phonological constituents. In (16) and (17), the word final /r/ of *dɔrzar* is retained as it is followed by a P-phrase boundary. In (16), where *sabipat* receives CF, a prosodic boundary is inserted before the focused constituent, and in (17) *dɔrzar* constitutes a P-phrase as a result of CF on it. On the other hand, in the contexts presented above, *dɔrzar sabipat* retains its prosodic phrasing in pre-focus (15) and (19), focus (20) and post-focus (18) environments. On such occasions, being placed in a phrase internal position, the word final /r/ of *dɔrzar* optionally undergoes deletion and is compensated by lengthening the vowel immediately preceding it.

In (21), we further see how spirantisation (see section 2.2.1) is accommodated across P-words constituting a P-phrase. For example in (21) and (22), [kʰ] spirantisation is accommodated and blocked respectively within and outside CF initiated P-phrase domain.

$$L^* \qquad H_P \quad L^*{+}H \qquad\qquad fH_P \qquad\qquad\qquad\qquad\qquad L_I$$

21) [[madʰɔb]$_P$ **[kɔmɔla kʰa-boloi]**$_P$ [kʰɔgɛn-ɔr    gʰɔr-ɔloi]$_P$   [go-is-ɛ]$_P$]$_I$

                [x]         [kʰ]         [ɣ]

Madhab    oranges  eat-to       Khagen-GEN house-DAT go-PRF-3

Madhab went to Khagen's house to eat oranges

$$L^* \quad H_P \ L^* \quad H_P \quad L^* \qquad fH_P \qquad\qquad\qquad\qquad L_I$$

22) [[madʰɔb]$_P$ [kɔmɔla]$_P$ **[kʰa-boloi]**$_P$    [kʰɔgɛn-ɔr    gʰɔr-ɔloi]$_P$ [go-is-ɛ]$_P$]$_I$

                [kʰ]            [kʰ]         [ɣ]

In (21), *kɔmɔla kʰaboloi* constitutes a P-phrase since it receives CF; as a result, the word initial [kʰ] of *kʰaboloi* gets an intervocalic environment across P-word boundaries, and consequently spirantises to [x]. The P-phrase boundary associated with the left edge of *kʰɔgɛnɔr* blocks such spirantisation of the initial [kʰ] of *kʰɔgɛnɔr*. Further, in the case of (22), the [kʰ] spirantisation of *kʰaboloi* reported in (21) is not seen, since CF on *kʰaboloi* leads to the insertion of a prosodic boundary before the focused constituent. Thus, we see how constituents with CF trigger p-phrase formation, which accommodates segmental processes within it.

### 5.1.3  Pre-focus constituent

Besides triggering a P-phrase corresponding to the focused constituent, CF exercises an optional phrasing effect on the pre-focus constituents, especially with shorter strings of utterances. The WF utterance in (23) is produced with four P-phrases: *rɔmɛnɛ*, *kʰɔgɛnɔk*, *matiboloi* and *goisɛ*, where *matiboloi* bears the nuclear accent. The intonational pattern of the utterance is shown in Figure 5.9.

$$\text{L*} \qquad \text{H}_P \qquad \text{L*} \qquad \text{H}_P \qquad \text{L*} \qquad \text{H}_P \qquad \qquad \text{L}_I$$

23)  [[rɔmɛn-ɛ]$_P$    [kʰɔgɛn-ɔk]$_P$    [mat-iboloi]$_P$   [go-is-ɛ]$_P$]$_I$

Ramen-NOM   Khagen-ACC   call-to          go-PRF-3

Ramen went to call Khagen.

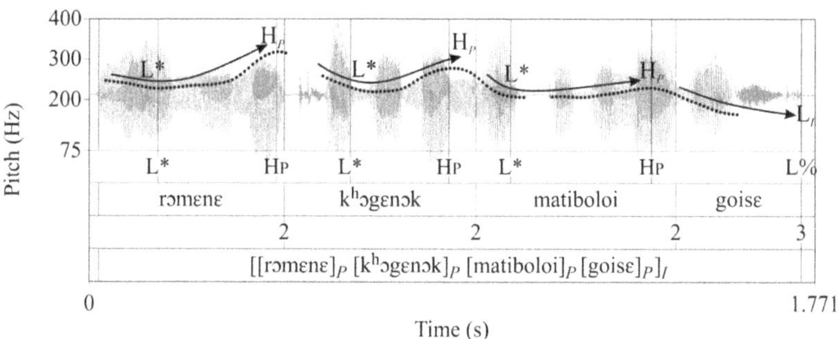



**Figure 5.9.** The WF rendering of the sentence *rɔmɛnɛ kʰɔgɛnɔk matiboloi goisɛ* 'Ramen went to call Khagen' [Speaker-4; Sex: Female; Variety: SCA].

When sentence (23) is produced with CF on *matiboloi*, as is the case in (24), we can see that the pre-focus constituents behave as a single P-phrase with bitonal pitch accent L*+H and high boundary tone H$_P$ (Figure 5.10).

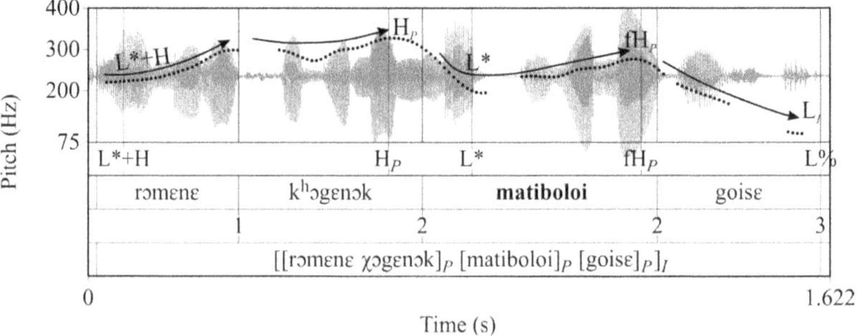

Figure 5.10. Annotated contour of the sentence *rɔmɛnɛ khɔgɛnɔk matiboloi gɔisɛ* (Ramen went to call Khagen) uttered with CF on *matiboloi*. [Speaker-4; Sex: Female; Variety: SCA].

$$L^*{+}H \qquad\qquad H_P \qquad L^* \quad fH_P \qquad\qquad L_I$$

24)  [[rɔmɛn-ɛ    kʰɔgɛn-ɔk]$_P$   **[mat-iboloi]**$_P$   [gɔ-is-ɛ]$_P$]$_I$

The intonationally marked pre-focus P-phrase in Figure 5.10 accommodates intervocalic spirantisation within its domain across P-word boundaries. The word initial [kʰ] in *kʰɔgɛnɔk* is produced as its fricativised version [x] (mentioned in the fourth tier of Figure 5.10). This segmental process of assimilation is blocked in (23), as *rɔmɛnɛ* and *kʰɔgɛnɔk* belong to two different phonological domains.

Although the rephrasing of pre-focus constituents is easily observable in the examples discussed above, in longer pre-focus strings this rephrasing pattern may not be maintained. For instance, in sentences (15), (16) and (19), pre-focus phrases (shown in Figure 5.3, 5.4 and 5.7 respectively) do not undergo prosodic rephrasing. One of the possible reasons may be that SCA speakers find it difficult to articulate longer strings of constituents as a single P-phrase domain with one pitch accent. In order to draw such a conclusion, however, further study will be required.

### 5.1.4   Post-focus constituents

Cross-linguistically, post-focus pitch compression (PFC) is a common phenomenon (Xu, 2011) which has been reported in many languages like Bengali (Hayes & Lahiri, 1991; Khan, 2008), Hindi (Patil et al., 2008), Tamil (Keane, 2014), French (Jun & Fougeron, 2000), Portuguese (Frota, 2000), Korean (Jun & Lee, 1998) and so on. SCA also maintains a complete post-focus pitch compression. We propose that, in SCA, the post-focus sequence undergoes PFC and, as a consequence, all the pitch accents and boundary tones (if there are any) remain unrealised. Since the PFC does not affect prosodic phrasing in the post-focus sequence, it cannot be related to dephrasing. In this chapter, our assumption derives its motivation from the segmental processes occurring in the post-focus constituents.

Here we are going to consider below the sentences given in (21) and (22), but with different focus realisations. The prosodic realisation of the sentence in WF condition (25) reveals how [kʰ] spirantisation is allowed within prosodic phrases and blocked across them.

$$L^* \quad H_p \quad L^* \qquad\qquad H_p \quad L^* \qquad\qquad H_p \qquad L_I$$

25)  [[madʰɔb]$_p$ [kɔmɔla kʰa-boloi]$_p$ [kʰɔgɛn-ɔr  gʰɔr-ɔloi]$_p$ [go-is-ɛ]$_p$]$_I$

                    [x]         [kʰ]        [ɣ]

Madhab       oranges   eat-to        Khagen-GEN  house-DAT  go-PRF-3

Madhab went to Khagen's house to eat oranges

The intonational manifestation of (25) has been instantiated in Figure 5.11, where the spectrogram shows how the segmental processes are maintained as per the schema given in (25).

In Figure 5.11, it has been demonstrated how, P-phrase internally, the segmental process of [kʰ] and [gʰ] fricativisation is accommodated. Word initial [kʰ] of *kʰaboloi* and [gʰ] of *gʰɔrɔloi* spirantise to [x] and [ɣ] respectively since the two words constitute P-phrases together with their preceding

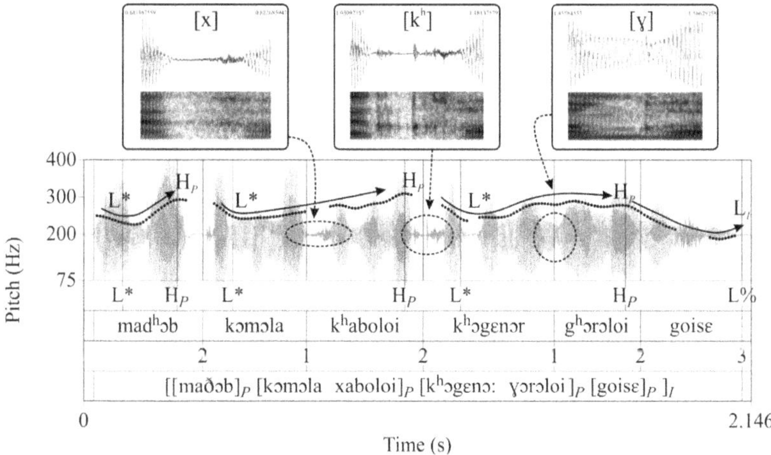


**Figure 5.11.** In the WF IP *madhɔb kɔmɔla khaboloi khɔgɛnɔr ghɔrɔloi goisɛ* 'Madhab went to Khagen's house to eat oranges' [kh] and [gh] spirantization, and /r/ deletion are accommodated P-phrase internally. [kh] of *khɔgɛnɔr* does not undergo assimilation since it aligns with P-phrase boundary. [Speaker-3; Sex: Female; Variety: SCA].

words. On the other hand, [kʰ] of *kʰɔgɛnɔr* does not experience such change although the word is preceded by a word that ends with a vowel (*kʰaboloi*). This shows that *kɔmɔla kʰaboloi* and *kʰɔgɛnɔr gʰɔrɔloi* constitute two separate phonological domains since spirantisation is permitted within the domains but blocked across them.

In IP (26), which bears CF on the IP initial constituent *madʰɔb*, it can be seen that CF leads to PFC on the post-focus P-phrases without affecting their prosodic phrasing.

$$L^* \quad fH_p \qquad\qquad\qquad\qquad\qquad\qquad\qquad\qquad\qquad L_I$$

26)  [[**madʰɔb**]ₚ [kɔmɔla  kʰa-boloi]ₚ [kʰɔgɛn-ɔr  gʰɔr-ɔloi]ₚ [go-is-ɛ]ₚ]ᵢ

$$\qquad\qquad [x] \qquad\qquad\quad [k^h] \qquad\qquad [ɣ]$$

Since the subject *madʰɔb* receives CF, it constitutes a P-phrase and bears the nuclear accent. As such, all the pitch accents and boundary tones (excluding $L_I$) realised on the post-focus constituents in WF rendering (see (25)) experience a complete tonal compromise. Such a compromise, as stated above, takes place only at the intonational level since their phrase level prosodic boundaries are retained.

In Figure 5.12, it has been demonstrated how post-focus P-phrases, in spite of losing their tonal specifications, strongly retain their prosodic boundaries so as not to accommodate phonological processes like

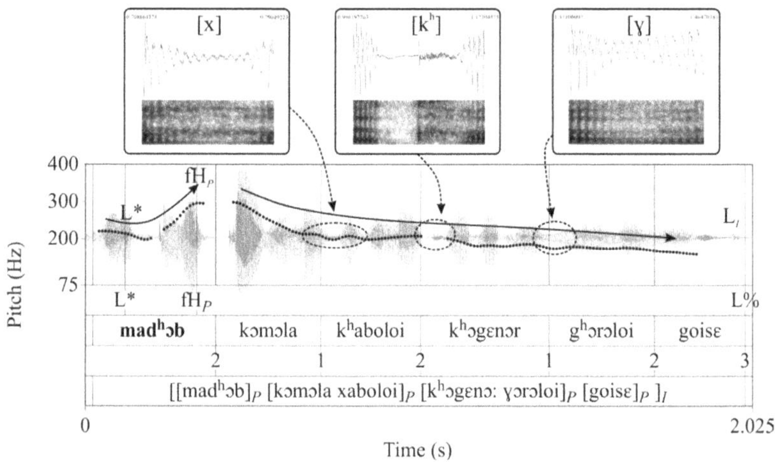


**Figure 5.12.** In the IP *madhɔb kɔmɔla khaboloi khɔgɛnɔr ghɔrɔloi goisɛ* 'Madhab went to Khagen's house to eat oranges' produced with CF on *madhɔb*, the post-focus sequence undergoes PFC. It does not dephrase the P-phrases *kɔmɔla khaboloi* and *khɔgɛnɔr ghɔrɔloi*. [Speaker-3; Sex: Female; Variety: SCA].

spirantisation across their domains: [kʰ] in *kʰɔgɛnɔr* does not undergo assimilation due to the P-phrase boundary (marked up with 2 in the third tier of Figure 5.12) preceding it. However, phrase internally such processes are accommodated: [kʰ] becomes [x] in *kʰaboloi* and [gʰ] becomes [ɣ] in *gʰɔrɔloi*.

This section shows that in SCA CF induces PFC on the post-focus sequence without disturbing the prosodic phrasing among the constituents.

## 5.2   CF phonology in NVA

In section 2.3.1 and section 2.3.2, we have seen that though SCA and NVA declarative utterances demonstrate rising pitch contours on non-final constituents, they mark nuclear accent differently. In the case of marking the nuclear accent of an IP with CF also, NVA adopts a different strategy. At the intonational level, similar to SCA, NVA marks a contrastively focused constituent with a rising contour; however this rise on the focused constituent is phonologically different from the rise we see in SCA. While in SCA, constituents with CF are preceded and followed by P-phrase boundaries, in NVA, such constituents are demarcated only by a preceding phrase boundary. Any P-phrase boundary among the constituents within the post-focus region gets deleted accommodating various segmental processes discussed in section 2.2.2. In the following sections, we will furnish evidence in support of our proposal: section 5.2.1 deals with the intonational aspect of CF in NVA, section 5.2.2 illustrates various segmental processes taking place across focus and post-focus constituents, and section 5.2.3 highlights how the pre-focus string in NVA shows a tendency to behave as a single prosodic domain. Since the focused constituent and the post-focus sequence do not form separate phonological domains, we will not discuss the prosodic aspect of post-focus constituents separately.

### 5.2.1   Intonational evidence

In NVA, a constituent with CF always initiates a P-phrase, which bears the nuclear accent of the IP domain. This is true for any constituent with CF at any position in an IP; such a constituent behaves as the most prominent prosodic constituent in the IP, and it is never followed by another pitch rise. The first syllable of the focused constituent receives a bitonal CF pitch accent (L*+fH), and as it is not demarcated by a prosodic boundary, it behaves as a single prosodic phrase together with all the constituents following it. In this and the following section, different CF realisations of the utterance given in (11) (reproduced in (27) for convenience) will be compared with its WF manifestation given in Figure 5.13.

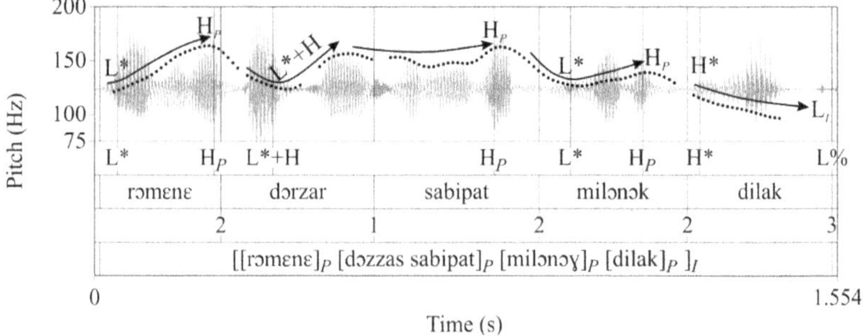


**Figure 5.13.** WF rendering of the sentence *rɔmɛnɛ dɔrzar sabipat milɔnɔk dilak* 'Ramen gave the door key to Milan'. [Speaker-1; Sex: Male; Variety: NVA].

$$
\begin{array}{llllll}
\text{L*} & \text{H}_P & \text{L*+H} & \text{H}_P & \text{L*} & \text{H}_P & \text{H*} & \text{L}_I
\end{array}
$$

27)    [[rɔmɛn-ɛ]_P    [dɔrza-r    sabi-pat]_P    [milɔn-ɔk]_P    [di-l-ak]_P]_I

[z] [s]

Ramen-NOM  door-GEN  key-CLS    Milan-ACC    give-PST-3

Ramen gave the door-key to Milan

Figure 5.13 shows that the first syllable in non-final P-phrases bears the low pitch accent, and the final syllable hosts the high boundary tone of the respective P-phrases. In the case of the bitonal pitch accent (L*+H), under the influence of the trailing tone (H), the $F_0$ track rises on the second syllable, after which it maintains a plateau or a sagging contour until the final syllable where the high boundary tone is realised.

With regard to nuclear accent placement, NVA differs from SCA; the H* pitch accent of the final P-phrase (here *dilak*) is considered phonologically the nuclear accent in an NVA declarative IP. The motivation for assigning a high pitch accent on the final constituent is derived from instances where the first syllable of the constituent shows a brief initial pitch plateau (see Figure 5.18).

Now if we observe the CF renderings of (27) we see that, in NVA, CF constituents are intonationally marked by bitonal focus pitch accent L*+fH. The starred tone is realised on the first syllable of the constituent where pitch value of the $F_0$ contour is at its lowest. After docking at its lowest value, the $F_0$ contour rises immediately, and this rise spreads over next adjacent syllables to the right; the spread of this rise may range from one to

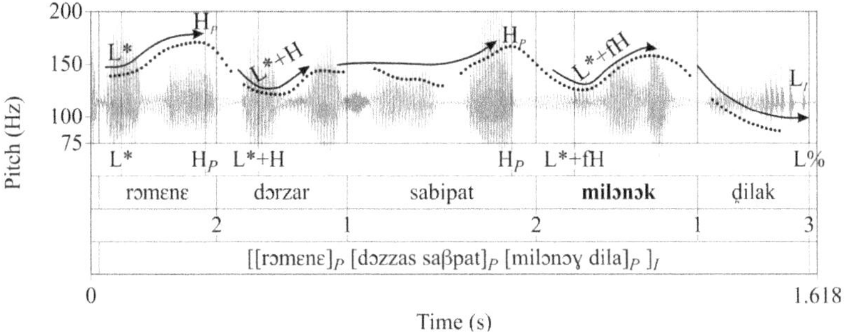


**Figure 5.14.** Intonational contour of the sentence *rɔmɛnɛ dɔrzar sabipat milɔnɔk ḍilak* 'Ramen gave the door key to Milan' with CF on *milɔnɔk*. [Speaker-2; Sex: Male; Variety: NVA].

two syllables. Here we may consider utterance (28), where the CF is on *milɔn-ɔk* 'Milan-ACC'.

$$L^*{+}fH \qquad L_I$$

28)   [[rɔmɛn-ɛ]_P  [dɔrza-r   sabi-pat]_P  [**milɔn-ɔk**  di-l-ak]_{P|I}

In (28), the focused constituent *milɔnɔk* is assigned L*+fH pitch accent on its first syllable which forms P-phrase together with the post-focus constituent *dilak*. Although the final syllable of *dilak* coincides with two prosodic boundaries – P-phrase and IP boundaries – the low IP boundary tone $L_I$ overrides the realisation of any possible P-phrase boundary tone. The intonational contour of the IP can be seen in Figure 5.14.

Figure 5.14, representing (28), displays how CF is marked by L*+fH pitch accent, where the low pitch accent aligns with the first syllable of *milɔnɔk* and the trailing focus high tone slurs over the following adjacent syllables. Apparently, besides a higher pitch excursion on the focused constituent, the intonational contour of (28) does not look different from that of the WF IP given in (27) (see Figure 5.13). However, if we look at the segmental realisation of the IP final constituent *dilak* in both instances, we can see that the constituent is realised in its reduced form (*dila*) in a post-focus position and non-reduced form (*dilak*) in a WF context. In the data collected for the present study, it is observed that in a WF context, an IP final verb is pronounced in its original form, whereas in a post-focus environment they undergo simplification. For instance, *kɔi-l-lak* (do-PST-3) becomes *kɔilla*, *gei-s-i* (go-PRF-3) becomes *gesi*. Therefore, although *dilak* in Figure 5.13 seems to show a smooth interpolation between P-phrase final $H_p$ on *milɔnɔk* and IP final $L_p$, we propose a high pitch accent H* on its leftmost prominent

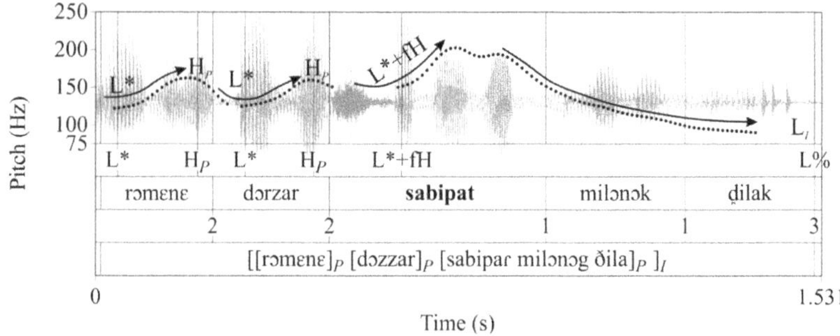


**Figure 5.15.** Intonational contour of the sentence *rɔmɛnɛ dɔrzar sabipat milɔnɔk dilak* 'Ramen gave the door key to Milan' with CF on *sabipat*. [Speaker-2; Sex: Male; Variety: NVA].

syllable. We can derive some more motivation in support of H* pitch accent on the IP final P-phrase from examples (32) and (33) given in section 5.2.2.

As far as the bitonal pitch accent (L*+fH) assignment to focused constituents is concerned, we may consider example (29), which contains the same string of words but bears CF on *sabipat*.

$$L^*+fH \qquad\qquad\qquad L_I$$

29)   $[[\text{rɔmɛn-ɛ}]_P \quad [\text{dɔrza-r}]_P \quad [\textbf{sabi-pat} \quad \text{milɔn-ɔk} \quad \text{di-l-ak}]_P]_I$

$\qquad\qquad\quad$ [z] $\qquad\qquad$ [ɾ] $\qquad$ [g]

In (29) the focused word *sabipat* constitutes P-phrase together with the post-focus sequence *milɔnɔk dilak*. How the IP manifests at the intonational level is shown in Figure 5.15.

In Figure 5.15, $F_0$ value on *sabipat* is at its lowest on the first syllable (*sa-*) and highest on the second syllable (*bi*); this justifies our proposal that CF high tone in NVA is in fact the trailing tone of bitonal pitch accent (L*+fH) rather than being a boundary tone. The pitch contour maintains a smooth fall across the post-focus constituents after the realisation of focus high tone, indicating the absence of phrase level prosodic boundary among these constituents.

## 5.2.2   *Segmental evidence*

So far we have seen how NVA marks the IP final pitch accent in WF IPs differently from that in CF IPs. We have further proposed that, in the latter, focused constituents form P-phrases embracing all the constituents following them, and pitch rise on the concerned constituents is initiated due to the bitonal focus pitch accent (L*+fH), which is the head of the sequence following it. If we assume this to be true, we also conclude that the entire string of constituents serves as a unitary phonological domain and, in that case, it must accommodate phonological processes such as /r/ assimilation, /kʰ/→[x] spirantisation or /kʰ/→[ɦ] debuccalisation within the domain. In this section, CF manifestations have been compared and contrasted with their WF variants (27 and 32) with reference to phonological domain internal segmental processes.

In the WF utterance (27), as has been displayed in Figure 5.13, all the four P-phrases, *rɔmɛnɛ*, *dɔrzar sabipat*, *milɔnɔk* and *dilak* are intonationally specified. As phonological domains, these P-phrases are also the domains of segmental assimilatory processes (see section 2.2.2.). For instance, the word final /r/ of *dɔrzar* assimilates to /s/ under the influence of the word initial /s/ of *sabipat* since the two words together constitute a phonological domain. Further, it has been discussed in the previous section (section 5.2.1) how the final constituent *dilak* forms a P-phrase and receives the IP final pitch accent (H*), and is manifested in its full form /dilak/.

When as a result of CF on *sabipat* (29) the constituent forms a P-phrase, the second occurrence of /r/ assimilation in *dɔrzar*, seen in (27) and (28), is blocked (Figure 5.15). This happens because *dɔrzar* and *sabipat* belong to two different phrase level phonological domains.

Now, interestingly, when *dɔrzar* receives CF (30), it is characterised by the rising pitch accent L*+fH on its first syllable and it forms a P-phrase in combination with the entire post-focus sequence.

$$\text{L*+fH} \qquad\qquad\qquad\qquad \text{L}_I$$

30)  [[rɔmɛn-ɛ]$_P$  [**dɔrza-r**  sabi-pat  milɔn-ɔk  di-l-ak]$_P$]$_I$

          [z] [s]      [ɾ]     [g]

The intonational contour of IP (30) has been illustrated in Figure 5.16 in which we can see how the assigned tones are manifested in terms of $F_0$ contour.

In Figure 5.16, the word initial /s/ of *sabipat* exercises an assimilatory influence on the final /r/ of *dɔrzar* compelling it to change to /s/, highlighting the absence of any prosodic boundary higher than the rank of P-word. This is in conformity with our claim that constituents with CF, together with all the post-focus constituents behave as single prosodic units.

The process of /r/ assimilation is also perceivable in (31), which bears CF on the IP initial constituent *rɔmɛnɛ*.

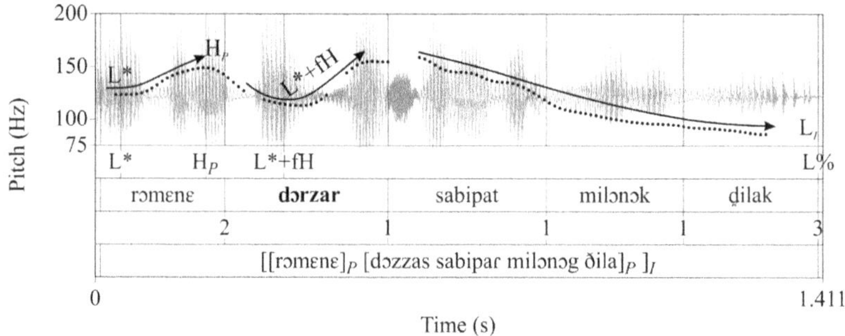


**Figure 5.16.** Intonational contour of the sentence *rɔmɛnɛ dɔrzar sabipat milɔnɔk dilak* 'Ramen gave the door key to Milan' with CF on *dɔrzar*. [Speaker-2; Sex: Male; Variety: NVA].

$$\text{L*+fH} \qquad\qquad\qquad\qquad\qquad\qquad\qquad \text{L}_I$$

31) [[**rɔmɛn-ɛ** dɔrza-r sabi-pat milɔn-ɔk di-l-ak]_P]_I

[z] [s]

In IP (31), *rɔmɛnɛ* forms a P-phrase together with all the constituents following it since, as we have already claimed, in NVA, CF constituents form P-phrases in combination with the post-focus sequence.

In Figure 5.17, the focused constituent *rɔmɛnɛ* shows a rising contour on it after which the $F_0$ contour drops smoothly. As can be seen in the third tier of Figure 5.17, all constituents are separated among one another by P-word boundaries, marked up with 1. The entire sequence, apart from being an IP, constitutes a P-phrase, which accommodates segmental processes such as /r/ assimilation within its domain. The P-phrases seen in (27) are dephrased into one P-phrase initiated by CF and headed by the CF pitch accent (L*+fH) realised on the focused constituent.

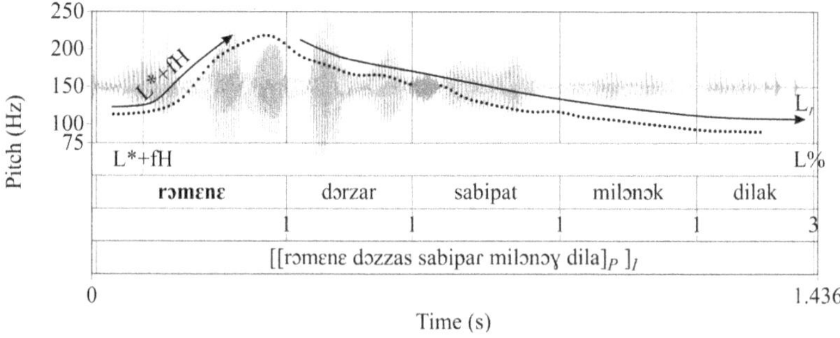


**Figure 5.17.** Intonational contour of the sentence *rɔmɛnɛ dɔrzar sabipat milɔnɔk dilak* 'Ramen gave the door key to Milan' with CF on *rɔmɛnɛ*. [Speaker-2; Sex: Male; Variety: NVA

As mentioned in section 2.2.2, in NVA, P-phrase internally the voiceless velar aspirated plosive /kʰ/ is debuccalised if it occurs in an intervocalic environment in the post-focus string. This intervocalic debuccalisation can be served as a cue to the phonological difference between WF and CF nucleus, and also to the phrasing of the post-focus constituents together with the focused constituent. In (32), the WF prosodic structure of the sentence *nɔgɛnɛ nɔjɛnɔk mala kʰuizlak* 'Nagen asked Nayan for a garland' has been given, and in Figure 5.18 its intonational contour is illustrated as per ToBI conventions.

32)      L*       H_{P}      L*   H_{P}     L* H_{P}    H*     L_{I}

     [[nɔgɛn-ɛ]_{P}   [nɔjɛn-ɔk]_{P}   [mala]_{P}   [kʰuiz-l-ak]_{P}]_{I}

     Nagen-NOM  Nayan-ACC  garland   ask-PST-3

     Ramen forbade Nagen

In WF context, the final constituent *kʰuizlak* bears the nuclear accent H* on its first syllable. The presence of the phrase level prosodic boundary to the left of *kʰuizlak* is supported by the segmental process of spirantisation. For instance, in (32) the word initial /kʰ/ of the verb *kʰuizlak*, as predicted in (8a), does not undergo /kʰ/→[x] spirantisation in spite of its occurrence between two vowels.

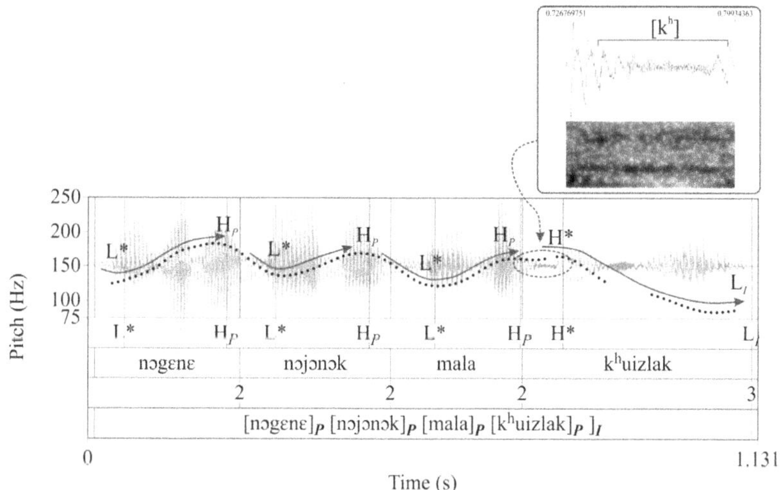


**Figure 5.18.** Intonational contour of the sentence *nɔgɛnɛ nɔjɔnɔk mala khuizlak* 'Nagen asked Nayan for a garland' in WF context. [Speaker-2; Sex: Male; Variety: NVA].

In Figure 5.18, after the realisation of high boundary tone on the final syllable of *mala*, a brief plateau can be seen on the first syllable of *kʰuizlak* designating the existence of high nuclear pitch accent H*[8]. Apart from the $F_0$ contour, the spectrogram also supports the existence of a prosodic boundary that blocks /kʰ/→[x] spirantisation in *kʰuizlak*.

Now let us have a look at utterance (33), which illustrates the post-lexical prosodic structure of the sentence given in (32) but uttered with CF on *mala*.

L*+fH          L$_I$

33)   [[nɔgɛn-ɛ]$_P$   [nɔjɔn-ɔk]$_P$   [**mala**   kʰuiz-l-ak]$_P$]$_I$

[ɦ]

Here, *mala* constitutes a P-phrase together with *kʰuizlak*, and the prosodic boundary between the two constituents is removed. As a result, the word initial /kʰ/ of *kʰuizlak* is provided with an intervocalic environment in post-focus position which compels it to undergo debuccalisation (/kʰ/→[x] → [ɦ]).

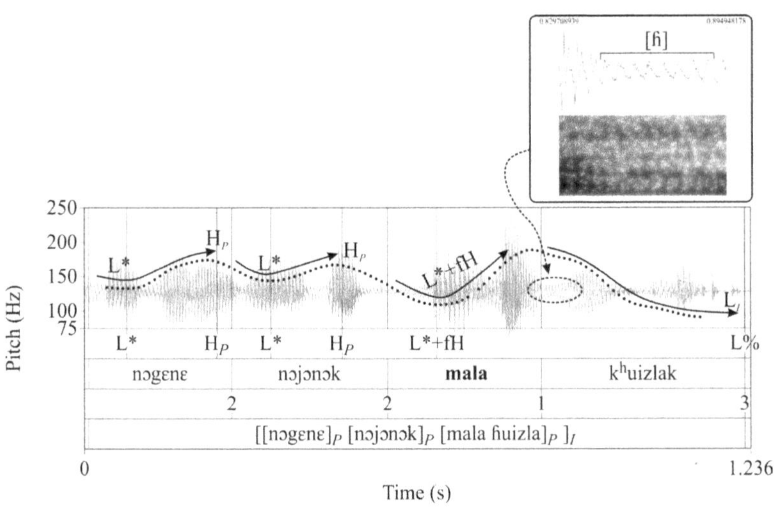


**Figure 5.19.** Intonational contour of the sentence *nɔgɛnɛ nɔjɔnɔk mala khuizlak* 'Nagen asked Nayan for a garland' with CF on *mala*. [Speaker-2; Sex: Male; Variety: NVA].

---

[8]   Though this brief plateau representing declarative nuclear pitch accent in NVA is not always apparent.

Figure 5.19 represents the intonational contour of the utterance given in (33). Here the rise on *mala* is caused by the bitonal focus accent L*+fH, unlike the previous instance (32) where it is caused by a high boundary tone; although the high tone seems to align with the right edge of *mala* in Figure 5.19, it is in fact the high trailing tone of CF pitch accent. In the fourth tier of Figure 5.19, it has been displayed how, placed in intervocalic environment, word initial /kʰ/ of *kʰuizlak* is produced as [ɦ].

In this section, we have demonstrated how CF creates a P-phrase domain taking the focused constituent and post-focus tail together. Within this domain, different phonologically bound segmental processes like /r/ assimilation and /kʰ/ debuccalisation take place across P-word boundaries.

### 5.2.3   Pre-focus constituent

In CF utterances, pre-focus constituents show a tendency to behave as a single phonological domain. Similar to the focus domain, this domain also is motivated by intonational patterns as well as different phonological processes occurring within it. Intonationally, the constituents within this domain share a single prosodic head (pitch accent) and a boundary tone to their right demarcating a prosodic boundary. Further, the segmental processes discussed in section 2.2.2 are allowed within this phonological domain across P-word boundaries. In this section, out of all the phonological processes discussed in section 2.2.2 only spirantisation is discussed.

The intervocalic spirantisation of aspirated velar plosives that has been reported in (9) takes place within a P-phrase domain. Now if we consider the WF and CF utterances given in (34) and (35) respectively, we see pre-focus constituents, *rɔmɛnɛ* and *kʰɔgɛnɔk*, form an independent P-phrase in (35), whereas they constitute two separate P-phrases in (34).

$$L^*\quad H_p \qquad L^*\quad H_p \qquad L^*\quad H_p \qquad H^*\quad L_I$$

34)  [[rɔmɛn-ɛ]_p   [kʰɔgɛn-ɔk]_p   [mait-pa]_p   [gei-s-i]_p]_I

Ramen-NOM   Khagen-ACC   call-to       go-PRF-3

Ramen went to call Khagen.

$$L^*+H \qquad\qquad H_p \qquad L^*+fH \qquad\qquad L_I$$

35)  [[rɔmɛn-ɛ   kʰɔgɛn-ɔk]_p   **[mait-pa**   gei-s-i]_p]_I

[x]

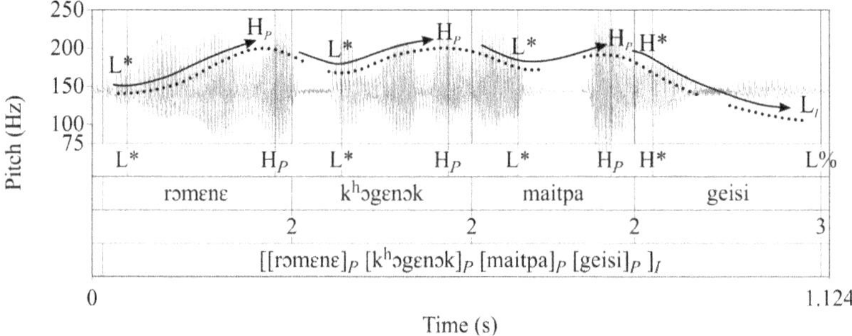

**Figure 5.20.** Intonational contour of the sentence *rɔmɛnɛ khɔgenɔk maitpa geisi* 'Ramen went to call Khagen' in WF context. [Speaker-1; Sex: Male; Variety: NVA].

In (34) each of the preverbal constituents forms P-phrase and is designated by $L^*H_p$ pitch specification. The final constituent *geisi* bears high nuclear accent $H^*$ on its first syllable.

In Figure 5.20, since the non-final P-phrases are characterised by $L^*H_p$ pitch structure, they show rising contours. When we consider (35), which bears CF on *maitpa*, we see that the constituents preceding the focused constituent are grouped within a single P-phrase characterised by bitonal pitch accent $L^*+H$ and high boundary tone $H_p$. The intonational representation of (35) has been presented in Figure 5.21.

Figure 5.21, which intonationally represents (35), displays how the two pre-focus constituents are demarcated by a boundary tone $(H_p)$ to their right and a pitch accent $(L^*+H)$ on the first syllable *rɔ* of *rɔmɛnɛ*. This prosodic phrasing is also supported by segmental evidence, which has been reported in the fourth tier in Figure 5.21. For instance, the absence of a phrase level prosodic boundary between *rɔmɛnɛ* and *khɔgenɔk* is evident from the fricativised production of /kʰ/ as [x]. Due to the lack of a strong prosodic

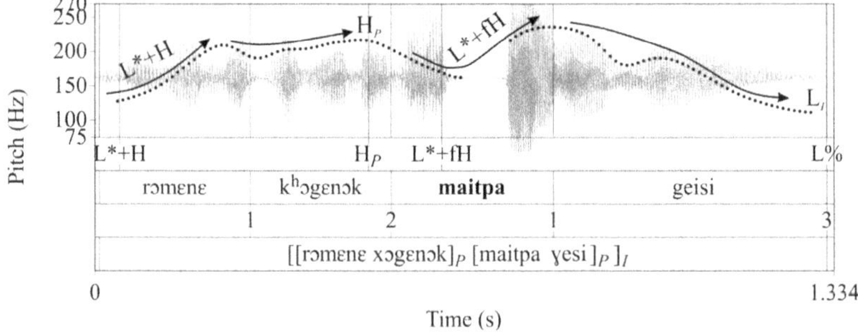

**Figure 5.21.** Intonational contour of the sentence *rɔmɛnɛ khɔgenɔk maitpa geisi* 'Ramen went to call Khagen' with CF on *maitpa*. [Speaker-1; Sex: Male; Variety: NVA].

boundary, /kʰ/ is placed in an intervocalic environment across two P-words which triggers /kʰ/→[x] spirantisation; this process is not accommodated across *rɔmɛnɛ* and *kʰɔgɛnɔk* in (34).

Thus, we see that constituents preceding CF nucleus (as in (35)) tend to behave as a unified phonological domain, which bears both phonological and intonational characteristics. However, with the increase in the number of constituents in the IP, this prosodic phrasing may not seem to be holding true. With longer strings of IP, the phrasing among the pre-focus constituents may adhere to their default phrasing pattern realised in WF condition. If we consider utterance (28), reproduced below in (36), we see that the pre-focus prosodic phrasing adheres to the phrasing structure seen in its WF realisation (27).

L*    H$_P$    L*+H        H$_P$    L*+fH        L$_I$

36)   [[rɔmɛn-ɛ]$_P$  [dɔrza-r  sabi-pat]$_P$  [**milɔn-ɔk**  di-l-ak]$_{P]I}$

This motivated us to conclude that although NVA exhibits a tendency towards forming a P-phrase out of the pre-focus constituents, with longer strings of constituents in the IP domain such phrasing may not materialise.

# 6   Discussion

After an extensive discussion in the previous sections on SCA and NVA intonation, and CF marking, we can conclude that the two varieties demonstrate different intonational contours with reference to WF declarative IPs, and they employ quite different ways of CF marking. SCA, apart from marking CF with IP nuclear tone, extensively employs a demarcative strategy in order to highlight a contrastively focused constituent. On the other hand, NVA concentrates on highlighting the prosodic prominence of the focused constituent by assigning a bitonal focus pitch accent L*+fH. The focused constituent is never demarcated to its right.

In SCA, the focused constituent forms an independent P-phrase with low pitch accent L* (L*+H in longer strings of focus constituents) and high focus boundary tone fH$_P$, which induces PFC on the following constituents. Consequently, although the post focus sequence retains its P-phrases, it has to compromise all its intonational manifestations. The hierarchical tree, given in Figure 5.22, representing the prosodic phrasing of IP (16), shows how the prosodic orientation of P-phrases in the post-focus string

Figure 5.22. In the SCA sentence *rɔmɛnɛ dɔrzar sabipat milɔnɔk dilɛ* 'Ramen gave the door key to Milan', the post-focus constituents, *milɔnɔk* and *dilɛ* retain their default prosodic phrasing.

remains unaffected by CF manifestation on a particular constituent. In the illustrated IP, CF is on *sabipat*.

On the contrary, in NVA, CF initiates a P-phrase by taking both focused and post-focus constituents, and the resultant P-phrase serves as a phonological domain. This P-phrase is headed by the CF pitch accent L*+fH and demarcated by the P-phrase boundary tone L$_p$. In Figure 5.23, the prosodic phrasing of IP (29), which bears CF on *sabipat*, has been illustrated by means of a prosodic hierarchy tree. Here, unlike SCA, the post focus constituents are dominated by a P-phrase node allowing segmental assimilations to take place across P-word domains.

In contrast to SCA, where CF initiates PFC on the post-focus constituents retaining their prosodic phrasing, in NVA, CF dephrases all the post-focus constituents into a single P-phrase, which is headed by the CF pitch accent L*+fH on the focused constituent. This CF initiated P-phrase accommodates various segmental processes such as /r/ assimilation, velar spirantisation, etc. within its domain (see section 5.2.2).

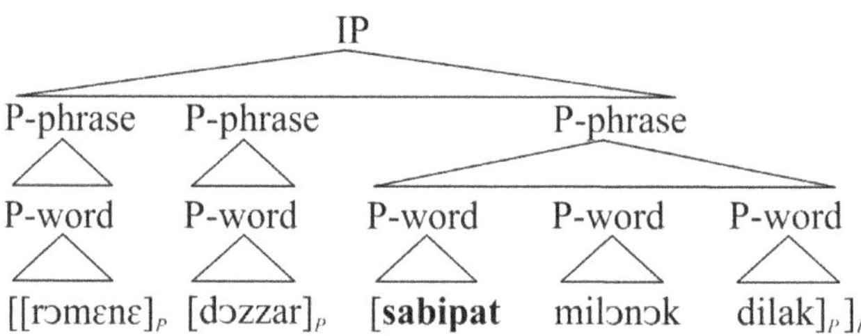

Figure 5.23. In the NVA sentence *rɔmɛnɛ dɔrzar sabipat milɔnɔk dilak* 'Ramen gave the door key to Milan', uttered with CF on *sabipat*, a single P-phrase node dominates the post-focus P-words: *milɔnɔk* and *dilak* together with focused constituent *sabipat*.

Since SCA demarcates constituents bearing CF with the focus high boundary tone, the listener is provided with a cue to the exact stretch of the focus domain. On the other hand, in NVA, due to lack of prosodic demarcation on the focused constituent to its right, the speaker may find it difficult to focus precisely on a string containing more than one P-word. In SCA utterance (38), CF on *kɔmɔla kʰaboloi* is characterised with bitonal pitch accent (L*+H) and high focus boundary tone (fH$_p$), whereas in (37) the focused word *kɔmɔla* is highlighted by L* and fH$_p$.

$$L^* \quad H_p \quad L^* \quad fH_p \qquad\qquad\qquad\qquad\qquad L_I$$

37) [[madʰɔb]$_p$ [**kɔmɔla**]$_p$ [kʰa-boloi]$_p$ [kʰɔgɛn-ɔr gʰɔr-ɔloi]$_p$ [go-is-ɛ]$_p$]$_I$

Madhab     oranges     eat-to     Khagen-GEN house-DAT go-PRF-3

Madhab went to Khagen's house to eat oranges

$$L^* \quad H_p \quad L^*{+}H \qquad\qquad fH_p \qquad\qquad\qquad\qquad L_I$$

38) [[madʰɔb]$_p$ [**kɔmɔla kʰa-boloi**]$_p$ [kʰɔgɛn-ɔr gʰɔr-ɔloi] [go-is-ɛ]$_p$]$_I$

Panel (a) and (b) in Figure 5.24 demonstrate the intonational manifestations of (37) and (38) respectively. In panel (a) and (b) of Figure 5.24, the focused constituents (*kɔmɔla* and *kɔmɔla kʰaboloi* respectively) are demarcated by L*/L*+H pitch accent and fH$_p$ boundary tone. Thus we see that focused constituents in SCA are intonationally demarcated on both sides: pitch accent on the leftmost prominent syllable and boundary tone on the rightmost syllable.

Now in the NVA variant of the utterance (38), given in (39) and displayed in panel (d) of Figure 5.24, CF on *kɔmla kʰaba* is marked by bitonal focus pitch accent L*+fH: the starred tone aligns with the first syllable and the trailing tone with the second syllable of the focused constituent. Unlike SCA, there is no prosodic boundary tone delimiting the focus boundary.

$$L^* \qquad H_p \qquad L^*{+}fH \qquad\qquad\qquad\qquad\qquad L_I$$

39) [[madʰɔb-ɛ]$_p$ [**kɔmla kʰa-ba** kʰɔgɛn-ɔr gʰɔr-ok ge-s-i]$_{P/I}$

              [ɦ]     [ɦ]      [ʕ]  [g]

Madhab-NOM oranges eat-to Khagen-GEN house-DAT go-PRF-3

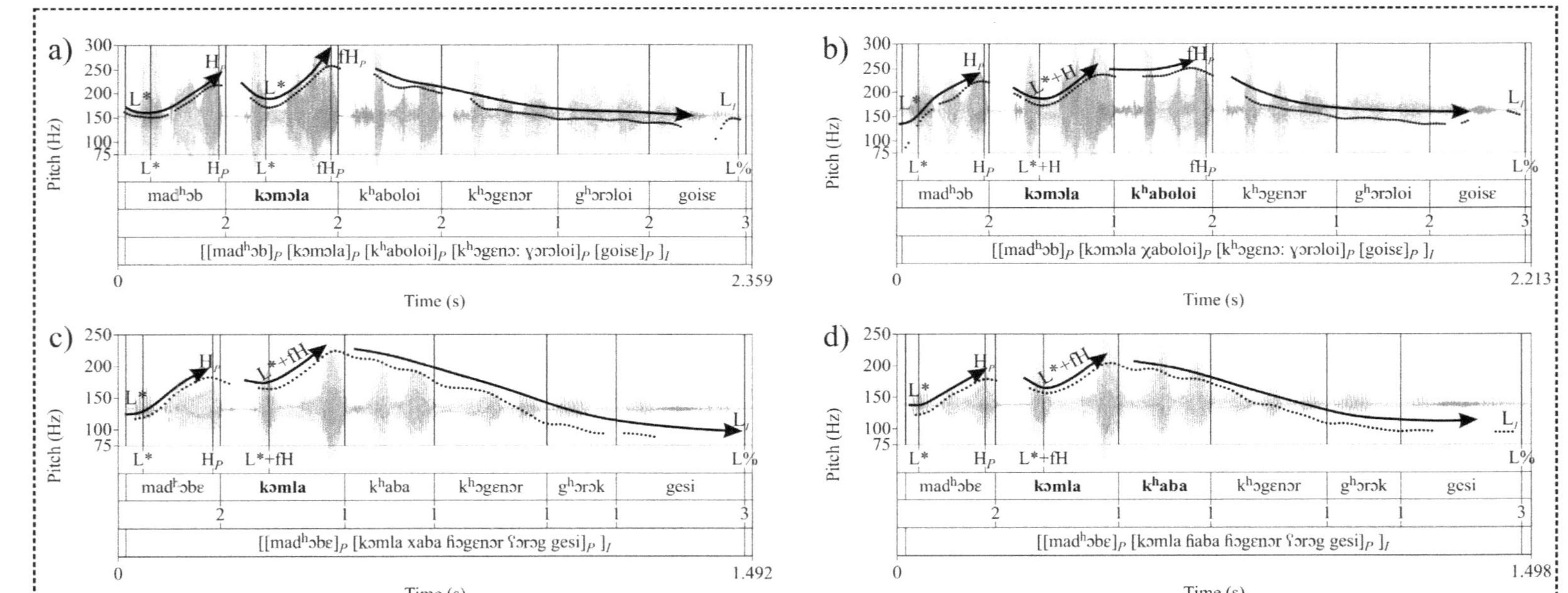

**Figure 5.24.** Panel (a) and (b) are the renderings of the SCA utterance *madhɔb kɔmɔla khaboloi khɔgɛnɔr ghɔrɔloi goisɛ* 'Madhab went to Khagen's house to eat oranges' with CF on *kɔmɔla* and *kɔmɔla khaboloi* respectively [Speaker-1; Sex: Male; Variety: SCA]. Panel (c) and (d) demonstrates two CF realizations of the NVA sentence *madhɔbɛ kɔmla khaba khɔgɛnɔr ghɔrok gesi* 'Madhab went to Khagen's house to eat oranges': CF in panel (a) is on *kɔmla* and in panel (b) on *kɔmla khaba*. [Speaker-2; Sex: Male; Variety: NVA].

In Figure 5.24, panel (d), the CF constituent *kɔmla kʰaba* is characterised by a pitch rise on *kɔmla* since the first syllable of *kɔmla* is assigned the CF pitch accent L*+fH. There is no demarcation of the focused constituent to its right since it forms a P-phrase together with the post-focus sequence; the $F_0$ contour drops smoothly after the realisation of the focus trailing tone fH on *kɔmla*. Now if we compare the phrasing pattern of (39) with that of (40), which bears CF on *kɔmla*, we see no difference between the two IPs.

$$\text{L*+fH} \qquad\qquad\qquad\qquad\qquad \text{L}_I$$

40)  [[madʰɔb-ɛ]$_P$  [**kɔmla**  kʰa-ba  kʰɔgɛn-ɔr  gʰɔr-ok  ge-s-i]$_{P/I}$

       [x]      [ɦ]      [ʕ]  [g]

The pitch contours of (39) and (40), given in panel (d) and (c) respectively, show how focus realisations of (39) and (40) look identical at the intonational level. The pitch contour visible in panel (c), demonstrating CF realisation on *kɔmla*, shows hardly any difference from the $F_0$ curve seen in panel (d), where focus is on *kɔmla kʰaba*. There is no prosodic cue traced in our investigated data for differentiating (39) from (40) other than the context. The tonal alignment on *kɔmla* is precisely the same in both the renderings.

# 7    Conclusion

In this study, we started with a rudimentary description of the prosodic structure of declarative IPs in SCA and NVA, and how various prosodic categories such as P-word, P-phrase and IP are hierarchically arranged in these two varieties of Assamese. It has been shown that the two varieties are different from each other as far as WF declarative utterances are concerned. While SCA places IP nuclear accent L* on the pre-verbal constituent, which is demarcated by high P-phrase boundary tone H$_p$, NVA declarative IPs place H* nuclear accent on the final constituent. Further, the studied varieties differ from each other in respect of CF marking. SCA shows a proximity to Kolkata Bengali (Hayes & Lahiri, 1991; Lahiri & Fitzpatrick-Cole, 1999) and Hindi (Patil, et al., 2008) since it demarcates focused constituents initially and finally at the prosodic level. In SCA, when constituents are focused, they receive low pitch accent (L*) and focus high boundary tone (fH$_p$). CF marking in NVA, on the other hand, demonstrates affinity to Bangladeshi variety of Bengali (Khan, 2008, 2014) and Korean (Jun & Lee, 1998). Like these languages, the focused constituent in NVA forms a P-phrase together with the post-focus sequence of constituents. NVA highlights focused constituents with bitonal focus pitch accent (L*+fH), which heads the succeeding sequence of constituents. As far as the pre-focus constituents are concerned, both varieties behave in an identical manner. They display an optional tendency to place the pre-focus constituents under a single P-phrase node. With longer pre-focus sequences, such phrasing may not be observed.

SCA and NVA are further found to marginalise the post-focus sequence by radically compressing the pitch variation in the sequence. Post-focus pitch compression has been reported in South Asian Languages like Bangladeshi (Khan, 2008) and Kolkata (Hayes & Lahiri, 1991; Lahiri & Fitzpatrick-Cole, 1999) Bengali and Hindi (Genzel & Kügler, 2010; Harnsberger, 1999; Patil et al., 2008). However, there are languages like Tamil (Keane, 2014), where such compression has not been reported. However, SCA and NVA adopt different phonological strategies to address the pitch compromise following CF. With regards to PFC, SCA can be compared with Japanese (Sugahara, 2005) which demonstrates PFC without compromising phrase boundaries in the post-focus domain. This is further supported by an instrumental experiment conducted by Twaha and Mahanta (2016b) which reveals that, in SCA, post-focus P-phrases do not maintain significant durational difference from their WF realisations. Even P-phrase final syllables do not undergo significant duration change. As opposed to complete PFC of pitch in SCA, CF dephrases the constituents occurring after the focused constituent in NVA; the entire post-focus string merges into the CF initiated P-phrase.

The intonational patterns for CF nucleus in the two varieties have been summarised in Table 5.1.

**Table 5.1.** Summary of Intonational marking of CF nucleus in SCA and NVA.

| *Variant* | *Pre-focus constituents* | | *Focused constituents* | | *Post-focus constituents* | |
|---|---|---|---|---|---|---|
| | Pitch Accent | Boundary tone | Pitch Accent | Boundary tone | Pitch Accent | Boundary tones |
| **SCA** | L*<br>Or<br>L*+H | $H_p$ | L*<br>Or<br>L*+H | $fH_p$ | Complete PFC of pitch | L% |
| **NVA** | L*<br>Or<br>L*+H | $H_p$ | L*+fH | ------ | Dephrased | L% |

# Appendix

## SCA sentences

1.  nɔgɛn-ɛ   nɔjɔn-ɔk   mala      kʰuz-il-ɛ
    Nagen-NOM      Nayan-ACC   mala      ask-PST-3
    Nagen asked Nayan for a garland

2.  rɔmɛn-ɛ   nɔgɛn-ɔk   mana      kɔr-il-ɛ
    Ramen-NOM      Nagen-ACC   forbid    do-PST-3
    Ramen forbade Nagen.

3.  nɔrɛn-ɛ   rɔmɛn-ɔk   mama      bul-il-ɛ
    Naren-NOM      Ramen-ACC   uncle     say-PST-3
    Ramen called Nagen uncle.

4.  nɔjɔn-ɛ   nɔrɛn-ɔk   lora      man-il-ɛ
    Nayan-NOM      Naren-ACC   son       consider-PST-3
    Nayan considered Naren as his son.

5.  ɔmɔl-ɛ   rɔbɛn-ɔk   gali      par-il-ɛ
    Amal-NOM      Raben-ACC   abuse     utter-PST-3
    Amal abused Raben.

6.  madʰɔb   kɔmɔla   kʰa-boloi   kʰɔgɛn-ɔr      gʰɔr-ɔloi      go-is-ɛ
    Madhab   orange   eat-to      Khagen-GEN     house-DAT      go-PRF-3
    Madhab went to Khagen's house to eat oranges.

7.  ram          aghʊn-ɔt       tɔka      ghot-iboloi        za-ɛ
    Ram          a month-LOC    money     earn-to     go-3
    Ram goes to earn money in the month of Aghon.

8.  ram-ɛ     xɔpʰura-t       geruwa      pʰul      bʰora-l-ɛ
    Ram-NOM   small box-LOC   saffron     flower    insert-PST-3
    Ram inserted saffron flowers in a small box.

9.  rɔmɛn    makʰɔn-ɔr     gʰɔr-ɔloi   kɔmɔla   kʰa-boloi go-is-ɛ
    Ramen    Makhan-GEN    house-DAT   orange   eat-to      go-PRF-3
    Ramen went to Makhan's house to eat oranges.

10. rɔmɛn-ɛ     atʰija   kɔl     kin-i     beja   thɔgɔn  kʰa-l-ɛ
    Ramen-NOM a name  banana buy-PRF bad   deceit  eat-PST-3
    Ramen badly got deceived by buying *atʰija* (a type of banana) banana.

11. rɔmɛn-ɛ     hotʰat   beja  thɔgɔn  kʰo-wa   kɔmɔl-ɔk   mat-il-ɛ
    Ramen-NOM suddently bad deceit  eat-PRF Kamal-ACC call-PST-3
    Ramen suddenly called badly deceived Kamal.

12. rɔmɛn-ɔr     gabʰoru  bʰɔnijɛk-zɔni  gus-i      go-l
    Ramen-GEN young     sister-CLS     move-PRF  go-PST3
    Ramen's unmarried young sister went away.

13. rɔmɛn-ɔr     bɔga    dʰʊl-tu    mati-t     por-i    go-l
    Ramen-GEN white   drum-CLS soil-LOC fall-PRF go-PST3
    Ramen's white drum fell on the ground.

14. rɔmɛn-ɛ     kʰɔgɛn-ɔk     mat-iboloi   go-is-ɛ
    Ramen-NOM Khagen-ACC  call-to     go-PRF-3
    Ramen went to call Khagen.

15. dʰirɛn-ɛ     azi    eta   daŋɔr  sʊr     dʰor-is-ɛ
    Dhiren-NOM today  one  big   thief  catch-PRF-3
    Today, Dhiren caught a big thief.

16. madʰɔb    makʰɔn  kʰa-boloi  kʰɔgɛn-ɔr    gʰɔr-ɔloi    go-is-ɛ
    Madhab  butter  eat-to   Khagen-GEN house-DAT go-PRF-3
    Madhab went to Khagen's house to eat butter.

17. nɔrɛn-ɛ     dawoni-k    nimɔkʰ  di-boloi   potʰar-oloi   go-is-ɛ
    Naren-NOM reaper-ACC salt    give-to   field-DAT   go-PRF-3
    Naren went to the field to give salt to reapers.

18. nɔrɛn      nimɔkʰ    an-iboloi   go-is-ɛ
    Naren     salt      bring-to   go-PRF-3
    Naren went to bring salt.

19. narajɔn     dɔkait    dʰɔr-iboloi   go-is-ɛ
    Narayan    robber   catch-to    go-PRF-3
    Narayan went to catch a robber.

20. nɔrɛn-ɛ     dʰirɛn-ɔk    an-iboloi    go-is-ɛ
    Naren-NOM Dhiren-ACC bring-to    go-PRF-3
    Naren went to bring Dhiren.

21. madʰɔb        kʰɔgɛn-ɔr        gʰɔr-ɔloi        makʰɔn    kʰa-boloi    go-is-ɛ
    Madhab        Khagen-GEN      house-DAT        butter      eat-to        go-PRF-3
    Madhab went to Khagen's house to eat butter.

22. rɔmɛn-ɛ          dɔrza-r        sabi-pat    milɔn-ɔk            di-l-ɛ
    Ramen-NOM      door-GEN      key-CLS    Milan-ACC          give-PST-3
    Ramen gave the door-key to Milan

## NVA sentences

23. nɔgɛn-ɛ            nɔjɔn-ɔk        mala            kʰuiz-l-ak
    Nagen-NOM      Nayan-ACC      mala            ask-PST-3
    Nagen asked Nayan for a garland

24. rɔmɛn-ɛ            nɔgɛn-ɔk        mana            kɔil-l-ak
    Ramen-NOM      Nagen-ACC      forbid          do-PST-3
    Ramen forbade Nagen.

25. nɔrɛn-ɛ            rɔmɛn-ɔk        mama          buil-l-ak
    Naren-NOM      Ramen-ACC      uncle          say-PST-3
    Ramen called Nagen uncle.

26. nɔjɔn-ɛ            nɔrɛn-ɔk        lora          main-l-ak
    Nayan-NOM      Naren-ACC      son            consider-PST-3
    Nayan considered Naren as his son.

27. ɔmɔl-ɛ            rɔbɛn-ɔk        gali          pail-l-ak
    Amal-NOM      Raben-ACC      abuse          utter-PST-3
    Amal abused Raben.

28. madʰɔb-ɛ        kɔmla    kʰa-ba    kʰɔgɛn-ɔr        gʰɔr-ɔk        ge-is-i
    Madhab-NOM    orange    eat-to    Khagen-GEN      house-DAT    go-PRF-3
    Madhab went to Khagen's house to eat oranges.

29. ram-ɛ        aghon-ɔt        taka        ghoit-pa        za-ɛ
    Ram-NOM    a month-LOC    money    earn-to        go-3
    Ram goes to earn money in the month of Aghon.

30. Ram-ɛ            xapʰar-kʰan        bhal-ke        mar-a        nai
    Ram-NOM        lead-CLS            good-ADV      kill-PRF      no
    Ram did not close the lead properly.

31. Ram-ɛ        bakɔs-ɔt      boga      pʰul      bhɔr-ais-i
    Ram-NOM      box-LOC       white     flower    insert-PRF-3
    Ram inserted white flowers in the box.

32. rɔmɛn-ɛ      makʰɔn-ɔr      gʰɔr-ɔt        kɔmla    kʰa-ba    ge-is-i
    Ramen-NOM    Makhan-GEN     house-DAT      orange   eat-to    go-PRF-3
    Ramen went to Makhan's house to eat oranges.

33. rɔmɛn-ɛ      aitʰa     kɔl       kin-i       beja    thɔg     kʰa-is-i
    Ramen-NOM    a name    banana    buy-PRF     bad     deceit   eat-PRF-3
    Ramen badly got deceived by buying *atʰija* (a type of banana) banana.

34. rɔmɛn-ɛ      hɔtʰat      beja    thɔg     kʰa-wa     kɔmɔl-ɔk    mait-l-a
    Ramen-NOM    suddently   bad     deceit   eat-PRF    Kamal-ACC   call-PST-3
    Ramen suddenly called badly deceived Kamal.

35. rɔmɛn-ɔr      boga     dʰʊl-tu      mati-t      por-i      gɛ-l
    Ramen-GEN     white    drum-CLS     soil-LOC    fall-PRF   go-PST3
    Ramen's white drum fell on the ground.

36. rɔmɛn-ɛ      kʰɔgɛn-ɔk      mait-pa      ge-isi
    Ramen-NOM    Khagen-ACC     call-to      go-PRF-3
    Ramen went to call Khagen.

37. dʰirɛn-ɛ      azi       eta     daɲar     sur      dʰois-s-i
    Dhiren-NOM    today     one     big       thief    catch-PRF-3
    Today, Dhiren caught a big thief.

38. madʰɔb-ɛ       makʰɔn    kʰa-ba    kʰɔgɛn-ɔr      gʰɔr-ɔk       ge-is-i
    Madhab-NOM     butter    eat-to    Khagen-GEN     house-DAT     go-PRF-3
    Madhab went to Khagen's house to eat butter.

39. nɔrɛn-ɛ      goru      dɔrakʰ      di-ba       pɔtʰr-ɔk      ge-is-i
    Naren-NOM    cow       tether      give-to     field-DAT     go-PRF-3
    Naren went to the field to tether cows.

40. nɔrɛn-ɛ       dɔrakʰ      ain-ba      ge-is-i
    Naren-NOM     tether      bring-to    go-PRF-3
    Naren went to bring a tether.

41. narajɔn-ɛ       dɔkait      dʰɔir-ba      ge-is-i
    Narayan-NOM     robber      catch-to      go-PRF-3
    Narayan went to catch a robber.

42.  nɔrɛn-ɛ        dʰirɛn-ɔk      ain-ba        ge-is-i
     Naren-NOM   Dhiren-ACC   bring-to      go-PRF-3
     Naren went to bring Dhiren.

43.  madʰɔb-ɛ        kʰɔgɛn-ɔr      gʰɔr-ɔt        makʰɔn   kʰa-ba   ge-is-i
     Madhab-NOM   Khagen-GEN   house-LOC   butter     eat-to   go-PRF-3
     Madhab went to Khagen's house to eat butter.

44.  rɔmɛn-ɛ        dɔrza-r      sabi-pat    milɔn-ɔk      di-l-a      k
     Ramen-NOM   door-GEN   key-DET   Milan-ACC   give-PST-3
     Ramen gave the door-key to Milan.

# References


Beckman, M. E., & Ayers Elam, G. (1997). *Guidelines for ToBI Labelling.* Retrieved from (original) English ToBI Homepage: https://www.ling.ohio-state.edu/research/phonetics/E_ToBI/

Beckman, M. E., & Pierrehumbert, J. B. (1986). Intonational structure in Japanese and English. *Phonology Yearbook, 3*, 255–309. https://doi.org/10.1017/S095267570000066X

Boersma, P., & Weenink, D. (2015). *Praat: Doing Phonetics by Computer [Computer Program].* Version 5.4.09. Retrieved from https://www.fon.hum.uva.nl/praat/

Bruce, G. (1977). *Swedish Word Accents in Sentence Perspective.* Lund: Gleerup.

Census Report. (2001). *Census of India – Statement1 (Abstract of speakers' strength of languages and mother tongues – 2001).* Retrieved in October 12, 2013, from Census of India: http://www.censusindia.gov.in/Census_Data_2001/Census_Data_Online/Language/Statement1.htm

Cruttenden, A. (1997). *Intonation* (2nd ed.). Cambridge: Cambridge University Press.

Dutta, H. (2010). *Role of Strength Relations in the Patterning of Segmental Speech Sounds: Evidence from Indian Langauges* (Doctoral dissertation). Retrieved in May 14, 2017, from http://shodhganga.inflibnet.ac.in/handle/10603/32183

Dutta Baruah, P. N. (2007). *A Contrastive Analysis of the Morphological Aspects of Assamese and Oriya.* Mysore: Central Institute of Indian Languages.

Féry, C. (2010). Indian languages as intonational 'phrase languages'. In I. Hasnain & S. Chaudhury (Eds.), *Problematizing Language Studies: Cultural, Theoretical and Applied Perspectives – Essays in Honor of Rama Kant Agnihotri* (pp. 288–312). Delhi: Aakar Books.

Féry, C. (2013). Focus as prosodic alignment. *Natural Language and Linguistic Theory*, 683–734. https://doi.org/10.1007/s11049-013-9195-7

Féry, C., Hörnig, R., & Pahaut, S. (2010). Correlates of phrasing in French and German from an experiment with semi-spontaneous speech. In C. Gabriel & C. Lleó (Eds.), *Intonational Phrasing in Romance and Germanic: Cross-linguistic and Bilingual Studies* (pp. 11–41). University of Hamburg: John Benjamins Publishing Company.

Fitzpatrick-Cole, J. (1991). The Minimal Word in Bengali. In A. Halpern (Ed.), *The Proceedings of the Ninth West Coast Conference on Formal Linguistics* (pp. 157–170). CSLI Publications.

Frota, S. (2000). *Prosody and Focus in European Portuguese. Phonological Phrasing and Intonation.* New York: Garland Publishing. 440 pp.

Genzel, S., & Kügler, F. (2010). The prosodic expression of contrast in Hindi. *Proceedings of Speech Prosody 2010*, Illinois, Chicago.

Goswami, G. (1982). *Structure of Assamese* (1st Ed.). Guwahati: Department of Publication, Gauhati University.

Goswami, G., & Tamuli, J. (2003). Asamiya. In G. Cardona & D. Jain (Eds.), *The Indo-Aryan Languages* (pp. 391–443). London: Routledge.

Goswami, U. (1958). *A study on Kamrupi, a Dialect of Assamese.* Guwahati: Gauhati University.

Gussenhoven, C. (1983). Testing the reality of focus domains. *Language and Speech, 26,* 61–80. https://doi.org/10.1177/002383098302600104

Harnsberger, J. D. (1999). The role of metrical structure in Hindi intonation. *Proceedings of South Asian Language Analysis Roundtable.* Urbana-Champaign: University of Illinois.

Hayes, B. (1989). The prosodic hierarchy in meter. In P. Kiparsky & G. Youmans (Eds.), *Rhythm and Meter. Phonetics and Phonology 1* (pp. 201–260). New York: Academic.

Hayes, B., & Lahiri, A. (1991). Bengali Intonational Phonology. *Natural Language & Linguistic Theory, 9*(1), 47–96. Retrieved November 7, 2010, from http://www.jstor.org/stable/4047788

Inkelas, S. (1990). *Prosodic Constituency in the Lexicon.* New York: Garland Publishing.

Jun, S.-A., & Fougeron, C. (2000). A Phonological model of French intonation. In A. Botinis (Ed.), *Intonation: Analysis, Modeling and Technology* (pp. 209–242). Dordrecht: Kluwer Academic Publishers.

Jun, S.-A., & Lee, H.-J. (1998). Phonetic and phonological markers of contrastive focus in Korean. In *Proceedings of the 5th International Conference on Spoken Language Processing* (pp. 1295–1298). Sydney, Australia.

Keane, E. (2014). The Intonational Phonology of Tamil. In S.-A. Jun (Ed.), *Prosodic Typology II: The Phonology of Intonation and Phrasing* (pp. 119–153). Oxford: Oxford University Press.

Khan, S. D. (2008). *Intonational Phonology and Focus Prosody of Bengali.* Unpublished Doctoral Dissertation. University of California, Los Angeles.

Khan, S. D. (2014). The intonational phonology of Bangladeshi Standard Bengali. In S.-A. Jun (Ed.), *Prosodic Typology II: The Phonology of Intonation and Phrasing* (pp. 81–117). Oxford: Oxford University Press.

Kiss, K. E. (1998). Identificational focus versus information focus. *Language, 74*(2), 245–273. https://doi.org/10.2307/417867

Kratzer, A. (2004). Interpreting focus: Presupposed or expressive meanings? A comment on Geurts and van der Sandt. *Theoretical Linguistics, 30*, 123–136. https://doi.org/10.1515/thli.2004.002

Ladd, D. (2008). *Intonational Phonology* (2nd Ed.). Cambridge: Cambridge University Press.

Lahiri, A., & Fitzpatrick-Cole, J. (1999). Emphatic Clitics and Focus Intonation in Bengali. In R. K. Zonneveld, *Phrasal Phonology* (pp. 119–144). Nijmegen: University of Nijmegen Press.

Liberman, M. Y. (1975). *The Intonational System of English.* Unpublished Doctoral Dissertation. Massachusetts: Massachusetts Institute of Technology.

Mahanta, S. (2001). *Some Aspects of Prominence in Assamese and Assamese English.* Unpublished Master Dissertation. Central Institute of English and Foriegn Languages, Hyderabad.

Moral, D. (1992). *Phonology of Asamiya Dialects: Contemporary Standard Mayong.* Unpublished Doctoral Dissertation. Deccan College, Pune, India.

Nespor, M., & Vogel, I. (1986). *Prosodic phonology.* Dordrecht: Foris Publications.

Patil, U., Kentner, G., Gollrad, A., Kugler, F., Féry, C., & Vasishth, S. (2008). Focus, Word Order and Intonation in Hindi. *Journal of South Asian Linguistics, 1*(1), 55–72.

Pierrehumbert, J. B. (1980). *The Phonology and Phonetics of English Intonation.* Doctoral Dissertation. Massachusetts: Massachusetts Institute of Technology, Distributed 1988. Indiana University Linguistics Club. Retrieved October 13, 2013, from Janet B. Pierrehumbert: http://faculty.wcas.northwestern.edu/~jbp/publications/Pierrehumbert_PhD.pdf

Pierrehumbert, J. B., & Beckman, M. E. (1988). *Japanese Tone Structure.* Cambridge, Massachusetts: MIT Press.

Rooth, M. (1992). A Theory of Focus Interpretation. *Natural Language Semantics, 1*, 75–116. https://doi.org/10.1007/BF02342617

Rooth, M. (1997). Focus. In S. Lappin (Ed.), *The Handbook of Contemporary Semantic Theory* (Blackwell Reference Online Ed.). Blackwell Publishing.

Selkirk, E. (1978). On Prosodic structure and its relation to syntactic structure. In T. Fretheim (Ed.), *Nordic Prosody II.* Trondheim: TAPIR: Indiana University Linguistics Club.

Selkirk, E. (1984). *Phonology and Syntax: The Relation Between Sound and Structure.* Cambridge, MA: MIT Press.

Selkirk, E. (1986). On derived domains in sentence phonology. *Phonology Yearbook, 3*, 371–405. https://doi.org/10.1017/S0952675700000695

Selkirk, E. (2002). Contrastive FOCUS vs. presentational focus: Prosodic evidence from English. In B. Bel, & I. Marlien (Ed.), *Proceedings of Speech Prosody 2002* (pp. 643–46), Aix-en-Provence, France.

Silverman, K., & Pierrehumbert, J. (1990). The timing of prenuclear high accents in English. In J. Kingston, & M. Beckman (Eds.), *Papers in Laboratory Phonology* (pp. 72–106). Cambridge: Cambridge University Press.

Sugahara, M. (2005). Post-focus prosodic phrase boundaries in Tokyo Japanese: Asymmetric behavior of an f0 cue and domain-final lengthening. *Studia Linguistica, 59*(2–3), 144–173. https://doi.org/10.1111/j.1467-9582.2005.00124.x

*The Leipzig Glossing Rules: Conventions for Interlinear Morpheme-by-Morpheme Glosses.* (2016, Oct 17). Retrieved from Max Planck Institute for Evolutionary Anthropology: https://www.eva.mpg.de/lingua/pdf/Glossing-Rules.pdf

Tomioka, S. (2009). Contrastive Topics Operate on Speech Acts. In M. Zimmermann & C. Féry (Eds.), *Information Structure: Theoritical, Typological, and Experimental Perspectives* (pp. 115–138). Oxford: Oxford University Press.

Twaha, A. I., & Mahanta, S. (2016a). The Phonology of Contrastive Focus in Standard Colloquial Assamese. In Ó. H. Gunnar, A. Farris-Trimble, K. McMullin & D. Pulleyblank (Eds.), *Proceedings of the 2015 Annual Meeting on Phonology.* Vancouver: Linguistic Society of America. http://dx.doi.org/10.3765/amp

Twaha, A. I., & Mahanta, S. (2016b). Phonetic cues to contrastive focus in Standard Colloquial Assamese. In *Proceedings of Tonal Aspects of Languages 2016* (pp. 152–156). Buffalo, New York.

Vallduvi, E., & Vilkuna, M. (1998). On Rheme and Kontrast. In P. W. Culicover & M. Louise (Eds.), *Syntax and Semantics, Vol. 29: The Limits of Syntax* (pp. 79–108). San Diego, CA: Academic Press.

Xu, Y. (2011). Post-focus compression: Cross-linguistic distribution and historical origin. In *Proceedings of the 17th International Congress of Phonetic Sciences* (pp. 152–155). Hong Kong.

Zimmermann, M. (2008). Contrastive focus and emphasis. *Acta Linguistica Hungarica An International Journal of Linguistics, 55*(3–4), 347–360. https://doi.org/10.1556/aling.55.2008.3-4.9

Zimmermann, M., & Onca, E. (2011). Focus marking and focus interpretation. *Lingua, 121*(11), 1651–1670. https://doi.org/10.1016/j.lingua.2011.06.002

Zubizarreta, M. L. (1998). *Prosody, Focus and Word Order.* London: The MIT Press.

**Asim. I. Twaha** is Assistant Professor of English at Barnagar College, Sorbhog under Gauhati University, Guwahati, Assam, India. His field of specialization is phonology, and the majority of his publications are in the areas of prosody, intonational phonology, and acoustic phonetics. He received a Teacher's fellowship from the University Grants Commission, India, to pursue his doctoral degree at the Indian Institute of Technology, Guwahati (2013- 2016). He is enthusiastic about exploring the phonology of post-lexical domains in different languages or language varieties.

**Shakuntala Mahanta** is Full Professor of Linguistics at the Department of Humanities and Social Sciences, Indian Institute of Technology, Guwahati. She specialized in phonology and her research interests and publications are mostly in the domains and intersections of theoretical phonology (Optimality Theory), acoustic phonetics, perception, prosody, as well as endangered languages. By virtue of being in Northeast India she takes a keen interest on various aspects of phonetics and phonology of the languages of Northeast India and has also published on the endangered languages of the region.

# 6
# Intonational phrasing and nuclear configurations of SVO sentences across varieties of Portuguese

Flaviane Fernandes-Svartman, Nádia Barros, Vinícius G. Santos & Joelma Castelo

## 1    Introduction

Intonational phrasing in Romance languages and their varieties has been the topic of a great deal of important recent research. Catalan, French, Italian, Portuguese, and Spanish display variation on how neutral declarative sentences in subject (S) – verb (V) – object (O) word order are phrased. Across these languages, SVO structures are usually phrased together, yielding the (SVO) grouping; alternatively, they may show a prosodic boundary after the subject, yielding the (S)(VO) grouping – with (SV)(O) and (S)(V)(O) phrasing patterns more restricted, or almost nonexistent. The different intonational phrasing patterns are triggered in Romance languages by interaction between syntactic and phonological factors, such as syntactic branching (constituency), prosodic branching (number of prosodic words – PWs), and constituent length (number of syllables), as shown by Avanzi, Christodoulides, and Delais-Roussarie (2014), D'Imperio, Elordieta, Frota, Prieto, and Vigário (2005), Elordieta, Frota, Prieto, and Vigário (2003), Elordieta, Frota, and Vigário (2005), Feldhausen, Gabriel, and Pešková (2010), Feldhausen (2011, 2014), Frota, D'Imperio, Elordieta, Prieto, and Vigário (2007), Prieto (2005), and Rao (2007, 2008).

Regarding Portuguese in particular, research on intonational phrasing in European Portuguese (EP) has shown variation on the distributions of (SVO) and (S)(VO) phrasing patterns for SVO sentences, as well as differences in the syntactic and prosodic factors affecting these patterns. In

Standard EP and Algarve EP, subject, verb, and object are predominantly phrased into the same intonational phrase (IP), whereas in Northern EP and Alentejo EP, the subject is commonly phrased into an IP, separately from verb and object (Cruz, 2013; D'Imperio et al., 2005; Elordieta et al., 2003, 2005; Frota & Vigário, 2007; Vigário & Frota, 2003). Despite this, constituent length and syntactic/prosodic branchingness may promote the (S)(VO) pattern for the first two EP varieties and the (SVO) pattern for the last two, with varying constraint degrees in each variety. The examples in (1a) and (1b), extracted from the corpus used in this study (see section 3), illustrate the (SVO) and (S)(VO) phrasing patterns in Portuguese, respectively.

(1)　　a.　[(A nora da mãe)$_S$ (mimava)$_V$ (meninos)$_O$]IP

　　　　　　The daughter-in-law of.the mother spoiled small children

　　　　　　'[(My mother's daughter in law)$_S$ (spoiled)$_V$ (small children)$_O$]IP'

　　　b.　[(A nora da mãe)$_S$]IP [(mimava)$_V$ (meninos)$_O$]IP

　　　　　　'[(My mother's daughter in law)$_S$]IP [(spoiled)$_V$ (small children)$_O$]IP'

As for other varieties of Portuguese, there are few studies on intonational phrasing, as far as we know (Fernandes-Svartman, Santos & Braga, 2018; Santos, 2020). The present chapter, aiming at a comparison of the intonational phrasing across three varieties of Portuguese – namely, European Portuguese (from Porto, Braga, Coimbra, Castelo Branco, and Évora), Brazilian Portuguese (from São Paulo and Rio Grande do Sul), and Guinea-Bissau Portuguese (from Bissau) contributes to the research in this barely explored field, taking into account unstudied varieties of Portuguese in terms of intonational phrasing patterns. Based on the results described by previous studies on intonational phrasing in EP and other Romance languages, we verified if the Portuguese varieties discussed here behave similarly or differently in terms of intonational phrasing in relation to those languages previously studied. With respect to EP varieties, our hypothesis is that Northern varieties (Porto and Braga) and Central-Southern varieties (Castelo Branco, Coimbra e Évora) show the same behaviour described in previous studies on other varieties of these same regions (see section 2.2). To attain our goal, we analysed pause insertions at boundaries and boundary tones and considered them as cues to identify IPs in all varieties. The nuclear contour configuration of final and non-final IPs was also analysed in order to discriminate similarities and differences among Portuguese varieties.

This chapter is organised as follows. Section 2 addresses previous results described in relevant literature on intonational phrasing in Romance languages, as well as the intonational configuration of nuclear contours and the intonational phrasing in neutral declarative sentences of Portuguese. In section 3, we present the data and the methodology adopted for the analysis. The results and their discussion are presented in section 4. Finally, in section 5, we present the conclusions and aspects of the investigation that need a more extensive research.

# 2 Theoretical background

## 2.1 Intonational phrasing in Romance languages

Romance languages show variation in the phrasing of SVO sentences. Comparative studies of Catalan, Spanish, Italian, and French show a tendency to (SVO) and (S)(VO) phrasing patterns across Romance languages, with different weight of syntactic (e.g. syntactic branching = constituency) and prosodic (e.g. prosodic branching = number of PWs; length = number of syllables) factors (Avanzi et al., 2014; D'Imperio et al., 2005; Elordieta et al., 2003, 2005; Feldhausen, 2011, 2014; Feldhausen et al., 2010; Frota et al., 2007; Prieto, 2005; Rao, 2007, 2008).

In Catalan and Peninsular Spanish, the most common phrasing pattern is (S)(VO), which is triggered by syntactic and prosodic branchingness, as well as constituent length (D'Imperio et al., 2005; Elordieta et al., 2003, 2005; Frota et al., 2007; Prieto, 2005). Nevertheless, the (SV)(O) phrasing pattern is also found in Catalan (D'Imperio et al., 2005; Elordieta et al., 2003; Frota et al., 2007; Prieto, 2005) and in Peninsular Spanish (D'Imperio et al., 2005), but much less frequently. (SV)(O) appears in Catalan as an effect of prosodic branchingness and constituent length: if the object is prosodically heavy (i.e. consisting of more than one PW), (SV)(O) is the preferential phrasing pattern (D'Imperio et al., 2005; Prieto, 2005). Feldhausen (2011) adds that (SV)(O) is the typical phrasing pattern in Catalan when the object is sentencial, e.g. a Complementiser Phrase object, regardless of whether it is light or heavy. This fact suggests that the syntactic structure has a direct effect on prosodic phrasing in that case, independently of prosodic weight.

Concerning the interaction between syntactic and prosodic structures, in a comparative study between Peninsular Spanish and (Standard) European Portuguese, Elordieta et al. (2005) pointed out that differences on the intonational phrasing patterns found for these languages – (S)(VO) and (SVO) respectively – reflect the different syntactic positions occupied by subjects in each language: in European Portuguese, the subject is within the Inflection Phrase (InfP), which contains the verb and the object, while in Spanish the subject occupies an external position with respect to the InfP, which contains the verb and the object.

Taking into account other varieties of Spanish apart from the peninsular variety, it is also possible to find variation in the phrasing of SVO sentences. Regardless of branchingness or speech rate, (S)(VO) is the most common phrasing pattern in two varieties of Argentinean Spanish: *porteño* (Buenos Aires) and the dialect of Neuquén (Northern Patagonia) (Feldhausen et al., 2010). (SVO) is the second most frequent phrasing pattern in these varieties, and (SV)(O) and (S)(V)(O) are almost nonexistent. In Lima Spanish (a variety of Peruvian Spanish), Rao (2007) observes that, in SVO sentences with three PWs, the preferential phrasing is that in which the first two PWs are prosodically grouped together: (SV)(O). SVO sentences with four PWs are divided into two phonological phrases (PhP) of equal length (each one composed of two PWs) in 94% of the data analysed by the author. On the other hand, SVO sentences with five PWs are divided into two PhPs with the first containing three PWs and the second containing two. This suggests that PhP weight is reduced with the progression of the utterance. Barcelona Spanish displays (S)(VO) as the preferential phrasing pattern in sentences composed by three PWs (Rao, 2008). In this type of sentence, there is a PhP containing the subject NP, and another PhP containing the two PWs belonging to the VP. The data from Barcelona Spanish analysed by the author also reveal that, as syntactic branching on subject and VP of sentences in this variety of Spanish increases, prosodic conditions (such as constituent length, weight balance in terms of number of PWs in PhPs, and symmetrical distributions of PhPs in sentences) seem to play a more crucial role than syntactic conditions in determining the phrasing of sentences in phonological phrases.

According to D'Imperio et al. (2005), Neapolitan Italian (a southern variety) displays both (SVO) and (S)(VO) phrasing patterns, with (SVO) as the main phrasing pattern and (S)(VO) appearing when triggered by the syntactic and prosodic branchingness of the subject (D'Imperio et al., 2005). Nevertheless, Feldhausen (2014) reports that in northern varieties of Italian (from Venice, Verona, and Siena), (S)(VO) is the main phrasing pattern. The author suggests that (S)(VO) vs. (SVO) distinguishes northern from southern Italian varieties.

In French, the (S)(VO) phrasing pattern is the most frequent, followed by (SVO) (Avanzi et al., 2014). Factors such as articulation rate and prosodic weight (calculated in terms of number of syllables or in number of PWs), but not syntactic branching, can affect the phrasing, so that S can be phrased

**Table 6.1.** Phrasing patterns in Romance languages.

| Language | Phrasing pattern | Conditions |
|---|---|---|
| Catalan | (S)(VO) | Main pattern |
| | (SV)(O) | Prosodically heavy object or CP object |
| Spanish (Peninsular) | (S)(VO) | Main pattern |
| Spanish (Argentina) | (S)(VO) | Main pattern |
| | (SVO) | Syntactic branchingness |
| Spanish (Peru) | (2PW)(1PW), (2PW)(2PW), (3PW)(1PW) | Number of PW |
| Spanish (Barcelona) | (S)(VO) | Main pattern |
| Italian (Northern varieties) | (S)(VO) | Main pattern |
| Italian (Neapolitan) | (SVO) | Main pattern |
| | (S)(VO) | Syntactic/prosodic branching subject |
| French | (S)(VO) | Main pattern |
| | (SVO) | Short subject or fast articulation rate |

independently, either in slow speech or if the constituent is long. According to the authors, S containing twelve syllables is more frequently phrased separated from the verb, in comparison with an S containing two syllables. Objects are rarely phrased autonomously.

The different phrasing patterns in Romance languages are summarised in Table 6.1.

## 2.2 Intonational phrasing and nuclear contours in Portuguese

Intonational phrasing in Portuguese has been mostly studied as regards the EP varieties. Recent comparative studies across EP varieties show some variation in phrasing patterns in SVO sentences, namely, different tendencies for (SVO) and (S)(VO) phrasing, as well as differences in the syntactic and prosodic factors which affect these patterns. In Standard European Portuguese (SEP), as spoken in Lisbon, (SVO) is the dominant phrasing pattern (D'Imperio et al., 2005; Elordieta et al., 2003, 2005; Frota, 2000, 2014; Frota et al., 2007). On the other hand, in Northern European Portuguese (NEP), as spoken in Braga, (S)(VO) is the dominant pattern (D'Imperio et al., 2005; Elordieta et al., 2005; Frota et al., 2007; Frota & Vigário, 2007;

Vigário & Frota, 2003). Comparisons between SEP and NEP reveal a tendency to form shorter prosodic constituents and a higher sensitivity to the number of words/constituent branchingness in NEP intonational phrasing (Frota & Vigário, 2007; Vigário & Frota, 2003). In the Central-Southern variety of EP (Cintra, 1971), the intonational phrasing was studied in two regions – Castro Verde, in Alentejo (Ale), and Albufeira, in Algarve (Alg) – where distinct dominant patterns were found: (S)(VO) in Ale, as in NEP, but (SVO) in Alg, as in SEP (Cruz, 2013; Cruz & Frota, 2013). In these regions, syntactic complexity and phonological length play different roles in prosodic phrasing: in Alg, the syntactic/prosodic branchingness promotes the (S)(VO) pattern, whereas in SEP, subject length (more than 8 syllables) promotes this phrasing pattern; in the case of Ale, as in NEP, both length and branchingness are determining factors on the (S)(VO) phrasing, although with different weight, since the length is more relevant in Ale, and branchingness is more relevant in NEP.

In Brazilian Portuguese (BP), as far as we know, previous analyses focusing on intonational phrasing patterns are scarce (Fernandes-Svartman, Santos & Braga, 2018). Nevertheless, Serra (2009) presents results for the perception of IP boundaries by BP speakers. According to the author: (i) pause is the main cue for the perception of IP boundaries by speakers; (ii) pre-boundary lengthening and pitch range variation are also cues for the perception of IP boundaries, although the relevance of these cues on the perception of IP boundaries vary; and (iii) constituent length also plays a role on the perception of IP boundaries, since boundaries of long IPs are more frequently perceived than boundaries of short IPs.

With regard to Guinea-Bissau Portuguese (GBP),[1] apart from the description of the tonal events association with the intonational contour of neutral declarative sentences in previous works (Santos, 2015; Santos & Fernandes-Svartman, 2014), there is no analysis in terms of intonational phrasing patterns of SVO sentences, so far.

The intonational configuration of the nuclear contour of neutral declarative sentences in Portuguese has a uniform pattern across varieties. In final IPs, a falling nuclear contour H+L* L% is found in most European and Brazilian varieties of Portuguese (for a representation of this tonal

---

[1] As distinct from Brazil and Portugal, where Portuguese is the first language spoken, in Guinea-Bissau Portuguese is the second language for most of the native speakers. In this country, Portuguese is the official language, that coexists with the Creole of Guinea-Bissau (national vehicular language, and the most spoken language of Guinea-Bissau), and with African languages of the West Atlantic and Mande group, which belong to the Niger-Congo family of languages (Couto & Embaló, 2010).

configuration, see Figure 6.4 in section 3). However, in EP, falling nuclear contour H+L* L% in the North (Porto–Por) and South (Ale and Alg) alternates with a low nuclear contour L* L% (for a representation of this tonal configuration, see Figure 6.4 in section 3), predominant in NEP, and alternative in Ale (Cruz & Frota, 2011; Frota, Cruz, et al., 2015; Vigário & Frota, 2003). In the latter region, the L* L% nuclear contour might trigger ambiguity with interrogatives, which share the same nuclear contour (Cruz & Frota, 2011). Regarding the nuclear contour of final IPs in NEP, Vigário and Frota (2003) show that, as distinct from the standard variety, the trailing tone H does not have a fixed alignment in the structure. For this reason, the authors account for the monotonal nuclear accent L* only. In non-final IPs, a rising contour, mainly L*+H H% (see a representation of this tonal configuration in Figure 6.4 in section 3), has been reported for SEP as the most frequent for inner parenthetical expressions (Frota, 2000, 2014). Topics, which also form separate IPs, show some variation: both L*+H H% and H+L* L% can be found associated with initial topics. In Barros (2014) and Barros and Frota (2015), the same pattern was found in Porto and Évora, where inner parentheticals form independent IPs, and show the same nuclear contour. The same studies report that pause is a frequent cue for inner IP boundary marking in Porto. In Ale and Alg (Cruz, 2013; Cruz & Frota, 2013), L*+H H% is also reported as the most frequent nuclear contour in the first IP of (S) (VO) sentences. Inner IPs are frequently marked with a High boundary tone in all varieties studied by the authors, regardless of the presence of a pause.

In BP varieties, the nuclear contour of final IPs of neutral declarative sentences follows the same nuclear tonal configuration (H+L* L%) as attested for EP (Castelo & Frota, 2015; Fernandes, 2007; Frota, Cruz, et al., 2015; Frota & Vigário, 2000; Serra, 2009; Silvestre, 2012; Tenani, 2002; among others). In contrast to EP, BP displays phonetic differences across its varieties in terms of the F0 scaling of pre-stressed syllables (which can be higher in northern varieties, cf. Cunha, 2000) – or regarding the alignment of the peak (which can be early in northern and late in southern varieties, cf. Castelo & Frota, 2015; Silvestre, 2012). Non-final IPs are characterised by a rising contour (Cunha, 2000; Frota, Cruz, et al., 2015; Serra, 2009; Tenani, 2002; among others), which is composed of a bitonal nuclear pitch accent L+H*/L*+H, followed by a high boundary tone H% in central varieties (for a representation of these tonal configurations, see Figure 6.4 of section 3). An alternative falling nuclear contour (H+L* L%) is also found in BP, in central and northern varieties (Cunha, 2000).

In GBP, the nuclear contour of final IPs of neutral declaratives is characterised by either a falling tonal configuration H+L* L% (Santos, 2015; Santos & Fernandes-Svartman, 2014) – as in BP and EP, or a low tonal configuration L* L% (Santos, 2015) – as in some varieties of EP. On the other hand, according to Santos (2015), the nuclear contour of non-final IPs in GBP neutral declaratives displays a rising tonal configuration L*+H H% or L* (L)H% (for a representation of these tonal configurations, see Figure 6.4 in section 3), both also found across Portuguese varieties.

Taking into account, on the one hand, the characteristics of the intonational phrasing in Romance languages and in Portuguese, and on the other hand the configuration of the neutral nuclear contour in Portuguese as described in this section, our purpose now is to identify the similarities and differences regarding these prosodic characteristics of Portuguese varieties discussed here in comparison with the same characteristics as described for those other languages. Our hypotheses are the following: (i) for intonational phrasing, the EP varieties considered here exhibit the same behaviour already described for other EP varieties of the same regions; and (ii) as for the nuclear contour of final and non-final IPs, EP, BP, and GBP varieties present the same types of contours already described in previous studies on EP, BP and GBP. To achieve our goals, we will use the corpus and methodology described in the next section.

# 3    Methodology

The speech material analysed in this study was collected through a reading task carried out within the scope of the Interactive Atlas of the Prosody of Portuguese (InAPoP). InAPoP is a project funded by the Foundation for Science and Technology (FCT) (PTDC/CLE-LIN/119787/2010) and coordinated by Sónia Frota (Frota, 2012–2015), which aims at developing research on the prosodic variation in Portuguese (European Portuguese, Brazilian Portuguese, and varieties of Portuguese spoken in Africa), building on a set of methodological procedures that enable cross-linguistic studies on prosody. One of the main outputs of the project is an interactive atlas, which can be accessed online at http://labfon.letras.ulisboa.pt/InAPoP/.

Data come from the adaptation, for all different varieties of Portuguese considered herein, of the structure of a corpus used in previous studies on Romance languages intonational phrasing: the Romance Languages Database (RLD) (D'Imperio et al., 2005; Elordieta et al., 2003, 2005; Frota et al., 2007; Frota & Vigário, 2007; Prieto, 2005).The RLD corpus, conceived to be comparable across Romance languages and to examine the influence of constituent length and syntactic branching on intonational phrasing, consists of SVO declaratives designed with all the combinations of two constituent length conditions (*short*: up to three syllables; *long*: five or more syllables) and three syntactic/prosodic branching conditions (*non-branching*: one lexical head/one prosodic word; *branching*: two lexical heads/two prosodic words; *double branching S/O*: three lexical heads/three prosodic words), yielding 76 different sentences. Examples of the sentences are given in (2), (3), (4), and (5).

(2)     Short non-branching Subject, short Verb and short non-branching Object (S = 3 syllables; V = 3 syllables; and O = 3 syllables):

A loura mirava morenos.

*'The blond girl looked at dark-haired boys.'*

(3)     Long non-branching Subject, long Verb and long non-branching Object (S = 6 syllables; V = 5 syllables; and O = 6 syllables):

A boliviana memorizava uma melodia.

*'The Bolivian girl memorised a melody.'*

(4)     Short branching Subject, short Verb and short Object (S composed by N+AP = 5 syllables; V = 3 syllables; and O = 3 syllables):

A nora loura mimava meninos.

*'The blond daughter-in-law spoiled small children.'*

(5)     Long branching Subject, short Verb and short non-branching Object (S composed by N+AP = 10 syllables; V = 3 syllables; and O = 3 syllables):

O boliviano mulherengo mirava morenas.

*'The Bolivian ladies' man looked at dark-haired girls.'*

For data collection, participants were presented to each utterance in a PowerPoint presentation individually (one slide per utterance) – or on a sheet of paper in the case of GBP – in random order. Speakers were instructed to read silently the context and the sentence, and then to produce the latter aloud at a normal rate of speech. Before the production of the target sentences, participants underwent a training session. All participants produced at least two renditions of each sentence.

In the present study, 56 out of the 76 different sentence types were taken into account in the analysis of intonational phrasing, comprising the short, long, branching and non-branching constituent conditions. Non-fluent readings (presenting non-grammatical pauses and hesitations) were excluded, so that a set of 1847 utterances from eight different varieties of Portuguese comprises the corpus of this study.

For EP, data were collected in five regions: Porto (Por), Braga (Bra), Coimbra (Cob), Castelo Branco (CtB), and Évora (Eva) (see Figure 6.1). Ten female monolingual native speakers (two for each region), educated (with different levels of education), aged between 20 and 45 years old produced the data. A total of 1066 utterances were selected for analysis (56 sentences × 2 speakers × 5 regions × 2 renditions – 54 non-fluent readings).

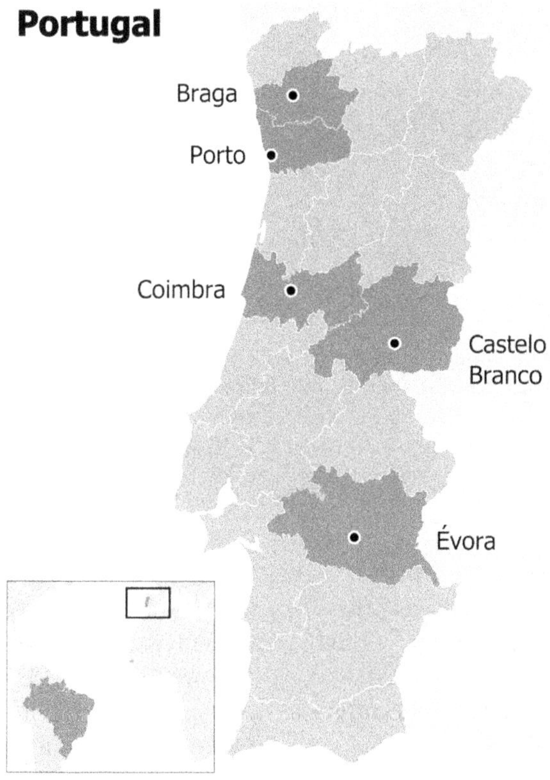


**Figure 6.1.** Map of European Portuguese regions: Braga, Porto, Coimbra, Castelo Branco, and Évora. Source: Adapted from "Map of Portuguese districts with names" by Pacoples/ Wikimedia Commons/Public domain (https://upload.wikimedia.org/wikipedia/commons/2/21/ Portuguese_Districts_Map_With_Names.svg) and "Location Guinea Bissau AU Africa" by Alvaro1984 18/Wikimedia Commons/Public domain (https://upload.wikimedia.org/wikipedia/ commons/f/fe/Location_Guinea_Bissau_AU_Africa.svg).

**Figure 6.2.** Map of Brazilian Portuguese regions: São Paulo and Rio Grande do Sul. Source: Adapted from "Brazil Labelled Map" by João Felipe C.S./Wikimedia Commons/CC BY-SA 3.0 (https://upload.wikimedia.org/wikipedia/commons/f/f6/Brazil_Labelled_Map.svg) and "Location Guinea Bissau AU Africa" by Alvaro1984 18/Wikimedia Commons/Public domain (https://upload.wikimedia.org/wikipedia/commons/f/fe/Location_Guinea_Bissau_AU_Africa. svg).

BP data were collected in two regions: São Paulo (SP) (capital of São Paulo State) and Porto Alegre (RGS) (capital of Rio Grande do Sul State) (see Figure 6.2). Productions of four female monolingual native speakers (two for each region), educated (graduated), aged between 20 and 45 years old were considered and a total of 335 utterances were selected for this work (56 sentences × 2 speakers × 2 regions × 2 renditions – 113 non-fluent readings).

For GBP, data were collected from one region: Bissau, Guinea-Bissau's capital city (see Figure 6.3). However, data collection took place in Brazil, where Guinean undergraduate exchange students, whose stay was no longer than four months at the time, were recorded. Speakers are females, educated (undergraduate students), aged 19, 20 and 27 years old, and bilingual in

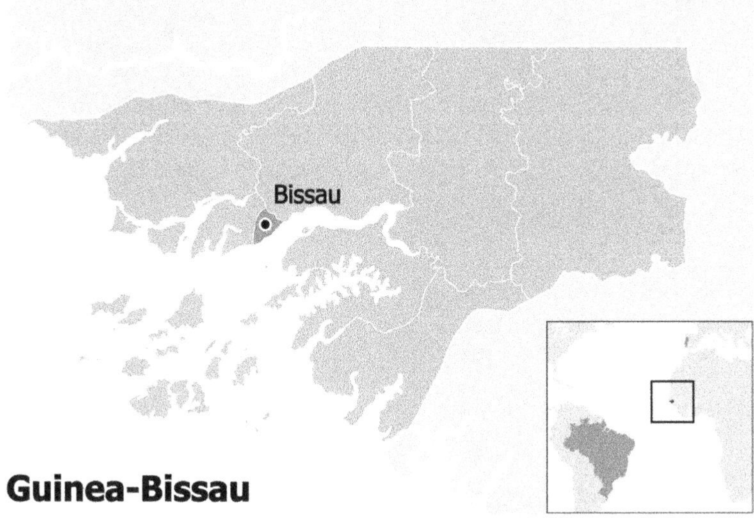


**Figure 6.3.** Map of Guinea-Bissau Portuguese region: Bissau. Source: Adapted from "Location map of Guinea-Bissau" by NordNordWest/Wikimedia Commons/CC BY 3.0 (https://upload. wikimedia.org/wikipedia/commons/6/64/Guinea-Bissau_location_map.svg) and "Location Guinea Bissau AU Africa" by Alvaro1984 18/Wikimedia Commons/Public domain (https:// upload.wikimedia.org/wikipedia/commons/f/fe/Location_Guinea_Bissau_AU_Africa.svg).

GBP and Guinea-Bissau Creole (first language). All speakers learned Portuguese in school, at age seven, and use Guinea-Bissau Creole at home, since their parents speak different African languages. For this variety of Portuguese, 333 utterances were selected (56 sentences × 3 speakers × 1 region × 2 renditions – 3 non-fluent readings).[2]

A prosodic and intonational analysis was made within the Prosodic Phonology (Nespor & Vogel, 2007; Selkirk, 1984, 1986) and the Autosegmental-Metrical approach to Intonational Phonology (Beckman & Pierrehumbert, 1986; Frota, 2000, 2014; Ladd, 2008; among others).

The cues considered to the IP boundaries marking were: boundary tones, signalled by a *High* tone (displaying a higher pitch than the average pitch level of the utterance) or a *Low* tone (displaying a lower pitch than the average pitch level of the utterance) marking a prosodic break, and pauses, defined as a stretch of silence present at the phrasing boundary (Frota et al., 2007). These cues were detected based on the perceptual and acoustic analysis of the data. The nuclear contour configuration of both final and

---

[2] Data for GBP were collected within the third author's Master dissertation (Santos, 2015).

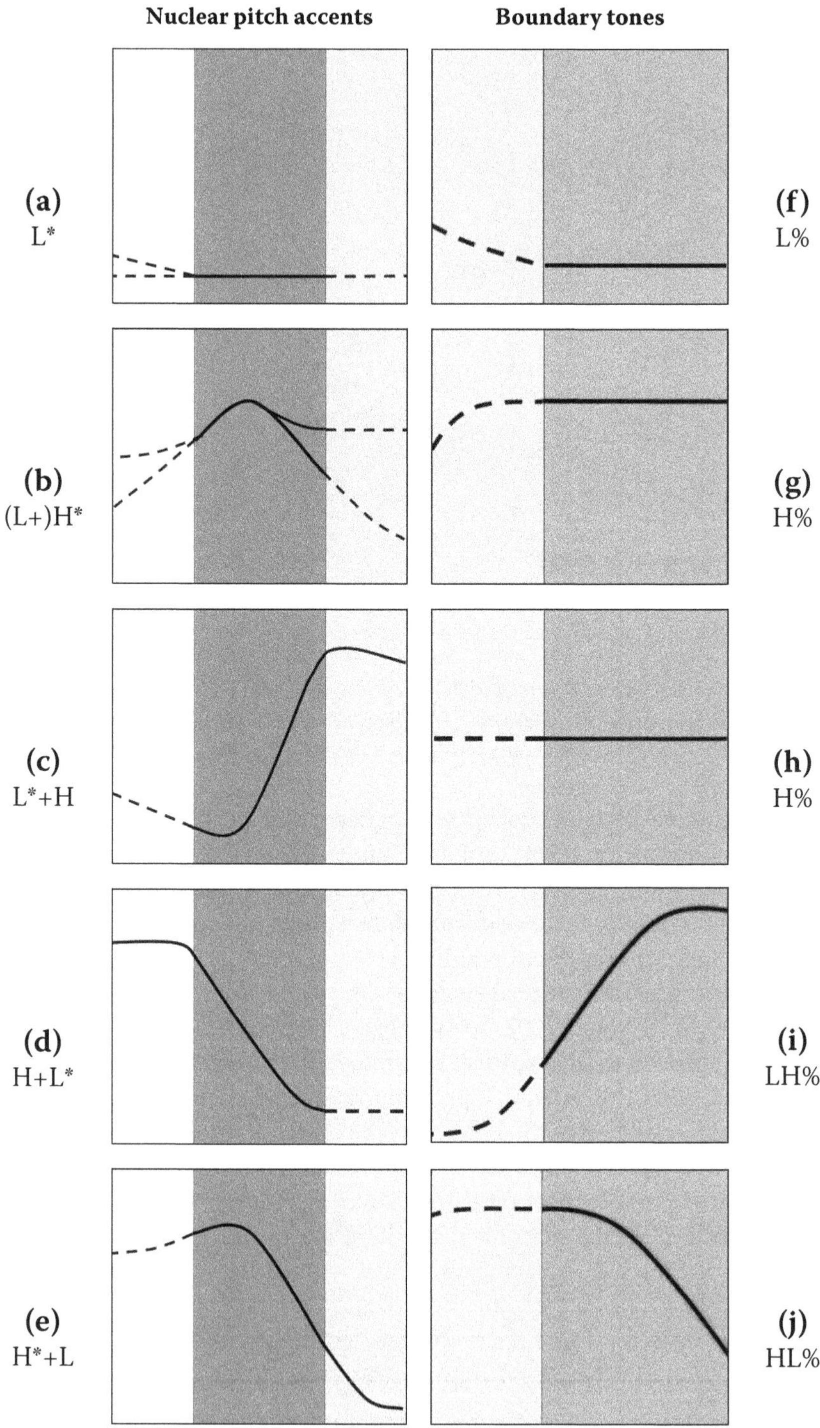



**Figure 6.4.** Inventory of nuclear pitch accents and boundary tones in Portuguese and their schematic representations according to P_ToBI (Frota, Oliveira, Cruz, & Vigário, 2015).

non-final IPs, i.e., the part of the intonational contour of final and non-final IPs with which the nuclear pitch accent and the boundary tone are associated, was also annotated, in order to analyse similarities and differences across varieties. Data were annotated in Praat (Boersma & Weenink, 2015), where three tiers were created: (i) 'Tones', where a phonological annotation of nuclear pitch accents and boundary tones was made, according to P_ToBI system of prosodic annotation (Frota, 2014; Frota, Cruz, et al., 2015; Frota, Oliveira, Cruz, & Vigário, 2015) for all varieties of Portuguese – see Figure 6.4 for the representation of nuclear pitch accents and boundary tones according to P_ToBI; (ii) 'Orthography', where a word by word orthographic transcription was made; and (iii) 'BI' (break indices), where prosodic boundaries of intonational phrases were annotated (using P_ToBI and InAPoP criteria, according to which: 0 = prosodic clitic, 1 = prosodic word, 2 = prosodic word group,[3] 3 = phonological phrase, and 4 = intonational phrase). Figure 6.5 illustrates this annotation.

Each data set of a variety of Portuguese was transcribed and annotated by one of the authors, native speakers of Portuguese (EP or BP), and whenever there were doubts concerning the annotation, another author among them was consulted.

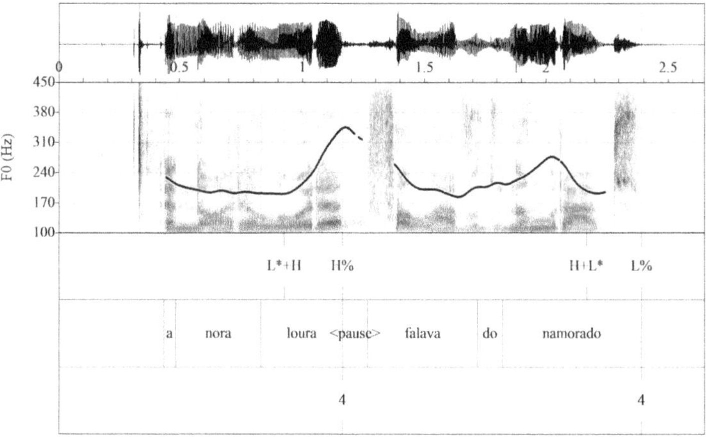



**Figure 6.5.** Example of segmentation and annotation of the sentence *A nora loura falava do namorado* 'The blond daughter-in-law spoke about the boyfriend,' produced by a speaker from CtB.

---

[3] On the prosodic word group, see Vigário (2007, 2010).

# 4    Results and discussion

## 4.1    European Portuguese (EP)

The results for European Portuguese (EP) show that (S)(VO) is the most frequent phrasing pattern in all regions investigated, except in Porto. In this region there is no preferred pattern, except in the branching subject condition, where (S)(VO) is also the main phrasing pattern (65%). Table 6.2 (northern varieties) and Table 6.3 (central-southern varieties) show the total percentage of realisation for each phrasing pattern, per region, as well as the total of realisation for each phrasing pattern, taking into account branching and non-branching subject conditions:

**Table 6.2.** Realization of (S)(VO) and (SVO) phrasing patterns, and (S)(VO) and (SVO) realization according to subject branchingness, in the northern varieties of Porto and Braga (%). Absolute values are presented in parentheses.

| | *Porto* | | *Braga* | |
|---|---|---|---|---|
| | *(S)(VO)* | *(SVO)* | *(S)(VO)* | *(SVO)* |
| **Phrasing pattern** | 49% (125) | 51% (99) | 78% (175) | 22% (44) |
| **Non-branching S** | 44% (42) | 56% (54) | 77% (72) | 23% (22) |
| **Branching S** | 65% (83) | 35% (45) | 83% (103) | 18% (22) |

**Table 6.3.** Realization of (S)(VO) and (SVO) phrasing patterns, and (S)(VO) and (SVO) realization according to subject branchingness, in the central-southern varieties of Castelo Branco, Coimbra and Évora (%). Absolute values are presented in parentheses.

| | *Castelo Branco* | | *Coimbra* | | *Évora* | |
|---|---|---|---|---|---|---|
| | *(S)(VO)* | *(SVO)* | *(S)(VO)* | *(SVO)* | *(S)(VO)* | *(SVO)* |
| **Phrasing pattern** | 73% (139) | 25% (44) | 58% (136) | 42% (83) | 63% (135) | 37% (86) |
| **Non-branching S** | 71% (53) | 30% (22) | 55% (52) | 46% (43) | 64% (60) | 36% (33) |
| **Branching S** | 80% (86) | 13% (22) | 68% (84) | 33% (40) | 59% (75) | 42% (53) |

Figures 6.6 and 6.7 illustrate (SVO) and (S)(VO) phrasing patterns, respectively, produced by a speaker from Porto.

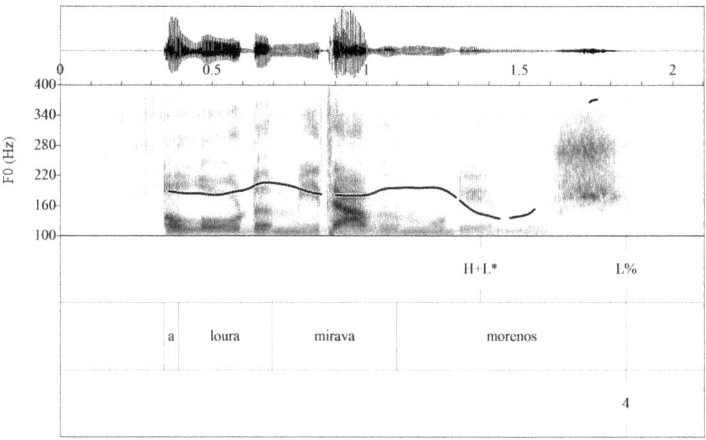


**Figure 6.6.** Intonational contour of the sentence *A loura mirava morenos* 'The blond girl looked at dark-haired boys,' (SVO) pattern, produced by a speaker from Porto.

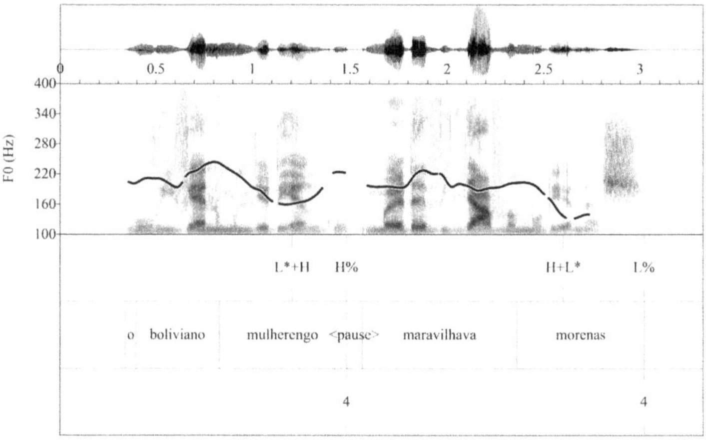


**Figure 6.7.** Intonational contour of the sentence *O boliviano mulherengo maravilhava morenas* 'The Bolivian ladies' man marvelled dark-haired girls,' (S)(VO) pattern, produced by a speaker from Porto.

**Table 6.4.** Realization of (S)(VO) and (SVO) phrasing patterns according to constituent branchingness, for short subjects and long subjects, in the northern varieties of Porto and Braga (%). Absolute values are presented in parentheses.

| | Porto | | Braga | |
| --- | --- | --- | --- | --- |
| *Branchingness* | *(S)(VO)* | *(SVO)* | *(S)(VO)* | *(SVO)* |
| **Phrasing pattern Short S** | 45% (58) | 55% (54) | 78% (85) | 22% (25) |
| **Phrasing pattern Long S** | 53% (67) | 47% (45) | 78% (90) | 22% (19) |
| **Non-branching Short S** | 40% (19) | 60% (29) | 79% (37) | 21% (10) |
| **Non-branching Long S** | 48% (23) | 52% (25) | 75% (35) | 26% (12) |
| **Short branching S** | 61% (39) | 39% (25) | 76% (48) | 24% (15) |
| **Long branching S** | 69% (44) | 31% (20) | 89% (55) | 11% (7) |

**Table 6.5.** Realization of (S)(VO) and (SVO) phrasing patterns according to constituent branchingness, for short subjects and long subjects, in the central-southern varieties of Castelo Branco, Coimbra and Évora (%). Absolute values are presented in parentheses.

| | Castelo Branco | | Coimbra | | Évora | |
| --- | --- | --- | --- | --- | --- | --- |
| *Branchingness* | *(S)(VO)* | *(SVO)* | *(S)(VO)* | *(SVO)* | *(S)(VO)* | *(SVO)* |
| **Phrasing pattern Short S** | 71% (68) | 29% (25) | 59% (72) | 35% (40) | 75% (78) | 25% (34) |
| **Phrasing pattern Long S** | 75% (71) | 22% (19) | 57% (64) | 43% (43) | 51% (57) | 49% (52) |
| **Non-branching Short S** | 70% (26) | 30% (11) | 54% (26) | 46% (22) | 79% (37) | 21% (10) |
| **Non-branching Long S** | 71% (27) | 29% (11) | 55% (26) | 45% (21) | 50% (23) | 50% (23) |
| **Short branching S** | 75% (42) | 25% (14) | 72% (46) | 28% (18) | 63% (41) | 37% (24) |
| **Long branching S** | 85% (44) | 15% (8) | 63% (38) | 37% (22) | 54% (34) | 46% (29) |

Table 6.4 (northern varieties) and Table 6.5 (central-southern varieties) show the percentage of realisation Lof both phrasing patterns, (S)(VO) and (SVO), according to subject branchingness, for short and long subjects.

It is clear that subject branchingness plays a major role in the (S)(VO) phrasing pattern in Porto, since non-branching subjects trigger high percentages of (SVO). Also in Coimbra branching subjects seem to increase (S)(VO), since the percentages for this pattern increase with subject branchingness.

Table 6.6 (northern varieties) and Table 6.7 (central-southern varieties) show the percentages of realisation of the same phrasing patterns according to subject and object branchingness and length.

Besides branching subjects promoting (S)(VO) in Porto, long branching objects also seem to favour this kind of phrasing pattern compared to the (SVO) phrasing pattern (see Tables 6.6 and 6.7). Considering branchingness

**Table 6.6.** Realization of (S)(VO) and (SVO) phrasing patterns, according to branchingness and length conditions for subjects and objects, in the northern varieties of Porto and Braga (%). Absolute values are presented in parentheses.

| | | Porto | | Braga | |
|---|---|---|---|---|---|
| *Branchingness* | *Length* | *(S)(VO)* | *(SVO)* | *(S)(VO)* | *(SVO)* |
| **Non-branching S** **and O** | **Short S** | 25% (4) | 75% (12) | 81% (13) | 19% (3) |
| | **Long S** | 44% (7) | 56% (9) | 67% (10) | 33% (5) |
| **Non-branching S/** **Short branching O** | **Short S** | 19% (3) | 81% (13) | 56% (9) | 44% (7) |
| | **Long S** | 38% (6) | 63% (10) | 69% (11) | 31% (5) |
| **Non-branching S/** **Long branching O** | **Short S** | 75% (12) | 25% (4) | 100% (15) | – |
| | **Long S** | 63% (10) | 38% (6) | 88% (14) | 13% (2) |
| **Branching S** | **Short S** | 61% (39) | 39% (25) | 76% (48) | 24% (15) |
| | **Long S** | 69% (44) | 31% (20) | 89% (55) | 11% (7) |

**Table 6.7.** Realization of (S)(VO) and (SVO) phrasing patterns, according to branchingness and length conditions for subjects and objects, in the central-southern varieties of Castelo Branco, Coimbra and Évora (%). Absolute values are presented in parentheses.

| | | Castelo Branco | | Coimbra | | Évora | |
|---|---|---|---|---|---|---|---|
| *Branchingness* | *Length* | *(S)(VO)* | *(SVO)* | *(S)(VO)* | *(SVO)* | *(S)(VO)* | *(SVO)* |
| **Non-branching S** **and O** | **Short S** | 57% (8) | 43% (6) | 44% (7) | 56% (9) | 81% (13) | 19% (3) |
| | **Long S** | 75% (12) | 25% (4) | 63% (10) | 38% (6) | 50% (8) | 50% (8) |
| **Non-branching S/** **Short branching O** | **Short S** | 71% (5) | 29% (2) | 56% (9) | 44% (7) | 75% (12) | 25% (4) |
| | **Long S** | 75% (6) | 25% (2) | 47% (7) | 53% (8) | 47% (7) | 53% (8) |
| **Non-branching S/** **Long branching O** | **Short S** | 81% (13) | 19% (3) | 63% (10) | 38% (6) | 80% (12) | 20% (3) |
| | **Long S** | 64% (9) | 36% (5) | 56% (9) | 44% (7) | 53% (8) | 47% (7) |
| **Branching S** | **Short S** | 75% (42) | 25% (14) | 72% (46) | 2% (18) | 63% (41) | 37% (24) |
| | **Long S** | 85% (44) | 1% (8) | 63% (38) | 37% (22) | 54% (34) | 46% (29) |

and length conditions for subjects, results in Tables 6.4 and 6.5 and in Tables 6.6 and 6.7 allow us to verify that long subjects are preferably phrased in a single IP, although in Porto non-branching subjects still trigger higher percentages of (SVO) phrasing, regardless of length. In this region, the syntactic branchingness seems to be more relevant in the intonational phrasing, while in the other regions both factors (branchingness and length) promote (S)(VO) phrasing, although in Coimbra and Évora non-branching subjects show different phrasing tendencies, (SVO), which are, nevertheless, not very high. It can also be observed that in Évora short subjects tend to be phrased more frequently in an IP different from the verb and object as compared to long subjects, both in branching and non-branching conditions. In Braga and Castelo Branco, with higher percentages than in the other regions, the general tendency is the (S)(VO) pattern, regardless of subject branchingness and length, although long branching subjects increase the frequency of the pattern. However, these results need a more careful analysis, namely one which includes double branching subjects and double branching objects (composed by more than two lexical heads/more than two PWs) and the verb length condition, which were not taken into account in this study, as well as the inclusion of more speakers. In future work, these factors will also be analysed in order to verify and confirm the role that constituent branchingness and length effectively play in intonational phrasing.

As for the nuclear contours, in non-final IPs, L*+H H% is the most frequent nuclear tonal configuration in Porto, Braga, Castelo Branco and Évora. In Coimbra, H+L* H% is the most frequent nuclear tonal configuration, although a L% boundary can occur. Table 6.8 shows the percentages of the most frequent types of nuclear contours for non-final IPs in utterances presenting the (S)(VO) phrasing pattern.

In Table 6.9, the percentages of the different kinds of tonal configurations of nuclear contours in final IPs, for both (S)(VO) and (SVO) phrasing patterns, can be observed.

In final IPs, in both (S)(VO) and (SVO) structures, the tonal configuration H+L* L%, which characterises neutral declaratives, is the most frequent nuclear contour, although L* L% also occurs (with low percentages), along the lines of what was found in previous work for several varieties of EP (Barros, 2014; Cruz, 2013; Frota & Vigário, 2007; Vigário & Frota, 2003). In future work, the distribution of each nuclear contour by phrasing pattern will be analysed.

As indicated above, different cues were used to identify IP boundaries in this study. In inner IPs, a rising contour was mostly found in all varieties, whether the boundary tone is a rising tone or a high boundary tone, which

**Table 6.8.** Realization of nuclear contours in non-final IPs, in EP (%). Absolute values are presented in parentheses.

| | Porto | Braga | Castelo Branco | Coimbra | Évora |
|---|---|---|---|---|---|
| | **Non-Final IP** | | | | |
| L*+H H% | 59.8% (134) | 55.6% (122) | 43.7% (80) | 20.9% (46) | 31.3% (69) |
| H+L* H% | 32% (72) | 25.6% (56) | 20.7% (38) | 34.9% (76) | 25.4% (56) |
| L* H% | 5.7% (13) | 4.4% (10) | 20.7% (38) | 5.4% (12) | 27.6% (61) |

**Table 6. 9.** Realization of nuclear contours in final IPs, in EP (%). Absolute values are presented in parentheses.

| | Porto | Braga | Castelo Branco | Coimbra | Évora |
|---|---|---|---|---|---|
| | **Final IP** | | | | |
| H+L* L% | 85.2% (191) | 97.7% (214) | 85.9% (157) | 91.5% (200) | 79.5% (176) |
| L* L% | 14.8% (33) | 2.3% (5) | 14.1% (26) | 8.5% (19) | 20.5% (45) |

will be explored in future work, in which F0 pitch range variation at the inner IP boundaries will be measured. Pause insertion is a recurrent cue to mark inner IP boundaries in Porto, with a percentage of insertion of 23%, and lower results in other varieties (3% in Braga, 19% in Castelo Branco, 10% in Coimbra, and 7% in Évora), which corroborates results from previous studies (Barros, 2014; Barros & Frota, 2015).

This preliminary analysis of phrasing tendencies in EP varieties allows us to confirm previous findings showing that EP varieties differ in their patterns of intonational phrasing: for the northern and central-southern varieties, the most frequent pattern is (S)(VO); for SEP and Alg, the most frequent pattern is (SVO). However, the varieties do not differ in the type of boundary cues: in this respect, for all varieties, inner intonational breaks are usually marked by a high boundary tone (H%), in presence or in absence of pause, and the final IP shows the nuclear tonal configuration H+L* L%, the most frequent nuclear tonal configuration for neutral declaratives.

## 4.2   Brazilian Portuguese (BP)

The phrasing patterns in the varieties of BP analysed in this study (SP and RGS) show differences and similarities with EP varieties. As presented above, some EP varieties (northern varieties and some central-southern varieties) show a preference to phrase the subject separately from the verb and object, either in branching or non-branching conditions. BP, on the other hand, presents a different behaviour, similar to standard European Portuguese (SEP) and Algarve (Alg). In the southern varieties of São Paulo (SP) and Rio Grande do Sul (RGS), subject, verb and object are phrased together in a single IP (SVO), presenting a frequency above 80%, be it in branching or non-branching condition. Importantly, the prosodic weight in terms of number of syllables or the syntactic branchingness are not relevant factors for the intonational phrasing in BP.

In Figure 6.8, the speaker from SP produces the (SVO) pattern, in the context of a branching subject, in the utterance *A nora loira levava velhinhas lindas* ('The blond daughter-in-law took beautiful old women'). In the sequence, Table 6.10 shows the percentages of realisation of each phrasing pattern for SP and RGS, and also the percentages of (S)(VO) and (SVO) phrasing patterns in non-branching and branching conditions, for each region.

Considering branchingness and length conditions, Table 6.11 shows the percentages of realisation of both (S)(VO) and (SVO) phrasing patterns in SP and RGS.

Table 6.11 shows that although in RGS subject and object branchingness seems to play a bigger role in (S)(VO) phrasing pattern than in SP, overall, this does not seem to affect the phrasing in BP, since (SVO) is still the main phrasing pattern in both regions, regardless of S and O branchingness and length.

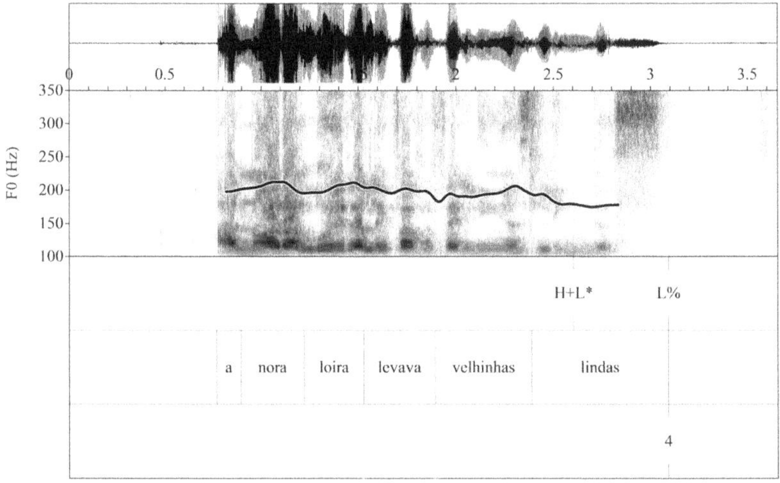


**Figure 6.8.** Intonational contour of the sentence *A nora loira levava velhinhas lindas* 'The blond daughter-in-law took beautiful old women,' (SVO) pattern, produced by a speaker from SP.

**Table 6.10.** Phrasing patterns in prosodic branching and non-branching conditions in BP as spoken in SP and RGS (%). Absolute values are presented in parentheses.

|  | São Paulo | | Rio Grande do Sul | |
|---|---|---|---|---|
|  | *(S)(VO)* | *(SVO)* | *(S)(VO)* | *(SVO)* |
| **Phrasing pattern** | 2% (5) | 98% (156) | 7% (18) | 93% (156) |
| **Non-branching S** | 1% (1) | 99% (85) | 4% (3) | 96% (84) |
| **Branching S** | 6% (4) | 94% (71) | 18% (15) | 82% (72) |

**Table 6.11.** Realization of (S)(VO) and (SVO) phrasing patterns, according to branchingness and length conditions for subjects and objects (%). Absolute values are presented in parentheses.

| | | São Paulo | | Rio Grande do Sul | |
|---|---|---|---|---|---|
| *Branchingness* | *Length* | *(S)(VO)* | *(SVO)* | *(S)(VO)* | *(SVO)* |
| **Non-branching S and O** | **Short S** | – | 100% (14) | – | 100% (14) |
| | **Long S** | – | 100% (12) | – | 100% (16) |
| **Non-branching S/ Short branching O** | **Short S** | 6% (1) | 94% (15) | 21% (3) | 79% (11) |
| | **Long S** | – | 100% (14) | – | 100% (16) |
| **Non-branchin S/ Long branching O** | **Short S** | – | 100% (15) | – | 100% (13) |
| | **Long S** | – | 100% (15) | – | 100% (14) |
| **Branching S** | **Short S** | 7% (2) | 93% (25) | 14% (8) | 86% (48) |
| | **Long S** | 4% (2) | 96% (46) | 23% (7) | 77% (24) |

However, BP varieties differ with regard to the alternative phrasing pattern. Although the (SVO) phrasing pattern is the preferred one, the alternative (S)(VO) has a higher frequency in RGS, with 7% of (S)(VO) cases against 2% of (S)(VO) cases in SP (see Table 6.10). In the utterance *A libanesa de Borborema rememorava a rima* ('The Lebanese from Borborema memorised the rhyme' – Figure 6.9), the speaker from RGS produces a long branching subject in an IP different from the IP in which the verb and object are found. The first IP is characterised by a rising nuclear contour (L*+H H%), the most frequent nuclear contour of non-final IPs in both varieties analysed in this study, as we will see further below.

Pause was the most frequent boundary cue found in BP, confirming previous results (Serra, 2009). It was inserted in 60% of inner IP boundaries

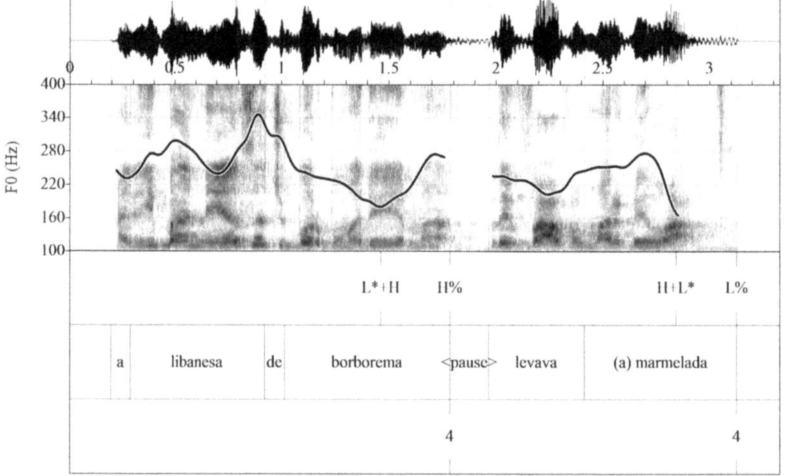


**Figure 6.9.** Intonational contour of the sentence *A libanesa de Borborema levava a marmelada* 'The Lebanese from Borborema took the marmalade,' (S)(VO) pattern, produced by a speaker from RGS.

(66% for SP and 57% for RGS). Other cues to mark inner IP boundaries were also observed, namely continuation rise and high boundary tone, which will be further analysed in future work.

As distinct from the phrasing patterns, EP and BP display the same nuclear contours both in final and non-final IPs. The most frequent nuclear contour of final IPs is composed by a falling pitch accent (H+L*) and a low boundary tone (L%) in both BP varieties. This tonal configuration (H+L* L%) is phonetically realised as a peak in the pretonic syllable and a falling contour along the tonic until the end of the utterance in SP (Figure 6.8) and RGS (Figure 6.10). The frequency of the nuclear tonal configuration H+L* L% is 98% in both varieties. The most frequent nuclear contour of non-final IPs in SP and RGS is composed by a rising pitch accent L*+H and a high boundary tone H%. This tonal configuration (L*+H H%) begins with a valley in the tonic syllable followed by a rise until the end of the internal IP (Figure 6.9). The nuclear tonal configuration L*+H H% is the tonal configuration most frequently found in non-final IPs of both varieties: 80% of cases in non-final IPs in SP data, and 96% in non-final IPs in RGS data (Table 6.12).

In sum, the (SVO) phrasing pattern is the most frequent across Brazilian varieties, showing the same results as SEP and Alg as regards nuclear contours. BP and EP also show similar results for the nuclear contour of final IPs: H+L* L% is the tonal configuration most generally associated with the nuclear contour of final IPs across varieties. BP shows a uniform non-final nuclear contour L*+H H%.

**Table 6.12.** Nuclear tonal configurations in final and non-final IPs in BP as spoken in SP and RGS (%). Absolute values are presented in parentheses.

| | *São Paulo* | *Rio Grande do Sul* |
|---|---|---|
| | ***Final IP*** | |
| H+L* L% | 98% (158) | 98% (170) |
| L* L% | 2% (3) | 2% (4) |
| | ***Non-final IP*** | |
| | *São Paulo* | *Rio Grande do Sul* |
| L*+H H% | 80% (4) | 96% (22) |
| H+L* L% | 20% (1) | 4% (1) |

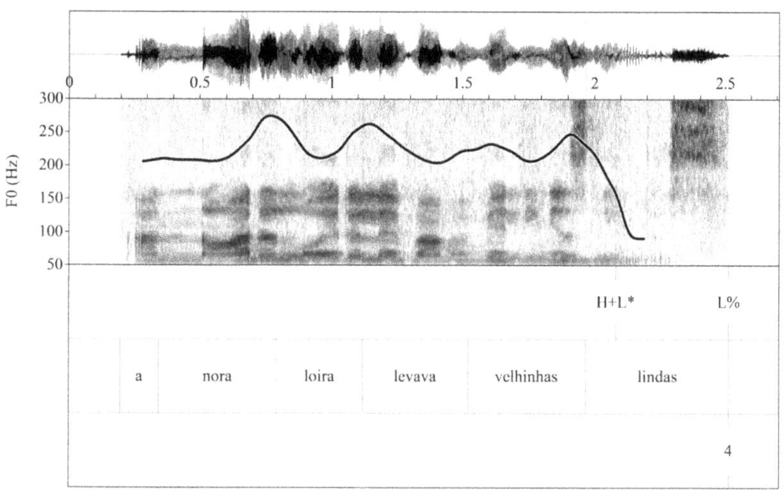


**Figure 6.10.** Intonational contour of the sentence *A nora loira levava velhinhas lindas* 'The blond daughter-in-law took beautiful old women,' (SVO) pattern, produced by a speaker from RGS.

## 4.3   Guinea-Bissau Portuguese (GBP)

Our results for GBP show that (SVO) is the most frequent phrasing pattern (81.1%), followed by (S)(VO) (14.7%) and by (SV)(O) (4.2%) phrasing patterns (see Table 6.13).

**Table 6.13.** Realization of (SV)(O), (S)(VO), and (SVO) phrasing patterns, and (SV)(O), (S)(VO), and (SVO) realization according to the subject branchingness in GBP (%). Absolute values are presented in parentheses.

|  | *(SV)(O)* | *(S)(VO)* | *(SVO)* |
| --- | --- | --- | --- |
| Phrasing pattern | 4.2% (14) | 14.7% (49) | 81.1% (270) |
| Non-branching S | 5.6% (8) | 4.9% (7) | 89.5% (127) |
| Branching S | 3.1% (6) | 22% (42) | 74.9% (143) |

Branchingness seems to play a relevant role in the intonational phrasing in GBP data, since the branching subject condition shows a higher overall percentage of (S)(VO) (22%) than non-branching subject condition (4.9%).

In fact, both syntactic/prosodic branchingness and constituent length may have an effect on the intonational phrasing of GBP sentences. Nevertheless, by observing in more detail the factors that have influence on the intonational phrasing of GBP sentences (subject and object branchingness and constituent length), we find that the most frequent pattern, considering different conditions, is still (SVO) (see Table 6.14). With respect to the two least frequent phrasing patterns presented in Table 6.14, i.e. (S)(VO) and (SV)(O), there is some variation. When S is non-branching and O is branching, there is a tendency to produce more cases of (SV)(O) in short S condition, and there is a slight tendency to produce more cases of (S)(VO) in long S condition, although percentages are very close. However, when S is branching, regardless of O branchingness and S and O length, a higher frequency of (S)(VO) is produced. In cases where both S and O are non-branching, (SVO) is the most frequent phrasing pattern.

The remarkable difference in the intonational phrasing, when we compare GBP and other varieties of Portuguese, is the possibility, in GBP, of the subject and verb to be phrased together in an IP apart from the object, i.e. (SV)(O), though with low frequency (4.2% – see Table 6.13). Although (SV)(O) is not attested in other Portuguese varieties so far, this phrasing pattern is found in other Romance languages, such as Catalan and Spanish (D'Imperio et al., 2005; Feldhausen, 2011; Prieto, 2005).

Regarding the nuclear tonal configuration of IPs, the most frequent configurations for final IPs in our data are H+L* L% (40.5%) and L* L% (59.5%) – see Table 6.15. The same configurations for final IPs are found in neutral declaratives across EP and BP varieties. Those are also the most frequent nuclear tonal configurations associated with the nuclear contour of final IPs attested by Santos (2015), whose study analysed a larger number of data: in

**Table 6.14.** Realization of (SV)(O), (S)(VO), and (SVO) phrasing patterns according to subject and object branchingness and constituent length in GBP (%). Absolute values are presented in parentheses.

| Branchingness | Length | (SV)(O) | (S)(VO) | (SVO) |
|---|---|---|---|---|
| Non-branching S and O | Short S | – | – | 100% (24) |
|  | Long S | – | 4.2% (1) | 95.8% (23) |
| Non-branching S/ Short branching O | Short S | 4.2% (1) | – | 95.8% (23) |
|  | Long S | – | 8.7% (2) | 91.3% (21) |
| Non-branching S/ Long branching O | Short S | 20.8% (5) | 4.2% (1) | 75% (18) |
|  | Long S | 8.7% (2) | 13% (3) | 78.3% (18) |
| Branching S/ Non-branching O | Short S | 2.1% (1) | 29.2% (14) | 68.8% (33) |
|  | Long S | 2.1% (1) | 25.5% (12) | 72.3% (34) |
| Branching S/ Short branching O | Short S | 6.3% (3) | 12.5% (6) | 81.3% (39) |
| Branching S/ Long branching O | Long S | 2.1% (1) | 20.8% (10) | 77.1% (37) |

**Table 6.15.** Nuclear tonal configurations of final and non-final IPs in GBP (%). Absolute values are presented in parentheses.

| Final IP | |
|---|---|
| H+L* L% | 40.5% (135) |
| L* L% | 59.5% (198) |

| Non-final IP | |
|---|---|
| L*+H H% | 38.1% (24) |
| L+H* H% | 3.2% (2) |
| L+H* L% | 3.2% (2) |
| L*+H L% | 4.8% (3) |
| L* L% | 3.2% (2) |
| L* LH% | 36.5% (23) |
| H+L* H% | 1.5% (1) |
| H+L* LH% | 9.5% (6) |

the utterances analysed by the author, H+L* L% corresponds to 52.5% and L* L% corresponds to 44.3% of tonal configurations associated with the nuclear contour of final IPs; the remaining 3.2% consists of other tonal configurations (Santos, 2015, p. 119).

As for the non-final nuclear contour of GBP, the following rising patterns are the most frequent in our data: L*+H H% (38.1%) and L* LH% (36.5%) (Table 6.14). However, as reported by Santos (2015), one should note that the high frequency of L* LH% is due to the high (and exclusive) occurrence of that tonal pattern in one of the speakers' data. In fact, apart from this one speaker, the most common and frequent tonal configuration associated with the nuclear contour of non-final IPs to all GBP speakers is L*+H H%. In addition, regardless of the configuration and the alignment of tones that are associated with non-final IP nuclear contours, rising tonal patterns are the most common ones and represent 70.2% of the author's data (see Santos, 2015, p. 120).

Figures 6.11, 6.12, and 6.13, respectively, exemplify the (SVO), (S)(VO), and (SV)(O) phrasing patterns found in GBP data.

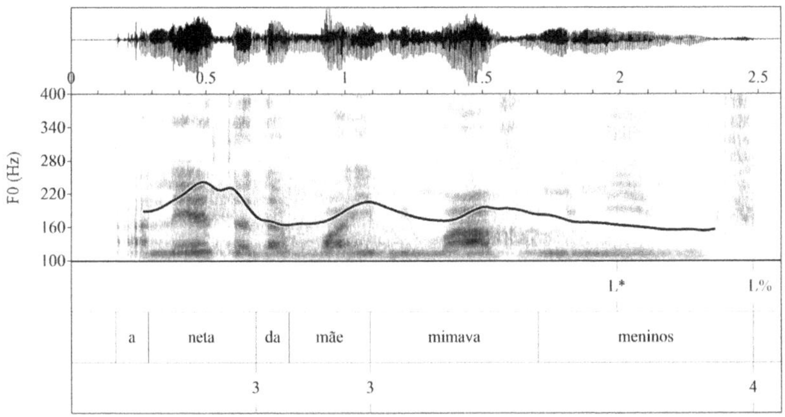


**Figure 6.11.** Intonational contour of the sentence *A neta da mãe mimava meninos* 'The granddaughter of (my) mother spoiled small children,' (SVO) pattern, produced by a speaker of GBP.

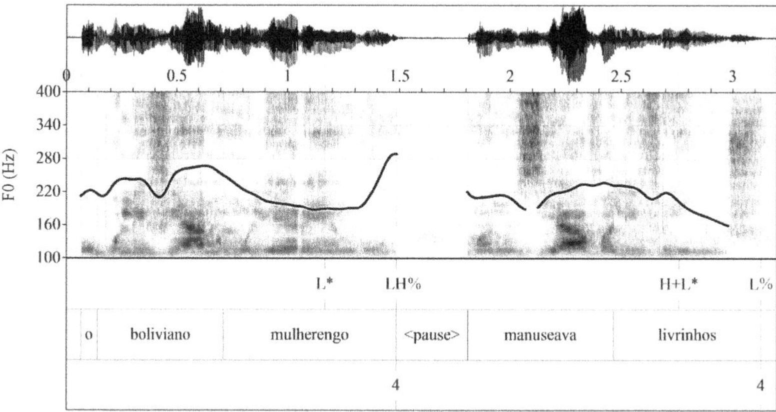

**Figure 6.12.** Intonational contour of the sentence *O boliviano mulherengo manuseava livrinhos* 'The Bolivian ladies' man handled little books,' (S)(VO) pattern, produced by a speaker of GBP.

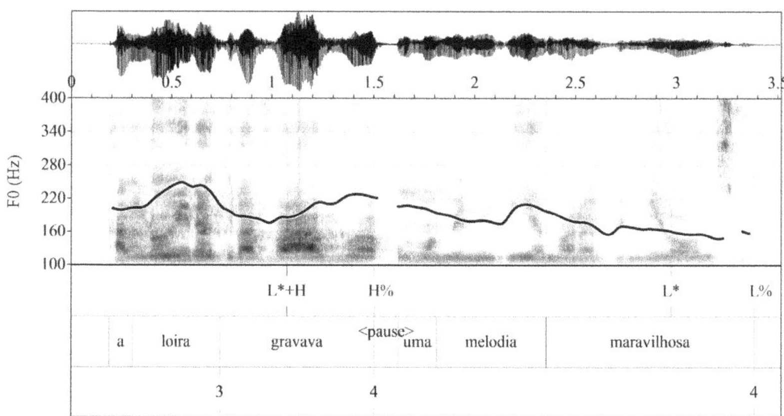

**Figure 6.13.** Intonational contour of the sentence *A loira gravava uma melodia maravilhosa* 'The blond girl recorded a wonderful melody,' (SV)(O) pattern, produced by a speaker of GBP.

# 5    Conclusions and directions for further research

The results obtained in this study confirm previous findings for the tonal configuration associated with the nuclear contour of final and non-final IPs of varieties of EP, BP, and GBP, and for intonational phrasing patterns of EP varieties. The results found for the intonational phrasing of the BP and GBP varieties explored here are completely new.

As regards the intonational phrasing, the results for the EP varieties analysed in this study (northern varieties of Porto and Braga and central-southern varieties of Castelo Branco, Coimbra, and Évora) confirm previous studies on the intonational phrasing of northern and central-southern EP (see all the references in section 2.2), showing that (S)(VO) is the most frequent phrasing pattern in all regions, except in Porto, where (SVO) is slightly more frequent. Nevertheless, in the branching subject condition, (S)(VO) is the main phrasing pattern also in Porto. In the other regions, subject branchingness and length are relevant factors that promote the (S)(VO) phrasing pattern. Although these results need further investigation and more careful analysis, they seem to confirm previous findings for EP, where constituent branchingness and length have a different weight in the prosodic phrasing of SVO sentences.

In BP varieties (SP and RGS), the most frequent intonational phrasing pattern is (SVO). The alternative phrasing pattern (S)(VO) is also found, with a slightly higher frequency in RGS than in SP in the branching subject condition.

In GBP, (SVO) is also the most frequent intonational phrasing pattern, although (S)(VO) and (SV)(O) are also attested in branching subject and branching object conditions respectively. The latter was found only in GBP, and is not attested in other varieties of Portuguese either in this study or in most previous investigations.

In comparison with other Romance languages, we note that all the varieties of Portuguese considered in this study, except for the northern variety of Braga and central-southern varieties of EP, are similar to Neapolitan Italian, since this variety displays (SVO) as the main phrasing pattern (D'Imperio et al. 2005). The northern and central-southern varieties of EP, which display (S)(VO) as the most frequent intonational phrasing pattern, are similar to Spanish, Catalan, French, and the northern varieties of Italian (see all the references in section 2.1). On the other hand, GBP is also similar to Catalan and Spanish, which present (SV)(O) as a possible intonational phrasing pattern (D'Imperio et al., 2005; Feldhausen, 2011; Prieto,

2005; Rao, 2007). As in Spanish (except for the Peruvian variety, in which (SV)(O) is the typical phrasing pattern, cf. Rao, 2007) and Catalan, in GBP (SV)(O) is also triggered by prosodic branchingness and constituent length, since long branching objects favor this pattern.

Regarding the cues to mark non-final IP boundaries, pause insertion and boundary tones are relevant cues to identify prosodic boundaries across Portuguese varieties.

With respect to the nuclear configuration, the rising tonal configuration L*+H H% is the most frequent tonal configuration associated with the nuclear contour of non-final IPs in all varieties analysed, confirming previous studies on Portuguese (see all the references in section 2.2), except in Coimbra, where H+L* H% is the most frequent tonal configuration found in this context. On the other hand, as also found in previous studies on Portuguese, the tonal configuration more frequently associated with the nuclear contour of final IPs is H+L* L%, both in EP and BP varieties. In GBP, both H+L* L% and L* L% are the most frequent tonal configurations in this same context – see Cruz (2013), Vigário and Frota (2003), and Frota and Vigário (2007) for L* L% as a possible tonal configuration associated with the nuclear contour of final IPs in Portuguese from Alentejo and in northern varieties of EP.

The different phrasing patterns and IP nuclear configurations in the Portuguese varieties considered in this study are summarised in Table 6.16 and Table 6.17 respectively.

This study provides a first analysis of intonational phrasing tendencies across the Portuguese varieties considered herein, contributing to the knowledge of intonational variation in Portuguese and in Romance languages, supported by a theoretical framework (the Autosegmental-Metrical approach to Intonational Phonology) and methodological procedures used in previous studies on intonational phrasing. However, note that, in contrast with D'Imperio et al. (2005) and Elordieta et al. (2005), where the phrasing level under analysis has been generally defined as a major prosodic phrase, we decided to systematically consider for analysis the Intonational Phrase level. If a major phrase (i.e., an intonational constituent covering the categories Intermediate Phrase and Intonational Phrase) was considered instead, as in the work mentioned above, the results might have been different, as we believe that the intonational constituents involved in the three varieties of Portuguese do not always coincide. Further investigation considering more data and other cues to identify IP boundaries, such as final lengthening, continuation rise, pitch reset after boundary, sustained pitch, and F0 pitch range variation at the boundary (Frota et al., 2007), is needed to clarify the phonological analysis of the phrasing differences across these Portuguese varieties and to determine the exact nature of the constituents

**Table 6.16.** Phrasing patterns in Portuguese.

| *Northern EP varieties* | *Phrasing pattern* | *Conditions* |
| --- | --- | --- |
| Porto | (SVO) | Main pattern |
| | (S)(VO) | Subject branchingness |
| Braga | (S)(VO) | Main pattern |
| | (SVO) | Subject branchingness and length |

| *Central-Southern EP varieties* | *Phrasing pattern* | *Conditions* |
| --- | --- | --- |
| Castelo Branco | (S)(VO) | Main pattern |
| | (SVO) | Subject branchingness and length |
| Coimbra | (S)(VO) | Main pattern |
| | (SVO) | Subject branchingness and length |
| Évora | (S)(VO) | Main pattern |
| | (SVO) | Subject branchingness and length |

| *BP varieties* | *Phrasing pattern* | *Conditions* |
| --- | --- | --- |
| São Paulo | (SVO) | Main pattern |
| Rio Grande do Sul | (SVO) | Main pattern |
| | (S)(VO) | Subject branchingness |
| *GBP variety* | *Phrasing pattern* | *Conditions* |
| Bissau | (SVO) | Main pattern |
| | (S)(VO) | Subject branchingness |
| | (SV)(O) | Object branchingness |

involved. This would also allow us to discuss the relationship between the different intonational phrasing patterns found – (SVO), (S)(VO), and (SV)(O) – and the syntax–phonology interface (as done in previous studies, such as Elordieta et al., 2005; Prieto, 2005; Feldhausen, 2011; among others), as well as on the relationship between the different intonational phrasing patterns and diatopic differences or different grammars.

**Table 6.17.** IP nuclear contours in Portuguese.

| Northern EP varieties | Non-final IP | Final IP |
|---|---|---|
| Porto | L*+H H% | H+L* L% |
| Braga | L*+H H% | H+L* L% |

| Central-Southern EP varieties | Non-final IP | Final IP |
|---|---|---|
| Castelo Branco | L*+H H% | H+L* L% |
| Coimbra | H+L* H% | H+L* L% |
| Évora | L*+H H% | H+L* L% |

| Southern BP varieties | Non-final IP | Final IP |
|---|---|---|
| São Paulo | L*+H H% | H+L* L% |
| Rio Grande do Sul | L*+H H% | H+L* L% |

| GBP variety | Non-final IP | Final IP |
|---|---|---|
| Bissau | L*+H H% | H+L* L%<br>L* L% |

# Acknowledgements

This study was supported by the InAPoP – Interactive Atlas of the Prosody of Portuguese (Frota, 2012–2015) (http://labfon.letras.ulisboa.pt/InAPoP/) (PTDC/CLE-LIN/119787/2010), Projeto Estratégico/Programático do Centro de Linguística da Universidade de Lisboa (UIDB/00214/2020), both funded by *Fundação para a Ciência e a Tecnologia* (FCT), *Fraseamento prosódico em português: comparações entre as variedades brasileira e africanas* (Fernandes-Svartman, 2015–2017) (CNPq, 459634/2014–3) project, *Variação e fraseamento prosódico em português: comparações entre variedades brasileiras e africanas* (Fernandes-Svartman, 2018–2021) (CNPq, 437021/2018–1), and *Variação e fraseamento prosódico em português brasileiro* (Fernandes-Svartman, 2019–2022) (CNPq, 313103/2018–6) projects, the PhD grants BD/102314/2014 to Nádia Barros, funded by FCT, and 0949/12–4 to Joelma Castelo, funded by CAPES, and the MSc grant 2013/08329–1 to Vinícius Santos, funded by FAPESP. We are grateful to the participants at ProVar – Workshop on Prosodic Variation (Lisbon, 9 July 2015) for their comments on an earlier version of this work, as well as to the three anonymous reviewers and to the editors Marisa Cruz and Sónia Frota. We thank Maria Clara Paixão de Sousa for the review of the chapter's text in English and all the speakers that produced the data analysed in this chapter.

# References


Avanzi, M., Christodoulides, G., & Delais-Roussarie, E. (2014). Prosodic phrasing of SVO sentences in French. In N. Campbell, D. Gibbon & D. Hirst (Eds.), *Proceedings of the 7th International Conference on Speech Prosody* (pp. 703–707), Dublin, Ireland.

Barros, N. (2014). *Fraseamento prosódico em Português: Uma análise entoacional de construções parentéticas e tópicos em duas variedades do Português Europeu.* Unpublished Master Thesis. University of Lisbon, Lisbon, Portugal. Retrieved from http://labfon.letras.ulisboa.pt/texts/Barros2014.pdf

Barros, N., & Frota, S. (2015). Prosodic phrasing in parentheticals and topics across varieties of European Portuguese. In The Scottish Consortium for ICPhS 2015 (Ed.), *Proceedings of the 18th International Congress of Phonetic Sciences.* Glasgow, UK: University of Glasgow. ISBN 978-0-85261-941-4. Paper number 0439.1-5

Beckman, M. E., & Pierrehumbert, J. B. (1986). Intonational structure in Japanese and English. *Phonology Yearbook, 3*(1), 255–309. https://doi.org/10.1017/S095267570000066X

Boersma, P., & Weenink, D. (2015). *Praat: Doing phonetics by computer* (Version 5.3.51) [Computer software]. Retrieved from http://www.praat.org/

Castelo, J., & Frota, S. (2015). Variação entoacional no Português do Brasil: Uma análise fonológica do contorno nuclear em enunciados declarativos e interrogativos. [Intonational variation in Brazilian Portuguese: A phonological analysis of the nuclear contour in declarative and interrogative utterances]. In A. Moreno, F. Silva, & J. Veloso (Eds.), *XXX Encontro Nacional da Associação Portuguesa de Linguística – Textos Selecionados* (pp. 113–131). Porto: Associação Portuguesa de Linguística.

Cintra, L. (1971). Nova proposta de classificação dos dialectos galego-portugueses. [New proposal for the classification of galician-portuguese dialects.] *Boletim de Filologia, 22*, 81–116. Lisboa: Centro de Estudos Filológicos.

Couto, H., & Embaló, F. (2010). *Literatura, língua e cultura na Guiné-Bissau: Um país da CPLP* [Literature, language and culture in Guinea-Bissau: A country of CPLP] [Special issue]. *PAPIA, 20.* Retrieved from http://revistas.fflch.usp.br/papia/issue/view/136

Cruz, M. (2013). *Prosodic variation in European Portuguese: Phrasing, intonation and rhythm in central-southern varieties.* Unpublished Doctoral Dissertation. University of Lisbon, Lisbon, Portugal. Retrieved from http://labfon.letras.ulisboa.pt/texts/MarisaCruz_PhDThesis_2013_V2.pdf

Cruz, M., & Frota, S. (2011). Prosódia dos tipos frásicos em variedades do Português Europeu: Produção e percepção. [Prosody of sentence types in European Portuguese varieties: Production and perception.] In M. A. Costa, I. Falé &, P. Barbosa (Eds.), *XXVI ENAPL: Textos Seleccionados 2010* (pp. 208–22). Lisbon: Associação Portuguesa de Linguística.

Cruz, M., & Frota, S. (2013). On the relation between intonational phrasing and pitch accent distribution: Evidence from European Portuguese varieties. *Proceedings of the 14th Annual Conference of the International Speech Communication Association* (Interspeech 2013), 300–304. Lyon, France.

Cunha, C. (2000). *Entoação regional no português do Brasil.* [Regional intonation in Brazilian Portuguese]. Unpublished Doctoral Dissertation. Federal University of Rio de Janeiro, Rio de Janeiro, Brazil.

D'Imperio, M., Elordieta, G., Frota, S., Prieto, P., & Vigário, M. (2005). Intonational phrasing in Romance: The role of syntactic and prosodic structure. In S. Frota, M. Vigário, & M. J. Freitas (Eds.), *Prosodies* (pp. 59–97). Berlin/New York: Mouton de Gruyter.

Elordieta, G., Frota, S., Prieto, P., & Vigário, M. (2003). Effects of constituent weight and syntactic branching on intonational phrasing in Ibero-Romance. In M. J. Solé, D. Recasens, & J. Romero (Eds.), *Proceedings of the 15th International Congress of Phonetic Sciences* (pp. 487–490), Barcelona, Spain. Retrieved from https://www.internationalphoneticassociation.org/icphs-proceedings/ICPhS2003/papers/p15_0487.pdf

Elordieta, G., Frota, S., & Vigário, M. (2005). Subjects, objects and intonational phrasing in Spanish and Portuguese. *Studia Linguistica, 59*(2–3), 110–143. https://doi.org/10.1111/j.1467-9582.2005.00123.x

Feldhausen, I. (2011). The prosodic phrasing of sentential objects. *Lingua, 121*(13), 1934–1964. https://doi.org/10.1016/j.lingua.2011.06.009

Feldhausen, I. (2014). Intonation and preverbal subjects in Italian. In S. Fuchs, M. Grice, A. Hermes, L. Lancia, & D. Mücke (Eds.), *Proceedings of the 10th International Seminar on Speech Production* (ISSP) (pp. 118–121), Cologne, Germany. Retrieved from http://www.issp2014.uni-koeln.de/wp-content/uploads/2014/Proceedings_ISSP_revised.pdf

Feldhausen, I., Gabriel, C., & Pešková, A. (2010). Prosodic phrasing in Argentinean Spanish: Buenos Aires and Neuquén. In *Proceedings of Speech Prosody 2010.* Chicago, IL.

Fernandes, F. R. (2007). *Ordem, focalização e preenchimento em português: Sintaxe e prosódia* [Order, focalization and filling in Portuguese: Sintax and Prosody]. Unpublished Doctoral Dissertation. State University of Campinas, Campinas, Brazil. Retrieved from http://www.bibliotecadigital.unicamp.br/document/?code=vtls000414150

Fernandes-Svartman, F. R. (Coord.) (2015–2017). *Fraseamento prosódico em português: Comparações entre as variedades brasileira e africanas* [Prosodic phrasing in Portuguese: Comparison across brazilian and african varieties]. Project funded by Conselho Nacional de Desenvolvimento Científico e Tecnológico – CNPq, 459634/2014-3.

Fernandes-Svartman, F. R. (Coord.) (2018–2021). *Variação e fraseamento prosódico em português: comparações entre variedades brasileiras e africanas* [Prosodic phrasing in Portuguese: Comparison across brazilian and african varieties]. Project funded by Conselho Nacional de Desenvolvimento Científico e Tecnológico – CNPq, 437021/2018-1.

Fernandes-Svartman, F. R. (Coord.) (2019–2022). *Variação e fraseamento prosódico em português brasileiro* [Variation and prosodic phrasing in Brazilian Portuguese]. Project funded by Conselho Nacional de Desenvolvimento Científico e Tecnológico – CNPq, 313103/2018-6.

Fernandes-Svartman, F. R., Santos, F. G., & Braga, G. (2018). Fraseamento prosódico em português: semelhanças e diferenças entre variedades africanas e brasileiras. [Prosodic phrasing in Portuguese: similarities and differences across African and Brazilian varieties]. *Filologia e Linguística Portuguesa*, 20(esp.), 119–38. https://doi.org/10.11606/issn.2176-9419. v20iEspecialp119-138

Frota, S. (2000). *Prosody and focus in European Portuguese: Phonological phrasing and intonation*. New York: Garland Publishing.

Frota, S. (2014). The intonational phonology of European Portuguese. In S.-A. Jun (Ed.), *Prosodic Typology II* (pp. 6–42). Oxford: Oxford University Press.

Frota, S. (Coord.) (2012–2015). *InAPoP – Interactive Atlas of the Prosody of Portuguese* Project funded by Fundação para a Ciência e a Tecnologia – FCT, PTDC/CLE-LIN/119787/2010 [http://labfon.letras.ulisboa.pt/InAPoP/].

Frota, S., Cruz, M., Fernandes-Svartman, F., Collischonn, G., Fonseca, A., Serra, C., Oliveira, P., & Vigário, M. (2015). Intonational variation in Portuguese: European and Brazilian varieties. In S. Frota, & P. Prieto (Eds.), *Intonation in Romance* (pp. 235–283). Oxford: Oxford University Press. https://doi.org/10.1093/acprof:oso/9780199685332.001.0001

Frota, S., D'Imperio, M., Elordieta, G., Prieto, P., & Vigário, M. (2007). The phonetics and phonology of intonational phrasing in Romance. In P. Prieto, J. Mascaró, & M. J. Solé (Eds.), *Segmental and Prosodic Issues in Romance Phonology* (pp. 131–153). Amsterdam: John Benjamins.

Frota, S., Oliveira, P., Cruz, M., & Vigário, M. (2015). *P-ToBI: Tools for the transcription of Portuguese prosody*. Lisbon: Laboratório de Fonética, CLUL/FLUL. http://labfon.letras.ulisboa.pt/InAPoP/P-ToBI/

Frota, S., & Vigário, M. (2000). Aspectos de prosódia comparada: Ritmo e entoação no PE e no PB. [Aspects of compared prosody: Rhythm and intonation in EP and BP]. In R. V. Castro, & P. Barbosa (Eds.), *Actas do XV Encontro Nacional da Associação Portuguesa de Linguística* (Vol. 1, pp. 533–555). Coimbra: Associação Portuguesa de Linguística.

Frota, S., & Vigário, M. (2007). Intonational phrasing in two varieties of European Portuguese. In T. Riad, & C. Gussenhoven (Eds.), *Tones and Tunes* (Vol. 1, pp. 265–291). Berlin: Mouton de Gruyter.

Ladd, R. (2008). *Intonational Phonology* (2nd ed.). Cambridge: Cambridge University Press.

Nespor, M., & Vogel, I. (2007). *Prosodic phonology: With a new foreword.* Berlin/New York: Mouton de Gruyter.

Prieto, P. (2005). Syntactic and eurhythmic constraints on phrasing decisions in Catalan. *Studia Linguistica, 59*(2/3), 194–222. https://doi.org/10.1111/j.1467-9582.2005.00126.x

Rao, R. (2007). On the phonological phrasing in the Spanish of Lima, Perú. *Southwest Journal of Linguistics, 26*(1), 81–111.

Rao, R. (2008). Observations on the roles of prosody and syntax in the phonological phrasing of Barcelona Spanish. *The Linguistics Journal, 3*(3), 85–131.

Santos, V. G. (2015). *Aspectos prosódicos do português de Guiné-Bissau: A entoação do contorno neutro* [Prosodic aspects of Guinea-Bissau Portuguese: The intonation of the neutral contour]. Unpublished Master Thesis. University of São Paulo, São Paulo, Brazil. https://doi.org/10.11606/D.8.2015.tde-29062015-153129

Santos, V. G. (2020). Aspectos prosódicos do português angolano do Libolo: entoação e fraseamento [Prosodic aspects of Angolan Portuguese as spoken in Libolo: intonation and phrasing]. Unpublished Doctoral Dissertation. University of São Pauylo, São Paulo, Brazil. https://doi.org/10.11606/T.8.2020.tde-03032020-174301

Santos, V. G., & Fernandes-Svartman, F. R. (2014). O padrão entoacional neutro do português de Guiné-Bissau: Uma comparação preliminar com o português brasileiro. [Neutral intonational pattern of Guinea-Bissau Portuguese: A preliminary comparison with Brazilian Portuguese]. *Estudos Linguísticos, 43*(1), 48–63. Retrieved from https://revistas.gel.org.br/estudos-linguisticos/article/view/418

Selkirk, E. (1984). *Phonology and syntax: The relation between sound and structure.* Cambridge: MIT Press.

Selkirk, E. (1986). On derived domains in sentence phonology. *Phonology 3,* 371–405. https://doi.org/10.1017/S0952675700000695

Serra, C. (2009). *Realização e percepção de fronteiras prosódicas no português do Brasil: Fala espontânea e leitura.* [Realization and perception of prosodic boundaries in Brazilian Portuguese: Spontaneous speech and reading]. Unpublished Doctoral Dissertation. Federal University of Rio de Janeiro, Rio de Janeiro, Brazil.

Silvestre, A. (2012). *A entoação regional dos enunciados assertivos nos falares das capitais brasileiras.* [The regional intonation of assertive utterances in Brazilian capitals' speeches]. Unpublished Master Thesis. Federal University of Rio de Janeiro, Rio de Janeiro, Brazil.

Tenani, L. E. (2002). *Domínios prosódicos no português: Implicações para a prosódia e para a aplicação de processos fonológicos.* [Prosodic domains in Portuguese: Implications for prosody and for the application of phonological processes]. Unpublished Doctoral Dissertation. State University of Campinas, Campinas, Brazil. Retrieved from http://www.bibliotecadigital.unicamp.br/document/?code=vtls000267023

Vigário, M. (2007). O lugar do grupo clítico e da palavra prosódica composta na hierarquia prosódica: Uma nova proposta. [The place of the clitic group and of the compound prosodic word in the prosodic hierarchy: A new proposal]. In M. Lobo & M. A. Coutinho (Orgs.), *XXII Encontro da Associação Portuguesa de Linguística – Textos Seleccionados* (pp. 673–688). Lisbon: Colibri Artes Gráficas.

Vigário, M. (2010). Prosodic structure between the Prosodic Word and the Phonological Phrase: Recursive nodes or an independent domain? *The Linguistic Review, 27*(4), 485–530. https://doi.org/10.1515/tlir.2010.017

Vigário, M., & Frota, S. (2003). The intonation of Standard and Northern European Portuguese. *Journal of Portuguese Linguistics, 2*(2), 115–137. https://doi.org/10.5334/jpl.31

**Flaviane Romani Fernandes Svartman** is Associate Professor of Philology and Portuguese Language in the Department of Classical and Vernacular Letters at the Faculty of Philosophy, Letters and Human Sciences at the University of São Paulo, São Paulo, Brazil. Her research addresses the study of phonetics and phonology of Portuguese with a special focus on prosody, the syntax-phonology interface and the comparison between African, Brazilian and European varieties of Portuguese.

**Nádia Barros** is a PhD student in Linguistics at The School of Arts and Humanities, University of Lisbon, and a teacher of English as a Foreign Language at the Center for Languages and Culture, Polytechnic Institute of Lisbon. She was a member of the research project *InAPoP - Interactive Atlas of the Prosody of Portuguese,* where she did research on prosodic variation and intonation.

**Vinícius G. Santos** is a postdoctoral researcher at the Department of Classical and Vernacular Languages and Literatures, University of São Paulo, Brazil. He obtained his PhD in 2019, focused on the phonological analysis of some prosodic features of the Angolan Portuguese as spoken in Libolo. His research interests include various aspects of prosody and intonational variation in African varieties of Portuguese.

**Joelma Castelo** is Lecturer at the Center of Human Sciences and Education of Universidade Estadual do Paraná, Brazil, and postdoctoral researcher at the University of São Paulo, Brazil. Her research focuses on the phonetics and phonology of intonational variation in Portuguese. Her most relevant publications are *Variação entoacional dos enunciados interrogativos, The yes–no question contour in Brazilian Portuguese* (Castelo & Frota, 2017), and *The perception of yes–no questions across varieties of Brazilian Portuguese* (Castelo et al., 2018).

# 7
# Hiatus resolution across words in European Portuguese dialects[1]

Nuno Paulino, Pedro Oliveira & Marina Vigário

## 1    Introduction

It is well documented that languages tend to avoid hiatuses, that is, sequences of adjacent vowels (Casali, 1997, 2011; Hall, 2011, 2013). Hiatus resolution (HR) in several Romance languages, including Portuguese, has been subject to intense investigation, making this a very productive area for crosslinguistic comparison (Alba, 2006; Cabré & Prieto, 2005; Chitoran & Hualde, 2007; Ellison & Viana, 1996; Fernandez Rei, 2002; Frota, 1995, 2000; Jenkins, 1999; Tenani, 2002; Vigário, 2003; and others). In this chapter, we are especially interested in the variation found in HR in one particular language variety, European Portuguese (EP). Using read and (semi-)spontaneous corpora and a limited set of vocalic sequences produced in controlled prosodic contexts, we will look at (i) the relative tolerance to hiatus, (ii) the phonological strategies available for hiatus avoidance, and (iii) the factors that may condition HR processes and their respective frequency in different regions of Portugal. We will then consider our results in light of the wider picture of prosodic variation in EP, in order to gain a better insight into the factors that may contribute to variation in hiatus phonology.

This chapter is organized as follows. In section 2 we survey some of the major prosodic dimensions that have been found to vary across Portuguese dialects. Several issues related to hiatus sequences in other languages and in EP are also reviewed, including the factors that may be involved in HR,

[1]    This investigation has been partially funded by the project InAPoP – Interactive Atlas of the Prosody of Portuguese (PTDC/CLE-LIN/119787/2010) and UIDB/00214/2020. Preliminary work on part of the data analysed here appears in Oliveira (2016), Oliveira, Cruz, Paulino and Vigário (2017), Oliveira, Paulino, Cruz and Vigário, (2014), Paulino (2016), and Paulino and Frota (2015).

the strategies available for HR and the conditions on HR. In section 3 we present the method for collecting the data that constitutes the empirical basis of this research. The results are reported in section 4, and a brief discussion follows (section 5). We conclude in section 6 with a synthesis of our major findings.

# 2 Background

## 2.1 Prosodic variation in European Portuguese dialects

In the last few years, several studies systematically analyzed different aspects of prosodic variation in EP, in particular within the InAPoP project (http://labfon.letras.ulisboa.pt/InAPoP/). Recent work by members of the dialectology and diachrony group of CLUL has also uncovered important aspects of segmental dialectal variation, both within and across words (Brissos, 2015; Brissos & Saramago, 2014; Segura, 2013). Research covers a wide range of areas within prosody and has been developed mostly within the framework of prosodic phonology and Autosegmental-Metrical approach to intonation (Frota, 2000, 2014; Ladd, 2008; Nespor & Vogel, 1986/2007; Vigário, 2003, 2010).

Work on intonation in several geographical areas where EP and Brazilian Portuguese (BP) is spoken has found variation in the tonal lexicon, i.e. the phonological shape of tonal categories, and in tonal density, i.e. amount of pitch accents found within intonational phrases (e.g. Castelo & Frota, 2015; Cruz & Frota, 2013; Frota, Cruz, et al., 2015; Frota, Castelo, et al., 2015; Frota & Vigário, 2000, 2007). Most noticeably, not only in BP but also in several regions of Portugal, there is a very high rate of pitch accent per prosodic word (like in Porto, Algarve and Alentejo), whereas Standard EP (SEP) has a much sparser pitch accent distribution (Frota, Cruz, et al., 2015, and references therein).

EP varieties have also been reported to differ in terms of prosodic phrasing preferences (Cruz, 2013; Elordieta, Frota & Vigário, 2005; Frota, Cruz et al., 2015; Frota & Vigário, 2007). It has been found that Subject–Verb–Object (SVO) sentences show greater tendency to be phrased into two intonational phrases, i.e. $(S)_{IP} (VO)_{IP}$, in the North (Braga) and Alentejo (Castro Verde), irrespective of size considerations, more so than in the Lisbon area and in the South (Albufeira), where the grouping of SVO sentences into a single major phrase is the preferred pattern, unless the Subject is long or branching, respectively.

Research on rhythm across Portuguese areas has looked at variation in the proportion of vocalic durations within the sentence (%V) and the durations of interconsonantal intervals (ΔC), two measures that were proposed in Ramus, Nespor and Mehler (1999) to correlate with the rhythmic classification of languages (Cruz, 2013; Frota & Vigário, 2001; Cruz, Oliveira, Palma, Neto & Frota, 2017; Frota, Vigário & Martins, 2002a, 2002b). In Portugal, it has been found that the Interior-Centre (Castelo Branco), Alentejo (Évora) and South (Albufeira) show values that pattern with stress-timed languages (for %V and ΔC dimension), whereas in Braga, Ermesinde, Lisbon and a southern zone of Alentejo (Castro Verde) the values obtained indicate a mixed rhythm (syllable-timed for %V dimension and stress-timed for ΔC dimension). In the North, furthermore, both Braga and Ermesinde regions show less syllable-timing in the %V dimension than Lisbon and Castro Verde.

Very recent investigation has also inspected the way Portuguese varieties and dialects treat tone crowding in intonational phrase final position. Tone crowding emerges when there is little space in the segmental string for complex tonal events, as when a fall–rise tune is associated with a stressed syllable in sentence final position (Frota et al., 2016). There are two main strategies to deal with emerging text–tune conflicts in Portuguese, which may consist in changing the tonal events (namely, via tone truncation) or changing the text (via vowel lengthening or split, schwa insertion, or blocking of word-final schwa deletion). While, unlike BP, EP favours strategies that involve text adjustment, there is dialectal variation, with more tune adjustment without changing the text in the North (in particular Northwest) and a crescendo of text adjustment strategies towards the South of Portugal.

Investigation on segmental processes across EP dialects indicates that resyllabification and fricatives' anticipatory voicing assimilation is found in all regions of Portugal and is bound by the intonational phrase (IP) (Aguiar, 2008; Cruz, 2013; Cruz & Frota, 2013). However, unlike in SEP, where the fricative before a vowel is anterior ([z]), it is produced as a [ʒ] in the Northeast area and there is variation in Southern regions (the later articulation being more frequent in Algarve than in Alentejo – Cruz, 2013).

In the realm of the variation in hiatus resolution processes in EP, one specific strategy, namely [j]-insertion to break a hiatus formed of two central vowels (as in *a* [j] *aula* "class") has been reported to be active only in the North and Centre of Portugal and in one location in São Miguel island (namely, Ponta Garça – Azores). This process has been noticed in the literature since the late XIXth century (Lopo, 1895; Pereira, 1906; Santos, 1897; Vasconcellos, 1901) and is still active, according to recent surveys (Oliveira, Paulino, Cruz & Vigário, 2014; Oliveira, Cruz, Paulino & Vigário, 2017;

Segura, 2013). Glide insertion (GI) has been shown to apply typically only when V1 is an oral vowel and the second vowel of the hiatus is stressed, it is an optional process spanning the intonational phrase domain, and there is great variation in terms of frequency of occurrence (Oliveira et al., 2014, 2017; more details on this process will be given in section 2.3, below).

Importantly, different areas seem to cluster together depending on specific prosodic aspects, and the prosodic classifications do not mirror the classical dialectal classification, established by Cintra (1971), based on a number of salient segmental features (see also Segura & Saramago, 2001; Segura, 2013). Under this view, there are two major dialectal areas in EP, the Northern Varieties and the Central-Southern Varieties, which are divided into smaller groups according to their behavior with respect to particularly noticeable segmental features. The Northern Varieties, which are characterized, for instance, by the neutralization on /b/~/v/, which contrast in the other regions, are divided into two major sub-areas, Transmontano and Alto-Minhoto, and Baixo-Minhoto, Duriense and Beirão. Transmontano and Alto-Minhoto has a consonantal system with four sibilants, where apical and predorsal (voiced and unvoiced) fricatives contrast, unlike in Baixo-Minhoto, Duriense and Beirão, where, as in SEP, only one anterior articulation is contrastive (apical and predorsal, respectively). Central-Southern Varieties are also subdivided, into Litoral-Centre and Interior-Centre and South sub-varieties. Sub-varieties of Central and Southern areas differ for instance in the realization of diphthongs. In particular, Interior-Centre and South shows monophthongization of /ej/ (>[e]).

One of our goals in this study is to determine if possible patterns of variation in hiatus resolution across the Portuguese regions under analysis go together with dialectal variation found in other specific areas of Portuguese phonology.


## 2.2 Hiatus resolution across (Romance) languages

Languages vary in the degree of tolerance to hiatus, the strategies available for HR, and the conditions under which hiatuses are tolerated (e.g. Casali, 1997, 2011; Hall, 2011, 2013). Common strategies for HR across languages include: (i) vowel coalescence (or vowel merger, fusion, degemination) V1 V2>V3 (e.g. *O árabe odi*[a] [o] *porco* > *...odi*[ɔ] *porco* "The arab hates pork", in Galician – Fernandez Rei, 2002); (ii) glide formation or semivocalization of V1 or V2 (e.g. *piano* > *p*[j]*ano*, "piano" in EP); (iii) deletion of one of the vowels V1 V2 > V2 or V1 (e.g. *oli esplendid* > *ol*[i]*splendid* "splendid oil" in Catalan – Cabré & Prieto, 2005); and (iv) insertion of a non-syllabic segment, i.e. a consonant or a glide (e.g. insertion of a consonant in Spanish /a/+/o/ > [aɣo] – Alba, 2006).

All of these strategies may be found in a single language, although not necessarily in the same contexts, as in most Romance languages, or in languages from many other language families, such as Bantu languages (e.g. Mudzingwa & Maxwell, 2011). The strategies for hiatus resolution, as well as the possibility or need to resolve the hiatus, may depend on a variety of factors:

- the quality of each vowel of the sequence and relative sonority (e.g. VV with rising sonority, as in *viola* "guitar", often allow glide formation of V1, as in many Romance languages, with varying degrees of probability – Chitoran & Hualde, 2007);
- word-level prominence on V1 or V2 or both – stress in both vowels usually blocks HR (like vowel merger), and the presence of stress on V1 or V2 often blocks processes that target stressless vowels (like semivocalization and deletion of the stressed vowel, as we will see further below);
- higher levels of prominence – phrasal prominence may disfavour HR at least when it originates a stress clash. According to Cabré and Prieto (2005), additionally, in many Romance languages, like Catalan and Galician, nuclear stress in V2 blocks HR irrespective of stress clash considerations.
- position of the vowels in hiatus within a phonological domain – V2 gliding or deletion as a strategy for HR may not be available word-initially, as in SEP (Vigário, 2003). HR strategies are also usually bound to a prosodic constituent – in Romance languages, in general, across word processes that yield resyllabification are bound by the Intonational Phrase (e.g. Frota, 2000; Nespor & Vogel, 1986/2007).

There is variation across Romance languages in terms of how some of these factors interact with HR. Notice nevertheless that in some cases, differences in terminology make it difficult to compare across languages. For example, vowel merger (VM) in BP, Galician and Catalan is reported to be possible when one of the vowels bears word-level stress, as in the Catalan examples *menú opcional* [u] "optional menu" and *destí incert* [i] "uncertain destiny", unlike in SEP, where word stress in either vowel blocks VM (Cabré & Prieto, 2005; Fernandez Rei, 2002; Frota, 2000; Tenani, 2002). However, at least in some of these cases, fusion may in fact correspond to vowel deletion. In BP, for example, Tenani (2002) assumes that there is fusion (or degemination) when two identical (central) vowels are merged and the result is a single vowel without a change in quality, as in *a aluna age sempre > a alun*[a]*ge sempre* "the student always acts", and as in the Catalan example above. For Frota (2000), Fernandez Rei (2002), and others, by contrast, vowel merger implies that the resulting vowel is different from each of the vowels that forms the hiatus.[2] Under this view, the examples above from BP and Catalan would be instances of vowel deletion instead of VM.

Irrespective of terminological issues, in all these languages VM (or vowel deletion) is blocked if V2 bears nuclear prominence. Thus, HR is possible in Catalan, for example, in *això obre la porta* "this opens the door" ([ɔ]), but not in *això obre* "this opens up" ([ɔ ɔ]) (Cabré & Prieto, 2005). Unlike in EP, in addition, in these languages V2 may semivocalize or delete (the latter possibly limited to V2 in closed syllables, as in *xampú excellent > xamp*[u]*xcellent* "excellent shampoo" and *Meu avó està enganado > Meu avó est*[a]*nganado* "my grandfather is wrong", in Catalan and Galician, respectively, taken from Cabré & Prieto, 2005, and Fernandez Rei, 2002). Semivocalization is also reported to be possible in Catalan when both vowels are stressed, although, like VM, it is only possible if V2 does not bear sentence nuclear stress (e.g. *algú obre la porta.* "someone opens the door" [w ɔ], but *algú obre.* [u ɔ]) "someone opens (it)".

What counts as a (minimal) stress clash configuration that must be avoided also varies across languages and language varieties (see the review in Frota, 2000: 113–118), and tolerance to hiatus may also depend on the availability of a given strategy to resolve hiatuses in the language. For example, in BP a V' V sequence, as in *sofá azul* "blue couch", may allow vowel merger because stress retraction is available in BP in this context (Bisol, 2003). Since stress retraction is not available in EP (Frota, 2000), and there are no alternative ways of resolving the hiatus, hiatuses with stressed V1 are always tolerated across words in EP, at least in the variety spoken in the Lisbon area.

Another domain of variation concerns the frequency of HR when optional processes are involved. A number of factors have been identified that play a role in the probability of HR. For example, a larger distance with respect to word-level stress seems to favour V1 semivocalization in Catalan (Cabré & Prieto, 2005) and the frequency of words or word combinations and/or word class (i.e. open vs. closed class) have also been reported to affect the probability of HR and the type of strategies available for resolving hiatuses (Alba, 2002, 2006; Chitoran & Hualde, 2007). Differences between groups of speakers in the frequency of glide formation in Catalan are seen in Cabré and Prieto (2005) to indicate a change in progress.

---

[2]    In this chapter, following Frota and others we assume that when the hiatus is formed of central vowels with different degrees for the open feature and the result is identical to one of these vowels, there is vowel deletion, instead of fusion.

## 2.3 A glimpse into hiatus resolution processes across words in European Portuguese

In present-day EP there are many lexical hiatuses. Word-internal hiatuses may be part of the basic underlying word-form, in many cases originally emerging from processes that applied in earlier stages of the language or emerge from morphological morpheme concatenation. A major additional source of hiatus in EP results from the combination of words.

Semivocalization and glide insertion are the two classes of productive processes that are available to resolve hiatus words internally in EP. Vowel deletion and fusion or vowel coalescence do not in general apply word internally, with the exception of very specific morphological contexts – for example, the theme vowel is usually present in verbal inflected forms, but it is systematically deleted when a following inflectional morpheme starts with a vowel, as in *com e + o > como* "(I) eat", and fusion of identical vowels is also found in inflected contexts, as in *dorm i + i > dormi* "(I) slept" (Mateus & Andrade, 2000).

Across words hiatuses are most often formed of a stressless [ɐ] or [u] followed by any of the phonetic vowels of EP, oral or nasal (with the exception of schwa), which may be stressless or bear word stress.

Although V2 semivocalization is reported to be possible in EP in Sá Nogueira (1938) and Ellison and Viana (1996), this seems to be at least very marked (Vigário, 2003).[3] The presence of word stress in V1, but not V2, is also incompatible with hiatus resolution, even with high vowels in the first position of the hiatus according to Frota (2000) (*javali ativo > *javali tivo* "active boar").

The investigation on hiatus resolution in EP has been especially concerned with the processes that may resolve hiatuses across words formed of a stressless [ɐ] or [u] or a stressed vowel ([i], [a] or [ẽ]) as V1 (Frota, 2000; Oliveira, 2016; Oliveira et al., 2014; Oliveira et al., 2017; Paulino & Frota, 2015). In particular (i) vowel merger (VM) of two central vowels hiatuses ([ɐ ɐ] > [a], as in *aluna africana > alun*[a]*fricana "african student"*), (ii) GI to break a hiatus formed of central vowels (e.g. *importava aves > importava* [j] *aves* "imported birds"); (iii) deletion of the round back vowel [u] (BVD), when followed by another vowel (e.g. *músico ama muito > músi*[kɐ]*ma muito* "the musician loves [it] very much"); (iv) semivocalization (SV) of

---

 Mateus & Andrade (2000) report that V1 semivocalization of exceptional stressless [i] in word final position is possible when followed by another vowel (*táxi antigo* "old taxi"). According to our intuitions, however, this is not possible. It is uncontroversial, in any event, that this vowel may not undergo deletion, unlike [u].

V1, when V1 is a high vowel (e.g. *músico ama muito > músi*[kwɐ]*ma muito* "the musician loves [it] very much").[4]

As we have seen above, several factors have been found to condition hiatus resolution, including (i) presence of stress in V2[5]; (ii) stress clash; and (iii) prosodic domain (see in particular Frota, 2000 and the references therein for EP). Specifically, Frota (2000) shows that (i) VM does not apply if one of the vowels bears word level stress, irrespective of phrasal prominence; (ii) BVD and SV may not target a stressed vowel; (iii) BVD may apply when V2 bears word-level stress, if it does not create a stress clash involving two adjacent phonological phrase heads or two clashing elements within a phonological phrase (PhP) (e.g. [*o bailarino*]$_{PhP}$ [*anda sempre*]$_{PhP}$ > [ok]*o bailarin_ anda sempre* "the dancer is always", but [*o dançarino*]$_{PhP}$ [*ama*]$_{PhP}$ *a bailarina russa* > **o dançarin_ ama a bailarina russa* "the dancer loves the Russian ballerina; [*o vestido âmbar*]$_{PhP}$ > **[o vestid__ âmbar* "the amber dress"; [*o músico*]$_{PhP}$ [*ama*]$_{PhP}$ > **o music_ ama* "the musician loves"); (iv) SV may apply when V2 bears word-level stress if it does not create a stress clash involving two adjacent phonological phrase heads (e.g. [*vestido âmbar*]$_{PhP}$ > [ok]*vestid*[w] *âmbar* "amber dress" but [...[*o dançarino*]$_{PhP}$ [*ama*]$_{PhP}$ ...]$_{IP}$> **o dançarin*[w] *ama* "the male dancer loves"); (v) distance between stresses in the string that results from the application of BVD and SV, also distinguishes the two processes, since, unlike SV, BVD is still blocked across PhP when V2 is the head of PhP and the result of deletion does not create strict adjacency of the two stressed syllables (e.g. [... [*o músico*]$_{PhP}$ [*ama*]$_{PhP}$ ...]$_{IP}$ > **o music ama* "the musician loves", but [... [*o músico*]$_{PhP}$ [*anda sempre*]$_{PhP}$...]$_{IP}$ > [ok]*o músic*[w] *anda sempre* "the musician is always") (vi) all these processes of HR apply within, but not across the intonational phrase (IP). Frota (2000) further shows that a number of other processes that apply across words in EP are bound by the IP.

Work on GI to break a hiatus formed with central vowels has shown that glide insertion is essentially found in the Northern and Central regions of Portugal, requires that V2 bears word-level stress, and is an optional

---

4    An additional process, possibly of a more superficial or phonetic nature, exists in various regions (Brissos, 2015), which happens in the standard language as well, consisting of the optional emergence of what looks like a transitional glide at least when V2 is stressed. This glide has the same value for the back feature as the right-adjacent non-central vowel (as in *a* [j] *égua* "mare", *a* [j] *Ema*; *a* [w] *hora* "hour", *a* [w] *ostra* "oyster"). The process at hand seems more gradual and less phonologised than the processes addressed in this chapter. In any event, this phenomenon has not been given much attention and requires further investigation.

5    In the literature there are also episodic references of glide insertion when V2 is stressless, namely in the area of Portalegre, in the Centre region (Brissos, 2015) and in the area of Viseu, a bit further to the North (Oliveira, 2016).

process that spans the IP domain. The frequency of insertion varies across prosodic conditions, and extra-linguistic conditions, such as geographic areas, speaking modalities and age groups (Oliveira, 2016; Oliveira et al. 2014, 2017). More on this process is presented in subsection 4.6.

# 3    Method – Materials and data collection

In this section we briefly describe the method used in the collection and processing of the data studied here.

The data analyzed in this chapter is part of a larger corpus collected within the *InAPoP* project.[6] For the present study we selected five regions from different parts of Portugal, two in the North, one in the Centre and two in the South. This allows us to capture some of the variation that may be found in hiatus resolution across the country. Specifically, the following urban areas were selected: *Arcos de Valdevez* (ArV – part of the administrative region (AR) of Viana do Castelo), *Vila Real* (VlR – AR of Vila Real), *Castelo Branco* (CtB – AR of Castelo Branco), *Évora* (Eva – AR of Évora) and *Alvor* (Alv – part of the AR of Faro) (see the map in Figure 7.1 further below). The data reported here come from a total of 1004 sentences, produced by 13 subjects distributed by the five areas.[7]

Besides the main data set, which is common to the five locations distributed across the country, another set of data collected within the InAPoP project was used here to allow us to have a better understanding of glide insertion, a phenomenon that has been found in previous research to occur less in read speech of younger subjects and in urban areas (Oliveira et al., 2014, 2017). This supplementary data set contains (i) read material, from a corpus of sentences specifically designed to investigate hiatuses formed of two central vowels with stress on the first or the second vowel, and (ii) semi-spontaneous speech (coming from a Map Task and an Interview). For the purpose of the present research, we have selected the material produced by 23 subjects in the reading task and 27 in the (semi-)spontaneous task, from six regions of the North and Centre of Portugal and two age groups (20–45 years old and more than 59 years old). Here, we will report on some of the overall results, which will provide relevant complementary information

---

[6] *Interactive Atlas of the Prosody of Portuguese* (Frota, coord., 2012–2015) – see http://labfon.letras.ulisboa.pt/InAPoP/.

[7] The distribution of participants and sentences analysed per location was the following: ArV – 3 subjects (246 sentences), VlR – 2 subjects (164 sentences), CtB – 3 subjects (239 sentences), Eva – 3 subjects (247 sentences) and Alv – 2 subjects (108 sentences).

related to the variation found in EP in the realization of hiatuses containing sequences of central vowels, and hiatus resolution more in general. Unlike the main corpus analyzed in this chapter, which was obtained in a reading task, in urban areas and with subjects aged 20–45 years old, the data from the second corpus includes not only read speech material but also (semi-) spontaneous speech, and was collected in several urban and rural areas, with the following distribution: Northwest – ArV (urban), CtL (rural); Northest – VlR (urban), StA (rural); Centre – CtB (urban) and UnS (rural) (see the map in Figure 7.1).

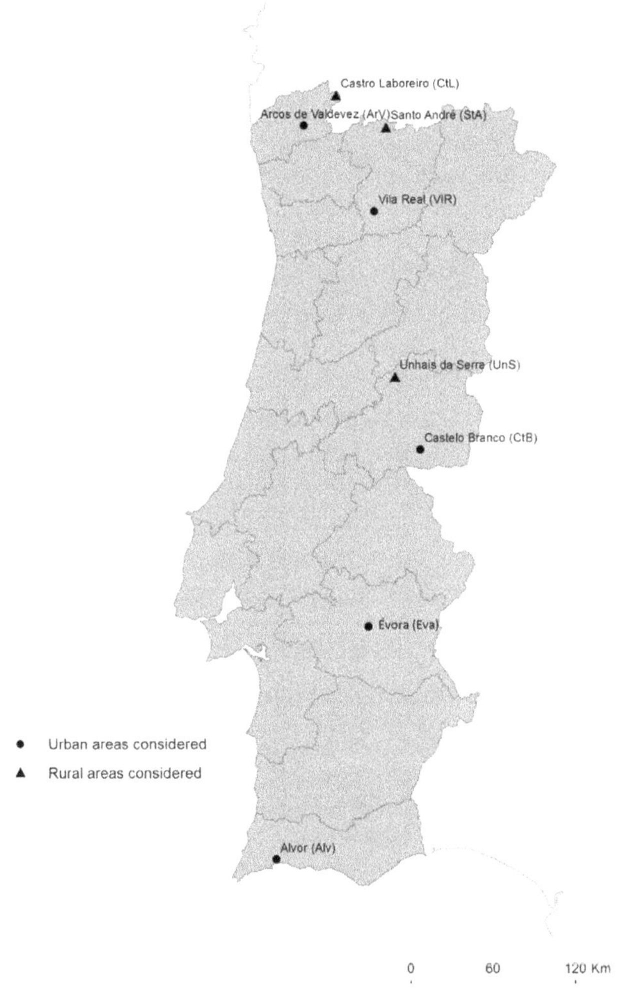



**Figure 7.1.** Geographic distribution of the locations where the speech materials analysed here were collected: Arcos de Valdevez (ArV), Castro Laboreiro (CtL), Vila Real (VlR), Santo André (StA), Castelo Branco (CtB), Unhais da Serra (CtB), Évora (Eva), Alvor (Alv).

The materials of this data set were produced by 27 speakers from two age groups: 12 aged between 20–45 years old and 15 over 59 years old (see the details in Oliveira, 2016).

The data were collected *in loco* and recorded to video (in .mov format) and to audio, with a JVC camera (model GY-HM11E) and an external ear microphone. At a later stage, the audio files were extracted from the video file with the program AoA Audio Extractor (ver.2.3.7). The extraction was saved as .wav format at a frequency of 22050 Hz and in mono.

The realization of lexical hiatuses was annotated perceptively by two experts plus a third one in case of disagreement (there was an agreement of 90% for the transcription of the realization of hiatuses formed of central vowels and of 80% for the realization of hiatuses formed of /u/+/a/). Perception was complemented by spectrographic inspection using *Praat* (Boersma & Weenink, 2007). For the prosodic analysis, we followed the criteria established for P-ToBI in Frota, Oliveira, Cruz and Vigário (2015). Different tiers were created with *Praat* for the annotation of various types of information, as illustrated in Figure 7.2.

The main corpus, collected in five regions, was firstly designed by Frota (2000) to investigate vocalic sandhi in SEP, spoken in the region of Lisbon. Among the possible vowels in hiatus, those selected, i.e. two central vowels (oral or nasal, corresponding to different spellings, and which we represent

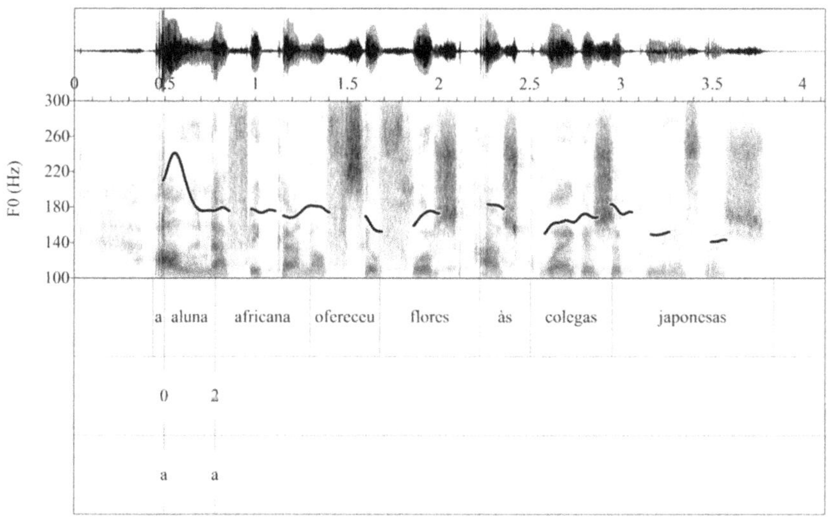


**Figure 7.2.** Multi-tier annotation using *Praat* – Tiers for the orthographic transcription, prosodic level at points relevant for the analysis and phonetic transcription of the target sequence (sentence *A aluna africana ofereceu flores às colegas japonesas*, produced by Subject AR, from CtB).

here as <a a>) and a high vowel (/i/ or /u/) plus a central vowel (represented here <u a>, always corresponding to the condition V1= unstressed, and <i a>, always corresponding to the condition V1= stressed), allow the investigation of vowel merger, vowel deletion and semivocalization. In this corpus, several prosodic conditions are also represented, such as: (i) lexical stress in V1 and/or V2, (ii) different levels of prominence in V1 and V2, (iii) sequences that may originate stress clash, and (iv) different positions within prosodic domains. Examples of the sentences that elicited the occurrence of hiatus in various prosodic conditions are listed in (1) below:

(1)  *Condition #1: Within PhP, both vowels unstressed (V V)*

[A alun**a a**fricana]_PhP ofereceu flores às colegas japonesas.

the student African gave flowers to-the colleagues Japanese

"The African student gave flowers to the Japanese colleagues."

[O músic**o a**fricano]_PhP cantou várias canções.

the musician African sang several songs

"The African musician sang several songs."

*Condition #2: Within PhP, V1 stressed (V' V)*

[O gal**ã a**fricano]_PhP enviou uma carta à cantora.

the movie star African sent a letter to-the singer

"The African movie star sent a letter to the singer."

[Ouv**i a**penas,]_PhP/IP não cheguei a ver o carro.

(I) listened only (I) not got to see the car

"I have just listened, I did not get to see the car."

*Condition #3: Within PhP, V2 stressed (V V'), V2 PhP head*

[A canet**a â**mbar]_PhP foi vendida ontem.

the pen amber was sold yesterday

"The amber pen was sold yesterday."

[O vestid**o â**mbar]$_{PhP}$ foi vendido ontem.

the dress amber was sold yesterday.

"The amber dress was sold yesterday."

## Condition #4: Across PhP, both vowels unstressed (V V)

[A aluna]$_{PhP}$ [**a**penas ofereceu flores]$_{PhP}$ ao professor de matemática.

the student only gave flowers to-the teacher of math

"The student only gave flowers to the math teacher."

[O músic**o**]$_{PhP}$ [**a**ceitou]$_{PhP}$ o emprego no restaurante.

the musician accepted the job at-the restaurant

"The musician took the job at the restaurant."

## Condition #5: Across PhP, V1 stressed (V' V)

[O gal**ã**]$_{PhP}$ [**a**ceita]$_{PhP}$ o papel de bandido.

the movie star accepted the part of-the bandit

"The movie star took the bandit's part"

[Ontem v**i**]$_{PhP}$ [**a**penas rapazes]$_{PhP}$ na festa.

yesterday (I) saw only boys at-the party

"Yesterday I saw only boys at the party."

## Condition #6: Across PhP, V2 stressed (V V'), V2 PhP Head

[A aluna]$_{PhP}$ [**a**ma]$_{PhP}$ o professor de matemática.

the student loves the teacher of math

"The student loves the math teacher."

[O músic**o**]$_{PhP}$ [**a**ma]$_{PhP}$ a bailarina russa.

the musician loves the dancer russian

"The musician loves the Russian dancer."

*Condition #7: Across PhP, V2 stressed (V V'), V2 PhP Non Head*

[A alun**a**]$_{PhP}$ [**a**ma muito]$_{PhP}$ o irmão mais novo

the student loves a lot the brother more young

"The student loves the younger brother very much."

[O músic**o**]$_{PhP}$ [**a**nda sempre]$_{PhP}$ de limusine preta.

the musician drives always a limousine black

"The musician always drives a black limousine."

*Condition #8: Across PhP, both vowels stressed (V' V')*

[O gal**ã**]$_{PhP}$ [**an**da]$_{PhP}$ de porche.

the movie star drives a porsche

"The movie star drives a Porsche."

*Condition #9: Across IP, both vowels unstressed (V V)*

[A alun**a,**]$_{IP}$ [**a**pós o exame,]$_{IP}$ foi para a discoteca.

the student after the examination went to the disco

"The student, after the examination, went to the disco."

*Condition #10: Across IP, V1 stressed (V' V)*

[O gal**ã,**]$_{IP}$ [**a**té partir,]$_{IP}$ não revelou a sua identidade.

the movie star before (to) leave not reveal his identity

"The movie star didn't reveal his identity before leaving."

[V**i,**]$_{IP}$ [**a**frontando o bandido,]$_{IP}$ um grupo de crianças.

(I) saw facing the bandit a group of children

"I saw a group of children facing the bandit."

*Condition #11: Across IP, V2 stressed (V V')*

[A alun**a,**]$_{IP}$ [**a**ntes de partir,]$_{IP}$ falou com os colegas.

the student before (to) leave talked with the colleagues

"The student has talked with his colleagues before leaving."

[O bailarin**o,**]$_{IP}$ [**a**ntes de partir,]$_{IP}$ falou com os amigos.

the dancer before (to) leave talked with the friends

"The dancer has talked with his friends before leaving."

For each type of hiatus, 20 sentences were elicited and produced twice by 13 speakers. Thus, for both the central vowels' hiatuses, and the hiatuses containing high vowel + central vowel, 520 productions were elicited ($20 \times 2 \times 13$), totalling 1040 sentences. Of the elicited sentences, 36 were excluded due to disfluent reading, and therefore a total of 1004 sentences were analyzed.

We have coded *VM* the realization as a single low vowel ([a] or [ã]) of two mid central vowels which are specified as non-low (either oral or nasal, i.e. [ɐ] or [ɐ̃]) by lexical phonological rules. In other words, in the present analysis vowel merger implies a postlexical change in vowel quality. Particularities in the segmental realization in the Northern regions explain why some hiatuses formed of central vowels that were reduced to a single low vowel may be instances of non-labial back vowel deletion (BVD$_a$) instead of VM. In ArV, for example, underlying low central vowels remain low ([a] or [ã]) before a nasal consonant in contexts where they are realized in other regions as mid (i.e. [ɐ] or [ɐ̃]). Thus, a sequence like *aluna ama* "student loves" is realized as *alun*[ɐ] [a]*ma* instead of *alun*[ɐ] [ɐ]*ma*. In these cases, the process for hiatus resolution does not yield a vowel different from at least one of the source vowels, since it is identical to V2 (e.g. *alun*[ɐ] [a]*ma muito* > *alun*[a]*ma muito* "student loves very much"; *a alun*[ɐ] [ã]*tes de partir* > *a alun*[ã]*tes de partir* "the student, before leaving"). In line with the notion of fusion present in Frota (2000), Fernandez Rei (2002), and others, these cases were not treated as instances of VM but of BVD$_a$. For the <u a> contexts, we coded as instances of SV the realization of V1 as [w] and as instances of BVD (or BVD$_u$) the cases where V1 does not surface.

As said above, in order to obtain complementary information on the realization of central vowels hiatuses in Northern and Central areas, we looked at data coming from another corpus, also part of InAPoP materials (see the Methodology tab at http://labfon.letras.ulisboa.pt/InAPoP/), which includes (semi-)spontaneous speech and read sentences, and which was specifically built to investigate the conditions on glide insertion. In this corpus the elicited sentences contained central vowels hiatuses with a stressed V2 in several prosodic conditions, allowing us to control the position within the prosodic domains, levels of phrasal prominence and phonological status of the word to which V1 belongs (a prosodic word or a clitic), as exemplified in (2):

(2) *Condition #1: V1 and V2 within PW*

    Nunca tinha ouvido falar da região de [Sima**á**ri]$_{PW}$ Cura, na África Oriental; e tu?

    never (I) had heard talk of-the region of Simaari Cura, in-the East Africa and you

    "I had never heard of Simaari Cura region, in East Africa; have you?"

*Condition #2: V1 and V2 across PW, within PWG*

    Sabes se há algum campeonato onde se joguem [os trint**a a**vos]$_{PWG}$ de final?

    (you) know if is some competition where they play the thirtieth of final

    "Do you know if there is a competition with a round of 60?"

*Condition #3: V1 and V2 across PWG, within PhP*

    Tive um amigo [que montav**a a**sas]$_{PhP}$ de aviões ultra-leves.

    (I) had a friend that assembled wings of aircrafts ultralight-PL

    "I had a friend that assembled wings in ultralight aircrafts"

*Condition #4: V1 and V2 across PhP.*

    Um amigo meu [importav**a**]$_{PhP}$ [**a**ves raras]$_{PhP}$ do Brasil.

    a friend mine imported birds rare from-the Brazil

    "A friend of mine imported rare birds from Brazil"

*Condition #5: V1 and V2, across IP*

[Quanto à Maria]$_{IP}$, [**a**ulas às oito da manhã]$_{IP}$ nunca lhe agradaram.

as to-the Mary classes at-the eight of-the morning never her pleased

As to Mary, classes at eight were never pleasant to her"


*Condition #6: W1=CL*

O Pedro falou [**da**]$_{CL}$ **A**na a uma antiga amiga

the Peter spoke of-the Ana to an old friend

"Pedro spoke about Ana to an old friend"

*Condition #7: Within PhP, W1=PW –*
*See examples in Condition #3.*


In the data set considered here we obtained 927 contexts for GI in the reading task, and 132 contexts for GI in the (semi-)spontaneous tasks (i.e. sequences of central vowels, the second of which was stressed). The second corpus is analyzed separately, in section 4.6.

The full list of sentences elicited in each corpus is given in Appendix 1.[8]


# 4　Results


In this section we look at the HR processes across regions, their relative frequency and the factors that condition the occurrence of the various processes.

In the following subsections we consider prosodic conditions that have been reported in the literature to constrain hiatus resolution phenomena: lexical stress in V1 or V2, prominence levels of W1 and W2, stress clash configurations, and position of the vowels within a prosodic domain. In each section, in the contexts where the two hiatuses may undergo changes,

---

[8]　In our corpus, V2 is always an open syllable. Possible effects of syllable structure on hiatus resolution in EP, which we do not anticipate, given the previous descriptions available, and our own informal observations, will be left for future research. The same applies to hiatuses containing vowels other than those included in our study.

we first look at the sequences of two central vowels, represented <a a> for ease of reference, which may be the target for VM, BVD$_a$ and GI, and then we look at the sequence of high vowel plus central vowel, which may be the target for SV and BVD, and of BVD$_a$, in the case of V2.

In the last subsection we present the results coming from the study of the supplementary corpus specifically designed to investigate the resolution of hiatuses composed of central vowels where V2 is stressed in the Northern and Central regions of Portugal. As said above, it has long been reported that glide insertion may apply in this region, and we now know that various factors may condition insertion. Thus, differently from what was done with the general corpus analyzed in sections 4.1–4.5, where only urban areas and speech from younger subjects in reading tasks are considered, in subsection 4.6 we will consider urban/rural differences, and variation across age groups and across speech modalities.

## 4.1   The effect of word level stress

Let us start by observing the effect of word stress in one of the vowels of the hiatus. When V1 is stressed, none of the processes apply.[9] In addition, V2 deletion is not possible across all regions. This means that in all of the dialectal areas considered V' V hiatuses are not resolved, as in *o galã apanhou*, "the movie star caught", *o galã aceita* "the movie star accepts", *ouvi apenas* "(I) only heard", *vi aparelhos* "(I) saw devices".

As shown in Figure 7.3, in our main corpus hiatuses composed of central vowels also tend not to be resolved if V2 bears word-level stress. In addition, when V2 is stressed all regions allow some amount of BVD$_a$, but not VM (with the exception of ArV, where the hiatus is always preserved in this condition). We may also notice that GI is only residually found, and only in CtB. The results depicted in Figure 7.4 show that when V1 is labial, SV and BVD may apply when V2 bears word stress, at least when no stress clash emerges, as we will see below (i.e. *o músico anda sempre…* "the musician is always…"). Nevertheless, the stress on V2 favours the occurrence of SV in all regions, relative to no stress. Conversely, when V2 is unstressed BVD is always more frequent than when it is stressed.

The results plotted in Figures 7.3–7.4 also show that the frequency of VM and especially of SV and BVD varies across regions. The frequency of VM

---

[9]   Since <i a> only appears in the hiatuses under analysis when V1 is stressed (see section 2), and given that hiatuses with stress on V1 are never resolved, as we have just seen, in what follows the hiatuses formed of a high vowel + /a/, will always involve only the labial vowel /u/, and will be represented <u a>.

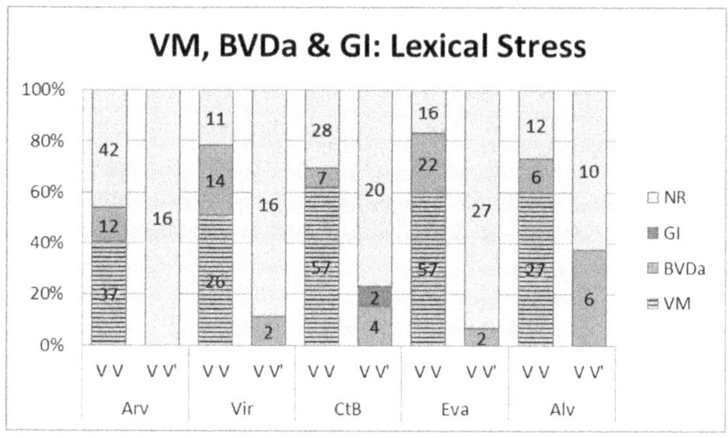


**Figure 7.3.**  Resolution of <a a> hiatuses when V2 is Unstressed vs. Stresssed.

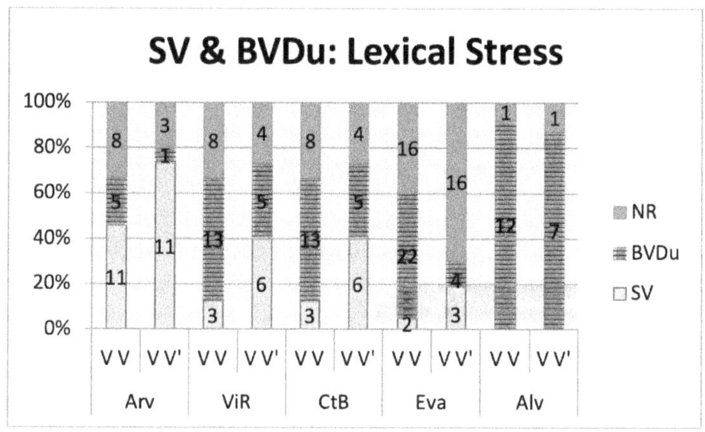


**Figure 7.4.**  Resolution of <u a> hiatuses when V2 is Unstressed vs. Stressed.

shows little fluctuation across all regions, although in the North it is slightly less frequent (between 40–45%) than in the Central and Southern regions (around 60% in all regions). Regions pattern very differently, however, in the preferred strategy for <u a> hiatus resolution: while in the Northwest region (ArV) semivocalization is favoured over vowel deletion, reaching close to 80% of the potential contexts of occurrence, in the Northeast (VlR) and Centre (CtB) semivocalization becomes less frequent, and this pattern is reinforced towards the South, with a very small rate of SV in Eva and no SV at all in the extreme South (Alv).

Comparing the rate of hiatus resolution in the two types of hiatus (<a a> and <u a>) when both vowels are unstressed (which is the stress condition under which both types of hiatuses may be avoided), no clear pattern emerges, since there seems to be a greater tendency for hiatus resolution when V1 is a labial vowel in ArV and Alv, but the reverse is found in VlR and a similar rate of hiatus resolution with both types of hiatus is found in the CtB and Eva. The fact that lexical stress on V2 blocks the resolution of central vowels' hiatuses whereas it does not in <u a> hiatuses implies that hiatus resolution is globally more frequent in the latter context throughout the territory.

## 4.2   Other levels of prominence in V2

Only in hiatuses formed of <u a>, which may be resolved when V2 bears word-level stress, may we evaluate the effect of higher levels of prominence in hiatus resolution, namely when V2 is head vs. non-head of PhP. Here we will not consider whether the result of hiatus resolution creates a stress clash, which will be systematically investigated in the next subsection.

As shown in Figure 7.5, in Northern and Central regions, hiatuses are more tolerated across PhP when V2 is not the head of PhP. The reverse pattern is observed in the Southern regions (Eva and Alv).

Figure 7.5 also shows the relative frequency of the two processes available for hiatus resolution, depending on the prominence level of the stress on V2. Here, all of the regions that use both SV and BVD pattern similarly, since SV is proportionally more frequent when V2 is the head of PhP than when it is not, and conversely, except in ArV, BVD is more frequent when V2 is not PhP head.

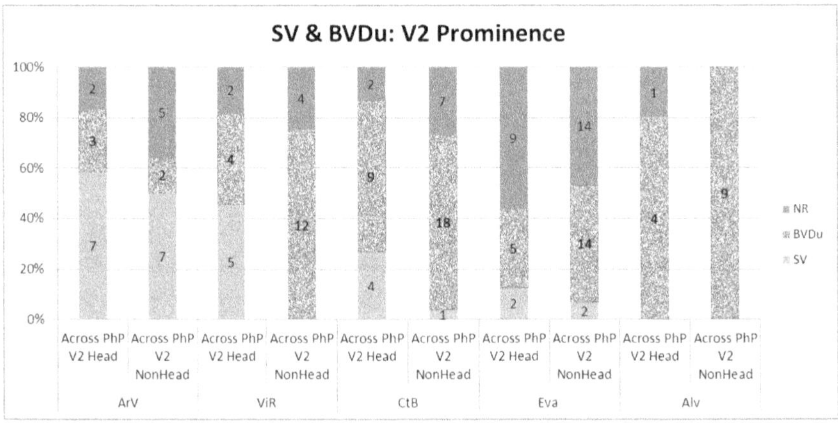


**Figure 7.5.** Resolution of <u a> hiatuses across PhP when V2 is Head or Non-Head of PhP.

## 4.3  Stress clash

Let us now consider specifically the effect of a clashing context in hiatus resolution across regions. Since the relevant context always involves V V' sequences, and this is not a context for VM, here too we will look only at the effect of stress clash on the processes involved in <u a> hiatus resolution. In the data analyzed in this subsection V1 and V2 belong to separate PhP and V2 may either be the head of PhP or only bear word-level prominence, and one or more underlying vowels may intervene between the stresses of W1 and W2. For example, in [o bailaRIno]$_{PhP}$ [Ama]$_{PhP}$ "the male dancer loves", there is one vowel that intervenes between two phrasal stresses, and in [o bailaRIno]$_{PhP}$ [Ama MUIto]$_{PhP}$ "the male dancer loves very much" there is also one vowel intervening between a PhP-level stressed syllable and a syllable bearing word-level, but not PhP-level prominence.

Figure 7.6 shows the effect on HR of a number of underlying vowels that intervene between stresses whether V2 bears phrasal prominence or not. We can see that in Eva and VlR hiatus resolution clearly tends to be blocked when V2 bears phrasal prominence and HR would result in two adjacent stresses. Importantly, in these regions HR frequently occurs if V2 does not bear phrasal prominence and/or HR does not originate adjacent stressed syllables. In Alv, by contrast, the difference in the rate of HR according to prominence and distance conditions does not exist or is residual. No blocking effect of phrasal prominence or underlying distance between stresses emerges in the other regions either.

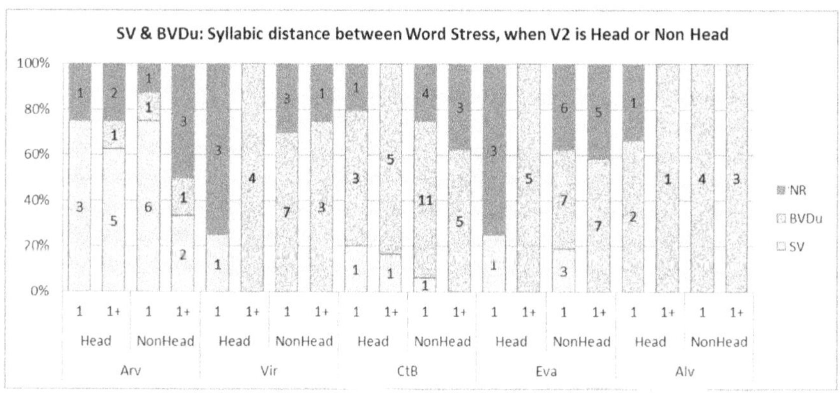


**Figure 7.6.** Resolution of <u a> hiatuses in contexts where there is 1 or more (underlying) vowels between W1 and W2 stresses (1 and 1+), when V2 is Head of PhP or not.

To sum up, only two locations show a clear effect of stress clash (VlR and Eva), since in configurations where a stress clash would emerge from HR, the hiatus is preserved. In several locations BVD is not blocked in configurations that create stress clash, in particular in the extreme Southern regions. In the locations where SV operates, it does not seem to be conditioned by stress clash either.

## 4.4   Position within prosodic domains

Let us now look at the effect on hiatus resolution of the position occupied by the two adjacent vowels within prosodic domains. In all of the regions, hiatus resolution processes are blocked across IP (see Figures 7.7 and 7.8).

In the other two prosodic conditions, i.e. inside and across PhP, there is some variation across regions in the rate of hiatus resolution. With central vowels hiatuses, in VlR, CtB, and Eva there is a clear decrease of hiatus resolution between PhP, compared to the condition inside PhP (Figure 7.7), whereas hiatuses in the two prosodic conditions pattern more similarly in ArV and Alv. With the exception of ArV, the reverse pattern is observed with <u a> hiatuses, that is, when these vowels are involved there is more HR across than inside PhP (Figure 7.8).

In both types of hiatus, prosodic conditions seem not to promote one strategy of HR over another.

In conclusion, all four phenomena are bound by the IP. For <a a> hiatuses, with the exception of ArV and Alv, the higher the domain the greater the tolerance to hiatus. Also, with the exception of ArV, the reverse pattern obtains with <u a> hiatuses in the other regions, where lower domains show higher rates of non-resolved hiatuses.

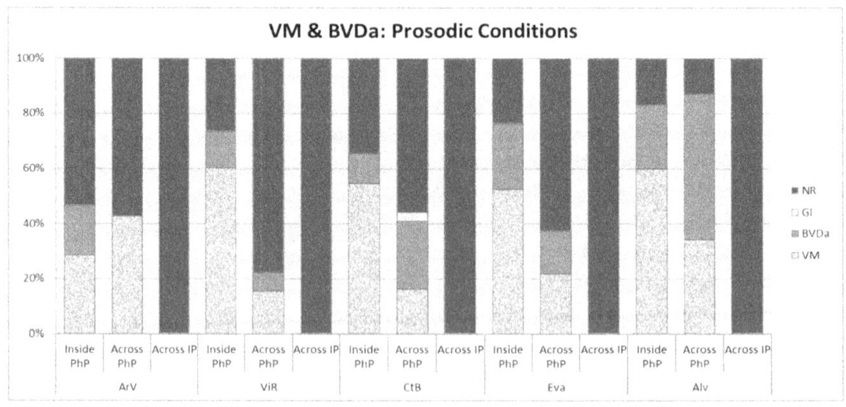


**Figure 7.7.**   Resolution of <a a> hiatus in all prosodic conditions.

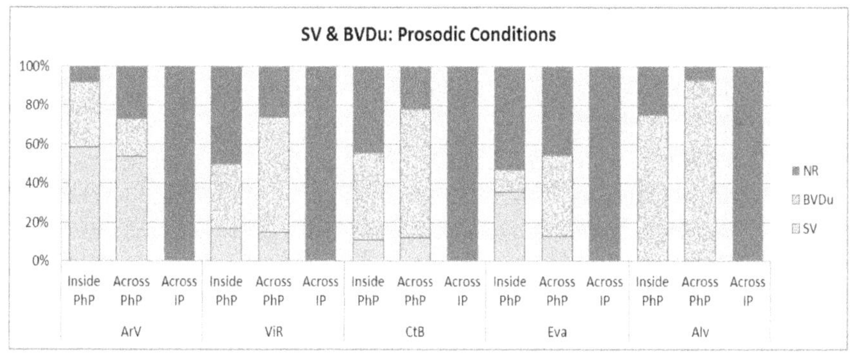



**Figure 7.8.**  Resolution of <u a> hiatus in all prosodic conditions

## 4.5  Overall tendency for hiatus resolution

Figure 7.9 shows the overall tendency for hiatus resolution in our main corpus across regions. The results indicate that there an increasing tendency for hiatus resolution towards the South, though not very expressive.

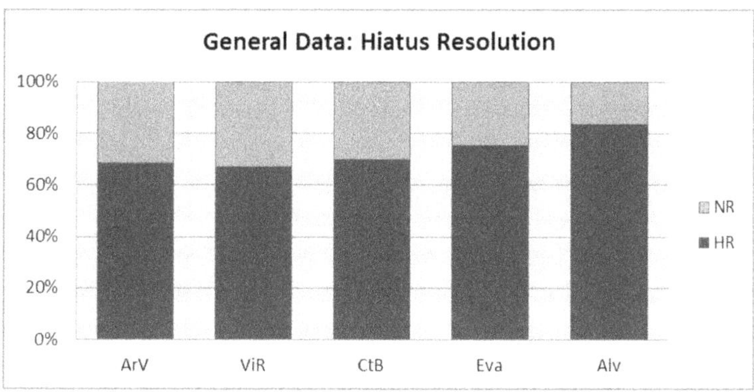



**Figure 7.9.**  Hiatus Resolution (all the phenomena – VM, $BVD_a$, $BVD_u$, GI) vs Non-Resolution, in all prosodic conditions within IP.

## 4.6  A closer look at glide insertion to break hiatuses formed with central vowels

In this subsection, we inspect in more detail the resolution of hiatuses formed of central vowels in the Northern and Central regions under investigation (ArV, VlR and CtB). The reason for having a closer look at hiatuses composed of central vowels in these regions is the fact that only in these areas do we find a particular strategy for <a a> hiatus resolution, which is [j]-insertion when V2 is stressed. However, in our main corpus, which was not specifically conceived to investigate this very context, GI was extremely rare. Recent research specifically focusing on GI has shown that a number of variables play a role in the emergence of GI, including the category of W1, urban vs. rural locations, speech modality, and age group. With respect to all these variables, the main corpus studied so far is expected to exhibit low rates of GI, because W1 is always a PW and not a clitic, the data selected for this study was collected in urban but not rural locations, there is no spontaneous speech nor data from subjects above 59 years old, variables that have been shown to promote GI. The data below is a selection of material in Oliveira (2016), Oliveira et al. (2014), and Oliveira et al. (2017).

In our data, this process only applies when V2 is stressed, as commonly described in the literature (e.g. Segura, 2013). Like the other hiatus resolution processes, GI is also never found across the intonational phase. Inside the IP, by contrast, it seems to apply freely and optionally in the three major regions investigated here, both in urban and rural locations, as shown in Figure 7.10 (in order to investigate the effect in GI of hiatuses position within prosodic phrases, in this case only the read material was considered).

The results in Figure 7.10 above indicate that not only GI but also $BVD_a$ coexist with NR. Besides that, <a a> hiatuses with stress on V2 tend to be avoided very often, unlike in SEP and other regions, where this type of hiatus is not resolved.

Ongoing investigation has shown that the prosodic status of W1 is relevant in the way GI operates, since insertion is usually much more frequent when W1 is a clitic (CL) than when it is a PW (Oliveira, 2016; Oliveira et al., 2017). Nevertheless, for the sake of comparison with the rest of the data in this chapter, here we will look at the effect of non-linguistic variables on GI considering only the data where W1 is a PW. The data in Figure 7.11, corroborate the description above in the sense that in urban regions, younger groups and, in the reading task, GI is quite rare. However, when considering the rural areas, the older group, and more informal speech modalities, it becomes clear that GI is in fact very productive. We can see in Figure 7.11 furthermore that, in the regions where the number of contexts produced was not too low or inexistent, there is an overall tendency to find more GI in the rural locations and in the older group. In addition, $BVD_a$ is only found in the reading task. GI is clearly promoted in the (semi-)spontaneous speech modalities.

We may note, nevertheless, a few deviations to the general pattern. In particular, in the reading task, where (i) the younger age-group of CtL (and

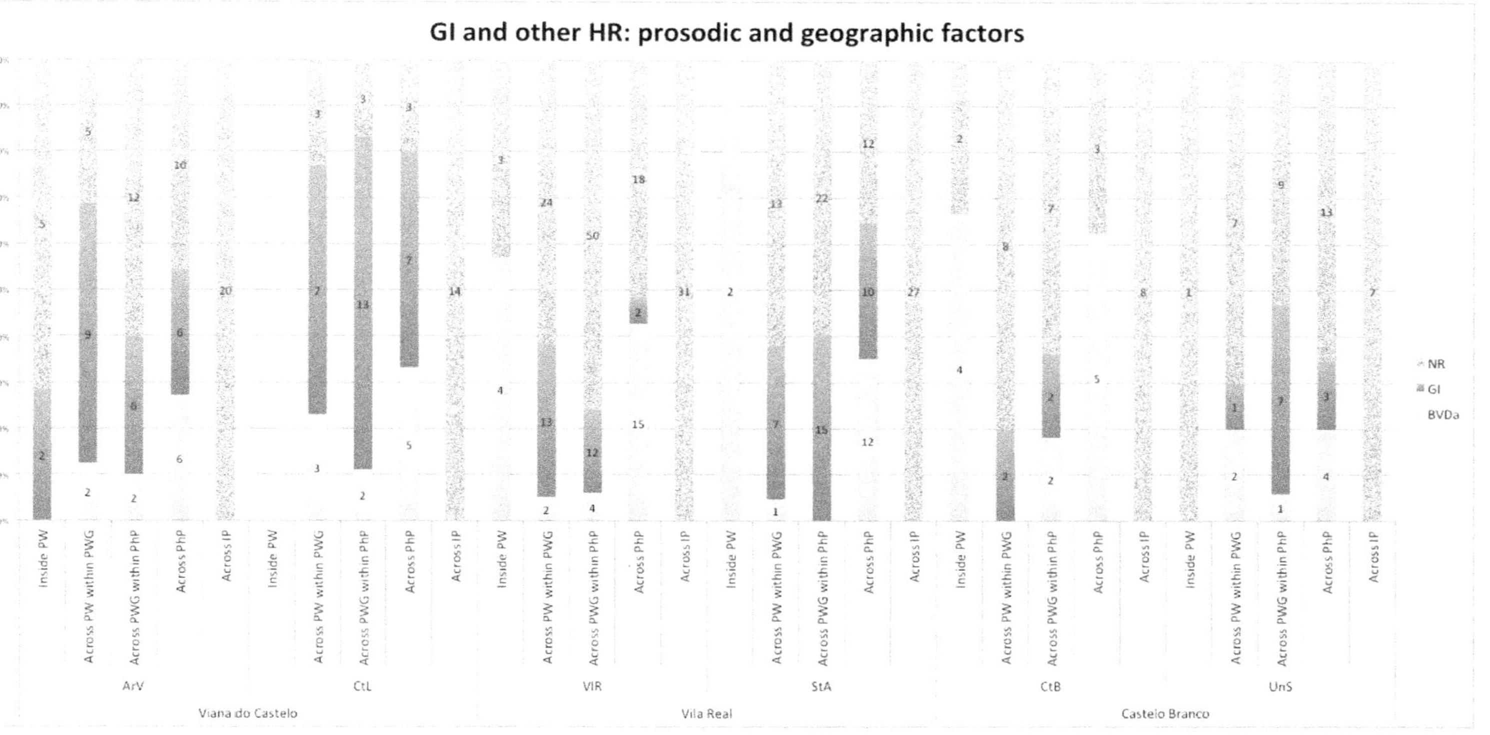


**Figure 7.10.** Resolution of <a a> hiatuses (V2 stressed) by position within prosodic domains in Northern and Central regions (second set of data, reading task only).

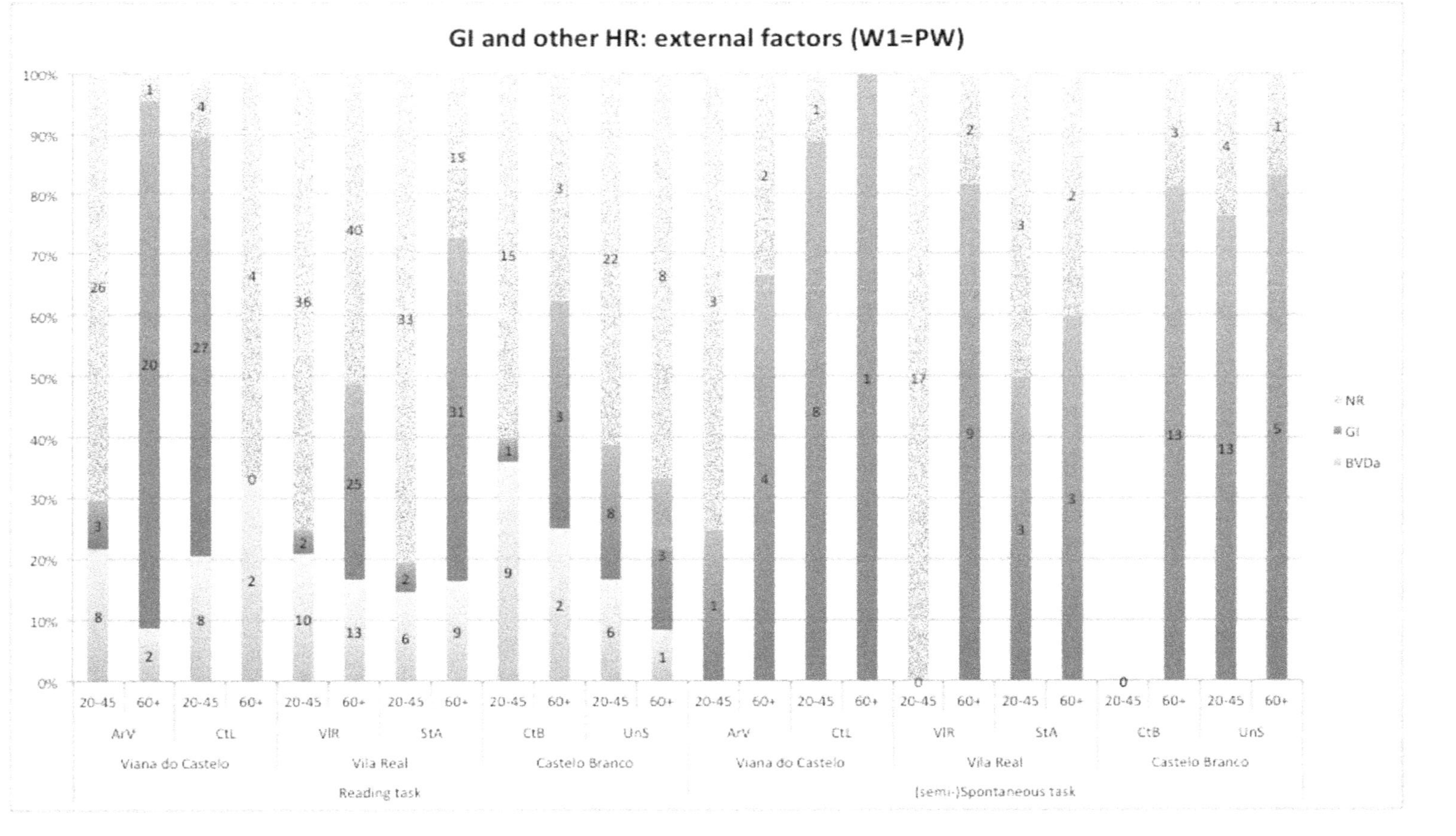


**Figure 7.11.** Resolution of <a a> hiatuses (V2 stressed) by region (Northwest: Viana do Castelo; Northeast: Vila Real; Central: Castelo Branco), urban (ArV, VlR, CtB) and rural locations (CtL, StA, Uns), age group (20–45 years old and more than 59 years old) and speech modality (reading and (semi-)spontaneous speech).

to a smaller extent of UnS) inserts more than the older group, where hiatus is preserved much more, (ii) there is no difference between the urban and rural areas of Castelo Branco, and (iii) the older group of the urban location of Castelo Branco inserts more than the same age group in the rural location. At least some of these effects are most certainly a consequence of subjects' low reading proficiency. Older participants from the urban location of Vila Real also show more GI than the participants of the same age group in the rural location, but this time in (semi-)spontaneous speech. In the region of Castelo Branco, in (semi-)spontaneous speech, the rate of GI is very high (around 80%) and the frequency of GI is very similar in both urban and rural areas, and across age groups.

To sum up, a closer look at GI in the Northern and Central regions shows that this is still an active strategy for avoiding hiatuses formed of central vowels, where V2 is stressed, it is fairly frequent across the regions, and several linguistic internal and external factors condition the frequency of occurrence of this particular strategy for breaking central vowels hiatuses.

# 5    Discussion

A number of commonalities were found across regions, which also characterize SEP (Frota, 2000). In none of the regions V2 deletion is a strategy to resolve hiatus, namely when V1 is stressed, as in *v*[i] [a]*penas* > **v*[i] *penas* "(I) only saw". In other Romance languages, V2 deletion has been reported to be possible at least with schwa or /e/ in closed syllables (Cabré & Prieto, 2005; Fernandez Rei, 2002). However, in contexts similar to those studied here, namely when V2 is in open syllable, there seems to be a general tendency for V2 not to delete. We interpret this as following from the prominent status of word initial position. In fact, SEP, like other dialects, shows evidence that PW initial position is stronger than word-internal positions, as indicated by phenomena such as word initial r-strengthening, weaker reduction of word initial unstressed vowels, initial stress and emphatic stress (Frota, 2000; Vigário, 2003).

Stress in V2 blocks VM in all of the regions, unlike what has been reported, for instance for BP and Catalan (Cabré & Prieto, 2005; Tenani, 2002). Here, however, it is important to acknowledge terminological differences, because while for us VM implies the fusion of two identical vowels and the quality of the resulting vowel changes, in the above mentioned work fusion (vowel merger) under identity does not have to result in a vowel of a quality different from V1 or V2 (e.g. *menú opcional* > *men*[u]*pcional* "optional menu", in Catalan). Notice, furthermore, that still another type of fusion is reported to occur in Galician when V2 is stressed. Here, *coalescencia* (or fusion) involves two different vowels ([a] and [o]) yielding a third different one ([ɔ]) (i.e. *recoñecía **o**lores* > *recoñecí*[ɔ]*lores* "(s/he) recognized smells"). In our data, when the hiatus is composed of central vowels with different values for the open feature, BVD$_a$ may apply when V2 bears word stress. However, when the two central vowels are identical, VM may not apply when V2 is stressed. In our view, this indicates that what we have coded as BVD$_a$ is indeed an instance of V1 deletion instead of vowel merger, since the process patterns like labial vowel deletion (BVD$_u$), i.e. it may apply when V2 bears word stress, unlike VM.

In our main corpus, stress on V2 tends to block central vowels' hiatus resolution. The same is not true of hiatuses with a labial V1. This seems to relate to the processes available to resolve the two types of hiatuses, namely VM, and more residually GI in this corpus, for the central vowels' hiatuses, and SV and BVD for the hiatuses with a labial V1. Unlike VM, SV and BVD may apply when V2 bears word level stress, a pattern found in SEP as well (Frota, 2000).

Also, similarly to SEP, the presence or absence of PhP-level prominence in V2 seems to have an effect in <u a> hiatus resolution, which nevertheless is variable across regions. Our results show that in Northern and Central regions, hiatuses are more tolerated across PhP when V2 is not the head of PhP and the reverse pattern is observed in the Southern regions (Eva and Alv). The effect observed may be a consequence of the predominance of SV in the Northern and, to some extent, Central regions – in contrast with the Southern regions, where BVD is clearly more frequent (or even the only process available, as in the case of Alv). Notice that in SEP, whereas BVD may not apply when V2 is Head of PhP, SV is always a possible strategy for HR (unless a stress clash occurs, as we have seen above).

The five locations do not show similar sensitivity to stress clash. Only in VlR and Eva, BVD and SV do not occur in contexts where the application of these processes originates a stress clash (i.e. two adjacent PhP-heads). Notice that in contexts where these processes do not originate a stress clash, hiatus resolution clearly predominates in these regions. In this respect, only VlR and Eva pattern like SEP, because hiatus resolution is blocked in contexts that create a stress clash. By contrast, in the other regions, there is no indication that stress clash may condition hiatus resolution. Most noticeably, in the extreme South (Alv), vowel deletion operates in every context where a stress clash emerges, unlike what was previously found for SEP. Thus, these regions may be patterning like languages such as Catalan, where only sentence nuclear stress on V2 seems to block V1 deletion and semivocalization (Cabré & Prieto, 2005).

The prosodic domains within which each of the processes under analysis operate is the IP, and internal domains do not block them. Variation across regions related to the prosodic configuration of hiatus within IP is observed only in terms of the frequency of HR in each type of hiatus. While with central vowels, with the exception of the most southern region (Alv), all regions show a greater tendency to preserve the hiatus across PhP in comparison to PhP-internal position, with hiatuses containing a labial V1, the reverse pattern is found, except for the most northern region (ArV). Importantly, it is often assumed that the higher the prosodic domains the less obligatory or frequently prosodic rules apply (see in particular Cabré & Prieto, 2005: 126 for HR strategies). Our data do not support this observation, in particular in what concerns HR processes involving a labial V1. We believe this topic deserves further investigation.

In terms of hiatus resolution strategies, two main differences were found across regions related to the presence/absence of GI and SV. Let us consider GI first. In our main corpus, coming from read speech material, produced by subjects aged 20–45 years old, from urban locations, GI is residual, even in Northern and Central regions. However, a closer inspection of GI in these regions shows that the process is quite frequent under certain conditions, since it was observed that not only language internal factors affect the frequency of occurrence of GI – such as position of hiatus within prosodic domains and prosodic status of W1 – but also external factors play a role in the frequency of this specific strategy for hiatus resolution – such as type of location (rural vs. urban), speech modality (read vs. (semi-)spontaneous speech), and age group (20–45 years old vs. more than 59 years old). A richer system of strategies for resolving hiatuses in the Northern and Central varieties could indicate that hiatuses are less tolerated. However, our global results show slightly less hiatus resolution in these regions. This, in our view, may be a consequence of a more general property of these dialects, namely a preference to preserve segments, a hypothesis developed in the following paragraphs.

We have seen in section 2 that, in cases of tone crowding, where there is a complex of tonal events to be associated with a small number of tone-bearing units, there is a crescendo towards the South of Portugal of changes in the tonal sequence as opposed to changes in the segmental string (Frota et al., 2016). In other words, in the North and Centre, there is a greater tendency to preserve lexical segments. If we admit that in these dialects, as in other languages, there is a pressure for hiatuses to be resolved, in particular when identical central vowels are involved, a way of achieving this without eliminating segmental and/or syllabic positions is to insert a non-vocalic element between the adjacent vowels.[10] Inserting a glide to break the hiatus allows the preservation of the segmental structure and, at the same time, resolves the hiatus.

The second observation related to the strategies found across regions for hiatus resolution concerns <u a> hiatuses. The relative frequency of SV and BVD varies across the country: the former is more frequent in the Northern regions and decreases towards the South, and the reverse is found with BVD. We believe that the clear predominance of SV over BVD in the Northwest region and the progressive decrease in the use of SV and the increasing presence of BVD may also be motivated by the greater tendency to preserve lexical segments found in the North, which gradually weakens towards the South (Frota et al., 2016). In fact, deletion of segmental material represents a more severe change in the segmental string than glide formation, which preserves a segmental position in the skeletal tier, unlike deletion.

Considering cross-dialectal variation in hiatus resolution in the larger context of segmental and prosodic variation across Portuguese dialects, a few observations are in place. The first one refers to the distribution of Glide Insertion as a strategy to break hiatus when V2 is stressed. The regions in which the process is attested, although with varying degrees of frequency, are located in the North and a smaller area of the Centre of Portugal (see also Oliveira et al., 2017). While it does not correspond exactly to the area of neutralization of /b/~/v/, because it expands into the Centre region, or of any other known segmental phenomenon, the distribution of GI seems to pattern like segmental isophones in that it seems to operate in a continuous space. This type of continuous pattern is also observed in the frequency of other segment preserving strategies in the resolution of hiatus, for instance, V1 deletes less in the Northern regions and is progressively more deleted towards the South, as well as in the frequency of segment preserving strategies to deal with tone crowding, as we have seen above. Such pattern of variation contrasts with other domains of phonological variation already identified, namely variation in pitch accent density, in phrasing preferences, and rhythm, which have been found to be geographically discontinuous (see the review in section 2.1). Our data seem to support Cruz et al.'s (2017) observations that variation in non-prosodic (i.e. segmental) features is more dependent on geography than variation of prosodic (i.e. suprasegmental) properties.

---

[10]  Other strategies that could allow HR without eliminating segments would be to change stress or duration patterns. These have not been found in our data in these regions.

# 6    Concluding remarks

This study has revealed a number of properties that are common to EP spoken in several regions from the North to the South of the country. Across the various regions the processes found for HR span the Intonational Phrase and are blocked by an IP boundary, HR phenomena do not target V2 or a stressed vowel, and VM is blocked when V2 bears word stress. While these features are found within the EP space investigated so far, the same does not hold for other Romance languages, including the Brazilian variety of Portuguese, since in other languages or language varieties hiatus resolution may apply across IP boundaries, there are reports of HR that target a stressed vowel, and VM is not necessarily blocked by word-level stress (possibly indicating that what is present in those languages is $BVD_a$, instead of VM). Some areas of variation within the EP space were also found, namely related to the frequency of hiatus resolution and the sensitivity to the conditions that may favor/inhibit HR, like phrasal stress on V2, position within/across PhP and stress clash creating contexts. Variation was also found in the preference for different strategies for HR. Most noticeably, only in the Northern and Central regions a specific strategy applies with central vowels hiatuses when V2 is stressed (namely, GI); and in the Northwest region there is a clear preference for resolving hiatuses containing a labial V1 via V1 gliding instead of deletion; whereas there is a progressively higher tendency to apply BVD towards the South. We have interpreted this as following from a more general tendency in the North, as opposed to the South, to preserve the segmental material, which has been proposed in Frota et al. (2016) to also explain why in tone crowding contexts, tone may be truncated in the North, with segments remaining unchanged, while towards the South there is an increasing tendency to preserve the melody and change the segmental material instead in order to create more space for tonal association.

Looking specifically at glide insertion to break central vowels hiatus, we have seen that external factors also play a role in the frequency of occurrence of the process, namely, speakers' age-group and provenance from rural/urban locations, as well as type of production task.

Globally, this work suggests that more crossdialectal and crosslinguistic comparison is necessary, in particular within the Romance languages area, which should also incorporate more dimensions of prosodic variation, besides hiatus resolution, as well as extralinguistic factors. We believe this will contribute to a deeper understanding of the factors underlying variation in the resolution of hiatuses.

# Appendix I

## Corpora used in the reading task

Subset of the materials of Frota, S. (Coords). (2012–2015) *Interactive Atlas of the Prosody of Portuguese.*

*CORPUS 1*

Sandhi Phenomena *corpus – Original source: Frota (2000)*

Sandhi 16. A aluna africana ofereceu flores às colegas japonesas.
Sandhi 17. A aluna aceitou o emprego no restaurante chinês.
Sandhi 18. A aluna apenas ofereceu flores ao professor de Português.
Sandhi 19. A aluna, após o exame, foi para a discoteca.
Sandhi 20. A caneta âmbar foi vendida ontem.
Sandhi 21. A tábula âmbar foi vendida ontem
Sandhi 22. A aluna ama o professor de matemática.
Sandhi 23. A astróloga ama o professor de matemática.
Sandhi 24. A aluna ama muito o irmão mais novo.
Sandhi 25. A astróloga ama muito o irmão mais novo.
Sandhi 26. A aluna, antes de partir, falou com os colegas.
Sandhi 27. A astróloga, antes de partir, falou com os colegas.
Sandhi 28. O galã africano enviou uma carta à cantora.
Sandhi 29. O galã afoito enviou uma carta à cantora.
Sandhi 30. O galã aceitou o papel de bandido.
Sandhi 31. O galã aceita o papel de bandido.
Sandhi 32. O galã apenas enviou flores à bailarina.
Sandhi 33. O galã apanhou sempre o melhor papel.
Sandhi 34. O galã, até partir, não revelou a sua identidade.
Sandhi 35. O galã, ameaçado pelo rival, revelou a sua identidade.
Sandhi 36. O músico africano cantou várias canções.
Sandhi 37. O músico aceitou o emprego no restaurante.
Sandhi 38. O músico apenas dedicou a canção à mãe.
Sandhi 39. O músico, após a audição, saltou para a plateia.
Sandhi 40. O vestido âmbar foi vendido ontem.
Sandhi 41. O púlpito âmbar foi leiloado ontem.
Sandhi 42. O músico ama a bailarina russa.
Sandhi 43. O dançarino ama a bailarina russa.

Sandhi 44. O músico anda sempre de limusine preta.

Sandhi 45. O bailarino anda sempre de limusine preta.

Sandhi 46. O músico, antes de partir, falou com os amigos.

Sandhi 47. O bailarino, antes de partir, falou com os amigos.

Sandhi 48. Ouvi apenas, não cheguei a ver.

Sandhi 49. Ouvi apitar, mas não cheguei a ver o carro.

Sandhi 50. Ontem vi antenas de televisão à venda.

Sandhi 51. Ontem vi aparelhos de televisão à venda.

Sandhi 52. Ontem vi apenas rapazes na festa.

Sandhi 53. Ontem vi animais domésticos na festa.

Sandhi 54. Vi, após o tiro, um vulto a fugir.

Sandhi 55. Vi, afrontando o bandido, um grupo de crianças.

## CORPUS 2

Glide Insertion *corpus – subset of* Set for the North

Iode 1. O Pedro falou da Ana a uma antiga amiga.

Iode 2. O Simão adoraria ser contratado pela equipa da águia.

Iode 3. A Ana saiu mais cedo da aula.

Iode 4. Sempre sonhei viajar pela Ásia distante.

Iode 5. O jornalista perguntou a Ana Moura pelo seu disco novo.

Iode 6. O irmão da Ana Lúcia comprou um novo cachimbo.

Iode 7. O Quim andava com ideias de trabalhar na AEG.

Iode 8. A AEP é uma associação de escuteiros, tal como o CNE.

Iode 9. A amiga da Anabela não estava à espera daquele presente de anos.

Iode 10. Aquele professor também dava aulas aos mais jovens.

Iode 11. Tive um amigo que montava asas de aviões ultra-leves.

Iode 12. Este agricultor só plantava **á**rvores baixas.

Iode 13. Um amigo meu importava aves raras do Brasil.

Iode 14. A matrícula do meu novo carro é JA-18-18.

Iode 15. O João era mesmo ganancioso, ultra-**á**vido de vencer!

Iode 16. Sabes se há algum campeonato onde se joguem os trinta avos de final?

Iode 17. Foi criada há pouco uma companhia aérea com as iniciais K.A.D.

Iode 18. Os políticos deram agora à J.A.E. a tarefa de vigiar a sinalização nas autoestradas Portuguesas.

Iode 19. O avô Joaquim andou por sítios de que nunca ouvi falar, como a cidade de Faátu e os Jardins de Cimabué.

Iode 20. Nunca tinha ouvido falar da região de Simaári Cura, na África Oriental; e tu?

Iode 21. A Maria há-de vir ajudar-nos na mudança.

Iode 22. Quanto à Joana, ela há-de vir visitar-nos no Verão.

Iode 23. Quanto à Maria, aulas às 8 da manhã nunca lhe agradaram.

Iode 24. A última década tem tido, segundo o Instituto Nacional de Estatística, anos de calor invulgar.

*Subset of* Set for the North *taken from Frota (2000) (C stands for* Context*)*

TopFoc 11. O galã anda de Porsche.

TopFoc 12. [C: Naquele filme é o vilão que anda de Porsche?]
O galã anda de Porsche.

TopFoc 15. O pintor retratou uma manhã âmbar

TopFoc 16. [C: Foi uma tarde âmbar que o pintor retratou?]
O pintor retratou uma manhã âmbar.

*Subset of* Set for the North *taken from Frota (2002) (C stands for* Context*)*

IntY/NN 2. [C: Não sei nada sobre esse filme.]
O galã anda de Porsche?

IntY/NN 3. [C: Ainda não vi a exposição.]
O pintor retratou uma manhã âmbar?

IntY/NF 8. [C: Vi esse quadro na exposição, mas não me recordo se o motivo era uma   manhã ou um entardecer âmbar]
O pintor retratou uma manhã âmbar?

IntWh 2.    [C: Ainda não vi a exposição]
Quem pintou uma manhã âmbar?

IntWh 3.    [C: Gostava de ouvir esse disco.]
Quem cantou uma manhã angelical?

*Subset of* Set for the North *taken from Frota (2014) (C stands for* Context*)*

Request 3.  [C: Gostarias de ver uma determinada imagem de cores num quadro e por isso pedes a um pintor amigo:]
Pinta uma manhã âmbar.

Request 6.  [C: Um amigo teu, pintor, gostaria de te oferecer um quadro pelo Natal e tu pediste-lhe:]
Pinta uma manhã âmbar.

*Subset of* Set for the North *taken from Frota (2003)*

IPeak 23.    O marmelo da Ásia não tem sabor nenhum.

# References

Aguiar, J. (2008). *Unidades e Processos Fonológicos no falar da região da Terra Quente: contributos para a Linguística Forense* [Phonological units and processes in the speech of Terra Quente region: Contribution for Forensic Linguistics.] Unpublished Master Thesis. Universidade do Minho, Braga, Portugal.

Alba, M. (2002). ¿Cómo se llega a l'escuela?: a study of usage effects on hiatus resolution in New Mexican Spanish. Paper presented at *NWAV-XXXI*. Stanford University.

Alba, M. (2006). Accounting for Variability in the Production of Spanish Vowel Sequences. In N. Sagarra, & A. J. Toribio (Eds.), *Selected Proceedings of the 9th Hispanic Linguistics Symposium* (pp. 273–85). Somerville, MA: Cascadilla Proceedings Project.

Bisol, L. (2003). Sandhi in Brazilian Portuguese. *Probus, 15*, 177–200. https://doi.org/10.1515/prbs.2003.007

Boersma, P., & Weenink, D. (2007). *Praat – doing phonetics by computer.* Version 5.3.56. www.praat.org

Brissos, F. (2015). Dialectos Portugueses do Centro-Sul: Corpus de fenómenos e revisão do problema da (des)unidade. [Central-Southern Portuguese dialects: A corpus of phenomena and review of the (dis)unity problem.] *Zeitschrift fur romanische Philologie, 131*(4), 999–1041. https://doi.org/10.1515/zrp-2015-0071

Brissos, F., & Saramago, J. (2014). O problema da diversidade dialectal do Centro-Sul português: Informação perceptiva versus informação acústica. [The problem of the dialectal diversity in the Portuguese of Center-South: Perceptive information versus acoustic information.] *Estudos de Linguística Galega*, 6, 53-80. https://doi.org/10.15304/elg.6.1781

Cabré, T., & Prieto, P. (2005). Positional and metrical prominence effects on vowel sandhi in Catalan. In S. Frota, M. Vigário & M. J. Freitas (Eds.), *Prosodies* (pp. 124-157). Mouton de Gruyter: The Hague.

Casali, R. (1997). Vowel elision in hiatus contexts: Which vowel goes? *Language, 73*, 493–533. https://doi.org/10.2307/415882

Casali, R. (2011). Hiatus resolution. In M. van Oostendorp, C. Ewen, E. Hume & K. Rice. (Eds.), *The Blackwell companion to phonology* (pp. 1434-1460). Malden, MA & Oxford: Wiley-Blackwell.

Castelo, J., & Frota, S. (2015). Variação entoacional no Português do Brasil: Uma análise fonológica do contorno nuclear em enunciados declarativos e interrogativos. [Intonational variation in Brazilian Portuguese: A phonological analysis of the nuclear contour of declarative and interrogative utterances.] In A. Moreno, F. Silva, & J. Veloso (Eds.), *Textos Selecionados do XXX Encontro da APL* (pp. 113-131). Porto: APL. ISBN: 978-989-97440-4-9.

Chitoran, I., & Hualde, J. I. (2007). From hiatus to diphthong: The evolution of vowel sequences in Romance. *Phonology, 24*, 37–75. https://doi.org/10.1017/S095267570700111X

Cintra, L. F. (1971). Nova proposta de classificação dos dialectos galego-portugueses. [New proposal for the classification of galician-portuguese dialects.] *Boletim de Filologia, 22*, 81–116.

Cruz, M. (2013). *Prosodic variation in European Portuguese: Phrasing, intonation and rhythm in Central-Southern varieties.* Unpublished Doctoral Thesis. University of Lisbon, Lisbon, Portugal.

Cruz, M., & Frota, S. (2013). On the relation between intonational phrasing and pitch accent distribution. Evidence from European Portuguese Varieties. Proceedings of the *14ᵗʰ Annual Conference of the International Speech Communication Association* (Interspeech 2013) (pp. 300–304). Lyon: France. ISSN 2308-457X.

Cruz, M., Oliveira, P., Palma, P., Neto, B., & Frota, S. (2017). Building a prosodic profile of European Portuguese varieties. The challenge of mapping intonation and rhythm. In M. P. Barbosa, M. C. Paiva & C. Rodrigues (Eds.), *Studies on variation in Portuguese* (pp. 81–110). Amsterdam/ Philadephia: John Benjamins Publishing.

Ellison, M., & Viana, M. C. (1996). Antagonismo e Elisão de Vogais átonas Finais em Português Europeu. [Unstressed final vowel clash and deletion in European Portuguese.] In I. Duarte & M. Miguel (Eds.), *Actas do XI Encontro Nacional da Associação Portuguesa de Linguística* (pp. 261–81). Lisboa: APL.

Elordieta, G., Frota, S., & Vigário, M. (2005). Subjects, objects and intonational phrasing in Spanish and Portuguese. *Studia Linguistica, 59* (2–3), 110–43. https://doi.org/10.1111/j.1467-9582.2005.00123.x

Fernandez Rei, E. (2002). *Regras fonolóxicas posléxicas e regras precompiladas de alomorfia sintagmática: Domínios prosódicos en galego* [Postlexical phonological rules and precompiled rules of sintagmatic alomorphy: Prosodic domains in Galician]. Unpublished PhD Thesis. Universidade de Santiago, Galiza, Spain.

Frota, S. (1995). Os domínios prosódicos e o Português Europeu: Fenómenos de sandhi. [Prosodic domains and European Portuguese: Sandhi phenomena.] In *Actas do X Encontro Nacional da Associação Portuguesa de Linguística* (pp. 221–37). Lisboa: APL/Colibri.

Frota, S. (2000). *Prosody and Focus in European Portuguese. Phonological phrasing and intonation.* New York: Garland Publishing.

Frota, S. (2014). The intonational phonology of European Portuguese. In S.-A. Jun (Ed.), *Prosodic Typology II* (pp. 6–42). Oxford: Oxford University Press.

Frota, S., Castelo, J., Cruz, M., Crespo-Sendra, V., Barros, N., Silvestre, A., & Vigário, M. (2015). Melodia ou Texto? Estratégias de acomodação entre melodia e texto no Português. [Melody or text? Tune-text accommodation strategies in Portuguese.] *Diadorim 17*(2), 12–33. https://doi.org/10.35520/diadorim.2015.v17n2a4067

Frota, S. (Coord). (2012–2015). *Interactive Atlas of the Prosody of Portuguese.* Project funded by Fundação para a Ciência e a Tecnologia (PTDC/CLE-LIN/119787/2010). Webplatform available at http://labfon.letras.ulisboa.pt/InAPoP/.

Frota, S., Cruz, M., Castelo, J., Barros, N., Crespo-Sendra, V., & Vigário, M. (2016). Tune or Text? Tune-text accommodation strategies in Portuguese. *Proceedings of Speech Prosody 2016*. Boston: Boston University.

Frota, S., Cruz, M., Fernandes-Svartman, F., Collischonn, G., Fonseca, A., Serra, C., Oliveira, P., & Vigário, M. (2015). Intonational variation in Portuguese: European and Brazilian varieties. In S. Frota & P. Prieto (Eds.), *Intonation in Romance* (pp. 235–83). Oxford: Oxford University Press.

Frota, S., Oliveira, P., Cruz, M., & Vigário, M. (2015). *P-ToBI: tools for the transcription of Portuguese prosody*. Lisboa: Laboratório de Fonética, CLUL/FLUL. ISBN: 978-989-95713-9-6. http://labfon.letras.ulisboa.pt/InAPoP/P-ToBI/

Frota, S., & Vigário, M. (2000). Aspectos de prosódica comparada: Ritmo e entoação no PE e no PB. [Aspects of compared prosody: Rhythm and intonation in EP and BP]. In V.R. Castro & P. Barbosa (Eds.), In *Actas do XV Encontro Nacional da Associação Portuguesa de Linguística* (pp. 533–55). APL: Coimbra.

Frota, S., & Vigário, M. (2001). On the correlates of rhythmic distinctions: The European/Brazilian Portuguese case. *Probus, 13*, 247–73. https://doi.org/10.1515/prbs.2001.005

Frota, S., & Vigário, M. (2007). Intonational phrasing in two varieties of European Portuguese. In T. Riad & C. Gussenhoven (Eds.), *Tones and Tunes I* (pp. 263–89). Berlin: Mouton de Gruyter.

Frota, S., Vigário, M., & Martins, F. (2002a). Language Discrimination and Rhythm Classes: Evidence from Portuguese. *Speech Prosody Proccedings* (pp. 315–18). Aix-en-Provence.

Frota, S., Vigário, M., & Martins, F. (2002b). Discriminação entre línguas: Evidência para classes rítmicas. [Languages discrimination: Evidence for rhythmic classes]. In *Actas do XVII Encontro da APL* (pp. 189–99). Lisboa: APL/Colibri.

Hall, N. (2011). Vowel epenthesis. In M. van Oostendorp, C. Ewen, E. Hume & K. Rice (Eds.), *The Blackwell companion to phonology* (pp. 1576–96). Malden, MA & Oxford: Wiley-Blackwell.

Hall, N. (2013). Acoustic differences between lexical and epenthetic vowels in Lebanese Arabic. *Journal of Phonetics, 41*(2), 133–43. https://doi.org/10.1016/j.wocn.2012.12.001

Jenkins, D. L. (1999). *Hiatus Resolution in Spanish: Phonetic Aspects and Phonological Implications from Northern New Mexican Spanish*. Unpublished PhD Thesis. The University of New Mexico, Albuberque, USA.

Ladd, D. R. (2008). *Intonational Phonology* (2nd ed.). Cambridge: Cambridge University Press.

Lopo, J. (1895). Linguagem Popular de Valpaços. [Colloquial language from Valpaços]. *Revista Lusitana, III*, 326.

Mateus, M. H. M., & Andrade, E. d' (2000). *The Phonology of Portuguese*. Oxford: University Press.

Mudzingwa, C., & Maxwell, K. (2011). Comparing Hiatus Resolution in Karanga and Nambya: An Optimality Theory Account. *Nordic Journal of African Studies, 20*(3), 203–40.

Nespor, M., & Vogel, I. (1986/2007). *Prosodic Phonology* (2nd ed.). Berlin/New York: Mouton de Gruyter,

Oliveira, P. (2016). *A prosódia da iode epentética em variedades do Português.* [The prosody of the epenthetic glide in varieties of Portuguese]. Unpublished Master Thesis. University of Lisbon, Lisbon, Portugal.

Oliveira, P., Cruz, M., Paulino, N., & Vigário, M. (2017). Glide insertion to break a hiatus across words in European Portuguese: The role of prosodic, geographic and sociolinguistics factors. In Barbosa, P. Paiva & C. Rodrigues (Eds.), *Studies on Variation in Varieties of Portuguese* (pp. 50–79). Amsterdam/Philadelphia: John Benjamins Publishing.

Oliveira, P., Paulino, N., Cruz, M., & Vigário, M. (2014). Onde ainda([j])há o fenómeno. Contributo para o estudo da inserção de glide entre vogais centrais. [Onde ainda([j])há o fenómeno. Contribution for the study of glide insertion between central vowels]. In A. Moreno, F. Silva, I. Falé, I. Pereira & J. Veloso (Eds.), *Textos Selecionados do XXIX Encontro da Associação Portuguesa de Linguística* (pp. 419–36). APL: Colibri.

Paulino, N. (2016). *Variação prosódica no Português Europeu. Análise comparada de fenómenos de sândi vocálico.* [Prosodic variation in European Portuguese. Compared analysis of vocalic sandhi phenomena]. Unpublished Master Thesis. University of Lisbon, Lisbon, Portugal.

Paulino, N., & Frota, S. (2015). Variação prosódica no Português Europeu: Análise comparada de fenómenos de sândi vocálico. [Prosodic variation in European Portuguese: Compared analysis of vocalic sandhi phenomena]. In *Textos Selecionados do XXX Encontro Nacional da Associação Portuguesa de Linguística* (pp. 435–48). Porto: APL.

Pereira, A. (1906). Tradições Populares e linguagem de Vila Real. [Popular traditions and coloquial language from Vila Real]. *Revista Lusitana, IX,* 229–58.

Ramus, F., Nespor, M., & Mehler, J. (1999). Correlates of linguistic rhythm in the speech signal. *Cognition, 73,* 265–92. https://doi.org/10.1016/S0010-0277(00)00101-3

Sá Nogueira, R. (1938) *Elementos para um tratado de fonética portuguesa.* [Elements for a treaty on portuguese phonetics]. Lisboa: Imprensa Nacional de Lisboa.

Santos, F. (1897). Linguagem Popular de Trancoso. [Colloquial language from Trancoso]. *Revista Lusitana, V,* 161–73.

Segura, L. (2013) Variedades dialectais do Português Europeu. [Dialectal varieties of European Portuguese]. In E. Raposo, M. B. Nascimento, M. A. Mota, L. Seguro & A. Mendes (Eds.), *Gramática do Português.* Volume 1. (pp 85–142). Lisboa: Fundação Calouste Gulbenkian/Centro de Linguística da Universidade de Lisboa.

Segura, L., & Saramago, J. (2001). Variedades dialectais portuguesas. [Portuguese dialectal varieties]. In M. H. M. Mateus (ed.), *Caminhos do Português: Exposição Comemorativa do Ano Europeu das Línguas* (pp. 221–37). Lisboa: Biblioteca Nacional.

Tenani, L. (2002). *Domínios prosódicos no Português.* [Prosodic domains in Portuguese]. Unpublished PhD Thesis. Universidade de Campinas, São Paulo, Brazil.

Vasconcellos, J. L. ([1901]1987). *Esquisse d'une dialectologie portugaise* (3rd ed.). [Outline for the portuguese dialectology]. Lisboa: Instituto Nacional de Investigação Científica/Centro de Linguística da Universidade de Lisboa.

Vigário, M. (2003). *The Prosodic Word in European Portuguese.* Berlin/New York: Mouton de Gruyter.

Vigário, M. (2010). Prosodic structure between the Prosodic Word and Phonological Phrase: Recursive nodes or an independent domain? *The Linguistic Review, 27*(4), 485–530. https://doi.org/10.1515/tlir.2010.017

**Nuno Paulino** is PhD Student at the Phonetics and Phonology Lab (Center of Linguistics of the University of Lisbon). His main interests are the phonetics and phonology of Portuguese spoken by adults and children. During his PhD he is studying sandhi acquisition in bilingual children of European Portuguese and another language. He is also an author and co-author of several presentations and published papers in both national and international journals.

**Pedro Oliveira** is Lecturer at the Faculté Arts, Lettres et Langues of Université Jean Monnet. He is a PhD student in Linguistics at Universidade de Santiago de Compostela. His PhD project focuses on the phonology and the prosodic domains of Asturian languages. He participated in the development of the scientific contents of the Museum of Portuguese Language, and was responsible for the data collection of Portuguese and Portuguese-based creole languages in South America, Portugal and Asia. His research focuses on phonetics and phonology, intonation and prosody.

**Marina Vigário** is Associate Professor at the University of Lisbon and Director of the Phonetics and Phonology Lab (Center of Linguistics of the University of Lisbon). Her research has focused on prosodic structure, rhythm and intonation, and frequency and grammar, both in adults and in children. She is the author of *The Prosodic Word in European Portuguese* (Mouton de Gruyter, 2003, 2011) and *Prosodic structure between the Prosodic Word and the Phonological Phrase: recursive nodes or an independent domain? (The Linguistic Review,* 2010). Besides fundamental research, she has long been committed to producing language resources and translational research within multidisciplinary teams.

# Index

CPSIA information can be obtained
at www.ICGtesting.com
Printed in the USA
JSHW050940150622
26655JS00006B/4